The Theory of Functional Grammar
Part 2

Functional Grammar Series 21

Editors

A. Machtelt Bolkestein
Casper de Groot
J. Lachlan Mackenzie

Mouton de Gruyter
Berlin · New York

Simon C. Dik

The Theory of Functional Grammar

Part 2: Complex and Derived Constructions

edited by

Kees Hengeveld

Mouton de Gruyter
Berlin · New York   1997

Mouton de Gruyter (formerly Mouton, The Hague)
is a Division of Walter de Gruyter & Co., Berlin.

∞ Printed on acid-free paper which falls within the guidelines of the
ANSI to ensure permanence and durability.

Library of Congress Cataloging-in-Publication-Data

> Dik, S. C. (Simon C.)
> The theory of functional grammar / Simon C. Dik ; edited
> by Kees Hengeveld. − 2nd, rev. ed.
> p.   cm. − (Functional grammar series ; 20−21)
> Includes bibliographical references (p.   ) and index.
> Contents: pt. 1. The structure of the clause. − pt. 2. Complex and derived constructions.
> ISBN 3-11-015404-8 (pt. 1 : alk. paper). −
> ISBN 3-11-015403-X (pt. 1 : pbk. : alk. paper) −
> ISBN 3-11-015406-4 (pt. 2 : alk. paper). −
> ISBN 3-11-015405-6 (pt. 2 : pbk. : alk. paper)
> 1. Functionalism (Linguistics)   I. Hengeveld, Kees,
> 1957−   .   II. Title. III. Series.
> P147.D54   1997
> 415−dc21   97-29611
>   CIP

Die Deutsche Bibliothek − Cataloging-in-Publication-Data

> **Dik, Simon C.:**
> The theory of functional grammar / Simon C. Dik. Ed. by Kees
> Hengeveld. − Berlin ; New York : Mouton de Gruyter
>   Pt. 2. Complex and derived constructions. − 1997
> (Functional grammar series ; 21)
> ISBN 3-11-015406-6

© Copyright 1997 by Walter de Gruyter & Co., D-10785 Berlin
All rights reserved, including those of translation into foreign languages. No part of this book may be reproduced in any form or by any means, electronic or mechanical, including photocopy, recording or any information storage and retrieval system, without permission in writing from the publisher.
Printing: Gerike GmbH, Berlin. − Binding: Lüderitz & Bauer-GmbH, Berlin.
Printed in Germany.

Preface

Preface by the author

This second part of *The Theory of Functional Grammar*, a sequel to part 1 (*TFG1*) which was published in 1989, deals with the functional grammar of complex and derived constructions. It presupposes the contents of *TFG1*, which will not be repeated, although brief summaries will be given at relevant junctions in the present volume.

As in *TFG1*, I should like to thank the many students and colleagues who, in writing and in oral discussion, have contributed to the development of Functional Grammar towards its present state. Particular thanks go to Kees Hengeveld for joint work on complex terms relevant to chapters 5-7; to Caroline Kroon for comments on a preliminary version of chapter 18; and to the working group on FG of the University of Copenhagen for a pleasant stay and lively discussions through the autumn of 1990. The responsibility for the present text is, of course, my own.

Finally, I would like to thank Elly Borghesi, Anne Mars, and Sabine Rummens for typing assistance.

Holysloot   Simon C. Dik

Preface by the editor

On 1 March 1995, Simon C. Dik died at the age of 55. The disease which led to his death had revealed itself three years earlier, and gradually prevented him from actively continuing his scientific work. When it had become apparent that it would not be possible for him to finish his two-volume *The Theory of Functional Grammar*, he asked me to assist him in preparing the manuscript for publication.

With the exception of chapters 16-18, the draft versions of all the chapters of this second volume were discussed with the author. The author's intention was to present an integrated theory of accessibility in chapter 16, but only the basic notions relevant to such a theory can be presented here. Chapters 17 and 18 needed very little revision. Since the text presented here is intended to reflect Simon Dik's views as closely as possible, references are made only to those publications that were known to the author, albeit sometimes in a preliminary version, at the time when I discussed the prefinal version of this volume with him.

Several persons and institutions have provided invaluable help while I was preparing this volume. The Faculty of Arts of the University of Amsterdam furnished financial support and exempted me from teaching duties during the academic year 1994-1995, which allowed me to advance much more rapidly than would otherwise have been possible. Machtelt Bolkestein and Lachlan Mackenzie read the entire text and provided many valuable comments. Hella Olbertz prepared the final camera-ready manuscript, including the references, and corrected numerous mistakes in the process. The Institute for Functional Research of Language and Language Use at the University of Amsterdam made their technical facilities available to me. Mouton de Gruyter and its staff gave technical and financial assistance throughout the editorial process. Finally, Matty Gaikhorst, Peter Kahrel, Lachlan Mackenzie, Harm Pinkster, Yvonne Sanders, and Willy van Wetter provided help of various kinds.

Amsterdam, May 1997   Kees Hengeveld

Table of contents

List of tables and figures xvii

Abbreviations used in FG-representations xix

1. Predicate formation 1
   1.0. Introduction 1
   1.1. The nature of predicate formation rules: an example 3
   1.2. A typology of predicate formation rules 5
        1.2.0. Introduction 5
        1.2.1. The form of the predicate 6
        1.2.2. The type of the predicate 7
        1.2.3. The quantitative valency 8
               1.2.3.1. Valency extension 8
               1.2.3.2. Valency reduction 9
        1.2.4. The qualitative valency 15
               1.2.4.1. Semantic functions 15
               1.2.4.2. Selection restrictions 17
   1.3. Explanatory notes on predicate formation 18
   1.4. The expression of the output predicate 21
   1.5. Conclusion 22

2. Verbal restrictors 1: general properties 23
   2.0. Introduction 23
   2.1. Participant identification 24
   2.2. Some terminological issues 25
   2.3. Verbal restrictors 28
        2.3.1. Verbal restrictors are extended predications 28
        2.3.2. Verbal restrictors are "open" predications 29
        2.3.3. Anaphorical relations 30
        2.3.4. Selection restrictions 31
        2.3.5. Stacking of verbal restrictors 32
               2.3.5.0. Introduction 32
               2.3.5.1. Stacking in English 33
               2.3.5.2. Stacking in Luganda 34
               2.3.5.3. Incorporating restrictions on stacking in FG 36

2.4. Non-restrictive usage of verbal restrictors 38
    2.4.1. Differences between restrictors and
           non-restrictors 39
    2.4.2. The semantic status of non-restrictors 41
    2.4.3. Non-restrictors and independent clauses 42
    2.4.4. The FG analysis of non-restrictors 44

3. Verbal restrictors 2: types 45
   3.0. Introduction 45
   3.1. Post-nominal verbal restrictors 47
      3.1.0. Introduction 47
      3.1.1. The formal expression of relative clauses 48
      3.1.2. On pronominal expression of the relativized
           variable 51
      3.1.3. Relative pronouns 54
   3.2. Prenominal verbal restrictors 55
      3.2.1. Participial restrictors 55
      3.2.2. Nominalized restrictors 57
      3.2.3. Closed predications as restrictors 58
      3.2.4. Appositive verbal restrictors 63
   3.3. Circumnominal verbal restrictors 65
   3.4. Correlative relative constructions 68

4. Verbal restrictors 3: explanations 71
   4.0. Introduction 71
   4.1. On the (non-)universality of verbal restrictors 72
   4.2. Prefield versus Postfield 74
   4.3. Scenarios for the creation of verbal restrictors 76
      4.3.1. From parataxis to verbal restrictor 77
      4.3.2. From embedded question to verbal restrictor 79
      4.3.3. From circumstantial satellite to verbal
           restrictor 82
           4.3.3.0. Introduction 82
           4.3.3.1. Circumstantial satellites 83
           4.3.3.2. Circumstantials in Orientation position 85
   4.4. Conclusion 92

5. Embedded constructions 1: semantic parameters 93
   5.0. Introduction 93
   5.1. Clausal terms 96

		5.1.1.	Direct speech	96
		5.1.2.	Indirect speech	98
		5.1.3.	Indirect speech complements have their own illocutions	100
		5.1.4.	Difference between direct and indirect speech	102
		5.1.5.	Not all elements can be converted into indirect speech	103
	5.2.	Propositional terms		106
		5.2.1.	Types of matrix predicates	106
		5.2.2.	Factivity	108
	5.3.	Predicational terms		110
		5.3.1.	Types of matrix predicates	110
		5.3.2.	Implicatives	114
	5.4.	Differences between types of embedded construction		116
		5.4.1.	*Believe* versus *persuade* versus *force*	116
		5.4.2.	Japanese complementizers	117
6.	Embedded constructions 2: functional and formal parameters			121
	6.0.	Introduction		121
	6.1.	Functional parameters		121
		6.1.1.	Semantic functions	121
		6.1.2.	Perspectival functions	123
		6.1.3.	Pragmatic functions	123
	6.2.	Formal parameters		125
		6.2.1.	The position of the embedded construction in the matrix domain	126
		6.2.2.	Formal subordination markers	135
		6.2.3.	Internal constituent ordering within the embedded construction	138
		6.2.4.	Finite or non-finite realization of the embedded predicate	138
		6.2.5.	Mood	140
7.	Embedded constructions 3: types			143
	7.0.	Introduction		143
	7.1.	Finite embedded constructions: subordinate clauses		144
	7.2.	Non-finite embedded constructions		145
		7.2.1.	Infinitival constructions	145
			7.2.1.1. Closed and open infinitival constructions . 147	
			7.2.1.2. Functions of infinitival constructions 150	

x   *The Theory of Functional Grammar 2*

               7.2.1.3. Infinitivals as complements to adjectives .. 152
        7.2.2. Participial constructions 154
        7.2.3. Nominalizations 157
               7.2.3.1. The possessive expression of arguments .. 160
               7.2.3.2. A cross-linguistic hierarchy of
                             nominalization types 162
               7.2.3.3. The treatment of nominalizations in FG ... 164

8. Polarity distinctions 169
    8.0. Introduction 169
    8.1. Negation: operator or satellite? 170
    8.2. Negation and Focus 171
    8.3. Illocutionary negation 172
    8.4. Propositional negation 174
    8.5. Predicational negation 177
    8.6. Negation at the predicate level 178
        8.6.0. Introduction 178
        8.6.1. Complementary formation 178
        8.6.2. Contrary formation 179
        8.6.3. Litotes 179
    8.7. Term negation or zero quantification 180
    8.8. Term negation versus predication negation 183
        8.8.1. Two strategies for talking about nothing 183
        8.8.2. Typological distribution 184

9. Coordination 189
    9.0. Introduction 189
    9.1. Coordination defined 189
    9.2. Ways of describing coordinate constructions 193
    9.3. Simple coordination 196
        9.3.1. Coordination of sentences and clauses 196
        9.3.2. Coordination of propositions and predications 200
        9.3.3. Coordination of terms 201
        9.3.4. Coordination of predicates 203
        9.3.5. Coordination of or inside restrictors 205
        9.3.6. Coordination of operators and functions 207
    9.4. Multiple coordination 209
    9.5. Simultaneous coordination 212

Table of contents xi

10. Anaphora 215
    10.0. Introduction 215
    10.1. Definitions 215
    10.2. Accessibility 218
    10.3. Expresssion 219
        10.3.0. Introduction 219
        10.3.1. Pragmatic factors 220
        10.3.2. Types of entities 223
            10.3.2.0. Introduction 223
            10.3.2.1. Anaphorical reference to properties and
                      relations 224
            10.3.2.2. Anaphorical reference to States of Affairs . 226
            10.3.2.3. Anaphorical reference to Possible Facts .. 227
            10.3.2.4. Anaphorical reference to Speech Acts 228
            10.3.2.5. Conclusion 228

11. The illocutionary layer 229
    11.0. Introduction 229
    11.1. The status of "illocution" 230
    11.2. Explicit and implicit performatives 232
        11.2.1. Explicit performatives 232
        11.2.2. Implicit performatives 234
    11.3. Sentence types as carriers of basic illocutions 236
    11.4. Illocutionary operators 239
    11.5. Illocutionary conversion 240
        11.5.1. Derived illocutions 240
        11.5.2. Types of grammatical conversion 242
        11.5.3. Types of illocutionary converters 245
        11.5.4. The borderline between grammatical and pragmatic
                conversion 249
        11.5.5. Embedded converted illocutions 250
        11.5.6. Indirect speech acts 251
    11.6. Explicit performatives again 252
    11.7. Conclusion 254

12. Interrogative clauses 257
    12.0. Introduction 257
    12.1. The illocutionary force of questions 258
    12.2. Different types of interrogative construction 260

12.3. Q-word questions 263
    12.3.1. The nature of Q-word questions 263
    12.3.2. The operators Int and Q 265
    12.3.3. Types of Q-constituents 267
    12.3.4. The representation of Q-constituents 269
    12.3.5. Accessibility to Q 270
        12.3.5.1. Questioning of terms 271
        12.3.5.2. Questioning of constituents within terms .. 271
        12.3.5.3. On questioning the predicate 274
12.4. The placement of Q-constituents 276
    12.4.1. Q-Pattern versus Q-Focus 280
    12.4.2. A question about pronoun retention 283
    12.4.3. The distribution of Q-Pattern and Q-Focus 284
12.5. Multiple Q-word questions 286

13. Focus constructions: basic patterns 291
  13.0. Introduction 291
  13.1. A note on terminology 291
  13.2. The prototypical Cleft construction 293
    13.2.1. The prototypical Cleft in FG 295
    13.2.2. Dummy head nouns 296
    13.2.3. On expressing Cleft constructions 298
    13.2.4. Selection restrictions 300
    13.2.5. The form of Focus term and agreement patterns
         in the Cleft construction 302
    13.2.6. Typological predictions 307
  13.3. Focus constructions with adpositional predicates 309

14. Predicate focus; cleft interrogatives; demarking of Focus
    constructions 313
  14.0. Introduction 313
  14.1. Focusing on the predicate 313
  14.2. Interrogative Focus constructions 318
  14.3. Demarking processes 325
    14.3.1. Demarking of Focus constructions 325
    14.3.2. Demarking of pragmatically marked construction
         types 329

15. Discrepancies between underlying clause structure and surface
    expression 331
    15.0. Introduction 331
    15.1. Types of discrepancies 332
    15.2. Formal discrepancy 333
        15.2.1. Non-nominative first arguments or Subjects 333
        15.2.2. Relative attraction 335
    15.3. Positional discrepancy 339
        15.3.1. Types of displacement 339
        15.3.2. On explaining displacement 341
    15.4. Formal and positional discrepancy 342
    15.5. On "Raising" 344
        15.5.1. Forms of Raising 344
        15.5.2. Constraints on Raising 346
        15.3.3. The pragmatic motivation of Raising 349
    15.6. Other forms of structural discrepancy 351
        15.6.1. First-order expression designates second-order
                entity 351
        15.6.2. Second-order expression designates first-order
                entity 355

16. Accessibility 357
    16.0. Introduction 357
    16.1. Operations 358
    16.2. Intrinsic constraints 359
    16.3. Hierarchical constraints 361
    16.4. Functional constraints 365
        16.4.0. Introduction 365
        16.4.1. Semantic and Syntactic Functions 366
            16.4.1.1. Keenan and Comrie's Accessibility
                      Hierarchy 366
            16.4.1.2. Reconsidering the Accessibility
                      Hierarchy 368
            16.4.1.3. Conclusion 375
        16.4.2. Pragmatic Functions 376
    16.5. Concluding remarks 377

17. Extra-clausal constituents 379
    17.0. Introduction 379
    17.1. On defining ECCs 380

17.2. Types of ECCs 383
    17.2.1. Interaction management 384
    17.2.2. Attitude specification 386
    17.2.3. Discourse organization 386
        17.2.3.0. Introduction 386
        17.2.3.1. Boundary marking 386
        17.2.3.2. Orientation 387
        17.2.3.3. Tails 401
        17.2.3.4. Integration of Theme and Tail into the clause 403
    17.2.4. Discourse execution 405
17.3. Conclusion 407

18. Towards a functional grammar of discourse 409
  18.0. Introduction 409
  18.1. Intention, content, interpretation, and knowledge 410
  18.2. Dynamic Discourse Models 412
  18.3. Three perspectives on a functional grammar of discourse ... 414
  18.4. Global discourse decisions: scope phenomena in discourse . 415
    18.4.0. Introduction 415
    18.4.1. Entering a discourse event 416
    18.4.2. Choosing a discourse genre 416
    18.4.3. Choosing a discourse style 417
    18.4.4. Type of discourse world created 417
    18.4.5. Discourse illocution 419
    18.4.6. Temporal decisions 421
    18.4.7. The introduction and maintenance of Discourse Topics 422
  18.5. Global structures in discourse 422
    18.5.1. The hierarchical structure of discourse 422
        18.5.1.0. Introduction 422
        18.5.1.1. Discourse layering 424
        18.5.1.2. Recursion in discourse structure 427
    18.5.2. Discourse units 428
        18.5.2.1. Interpersonal units 429
        18.5.2.2. Representational units 430
    18.5.3. Discourse relations 431

Table of contents xv

    18.6. Discourse coherence 433
        18.6.0. Introduction 433
        18.6.1. Frames as a source of coherence 433
        18.6.2. Iconic sequencing 435
        18.6.3. Topical continuity 436
        18.6.4. Focality 438
        18.6.5. Tail-Head Linking 438
        18.6.6. Connectors 440
    18.7. Conclusion 441

References 443

Index of languages 465

Index of names 467

Index of subjects 471

List of tables and figures

Tables

1. Types of entities as referred to by terms 93
2. Terms for higher order entities 94
3. Types of entities which can be anaphorically referred to 224
4. Sentency types in seven languages 238

Figures

1. A model of verbal interaction 410

Abbreviations used in FG-representations

Word classes

T	any word class
A	adjective
N	noun
V	verb

Syntactic functions

Obj	object
Subj	subject

Pragmatic functions

Foc	focus
GivTop	given topic
NewTop	new topic
Or	orientation
ResTop	resumed topic
SubTop	sub-topic
Top	topic

Semantic functions

Ø	zero
Ag	agent
Ben	beneficiary
Circ	circumstance
Comp	company
Dir	direction
Exp	experiencer
Fo	force
Go	goal (patient)
Instr	instrument
Loc	location
Man	manner
Po	positioner
Poss	possessor
Proc	processed
Rec	recipient
Ref	reference
So	source
Temp	time

Layers

f	predicate
x	term
e	predication
X	proposition
E	clause

Satellites

σ_1	any predicate satellite
σ_2	any predication satellite
σ_3	any proposition satellite
σ_4	any illocutionaty satellite

Π-operators

Π_1	any predicate operator
Π_2	any predication operator
Π_3	any proposition operator
Π_4	any illocutionary operator
Ant	anterior

Decl	declarative
Excl	exclamative
Gen	generic
Hab	habitual
Imp	imperative
Impf	imperfective
Int	interrogative
Neg	negative
Perf	perfect
Pf	perfective
Poss	possibility
Post	posterior
Pres	present
Progr	progressive
Req	request
Sim	simultaneous
Subs	subsequent

Term operators

Ω	any term operator
Ø	zero quantifier
1	singular
A	anaphoric
coll	collectivizing
d	definite
dem	demonstrative
g	generic
i	indefinite
ind	individuating
m	plural
$n°$	n-th
prox	proximate
Q	questioned
R	relative
rem	remote
-s	non-specific

1. Predicate formation

1.0. Introduction

Most languages have a system of productive rules through which new predicates can be derived from given predicates. For example, English has a productive rule of Agent Noun formation so that, given any action verb such as *write*, we can derive the corresponding Agent Noun *writer*. This is an example of productive *word formation*, since the output of this rule consists of a word. However, neither the input nor the output of productive rules of this type necessarily consists of words. They may consist of items smaller than words ("stems"), or of analytical items, consisting of several words.

Consider, for example, the formation of derived causative predicates across languages. In many languages derived causative predicates are expressed morphologically, as in Turkish:

(1) *öl-* 'die'   ---> *öl-dür* 'cause to die'

In many other languages, such derived predicates are expressed analytically, as in French:

(2) *mourir* 'die'   ---> *faire mourir* 'cause to die'

This expression difference does not necessarily correspond to a difference in method of construction. Both the Turkish and the French derived causative predicate can be described through a rule of causative predicate formation (see below, 1.2.3.1.). In cases of analytical expression it must be demonstrated, of course, that the words in question together behave as one complex predicate rather than as two independent predicates. The fact that derived predicates do not necessarily consist of single words implies that languages which do not have any word-internal morphological structure may nevertheless have predicate formation processes, expressed in analytical form. If synthetic formation processes as exemplified in (1) and analytic formation processes as in (2) are treated under the general heading of "predicate formation" this also means that more significant generalizations across languages can be made, which adds to the typological adequacy of the theory.

Predicate formation rules thus cover the area of (productive) composition and derivation (together: stem or word formation), but they also allow for the creation of derived predicates which are analytically expressed through a combination of words.

A basic idea of FG is that a predicate (whether basic, and thus coded in the lexicon, or derived by predicate formation) is never an isolated item, but always a structure: predicates exist only as part of *predicate frames*, which define not only the form, but also the type and the quantitative and the qualitative valency of the predicate. Since predicates only exist in predicate frames, it follows that predicate formation rules are rules which can productively derive new predicate frames from given predicate frames. They are thus rules which map predicate frames onto predicate frames. This point has important consequences for our conception of predicate formation: since the type and the valency of predicates are available both in the input and in the output of predicate formation rules, we can easily formulate conditions on predicate formation which depend on the type and valency properties of the input predicates, and we can easily specify effects that a predicate formation rule may have on the output type and valency. Furthermore, a study of the possible effects on the output type and valency allows us to arrive at a natural typology of predicate formation processes.

Predicates designate properties or relations. All languages have a stock of basic predicates in their lexicon. These predicates specify the most basic properties and relations that can be talked about in the language in question. If a language has a system of predicate formation rules, these rules allow this set of basic properties / relations to be projected into a wider set of properties / relations that can be talked about by means of predicates. The rationale of predicate formation rules is thus that they extend the set of basic properties / relations that can be designated in the language.

Clause structures are built up around predicate frames. The rules and strategies for construing clause structures can make use of the full set of predicates (basic and derived) available in the language. For this reason, we say that both basic and derived predicates (together with basic and derived terms) are contained in the "Fund" of the language. The Fund thus contains all predicate frames and all term structures that can be used in the creation of clause structures. In this chapter we give a survey of the most important types of predicate formation rules as found across languages.[1]

---

1. Within FG a considerable amount of work has been done with respect to predicate formation processes in a variety of languages. This work can be tabulated as follows: Arabic (Moutaouakil 1986, 1987, 1990), Bantawa (Gvozdanović 1990),

1.1. The nature of predicate formation rules: an example

Let us first consider one simple example to see what predicate formation rules can do, and how they can be represented. Given any action verb in English, we can in principle productively derive the agent noun corresponding to that verb. Thus, from *write*, *run*, *drive*, and *skate* we can derive *writer*, *runner*, *driver*, and *skater*. We can say that a nominal predicate frame can be productively formed on the basis of the appropriate verbal predicate frame, through a rule which effects a systematic modification of both form and meaning of the input predicate frame. We can represent this kind of rule as follows:

(3)   Agent Noun Formation
        input: pred [V,+contr] $(x_1)_{Ag/Pos}...(x_n)$ $[n \geq 1]$
        output: {Ag pred} [N] $(x_1)_\emptyset ...(x_n)$
        meaning: 'a person who has the property of being (habitually) involved in the action of pred-ing'

The input to this rule must in general be a [+control] predicate (i.e. a predicate frame with a first argument in the function Agent, as in *write* --> *writer*, or Positioner, as in *hold* --> *holder*) of arbitrary quantitative valency. Note that these conditions can be easily coded in the type of the input predicate frame. The output is a nominal predicate frame of the same quantitative valency. The element "Ag" in the output predicate frame symbolizes the abstract element which serves to trigger the appropriate expression rule (in this case, the rule which introduces the affix *-er*).

Let us consider some further properties of this type of predicate formation rule:

Bulgarian (Stanchev 1990), Dutch (Dik 1980; Kahrel 1985a, 1985b; Mackenzie 1985b; Vet 1986c), English (Brömser 1985; Kahrel 1985a, 1985b; Mackenzie 1985a), French (Afman 1985; Vet 1985, 1986b), Greek (Risselada 1987), Hebrew (Junger 1985a, 1985b, 1987a, 1987b), Hungarian (De Groot 1984, 1986, 1987, 1989), Latin (Bolkestein 1985; Bolkestein—Risselada 1985), Polish (Siewierska 1990), Russian (W. de Groot 1982), Saramaccan (Kahrel 1987), Serbo-Croatian (Dik—Gvozdanović 1981; Kučanda 1984, 1987), Spanish (Moreno 1990), Swedish (Tweehuysen 1988a, 1988b), Turkish (van Schaaik 1985). I refer to these publications for further details on the manifestation of predicate formation in the different languages mentioned.

4   *Predicate Formation*

(i) The rule must be productive. This means that a speaker who knows the input predicate and the rule must be able to correctly derive the output, both as regards form and meaning. There must thus be a systematic formal and semantic relationship between input and output.

(ii) It often happens that the presumed output of some predicate formation rule has certain unpredictable formal or semantic properties. Consider the following examples in relation to this particular rule. We might want to derive an agent noun such as *author* in a similar way to *writer*. However, there is no verbal predicate **auth* which could serve as an input to this rule. Therefore, *author* will have to be considered as a basic predicate, to be entered in the lexicon. Further, we might want to consider *cook* as an Agent noun to be derived from the verb *cook*. But there is no productive formal relationship between the two. Again, the noun *cook* will have to be considered as a basic predicate, coded in the lexicon. Note, however, that we could use the following lexical representation for this noun:

(4) $cook$ [N] $(x_1)_\emptyset$ $(x_2)_{Go}$ = {Ag $cook$} [N] $(x_1)_\emptyset$ $(x_2)_{Go}$

This lexical definition says that *cook* is "the Agent noun of the verb *cook*", and thus signals that the noun *cook* fills the "gap" of what would otherwise be derived as **cooker*. Procedurally, we could now arrange our grammar as follows. If an Agent noun of some action verb is needed, rule (3) is applied to that verb. With the output of that rule, the lexicon is checked for entries such as (4). If such an entry is found, the lexical noun listed there is selected, and the regular expression of the output of the predicate formation rule is blocked; otherwise, that output is regularly expressed through the expression rules. This procedure is another example of the principle of "lexical priority" discussed in *TFG1*: chapter 14.

(iii) Note that a noun like *runner* can only be derived through (3) in the basic sense of 'person who has the property of being (habitually) involved in the action of running'. Other, more specialized senses, such as 'messenger', 'scout', 'smuggler', cannot possibly be derived through this productive rule, since the specialized meanings cannot be productively construed on the basis of the meaning of the input predicate. Such forms with specialized meanings must therefore again be thought of as coded in the lexicon in "ready-made" form. This is in accordance with our general principle that the lexicon contains all the lexical information which a speaker must know as such, and cannot derive by himself. The implication is that one and the same form (e.g. *runner*) may occur in the lexicon with certain specialized (lexicalized) meanings, as well as being the output of a predicate formation rule in the meaning productively derivable from the rules.

(iv) We see from these examples that derived predicates may develop formal and semantic idiosyncracies which, in the course of time, move them from the set of derived predicates in the Fund to the set of basic predicates in the Lexicon. This is a pervasive form of *lexicalization* which plays an important role in the historical development of any language.

(v) Note that the output predicate in (3) retains the argument structure of the verbal input predicate. In the case of one-place (intransitive, n = 1) predicates, this is irrelevant. In the case of many-place predicates, however, it allows us to explain such correspondences as the following:

(5) a. *John Brown wrote this book.*
    b. *John Brown is the writer of this book.*

It is a well-known problem for linguistic analysis how one is to analyse the constituent *of this book* in (5b). On the one hand, it seems to entertain a kind of "genitival" relation with the noun *writer*; on the other hand, the fact must somehow be accounted for that *this book* has in some sense the same relation to *writer* as it has to *wrote* in (5a), whence such terms as "objective genitive" to indicate the status of *this book* in (5b). In our analysis we could say the following: the derived noun *writer* still has a slot for a Goal argument, a property which it inherits from the input verbal predicate; in the domain of a noun, the Goal function will be mapped onto *of* by the expression rules (just as many other noun-noun relations are expressed by *of*), whereas in the verbal domain the Goal function is not overtly expressed. This seems an appropriate way of accounting for both the similarities and the differences between derived Agent Nouns and the underlying verbal predicates from which they are derived.[2]

1.2. A typology of predicate formation rules

1.2.0. Introduction

Predicate formation rules take a predicate frame as input and deliver a derived predicate frame as output. We may assume that any property of the input predicate frame is liable to modification through predicate formation. This

---

2. See below, section 7.2.3., on nominalization.

means that the various properties which are coded in the predicate frame provide a natural basis for distinguishing different types of predicate formation processes. A predicate frame codes the following types of information:[3]

(6) 1. the form of the predicate
     2. the type of the predicate
     3. the valency of the predicate
        3.1. the quantitative valency
        3.2. the qualitative valency, i.e.
             3.2.1. the semantic functions,
             3.2.2. the selection restrictions

We do indeed find predicate formation processes which affect each of these features of the predicate frame. Very often, one complex predicate formation rule will affect several of these features simultaneously. For the sake of clarity, however, I will discuss each of the possible modifications effected by predicate formation as if it were a separate process.

1.2.1. The form of the predicate

In earlier discussions of predicate formation in FG (see e.g. Dik 1990a), the way in which the form of the input predicate was affected by the predicate formation rule was directly given in the rule itself. In the modified approach proposed here, instead of specifying the actual form of the output predicate, an auxiliary operator (cf. *TFG1*: 14.6.2.), i.e. an abstract element such as "Ag" in (3), represents the formal adaptation the input predicate will have to undergo in the expression rule component. I assume that all predicate formation rules introduce such abstract elements, which will then be mapped onto concrete formal material by the expression rules. This adds to the general validity of the rules in question. For example, much the same rule can be used for Agent Noun formation in many languages which have such a rule. The formal differences will then come out in the expression rules of each individual language. In 1.4. an overview of the ways in which the input predicate may be affected by these expression rules will be given.

---

3. Cf. *TFG1*: 4.2.

1.2.2. The type of the predicate

In (3) I illustrated a form of predicate formation which changes a verbal predicate into a derived nominal predicate. This is a form of class-changing predicate formation. On the other hand, there are predicate formation rules which do not change the category of the input predicate, but modify or modulate it in one way or another. For example, the very productive predicate formation rule of diminutive formation in Dutch (which derives *boek-je* 'little book' from *boek-*, etc.) is an instance of "class-maintaining" predicate formation: both the input and the output are nominal predicates. However, there is a difference in sub-type in this sense that the derived diminutive predicate necessarily has neuter Gender, independently of the Gender of the input predicate.

Through various types of class-changing predicate formation, the basic categories of a language can be put to derived uses. The relevant relationships can be represented as follows:

(7)

The basic categories V, N, and A can be defined in terms of their most typical functions (cf. *TFG1*: 8.1.), as follows:

(8)   V: main predicate of a predication
       N: first restrictor in a term structure
       A: second restrictor in a term structure

Thus, we find these categories in their basic functions in an expression such as:

(9)   *The old* (A) *man* (N) *died* (V).

Through class-changing predicate formation along the lines of schema (7), however, each of the basic categories can (depending, of course, on the possibilities available in the language involved) in principle be put to the uses of any of the others. For some examples, consider:

8   *Predicate Formation*

(10)   V --> N   *write --> writer*
       V --> A   *write --> writing*
       N --> V   *father* [N] *--> father* [V]
       N --> A   *colour --> coloured*
       A --> V   *red --> redden*
       A --> N   *red --> redness*

One particularly important aspect of category-changing predicate formation is that terms can be changed into predicates, as in:

(11) a.   *John is an intelligent boy.*
     b.   *John is in the garden.*

In order to allow for this, we assume that there is a very general predicate formation rule, which takes a term (possibly provided with a semantic function) as input, and turns it into a one-place predicate, which can then be used in such constructions as (11a-b) (cf. *TFG1*: 8.4.). We will thus say that *an intelligent boy* in (11a) is a term, construed from the predicates *intelligent* and *boy*, and that the term as a whole is then again turned into a predicate. Note that since term structures have recursive properties, this form of "term predicate formation" in principle yields an infinite number of derived predicates.

1.2.3. The quantitative valency

As to the quantitative valency of a predicate, i.e. the number of arguments with which it combines, this can be affected in two ways by predicate formation: (i) valency extension, and (ii) valency reduction. Let us consider these two processes in turn.

1.2.3.1. Valency extension. The quantitative valency of a predicate is extended when, for example, an intransitive predicate is turned into a transitive one, as in the following example:

(12) a.   *The soldiers marched to the camp.*
     b.   *The corporal marched the soldiers to the camp.*

The rule which underlies this process could be represented as follows:

(13) input: pred [V] $(x_1)_{Ag}$
      output: {Tr pred} [V] $(x_0)_{Ag}(x_1)_{Go}$
      meaning: 'x_0 makes x_1 pred'

Note the following properties of this particular rule: (i) it is class-maintaining, although the output enters into another subcategory of V; (ii) the output predicate form is (in this case) zero-marked; (iii) the input predicate frame is extended by one argument position, (iv) the original Agent argument is "demoted" to the semantic function of Goal. We return to this latter property below.

The most typical form of valency extension is the rule of causative predicate formation, which we find in various guises in a great many languages. The general schema of the causative rule can be given as follows:

(14) Causative Predicate Formation
      input: pred [V] $(x_1) ... (x_n)$ [$n \geq 1$]
      output: {Caus pred} [V] $(x_0)_{Causer}(x_1)_{Causee} ... (x_n)$
      meaning: 'x_0 brings it about that x_1 pred-s ... (x_n)'

Note the following properties of this rule: (a) an extra argument (x_0), representing the Causer, is added to the input predicate frame; (b) the original first argument gets the semantic function Causee, in addition to its original semantic function; (c) the output predicate is provided with the causative marker "Caus", which may finally be expressed by zero, by a causative affix on the predicate, or by a causative auxiliary such as *let* in English, *laten* in Dutch, or *faire* in French.

The causative predicate formation rule creates a kind of problem for the expression rules: there is in a sense "one argument too many" as compared to the non-derived predicate frames of the language. Many properties of causative constructions across languages can be understood as resulting from different strategies to solve this problem. I return to this point in 1.3. below.

1.2.3.2. Valency reduction. In valency reduction, the quantitative valency of an input predicate is reduced by (at least) one argument position. Across languages, valency reduction has a rich spectrum of manifestations and implications, which show remarkable degrees of similarity. Let us first consider an example of some constructions which may be produced through valency reduction, and then outline the typology of valency reduction in a more general way. Consider the following examples from English:

(15) a. *Mary is washing.*
     (a) 'Mary is washing something'
     (b) 'Mary is washing herself'
  b. *These clothes don't wash.*
    'These clothes are such that it is impossible to wash them'

In (15a) we have an otherwise two-place verb with only the Agent argument expressed. If this construction only had interpretation (a), we could simply say that the second argument has been left unspecified; but this does not naturally lead us to the "reflexive" interpretation (b). In (15b) we have the same predicate, but now with only the second argument expressed; the interpretation is such that a property is assigned to *these clothes*, where the property resides in the impossibility of washing them. (15b) is a kind of "pseudo-passive" with a modal aspect to it.

How can these apparently disparate facts be brought into a unified explanatory framework? We believe that the general theory of valency-reducing predicate formation provides such a framework. This theory can be sketched in the following way.

There are several different types of predicate formation rule which reduce the valency of the input predicate frame by one argument position. The most important of these are: (i) Incorporation, (ii) First Argument Reduction, and (iii) Second Argument Reduction.

(i) *Incorporation*[4]
Incorporation produces such constructions as:

(16)   *John bird-catches.*
       'John is bird-catching'
       'John is a bird-catcher'

In languages which have this type of construction, it has a number of recurrent properties: (a) the output predicate is typically intransitive rather than transitive; (b) the incorporated nominal cannot be modified or determined in any way, and is non-referential; (c) the resulting complex verb often gets a "de-actualized" (generic, habitual, virtual, dispositional) interpretation.

We account for fact (a) by assuming that in the incorporation rule, the input

---

4. For more extensive discussion see Mardirussian (1975), Dik (1980), Anderson (1985).

predicate (e.g. *catch*) is reduced by its second argument position; for fact (b) by assuming that it is the nominal predicate *bird* rather than a full term which is incorporated; and fact (c) follows from this: terms refer, but predicates do not; and if no specific reference to "birds" is involved, then the derived predicate will naturally receive a generic interpretation.

The relevant predicate formation rule for Goal Incorporation can thus be formulated as follows:

(17) Goal Incorporation
  input: (a) pred1 [V] (x_1) $(x_2:<sel>)_{Go}$
  (b) pred2 [N,sel] (x_2)
  output: {Inc pred1-pred2} [V] (x_1)

In this rule, "sel" expresses that the type of the nominal input predicate (e.g. *bird*) should be compatible with the selection restriction imposed on the second argument position of the verbal input predicate (e.g. *catch*).

Across languages, nominal predicates corresponding to different semantic functions may be incorporated into the verbal predicate:

(18) Incorporated nominal corresponds to argument
  a. Goal   : *John is bird-catching*
  b. Agent   : *The cart was horse-drawn*
  c. Force   : *This engine is fuel-powered*
  d. Processed : *It was rain-falling*

  Incorporated nominal corresponds to satellite-1
  e. Instrument : *John hand-polished the car*
  f. Direction : *John is school-going*
  g. Location   : *John was chair-sitting*
  h. Manner   : *You must quiet-sit*
  i. Speed   : *John fast-ran to the station*

As these examples show, it is arguments and satellites of level 1 (cf. *TFG1*: 9.1.3.) which can be incorporated (cf. Dik et al. 1990).[5] In other words, the

---

5. I assume here that in *sit on a chair* the constituent *on a chair* is an "inner locative" satellite-1, whereas in *sit (on a chair) in the kitchen* the constituent *in the kitchen* is an "outer locative" satellite-2. The prediction would be that *chair-sitting* but not *kitchen-sitting* would constitute a potential output of Incorporation rules

domain of incorporation rules appears to be the core predication.

Note that although incorporation is often considered as a feature of "exotic" languages, we do in fact need it for English as well. For although (16) is not grammatical as it stands, we need a derived predicate *bird-catch* for such forms as *bird-catching* and *bird-catcher*. For the latter form, we shall assume that the output of a rule of Goal Incorporation can be input to the rule of Agent Noun formation formulated in (3). In order to be input to this rule, the stem *bird-catch* must be considered a verbal predicate (so as to conform to the input conditions holding for (3)). It is, however, a verbal predicate which cannot be used as a finite verb in English. This property will have to be stipulated along with the creation of the derived verbal predicate.

(ii) *First Argument Reduction*
The general schema for First Argument reduction can be formulated as follows:

(19)   First Argument Reduction
       input: pred [V] (x_1) (x_2)...(x_n) [$n \geq 1$]
       output: {R pred} [V] (--) (x_2)...(x_n)
       meaning: 'pred applies to only (x_2)...(x_n)'

The "R" in the output symbolizes some kind of reduction marker, which may be expressed by zero, by a verbal affix, or by a particle (in the latter case, many languages use an originally "reflexive" element, such as *se* and cognates in Romance and Slavic languages (with the affixal form *-sya* in Russian), and *-s* and cognates in Scandinavan languages). The meaning specification can be interpreted as a kind of riddle: how can an n-place predicate apply to (n-1) arguments? The answer to this riddle is that in the output predicate it is completely irrelevant what the identity of the first argument is.

"Pure" application of (19) yields such constructions as (20b) on the basis of underlying predicate structures as in (20a):

(20) a.   *John catches butterflies.*
     b.   *(It) catches-R butterflies.*

Since in (20b) no Agent whatsoever is involved, the construction can only be interpreted in a general sense: 'A catching of butterflies is going on'. In this

---

across languages.

usage, the original Goal argument retains the expression typical for Goals in the language (e.g. accusative case).

Constructions such as (20b) are usually subjected to a further process, however, through which the original second argument "usurps" the rights of the first argument. This process of "argument shift" yields constructions of the form:

(21)   *Butterflies catch-R.*
       'There are butterflies being caught'

Probably because this is not very informative, First Argument Reduction is often in a sense compensated by the addition of a satellite to the output frame (satellite absorption). Compare the following constructions:

(22) a. *John writes on this typewriter.*
     b. *?*This typewriter writes-R.*[6]
     c. *This typewriter writes-R nicely.*

Construction (22b), without any extension, is hardly grammatical in English; with the extension of a Manner satellite, as in (22c), it is perfect.[7] Note, finally, that (22c), which can be derived by First Argument Reduction, argument shift, and satellite absorption, designates a property rather than an event. Thus, the Action-feature of the input predicate *write* has been neutralized through these various operations.

(iii) *Second Argument Reduction*
The general schema for Second Argument reduction can be formulated as follows:

(23)   Second Argument Reduction
       input: pred [V] (x_1) (x_2)...(x_n) [$n \geq 2$]
       output: {R pred} [V] (x_1) (--)...(x_n)
       meaning: 'pred applies to (x_1)...(x_3)...(x_n)'

The meaning specification again provides a kind of riddle: how can an

---

6. Note that R is expressed by Zero in English.
7. See Kahrel (1985a) for discussion of these various features of English detransitivization.

originally transitive predicate be interpreted as not applying to a Goal argument? For this riddle, there seem to be just three possible solutions, which can be exemplified as follows:

(24)   *Real men do not wash-R*
    (a) non-specific interpretation:
        'Real men do not engage in the activity of washing (anything, whatever it is)'
    (b) reflexive interpretation:
        'Real men do not wash themselves'
    (c) reciprocal interpretation:
        'Real men do not wash each other'

In many typologically diverse languages, we find this same cluster of possible interpretations for derived predicates which may be understood in terms of Second Argument Reduction.

(iv) *General properties of valency reduction*
We saw that valency reduction sometimes leads to a "de-actualized" interpretation. We can now be a little more specific about the conditions in which this occurs, and on the ways in which it manifests itself. Note that valency reduction means that the original n-place predicate ends up with only n-1 arguments. The derived predicate in a sense has one "open" valency which must be satisfied. In the reflexive interpretation, that valency is satisfied by connecting the predicate twice to the same argument; the same applies, in a more complex way, in the reciprocal interpretation. It is only when the missing argument is interpreted as completely unspecified, i.e., in First Argument Reduction and in Second Argument Reduction with a non-specific interpretation, that we see the tendency towards de-actualization. This is understandable, since an "actual" interpretation will usually require a sufficient number of specific arguments.

Under the general label of "de-actualization", we may distinguish at least the following different values: (a) generic (the derived predicate designates a general property), (b) habitual (a habit), (c) virtual / potential (a tendency, a liability), (d) dispositional / volitional (a wish, a positive feeling with respect to getting involved in the SoA). The latter reading is especially favoured if the construction contains a personal Experiencer (typically in the dative). These various types of de-actualization can be illustrated with the following examples:

(25) a. *Dogs bite-R.* (generic)
  'It is a generic characteristic of dogs that they bite'
 b. *It goes-R to school by car.* (habitual)
  'They have the habit of going to school by car'
 c. *These glasses break-R.* (virtual / potential)
  'These glasses are breakable'
 d. *It eats-R porridge to me.* (dispositional / volitional)
  'I like / feel like / would like to eat porridge'

Again, these various shades of de-actualization are found, in similar form, in a great number of languages.

1.2.4. The qualitative valency

The qualitative valency of the input predicate is involved when the semantic functions or the selection restrictions (or both) are modified through predicate formation.

1.2.4.1. Semantic functions. Some examples of modification of semantic function have already been presented above. In causative formation (14), a Causee function is added to the original second argument. In argument shift, an original Goal argument may be shifted to first argument role and receive either the function Processed (if a process-interpretation is assigned to the derived predicate) or Zero (if that predicate indicates the state of having some property). More interesting cases of semantic function shift are found in such Dutch and English pairs as:

(26) a. *Jan plantte wilgen in zijn tuin.*
 b. *John planted willows in his garden.*
 c. *Jan beplantte zijn tuin met wilgen.*
 d. *John planted his garden with willows.*

For several reasons such constructions cannot, according to the principles of FG, be derived from the same underlying predicate frame. Most importantly, there is a semantic difference between (26a-b) and (26c-d), which must be coded in the underlying predicate frame. Second, it would be difficult to formulate generally applicable rules which, starting out with one underlying predicate frame, would yield the two alternative constructions in a natural way. Third, as we see in the Dutch version (but not in English), there seems to be a morphological relationship involved (*planten* vs. *beplanten*) which is typical for predicate formation. For this reason such relations as between (26a-b) on the one hand and (26c-d) on the other will be described through a predicate formation rule of the following form:

(27) Completive Predicate Formation
 input: pred [V] $(x_1)_{Ag}$ $(x_2)_{Go}$ $(x_3)_{Loc}$
 output: {SFS pred} [V] $(x_1)_{Ag}$ $(x_3)_{Go}$ $(x_2)_{Instr}$
 meaning: '(x_1) pred-s (x_3) completely with (x_2)'

in which SFS symbolizes the element which will trigger the expression appropriate for semantic function shift in the language in question (in English *Ø*; in Dutch, *be-*).

Although many languages have pairs such as illustrated in (26), the usages made of the opposition are not necessarily the same, and thus require detailed research in each particular language. Let me give two examples of this.

Bolkestein (1985) and Bolkestein—Risselada (1985) studied pairs of three-place predicates in Latin which relate to each other in the following way:

(28) a. *oppidum   fossa   circumdare*
 fortress-acc ditch-abl encircle
 'encircle the fortress with a ditch'
 b. *fossam   oppido   circumdare*
 ditch-acc fortress-dat encircle
 'encircle a ditch around the fortress'

They found no clear semantic differences between such pairs. Nevertheless, the choice of one or the other is not arbitrary, but the factors involved appear to be of a textual or discourse nature rather than residing in the potential to designate different SoAs. To put it informally: if there are more contextual "strings attached" to the 'fortress', then *oppidum* will have a strong preference for the accusative (second argument) position; if there are more contextual "strings attached" to the 'ditch', *fossa* will much more often qualify for the accusative position. For example, if *oppidum* has been the discourse topic for a while, or is going to be so in the rest of the text, there will be a strong tendency for it to appear in the accusative (cf. *TFG1*: 13.3.).

That the usage of the alternative patterns is pragmatically monitored is not necessarily incompatible with the idea that they are related through predicate formation, for the following reason: Latin also has pairs in which different lexical predicates occur in alternative case patterns, as in:

(29) a. *adimere   aliquid   alicui*
         take away   something-acc   someone-dat
         'take away something from someone'
    b. *privare   aliquem   aliqua re*
         bereave   someone-acc   something-abl
         'bereave someone of something'

Such pairs, which have more or less the same meaning, will need separate entries in the lexicon, since they are built around different predicates altogether. Nevertheless, the same factors of "textual cohesion" determine strong preferences for either the 'something' or the 'someone' to appear in the accusative position. Thus, pragmatic factors co-determine lexical choice. In the same way, such factors may co-determine the choice of either the basic or the derived predicate frame in such cases as (26a-b).

For a second example, consider the following pair from Hungarian, studied in De Groot (1986, 1987, 1989):

(30) a. *János   vaj-at   ken   a   kenyér-re.*
         John   butter-acc   spread   the   bread-sublative
         'John spreads butter onto the bread'
    b. *János   vaj-jal   keni   a   kenyer-et.*
         John   butter-instr spread   the   bread-acc
         'John spreads the bread with butter'

De Groot demonstrates that (30b) does not differ from (30a) in having a "completive" meaning absent in (30a). In fact, both (30a) and (30b) can be turned into "completive" expressions by choosing the perfective rather than the imperfective aspectual form of the verb. However, when the perfective is chosen in (30a), it is the 'butter' which receives the "holistic" interpretation (i.e., all the butter has been used in smearing the bread); if perfective is assigned to (30b), this interpretation is assigned to the 'bread' (i.e., all the bread has been smeared with butter).

Both in Latin and Hungarian, though in different ways, the second argument position, realized in the accusative, appears to have special semantic / pragmatic significance. Further cross-linguistic research will hopefully throw more light on the privileges of the second argument position.

1.2.4.2. Selection restrictions. There may also be predicate formation rules which exclusively affect the selection restrictions of the input predicate frame. Examples of this may be found in the Algonquian languages (as in Cree, cf.

Wolfart—Carroll 1981), in which verbal predicates fall into four main classes:

(31) a. AI = Animate Intransitive, as in *The mouse squeaks*.
 b. II = Inanimate Intransitive, as in *The door squeaks*.
 c. TA = Transitive Animate, as in *I see the mouse*.
 d. TI = Transitive Inanimate, as in *I see the door*.

The four verb classes differ from one another in (i) the stem forms of the verbal predicate, (ii) the inflections of these stems with respect to Person and Number. In a limited number of cases, II stems can be productively derived from AI stems, and TI stems from TA stems, as in the following Cree examples:

(32) a. *ohpiki-*   AI 'grow up' (as said of a child)
 b. *ohpikin-* II 'grow up' (as said of tomatoes)
(33) a. *waapam-* TA 'see' (a person)
 b. *waapaht-* TI 'see' (something)

A derivation such as (32) could be formulated in the following predicate formation rule:

(34) AI-to-II conversion
   input: pred [V] $(x_1: <anim>)_{Proc}$
   output: {II pred} [V] $(x_1: <inanim>)_{Proc}$

in which "II" symbolizes the "inanimate intransitive" nature of the derived predicate.

Such a rule would then only affect the selection restriction on the argument position of the input predicate.

1.3. Explanatory notes on predicate formation

Let us consider how the predicate formation component of natural languages can be functionally understood. On this topic we can make the following remarks:

(i) *General functions of predicate formation*
Basic predicates, as stored in the lexicon, represent the most fundamental properties and relations expressible in the language. All these predicates,

together with their combinatory properties as coded in the predicate frames, have to be separately learned and memorized if the speaker is to be able to use them at all. There are obvious psychological limits to the number of basic predicates that a language can contain at any one stage in its development. Productive predicate formation rules now warrant the projection of these basic properties / relations onto a much wider set of properties / relations, on the basis of such schemata as the following:

(35)   If property / relation A is designated by predicate frame B, then property / relation A' may be designated by predicate frame B', where B' can be derived from B by a predicate formation rule, the meaning specification of which systematically relates A' to A.

The functionality of this type of projection with respect to the expressibility of properties / relations in a language will be obvious.

(ii) *Specific functions of predicate formation*
Predicate formation rules may have more specific functionality, as we saw in the discussion of semantic function shift in section 1.2.4.1.: in the examples from Latin and from Hungarian there appeared to be something special attached to the second argument position, such that if certain conditions are met terms are preferably placed in that rather than in any other argument position. Predicate formation rules may help in getting terms from non-preferred into preferred argument positions with respect to the criteria in question.

(iii) *Functional explanation of the expression of derived predicate frames*
Derived predicate frames may have expression patterns which are not immediately expected on the basis of their underlying semantic properties. Let us illustrate this point with one example. In French causative constructions, the Causee can be expressed in two different ways:

(36) a. *Jean   a   fait   ouvrir   la   porte   par Pierre.*
         John   has made   open   the   door   by Peter
         'John caused the door to be opened by Peter'
    b. *Jean   a   fait   ouvrir   la   porte   à   Pierre.*
         John   has made   open   the   door   to Peter
         'John made Peter open the door.'

In (36a) the expression *par Pierre* is to be expected on the basis of the underlying Agent function of the Causee. In (36b), however, we find the expression *à Pierre*, which is normally reserved for Recipients in French. At the same time, there is a subtle semantic difference between the two constructions. This difference seems to be that in (36a) the Causee is presented as still controlling the action of closing the door, whereas in (36b) the Causee is presented as not having had much choice other than to obey John's order. The causation is more "direct" in (36b) than it is in (36a).

In Dik (1985a) I have tried to explain these and other related facts by means of the following two principles:

(37)   *Principle of Formal Adjustment* (PFA)
        Derived constructions of type T tend to mould their expression after the typical expression model of non-derived constructions of type T.

(38)   *Principle of Semantic Adjustment* (PSA)
        To the extent that PFA is yielded to, the derived construction will also tend to adjust to the semantics of non-derived constructions of type T.

Let us see how these principles work out in the case of (36). This type of causative formation builds a derived three-place predicate from a two-place input predicate (see rule (14) above). The typical expression model for non-derived three-place predicates is the Agent-Goal-Recipient model as found in:

(39)   *Jean   a   donné   un   cadeau   à   Pierre.*
        John   has   given   a   present   to   Peter
        'John gave a present to Peter.'

We can now say that (36a) has not yielded to PFA: the Causee is still expressed according to its underlying Agent function. Correspondingly, there is no semantic adjustment: the Causee is still fully agentive, and thus in control of the action. (36b), however, has yielded to PFA and adopted the expression model of (39); correspondingly, PSA has dimished the agentive, controlling character of the Causee into a secondary, submissive role in which no room is left for personal initiative.

That PFA and PSA together have considerable explanatory power appears from the fact that they make correct predictions, not only with respect to the manifestations of the causative construction in a great many different languages, but also with respect to other construction types (such as nominalizations), which have no immediate connection with the phenomena discussed here. See chapter 7 for some discussion of this.

1.4. The expression of the output predicate

The abstract elements specified in predicate formation rules can trigger expression rules which modify the form of the input predicate in the following ways:

(i) *Zero modification*
In the case of zero modification there is no change in the form of the predicate, as in *play* (verb) --> *play* (noun), or in a relation such as *plant X in Y* --> *plant Y with X*.

(ii) *Prosodic modification*
Prosodic modification is involved when the output predicate form has accentual or tonal properties different from the input form.

(iii) *Reduplication*
Reduplication may be partial, as when only (part of) an initial or final syllable is reduplicated (e.g. *kalam* --> *ka-kalam, kalam-am*), or complete, as in *kalam* --> *kalam-kalam*). Partial reduplication may be accompanied by "vowel harmony", when the vowel in the reduplicated part adjusts to the vowel value of the initial or final part of the stem (as in *kalam* --> *ka-kalam*, but *tutam* --> *ku-tutam*). In such a case the reduplicated part can be written as *kV-*, where the value of the vowel V must be derived from the relevant stem vowel).

(iv) *Addition of an affix*
The derived predicate may differ from the input predicate through the addition of an affix (prefix, infix, suffix), or a combination of affixes.

(v) *Productive mutation of the stem*
Predicate formation may lead to systematic modification of the form of the stem, e.g. through vowel or consonant mutation. Since predicate formation rules must necessarily be productive, it follows that non-productive mutations cannot be accounted for by such rules; the relevant forms will constitute at most a regularity in the lexicon.

(vi) *Addition of some auxiliary word*
Predicate formation may lead to the addition of an auxiliary word (an auxiliary verb or adverbial particle) in the case of analytic expression of the output predicate.

(vii) *Any combination of (i)-(vi)*
In the expression of actual predicate formation processes, various of these expression devices often combine (to the extent that they are combinable at all).

1.5. Conclusion

The predicate formation component provides us with a powerful mechanism to capture productive processes by means of which new predicates are derived from given predicates. In the modified approach proposed in this chapter, the effects of predicate formation rules on the form of the input predicate are captured by auxiliary operators, and are treated in exactly the same way as those of other types of expression rules. This approach, while maintaining the basic division between derivational and inflectional rules, allows for a unified treatment of all the rules affecting the form of a predicate.

2. Verbal restrictors 1: general properties

2.0. Introduction

In *TFG1*: chapter 6 we analysed terms according to a general schema of the following form:

(1) $(\omega x_i: \varphi_1(x_i): \varphi_2(x_i): ... : \varphi_n(x_i))$

in which each $\varphi(x_i)$ indicates a "restrictor": an open structure in x_i which restricts the potential reference of the term. An instantiation of such a schema is the underlying structure (2a),[1] with the paraphrase (2b) and the realization (2c):

(2) a. $(d1x_i: \textit{dress} \text{ [N]}: \textit{black} \text{ [A]}: \{(\textit{the girl})_{Poss}\}:$
          $[\text{Past e}: \textit{ruin} \text{ [V]} (\textit{John})_{AgSubj} (x_i)_{GoObj}])$

   b. 'definite singular entity x_i such that x_i has the property "dress", such that x_i has the property "black", such that x_i has the property "of the girl", such that x_i has the property that John ruined x_i'

   c. *the girl's black dress which John ruined*

As is clear from this example, restrictors may be of different types. Nouns such as *dress* are typically used as "first restrictors": they represent standardized (bundles of) properties in terms of which a first categorization is projected onto the ensemble of potential referents. Adjectives such as *black* (in the languages that have them) typically function as "second restrictors", adding further detail to what has already been defined in the noun. Adjectives differ from nouns in that they can typically also be used in predicative function. A third type of restrictors is formed by term predicates, which may entertain different relations with the head noun:

---

1. The underlying structure will be further detailed and motivated in the course of our discussion.

(3) a. the girl's *dress*
    b. *the girl* with the red hat
    c. *the chair* in the garden

Apart from these various non-verbal restrictor types, there are different kinds of restrictors which are construed around verbal predicates, such as *which John ruined* in (2a). Some further examples are:

(4) a. *the man* who is working
    b. *the* working *man*
(5) a. *the man* who is working in the garden
    b. *the man* working in the garden

Such restrictors will be called "verbal restrictors" (VRs). VRs are either formed on the basis of an underlying verbal predicate, as in (4)-(5), or of an underlying non-verbal predicate made verbal through copula support, as in:

(6)   *a dress* which is black

2.1. Participant identification

The various types of VR illustrated above have in common that they help identify the referent of a term phrase by specifying a State of Affairs this participant is engaged in. For example, in the expression *a man who is smoking a cigar* we identify the man in question as being a participant in the Action of "smoking a cigar". This identifying strategy I shall call the strategy of "Participant Identification". The universally relevant pragmatic problem of Participant Identification may be solved by VRs in those languages that have them, but also by various other means in languages that do not have them. Participant Identification can be characterized as follows:

(7)   The speaker wishes to refer the addressee to some entity x_i, where x_i can be identified as being a participant in some State of Affairs.

It is useful to look at the typology of VRs in terms of Participant Identification for three main reasons:
   (i) only through retracing the function of VRs to the universally relevant operation of Participant Identification can we understand the properties of VRs in terms of universal strategies of verbal interaction (this chapter);

(ii) looking at VRs in terms of Participant Identification leads to a better understanding of the properties of different types of VRs (chapter 3);

(iii) the "other means" available for solving the problem of Participant Identification may shed light on the sources from which VRs may develop diachronically (chapter 4).

2.2. Some terminological issues

The notion "relative clause", which traditionally covered restrictors expressed with a finite verb, as in (2), has undergone a certain extension in the recent typological literature on verbal restrictors, so as to include various more or less equivalent construction types without a finite verb (Schwartz 1971, Keenan—Comrie 1977, Comrie—Keenan 1979, Downing 1978, Comrie 1981, Mallinson—Blake 1981, Lehmann 1984, 1986, Keenan 1985).[2] Such equivalents come in many different forms, including participial and nominalized construction types. Instead of distinguishing these types from relative clauses proper, typologists have tended to generalize the notion "relative clause" itself to include all these types.[3] With this usage of "relative clause", however, there is little hope of arriving at a universally valid characterization of this notion in terms of recurrent morpho-syntactic properties. The conclusion which has usually been drawn from this situation is that we need a semantic rather than a syntactic definition of "relative clause", in terms of which we can then study the ways in which languages formally express the relevant semantic configuration (Comrie 1981: 136):

(8) *Semantic definition of "relative clause"*
 A relative clause is a proposition[4] embedded within a construction with a nominal head, which restricts the set of potential referents of that nominal head to a subset of which the proposition is (also) true.

---

2. Let me add here that many of the generalizations formulated in this and the following chapters are due to these authors.

3. Keenan (e.g., 1985) rather idiosyncratically uses the term "relative clause" to include the head noun and its determiner(s). In this usage, which I will not follow here, the term "relative clause" covers whole noun phrases such as *the man who wrote the book* rather than the restrictor *who wrote the book*.

4. Below it will be argued that in FG terminology, "predication" is more appropriate here than "proposition".

Thus, the relative clause *which John ruined* in (2) restricts the potential reference of the term to that particular "black dress of the girl" of which it is (also) true that John ruined it.

It is evident that this characterization is also applicable to a construction of the form:

(9)   *the dress* ruined by John

This means that the difference between a finite relative clause, as in (2), and a participial restrictor, as in (9), is judged to be irrelevant to the definition of the notion "relative clause" as given in (8). In both (2) and (9), the part in roman type is judged to be the formal expression of a "relative clause".

One consequence of this view is that other types of restrictive modifier can claim the title of "relative clause" with much the same right as those exemplified in (2) and (9). Consider the following:

(10) a. *Only children* who are intelligent *can go to that school.*
     b. *Only* intelligent *children can go to that school.*
(11) a. *The school* which is in the centre of town *is not very good.*
     b. *The school* in the centre of town *is not very good.*

The a-constructions present genuine relative clauses in the more restricted sense that I will adhere to. The italicized constituents in the b-constructions, however, can be regarded as alternative formal expressions of a similar semantic configuration. The conclusion would then have to be that attributive adjectives, as in (10b), and attributive adpositional phrases, as in (11b), also exemplify "relative clauses".

Indeed, it has often been proposed that the attributive modifiers in the b-constructions should be regarded as "reduced relative clauses", to be derived from the structures underlying the corresponding a-constructions by a rule of "relative clause reduction", which deletes the relative pronoun and the copula, and in the case of adjectives also reverses the order of constituents.

We do not wish to follow this line of reasoning, for several reasons.

(i) In FG we wish to avoid deletion of specified material wherever possible. Thus, there is no room for some such rule as "relative clause reduction" (see *TFG1*: 1.7.1.).

(ii) Nor is there any NEED for such a rule. As was argued in *TFG1*, chapter 8, attributive adjectives and prepositional phrases as in (10b) and (11b) can be treated as predicates in their own right, and need not be described via the detour of relative clauses as in (10a) and (11a).

(iii) Languages may have attributive modifiers which cannot be realized in the form of relative clauses. A case in point is provided by Luganda (Walusimbi—Givón (1970)), where adjectival predicates can never be realized in relative clause form:

(12) *omusajja   o-mulungi*
       man   good
       'the good man'
(13) *omusajja   *e*   *ali*   *(o)-mulungi*
       man   who be   good
       'the man who is good'

For such constructions as (12) to be derived through "relative clause reduction" one would have to postulate an underlying structure which would NECESSARILY have to be reduced in order to be expressed. This would amount not simply to a detour in describing attributive adjectives, but to a detour for which there is no independent motivation.

(iv) With respect to form, ordering, and usage, attributive adjectives have quite different typological properties from relative clauses proper. And in practice, those who propose the semantically oriented definition of "relative clause" given in (8) do not usually discuss attributive adjectives as falling under that definition. But there is nothing in the definition which excludes them.

It is clear that what is defined in (8) is in fact our notion of "restrictor": a predication, embedded within a term, which restricts the set of potential referents of that term. Rather than identify "relative clause" with "restrictor", I should like to regard relative clauses[5] as a subclass of restrictors, characterized by certain distinguishing expression properties. Therefore, I shall adopt the following terminology in the further course of the discussion:

A *Verbal Restrictor* (VR) = a restrictor which contains a verbal predicate. That verbal predicate may either be verbal underlyingly, or formed through the application of the rule of Copula Support.

A *Relative Clause* (RC) = a VR, the predicate of which is realized as a finite verb. Since "finite verb" by and large coincides with "verb on which Tense is or can be expressed", the notion of RC in this definition is practically

---

5. Note that the term "clause" is here retained in order to avoid discontinuity with traditional terminology. Below it will be argued that the restrictive relative clause in terms of FG has the underlying status of an "extended predication".

equivalent to "tensed restrictor".

A *Participial Restrictor* = a VR, the predicate of which is realized as a participle.

A *Nominalized Restrictor* = a VR, the predicate of which is realized as a nominalized verb.

The following constructions exemplify these subtypes of VRs:

(14) a. *the watch* which the father gave to his son
         (Relative Clause)
     b. *the* by the father to his son given *watch*
         (Participial Restrictor)
     c. *the watch* of the father's giving (it) to his son
         (Nominalized Restrictor)

Note that these construction types are primarily considered as subtypes of "restrictor". This implies that we confine ourselves for the time being to the "restrictive" usage of these construction types; so-called "non-restrictive" uses will be discussed below in 2.4.

2.3. Verbal restrictors

2.3.1. Verbal restrictors are extended predications

It appears that VRs, in their basic restrictive function (and contrary to non-restrictors), cannot freely contain "subjective" attitudinal operators and satellites of level 3. Consider:

(15) a. **I'm looking for a person* who can probably help me.
     b. **I'm looking for a person* who allegedly can help me.
     c. **I'm looking for a person* who, I believe, can help me.

Since such subjective modal elements cannot easily occur within the confines of the VR, it may be assumed that the latter indeed (maximally) has the underlying status of an extended predication. That predication specifies the SoA that an entity must be involved in if it is to qualify as a potential referent of the term in question.

If the extended predication is the maximal domain that VRs can contain, this does not mean that all types of VR necessarily contain all the elements

Some general properties of verbal restrictors 29

which can be specified within this domain. One difference between relative clauses on the one hand and participial/nominalized VRs on the other is, for example, that the latter, in contrast to the former, usually do not allow for the specification of tense distinctions, while they do allow for aspectual distinctions. Thus, depending on the nature of the VR, various distinctions potentially specifiable within the domain of the extended predication may be absent.

2.3.2. Verbal restrictors are "open" predications

VRs are typically "open" extended predications in the term variable x_i (cf. *TFG1*: 4.2.). If we start from a closed extended predication as in (16), we can form different "open" variants of this predication by inserting the term variable x_i in one of the term positions, as in (17). Such open predications can be interpreted as specifying properties of x_i:

(16)   Past e: [*give* [V] (*the boy*)$_{Ag}$ (*the book*)$_{Go}$ (*the girl*)$_{Rec}$] (*the library*)$_{Loc}$
        'The boy gave the book to the girl in the library'

(17) a.   Past e: [*give* [V] (x_i)$_{Ag}$ (*the book*)$_{Go}$ (*the girl*)$_{Rec}$] (*the library*)$_{Loc}$
        'the property of being the person who gave the book to the girl in the library'

    b.   Past e: [*give* [V] (*the boy*)$_{Ag}$ (x_i)$_{Go}$ (*the girl*)$_{Rec}$] (*the library*)$_{Loc}$
        'the property of being the thing which the boy gave to the girl in the library'

    c.   Past e: [*give* [V] (*the boy*)$_{Ag}$ (*the book*)$_{Go}$ (x_i)$_{Rec}$] (*the library*)$_{Loc}$
        'the property of being the person to whom the boy gave the book in the library'

    d.   Past e: [*give* [V] (*the boy*)$_{Ag}$ (*the book*)$_{Go}$ (*the girl*)$_{Rec}$] (x_i)$_{Loc}$
        'the property of being the place where the boy gave the book to the girl'

Such open extended predications can then be used as restrictors in term structures, as in (18), in which (17c) is used as a restrictor:

(18)   (d1x_i: *lady* [N]:
        [Past e: [*give* [V] (*the boy*)$_{Ag}$ (*the book*)$_{Go}$ (x_i)$_{Rec}$] (*the library*)$_{Loc}$])
        'the lady to whom the boy gave the book in the library'

Within the domain of the open predication different forms of Subj/Obj assignment may be possible. For example, the following would be a possible configuration in English:

(19)   (d1x_i: *lady* [N]:
[Past e: [*give* [V] (*the boy*)$_{Ag}$ (*the book*)$_{Go}$ (x_i)$_{RecSubj}$] (*the library*)$_{Loc}$])
'the lady who was given the book by the boy in the library'

As Kwee (1981) has shown, we must not interpret the notion of "open predication" procedurally, where the procedure would involve selecting an extended predication schema, inserting terms in all term positions but one, and then using the result as a restrictor in building up a term structure. This procedure would not guarantee that the open term position would be relativizable and semantically appropriate to the term-as-constructed-so-far, a fact which would lead to unwanted filtering in the grammar. The correct procedure is thus to first select a relativizable term position in an extended predication schema and then fill in the rest of the term positions.

2.3.3. Anaphorical relations

The open term position in the VR stands in an anaphorical relation to the variable of the term in which it occurs, as comes out in such paraphrases as:

(20)   *the lady who was given the flowers*
"the lady such that *she* was given the flowers"

Many languages do indeed have pronominal expression of the open term variable as in the paraphrase of (20) — a phenomenon to which we return below — and relative pronouns can be regarded as the fused expression of the relativized and the anaphorical character of the relativized variable.

    The anaphorical nature of the open term variable is already clear from the identity of indices of the x_i variables used in the examples given so far. To make this anaphorical nature of the open term position even more explicit, I shall use the anaphorical operator "A" to mark the variable in this position. Thus, the structure given in (19) can be more clearly specified as:

(21)   [Past e: [*give* [V] (*the boy*)$_{Ag}$ (*the book*)$_{Go}$ (Ax_i)$_{RecSubj}$]
(*the library*)$_{Loc}$])

In the case of relative clauses, the anaphorical variable will also be called the relativized variable.

2.3.4. Selection restrictions

It is not the case that just any open predication can be inserted into just any term structure.[6] Compare:

(22) a. *The horse neighed.*
 b. **The house neighed.*
(23) a. *the horse which neighed*
 b. **the house which neighed*

The predicate *neigh* is selectionally restricted to horses:

(24) *neigh* [V] (x_1: <horse>)$_{Ag}$

Thus, (22a) is acceptable since a term designating a horse is inserted into the argument position of (24), but (22b) is not. In the case of terms such as (23) the situation is a little bit more complex. Consider the term structure underlying (23a):

(25) (d1x_i: *horse* [N]: [Past e: *neigh* [V] (Ax_i: <horse>)$_{Ag}$])

In this case the selectional rule must be formulated as follows: the extended predication underlying the VR must be chosen in such a way that the selection restriction on its "open" term position is compatible with the semantic properties of the head noun (the initial restrictor). This again shows that the best method of constructing a VR is to first decide which is going to be the "open" position in the restrictor, and then insert terms into the remaining positions (see also Kwee 1981). This presupposes a step-by-step procedure for the construction of term structures, in which restrictors are stacked onto one another one by one, in such a way that the term-as-constructed-so-far may constrain the choice of further restrictors.

This "dynamic" view of term construction is reinforced by the fact that not

---

6. On the problem of choosing an appropriate restrictor, as seen from a computational point of view, see Kwee (1981).

only the head noun, but also the other restrictors as chosen so far may influence the appropriateness of a VR (cf. *TFG1*: 6.4.1). Compare:

(26) a. *the girl who is pregnant*
 b. **the boy who is pregnant*
(27) a. *the professor who is pregnant*
 b. *the female professor who is pregnant*
 c. **the pregnant professor who is female*
 d. **the male professor who is pregnant*

The examples in (27) provide several arguments for a dynamic term construction procedure: first, in (27d) it is the adjectival restrictor *male* rather than the head noun which blocks the choice of *pregnant* in the VR; second, the difference between (27b) and (27c) shows that if first *female* is chosen and then *pregnant*, the result is all right, but if first *pregnant* is chosen and then *female*, the result is redundant (cf. Dahl 1971). This is because "pregnant" already implies "female". These phenomena thus show that a restrictor must be compatible with the term-structure-as-construed-so-far. In the next section we will find another argument for this form of dynamic term construction.

2.3.5. Stacking of verbal restrictors

2.3.5.0. Introduction. The underlying structure which we assume for terms is such that restrictors can be "stacked" onto one another (as expressed by ":" in schema (1) above), thus progressively limiting the ensemble of potential referents of a term. Note that "stacking" applies to a series of restrictors, related through ":", such that each following restrictor applies to the same term variable x_i. This should be distinguished from recursion within VRs, as in:

(28) *the dog [that chased the cat [that caught the mouse]]*

Here, the VR *that caught the mouse* restricts the term headed by *cat*, whereas the VR *that chased the cat that caught the mouse* restricts the term headed by *dog*. Such recursion is allowed in most languages within the limits of interpretable complexity.

Stacking rather than recursion is involved in a construction such as:

(29)   a hard-working man who loved his job

In this case, the potential referent is first restricted by "man", then by "hard-working", and then by "who loved his job". These restrictors are stacked onto one another rather than being recursively nested inside one another.

So far we have not put any limitation on the number and kinds of restrictors which can be stacked onto each other. It appears to be a universal fact about natural languages, however, that the possibilities for stacking restrictors in the actual construction of terms are constrained in various ways, and that the constraints are especially restrictive in the case of VRs (more particularly, in the case of VRs realized as RCs). The question is, then, how we are going to build these constraints into our description of term structures.

In order to tackle the problem of restrictions on stacking I will proceed in the following way. First, I give the facts as they are found in two languages, English and Luganda. Then, I show how the rules of term formation can be formulated in such a way that any output that is ungrammatical in terms of stacking is systematically avoided.

2.3.5.1. Stacking in English. Stockwell et al. (1973:442) give a neat survey of the facts of stacking in English. These facts can be summarized as follows:

(i) adjectival and nominal restrictors can be quite freely stacked onto one another, as in:

(30)   ten square black Chinese paper boxes

This term can be given an interpretation such that *box, paper, Chinese, black,* and *square* successively restrict the set of potential referents.

(ii) RCs can be stacked onto prepositional modifiers:

(31)   a car with rear engine drive that holds the road well

(iii) in some dialects of English, RCs cannot normally be stacked onto one another. In other dialects this is marginally possible:

(32) a.   ?a watch that keeps good time that is cheap
     b.   ?a box that is Chinese that is black
     c.   ?a car that has a rear engine that holds the road well

(iv) in probably no dialect of English can more than two RCs be stacked onto one another:

34   *Verbal restrictors 1*

(33)   **a watch that keeps good time that is cheap that I want to buy*

(v) on the other hand, in certain types of construction, stacking of two RCs onto one another is grammatical in all dialects of English:

(34)   *the first book that I read that really amused me*

I do not think that this last example can be explained away by assuming some special underlying structure for it. It seems quite clear that the term operator (ordinator) *first* has the entire following construction in its scope in the sense that the referent of (34) is intended to be the first entity in a series of entities such that each of these entities x_i has the properties defined by:

(35) a. *book* [N]
     b. [Past e_i: *read* [V] $(I)_{Ag}$ $(Ax_i)_{Go}$]
     c. [Past e_j: *amuse* [V] $(Ax_i)_{Fo}$ $(me)_{Go}$]

The facts of English clearly show (i) that stacking of restrictors must be possible in underlying term structure, while (ii) there are heavy restrictions on stacking, especially if the restrictors are to be realized in the form of RCs.

2.3.5.2. Stacking in Luganda. The following account of stacking restrictions in Luganda is based on Walusimbi—Givón (1970). The interpretation in terms of FG is mine. Walusimbi and Givón present the following facts about term formation in Luganda.

Attributive adjectival modifiers in Luganda are distinguished from predicative adjectives by means of a prefix. As noted above, adjectival modifiers cannot be expressed by means of RCs, as is evident from the grammaticality of (12) as against the ungrammaticality of (13).

Adjectival restrictors of type (12) can be stacked onto one another. Their order reflects the order of restrictors as we would have it in underlying term structure:

(36)   *omusajja   o-mulungi   o-munene*
        man   good   big
        'the big good man'
(37)   *omusajja   o-munene   o-mulungi*
        man   big   good
        'the good big man'

The fact that (36) and (37) are not synonymous is (further) evidence that the restrictors must be stacked rather than conjoined in underlying structure.

Adjectival modifiers can also be stacked onto RCs, and the other way around, as in:

(38) a. *omusajja   gwe   na-laba   o-mulungi*
        man   whom   I saw   good
     b. *omusajja   o-mulungi gwe   na-laba*
        man   good   whom   I saw
        'the good man whom I saw'

And RCs can be stacked onto one another, as in:

(39) *omusajja   gwe   o-labye   (e)   a-badde   wano*
     man   whom   you-saw   who   was   here
     'the man whom you saw who was here'
(40) *omusajja   (e)   a-badde   wano   gwe   o-labye*
     man   who   was   here   whom   you-saw
     'the man who was here whom you saw'

There are interesting restrictions, however, on this mutual stacking of RCs: a Subj relativizing restrictor can be stacked onto an Obj relativizing one, as in (39), and the other way around, as in (40), but two Subj relativizing restrictors or two Obj relativizing restrictors cannot be stacked onto one another: for two RCs to be stacked onto one another, then, they must differ as to the syntactic function of the relativized term.

This functional non-identity of the relativized variable seems to be a general condition on stacking of RCs. For example, the only type of English construction said to allow stacking of RCs in all dialects ((34) above) also has the property that the two relativized term positions have different syntactic functions. The same is true of the only example of grammatical stacking in English given by Jacobsen (1977:354):

(41)   *People* [that I know][that want to invest] *never seem to get a chance.*

And the example given in Van der Auwera (1985:21) of grammatical stacking in French also has this property:

(42) Julie   est   la   seule   femme   que je   connaisse
      Julie   is   the   only   woman   that I   know
         qui   sache   faire   la   cuisine.
         who   knows   do   the   kitchen
      'Julie is the only woman that I know who can cook'

Though the Luganda facts are different from those of English and French in detail, they strikingly confirm the general pattern: stacking of restrictors is possible, but heavily constrained in the case of RCs.

2.3.5.3. *Incorporating restrictions on stacking in the grammar.* In discussing the restrictions on stacking in Luganda, Walusimbi—Givón (1970) suggest that these could be accounted for in terms of "perceptual strategies" which disfavour stacking constructions when these exceed a certain limit of complexity. Something like this may well be the case, but the basic principles of FG are not compatible with the idea that there is a dichotomy between the grammar on the one hand and perceptual strategies on the other, such that the latter may be used to filter out unacceptable output of the former. Speakers certainly know how to avoid producing constructions which the Addressee would be unable to interpret. That is, while perceptual mechanisms may explain why the rules of grammar are the way they are, they do not release us from the duty to formulate these rules in such a way that ungrammatical output is avoided.

The only solution open to FG, then, is to constrain term formation rules in such a way that no term structures can be formed which could not be properly expressed. In other words, the restrictions on stacking will have to be built into the procedures for term formation. Therefore, these procedures must be formulated in such a way that configurations of the form:

(43)   ... $\varphi_m(Ax_i): \varphi_n(Ax_i): ...$

can be formed only under extremely limited circumstances. Let us suppose that the condition in English, just as in Luganda, is that configurations of type (43) only lead to completely well-formed constructions if the two variables have different syntactic functions. This would further restrict the type of configuration allowed in underlying term structures to such cases as:

(44)   (d1 first x_i: *book* [N]:
        [Past e_i: *read* [V] $(I)_{AgSubj} (Ax_i)_{GoObj}$]:
        [Past e_j: *amuse* [V] $(Ax_i)_{FoSubj} (I)_{GoObj}$])

in which the first (Ax_i) has Obj function, the second (Ax_i) Subj function (or the other way around).

The next question is: how do we bring it about that only configurations of type (44) are admitted to underlying term structures, and all other double (Ax_n) configurations excluded? This can be achieved if the following procedure is followed:

— term structures are built up gradually, the successive restrictors being added one by one;

— whenever a restrictor has been added, it is decided what syntactic function will be assigned to the relativized variable.

This procedure implies that there will be a moment in the construction of (44) at which the term-under-construction will have the following form:

(45)   (d1 first x_i: *book* [N]: [Past e_i: *read* [V] $(I)_{AgSubj}$ $(Ax_i)_{GoObj}$].....

It is now not difficult to either decide not to add another verbal restrictor, or to choose a further restrictor in such a way that the (Ax_i) variable is in a position in which it can receive another syntactic function than Obj.

It would seem that any other procedure than this gradual building up from left to right will lead to situations where something will have been construed which cannot be expressed, so that it must be filtered out. Note, however, that this provides another argument for the dynamic term construction procedure argued for in 2.2.4.

In a situation such as (45), in which it is either difficult or impossible to add another relativized restrictor, there is always a way to achieve just about the same communicative effect. This is to conjoin the next restrictor to the last one,[7] so as to result in:

(46)   (d1 first x_i: *book* [N]:
         [Past e_i: *read* [V] $(I)_{AgSubj}$ $(Ax_i)_{GoObj}$]
         and
         [Past e_j: *really like* [V] $(I)_{ExpSubj}$ $(Ax_i)_{GoObj}$])
         'the first book which I read and which I really liked'

Such conjunction of restrictors is not constrained in the way that stacking is, neither in English nor in Luganda. It is probably universal that restrictors can be conjoined *ad libitum*, again up to the limit of interpretable complexity.

---

7. For conjoining of restrictors, see 9.3.5.

2.4. Non-restrictive usage of verbal restrictors[8]

In many languages a distinction can be made between restrictive and non-restrictive (descriptive, appositional) usage of VRs. The difference can be illustrated with:

(47) RESTRICTIVE:
The students who have passed the exam *can take the advanced course.*
('only the students who have passed the exam')

(48) NON-RESTRICTIVE:
The students, who have passed the exam, *can take the advanced course.*
('all the students')

In (47) the relative clause restricts the ensemble of intended referents to the sub-ensemble of students for whom it is true that they have passed the exam. In (48), on the other hand, it is stated that all the (relevant) students can take the advanced course. By way of additional information about these students, it is said that they have passed the exam.

The same distinction can be made in the case of participial restrictors:

(49) a. *The 16 players selected for the team were sent on a training tour.*
  b. *The 16 players, selected for the team, were sent on a training tour.*

In fact, the same distinction is also relevant to attributive adjectives and term predicates, as in:

---

8. For discussion of non-restrictive relatives see Touratier (1980: 370-372), Mallinson—Blake (1981: 359-366), Lehmann (1984: 261-267); within the context of FG, Rijksbaron (1981), Hannay—Vester (1987), Vester (1987), and Van der Auwera (1992).

(50) a. *The three intelligent children were given a scholarship.*
b. *The three — intelligent — children were given a scholarship.*
(51) a. *The trees in the back of the garden will have to be cut down.*
b. *The trees — in the back of the garden — will have to be cut down.*

In (50a) the "three intelligent children" are opposed to other, less intelligent children; in (50b) only three children are involved, and these are said to be intelligent. Similarly, in (51a), but not in (51b), it is presupposed that there are other trees than those in the back of the garden. In their non-restrictive usage, the relevant constituents may be called "non-restrictors".

2.4.1. Differences between restrictors and non-restrictors

Non-restrictors very often have the same segmental form as the corresponding restrictors, but they will characteristically be distinguished from the latter in their suprasegmental, prosodic properties. Whereas restrictors are integrated into the prosodic contour of the term structure in which they occur, non-restrictors are characteristically "punctuated", set off within that structure by prosodic inflections which more or less literally put them between brackets. This prosodic difference, which is generally similar across languages, iconically symbolizes the less integrated, more independent status of the information contained in non-restrictors.[9]

There may also be segmental differences between restrictors and their non-restrictive counterparts. Consider the following differences in English:

(52) a. *The three books which/that/Ø John sold brought in quite a lot of money.*
b. *The three books, which/*that/*Ø John sold, brought in quite a lot of money.*

Non-restrictive relative clauses in English can only take the relative pronoun, and not the relative marker *that* or Ø marking. Similar differences are found in other languages: thus, Persian has a suffix -*i* which can be interpreted as "announcing" that the following constituent is going to be a restrictor. This suffix is not used when a non-restrictor follows (cf. Comrie 1981:132). In

---

9. Cf. Quirk et al. (1972) on the "parenthesis" intonation of non-restrictive relatives.

Bahasa Indonesia, restrictors are distinguished from non-restrictors through the position of the demonstrative elements *ini* 'this' and *itu* 'that', which are usually term-final (Sie Ing Djiang 1989):

(53) a. *Biduan   yang   berasal   dari   Solo   ini   tinggal   di*
       vocalist RM   come   from   Solo   this   live   in
       Jakarta.
       Jakarta
       'This vocalist who comes from Solo lives in Jakarta.'
   b. *Biduan   ini,   berasal   dari   Solo,   tinggal   di   Jakarta.*
      vocalist this   come   from   Solo   live   in   Jakarta
      'This vocalist, who comes from Solo, lives in Jakarta.'

Note that again this difference in formal structure suggests that the non-restrictor falls outside the structure of the term proper.[10]

Semantically, too, non-restrictors in a sense stand outside the term which they modify. This is clear from such properties as the following:

(i) Non-restrictors do not restrict the ensemble of potential referents of the term in question. They add information to the term, but that information is not essential for identifying the referents of the term.

(ii) Consequently, when we leave out a non-restrictor from a term, we do not thereby change the potential referent ensemble of that term. The remaining construction has the same domain of referential application as the original one.

(iii) Since non-restrictors do not restrict the ensemble of referents of a term, they can be added to terms of which the referent ensemble set is already uniquely determined, this in contradistinction to restrictors. Compare:

(54) a. *John, who is a good friend of mine, is staying with us.*
   b. **John who is a good friend of mine is staying with us.*

This does not mean that restrictors are absolutely incompatible with proper nouns, but when they are added, the implications are different. Compare:

(55) a. *The Eiffel Tower, which was finished in 1889, is a technical miracle.*
   b. *The Eiffel Tower which was finished in 1889 is a technical miracle.*

---

10. For similar such differences in other languages see Mallinson—Blake (1981: 359-366).

(55b) cannot be ruled out as ungrammatical, but (contrary to (55a)) it presupposes that there is at least one other Eiffel Tower which was not finished in 1889.

(iv) Non-restrictors fall outside the scope of the term operators of the term which they accompany. Thompson (1971:87) gives the following examples:

(56) a. *Three boys who had beards were at the party.*
b. *Three boys, who had beards, were at the party.*

It is evident that *three* in (56a) quantifies "boys who had beards", whereas in (56b) it quantifies only "boys".

(v) When anaphoric reference is made to a term accompanied by a non-restrictor the content of the non-restrictor is not in the scope of the anaphoric element. McCawley (1978:151) gives the following example:

(57) a. *Tom has two cats that once belonged to Fred, and Sam has one.*
b. *Tom has two violins, which once belonged to Heifetz, and Sam has one.*

It seems impossible to interpret (57b) as saying that Sam has one violin which (also) once belonged to Heifetz.

(vi) A non-restrictor cannot be added to a term which introduces an empty ensemble (Keenan 1985: 169). Compare:

(58) a. *On my way home I saw no man who was carrying a gun.*
b. **On my way home I saw no man, who was carrying a gun.*

2.4.2. The semantic status of non-restrictors

In contrast to restrictors, non-restrictors freely admit attitudinal and illocutionary satellites:[11]

---

11 Cf. Pinkster (1988: 125) for some Latin examples.

(59) a. *The students who worked hard passed the exam.*
b. **The students who probably worked hard passed the exam.*
c. *The students, who probably worked hard, passed the exam.*
d. **The students who, frankly, worked hard passed the exam.*
e. *The students, who, frankly, worked hard, passed the exam.*

In the preceding we have analysed restrictive VRs as extended predications. Such predications do not contain illocutionary and attitudinal elements. We now see that non-restrictors are different in type. They can be analysed as full clause structures with their own illocutionary and attitudinal layers. This also explains why non-restrictors can differ in illocution from the clause in which they are embedded. This was noted by Ross (1967) with the following example:

(60) *Is even Clarence, who is wearing mauve socks, a swinger?*

The same observation is made by Lyons (1977: 760, note 19), who compares the following constructions:

(61) a. *Is that man, who broke the bank at Monte Carlo, a mathematician?*
b. *Is that man - he broke the bank at Monte Carlo - a mathematician?*

In these examples the non-restrictor has declarative illocutionary value, even though occurring within an interrogative matrix clause.

2.4.3. Non-restrictors and independent clauses

The last example gives further evidence for the relative independence of non-restrictors from the term they modify: many linguists have pointed out the close relations between non-restrictors, parenthetical constituents, and freely conjoined clauses:

(62) a. *The students, who have passed the exam, can take the advanced course.*
b. *The students - they have passed the exam - can take the advanced course.*
c. *The students have passed the exam and (they) can take the advanced course.*

In the early days of Transformational Grammar this was often taken as a ground for deriving sentences with non-restrictors from corresponding pairs of conjoined clauses (cf. Thompson 1971, Jacobsen 1977: 344). But such an analysis is not without problems.

First, there is a hierarchical relation between the information contained in the main clause and that contained in the non-restrictor which is not present in the corresponding conjoined clauses:

(63) a. *The plane, which had never flown well anyway, finally crashed.*
   b. *The plane finally crashed, and it had never flown well anyway.*

The non-restrictive information in (63a) is semantically subordinate to the main clause in a way which is not mirrored in (63b). Often, the subordinated information will be pragmatically interpreted as providing the ground or motivation for why the content of the main clause can be asserted. This relation may be made explicit in certain segmental elements:

(64) a. *The book, which* after all *is not very expensive, can be recommended to undergraduates.*
   b. *The book, cheap* as it is, *can be recommended to undergraduates.*

The potential illocutionary difference between matrix clause and non-restrictor also militates against a derivation from conjoined clauses. Consider example (60). In such a case, Ross (1967) argues, the underlying source cannot be a pair of conjoined clauses as in:

(65)   **Is even Clarence a swinger and he is wearing mauve socks.*

The only potential source would then be a combination of independent sentences such as:

(66)   *Is even Clarence a swinger? He is wearing mauve socks.*

But that presupposes a model in which certain complex sentences can be derived from combinations of independent sentences, a procedure not commonly accepted even in Transformational Grammar.

2.4.4. The FG analysis of non-restrictors

In FG, obviously, we would like to avoid such derivations. How, then, can we analyse non-restrictors in a way which does justice to the fact that (i) they are subordinated within the clause in which they occur, while (ii) they have a certain degree of formal and semantic independence within that clause?

This problem can be solved by analysing non-restrictors as open clauses adjoined by way of parenthesis to a term which is complete in itself.[12] This parenthetical relation may be symbolized by =(...)=. Compare the following term structures:

(67) a. *the books which John sold*
      $(dmx_i: book [N]: [Past e: sell [V] (John)_{Ag} (Ax_i)_{Go}])$
   b. *the books, which John sold, ...*
      $(dmx_i: book [N]) = (Decl\ E: X: Past\ e: sell [V] (John)_{Ag} (Ax_i)_{Go}) =$

The bracketing in (67b) now correctly shows that the term *the books* is complete in itself, and is available as a target for various operations (e.g. anaphorical reference). It also indicates that the term operators of that term do not extend their scope into the non-restrictor. The formal differences between (67a) and (67b) can be used to trigger their differences in expression (qua intonation and qua selection of initial marker). On the other hand, the structures of (67a) and (67b) are sufficiently similar to show how they can be expressed in much the same segmental form.

Metaphorically speaking, we can say that a non-restrictor is a semantically independent but subordinate (open) clause which is adjoined to a term, and is then "caught" by the rules and principles which determine the form and the order of constituents in the expression of underlying term structures.

---

12. Cf. Rijksbaron (1981), De Groot—Limburg (1986).

3. Verbal restrictors 2: types

3.0. Introduction

As is already clear from the various examples given in chapter 2, VRs may differ in various respects, such as:

(i) whether they contain a finite verb or not. The former were called "relative clauses", the latter "participial restrictors" or "nominalized restrictors", as the case may be.

(ii) whether they precede the head noun (occur in the Prefield), or follow it (occur in the Postfield). The former will be called "prenominal VRs", the latter "postnominal VRs". There is also a type of VR in which the head noun seems to appear inside VRs, which may be called "circumnominal VRs".[1]

Since the VR is a modifier of the head noun of a term, we would expect the following basic distribution in Prefield and Postfield languages:

(1)   Prefield   Postfield
         VR - N   N - VR

Since Greenberg (1966) it has been known that this correlation does hold to a certain extent.[2] Clear Postfield languages of the V-initial type almost invariably have the order N-VR, and clear V-final languages predominantly have the order VR-N. The correlation is not complete, however: prefield languages may have N-VR ordering (especially if the VR is a relative clause), either categorically or as an optional variant to VR-N. The correct picture is thus as follows:

(2)   Prefield   Postfield
         VR - N   N - VR
         N - VR

---

1. For the terminology used here, compare Downing (1978) and Lehmann (1984).

2. Greenberg (1966), well aware of the differences between prenominal and postnominal VRs, was careful to use the term "relative expression" rather than "relative clause".

This implies that, when considered across all languages, postnominal VRs predominate over prenominal VRs.[3] I return to the question of how this distribution could be explained in 4.1.

When we speak of VR-N and N-VR as we have done so far, the impression is easily established that prenominal and postnominal VRs are birds of one feather, and that the only crucial difference lies in the order of VR and N. This impression, however, is quite misleading. Prenominal and postnominal VRs typically have quite different properties:

(3) TYPICAL PROPERTIES OF VRs:
	prenominal	*postnominal*
(i)	non-finite verb	finite verb
(ii)	final marker, if any	initial marker, if any
(iii)	no relative pronouns	relative pronouns possible
(iv)	rare pronominal expression	frequent pronominal expression

Property (i) defines postnominal VRs as typically taking the form of relative clauses in the more restricted sense which we have assigned to this term in 2.2. Prenominal VRs typically have the status of participial or other non-finite restrictors. This difference is especially clear in languages which have VRs of both types, as we shall see in the next chapter.

Property (ii) is in accordance with the Relator Principle (see *TFG1*: 16.4.2.), which in this case defines the preferred ordering as follows (where RM is the marker of the verbal restrictor):

(4) (VR ... (RM)) Noun ((RM) ... VR)

(5) a. prenominal: *potatoes eating-RM man*
     b. postnominal: *man RM eats potatoes*

Properties (iii) and (iv) will be discussed below.

A further difference between prenominal and postnominal VRs is that

---

3. N-VR is the "dominant" construction in the sense of Greenberg (1966) (cf. Keenan (1985)). The statement that there is a correlation between SOV order and prenominal relative clause, which is sometimes found in the literature, is in two ways an oversimplification: first, many SOV languages have postnominal VRs; second, prenominal VRs do not have the properties of "relative clauses" in the more restricted sense of the term.

whereas postnominal VRs are quite uniform in structure, prenominal VRs have a much richer variety of different manifestations. In this chapter the various types of VR will be discussed one by one. I will now first concentrate on the properties of postnominal relative clauses. In chapter 4 I will then discuss some general questions pertaining to the ways in which the variety and the recurrent properties of VRs could be explained.

3.1. Postnominal verbal restrictors

3.1.0. Introduction

Postnominal VRs typically contain a finite verb and thus have the status of relative clauses. They are initially marked, if at all. They may contain relative pronouns and often exhibit pronominal expression of the relativized variable. Let us have a closer look at these different properties.

Finite relative clauses were shown above to be based on open extended predications in which free choice of Tense is possible. This means that the presence of a specified Tense operator in a VR can in itself already be seen as necessarily triggering expression as a relative clause, whereas absence of specified Tense in the VR would trigger non-finite (participial or nominalized) realization of the VR (cf. De Groot 1989). For the sake of clarity, however, I will add an operator "R" (for Relativization) to those VRs which are to be realized as relative clauses. We will then get such underlying structures as:

(6) $(d1x_i: book [N]: R [Past e_i: read [V] (John)_{AgSubj} (Ax_i)_{GoObj}])$
        'the book which John read'

Such a structure can (in English) be realized in different ways:

(7) a. *the book Ø John read Ø*
    b. *the book that John read Ø*
    c. *the book which John read*

We can now say that in (7a) neither the R operator nor the (Ax_i) variable gets any formal expression. In (7b), the R operator is expressed by the invariable subordinator or relativization marker (RM) *that*, whereas the (Ax_i) variable is again not expressed.[4] In (7c), the relative pronoun *which* can be interpreted as a fused expression of both the operator R and the relativized variable (Ax_i).

Let us now consider these various forms of relative clause expression from a more cross-linguistic perspective.

3.1.1. The formal expression of relative clauses[5]

There are three types of markers which, in different combinations, are used to formally characterize postnominal relative clauses:

(i) *invariable relativization markers* (RM), comparable to subordinators, such as English *that*; these markers give explicit information on the subordinate status of the relative clause, but they give no direct information on the nature of the relativized variable.

(ii) *personal pronouns*, such as *he, his, him*; such pronouns, in the context of the relative clause, give information about the nature of the relativized variable, but they give no information about the relativized nature of the relative clause.

(iii) *relative pronouns*, such as English *who, whose, whom*; such elements contain information both on the relativized status of the relative clause and on the nature of the relativized variable.

Together these elements define the following most common patterns for the expression of postnominal relative clauses, where P1 is the first position in the relative clause:

(8)   FORMAL MARKING OF POSTNOMINAL RELATIVE CLAUSES

	P1 position	*Pattern position*
a.	Ø	Ø
b.	RM	Ø
c.	Ø	personal pronoun
d.	RM	personal pronoun
e.	RM + personal pronoun	Ø
f.	relative pronoun	Ø

---

4. I here tacitly assume that English relative *that* is an RM, not a relative pronoun. The long-standing debate on the status of relative *that* is exhaustively discussed in Van der Auwera (1984), whose final conclusion, however, is different from the present view.

5. Cf. Keenan (1985).

The following constructions illustrate these different patterns:

(9) a. the book   Ø   John read Ø
    b. the book that John read Ø
    c. the book   Ø   John read it
    d. the book that John read it
    e. the book that it John read Ø
    f. the book which John read Ø

Note the following points: the RM and relative pronoun always take initial position in the relative clause; thus, if the relative status of the relative clause is marked at all, it is marked at the beginning of the relative clause. When an relative clause contains a pronominal element we speak of "pronominal expression" of the anaphorical (relativized) variable. Such a pronominal element, if it occurs, is typically placed in pattern position (= that position which a pronoun would take in a non-relative clause); it may also be attracted to initial position (type (9e)). Note, finally, that relative pronoun and personal pronoun exclude each other. That is, we have not found convincing cases of constructions corresponding to:

(10)   *the book which John read it.

This fact (if confirmed by further research) allows us to say that relative pronoun does indeed simultaneously express R and (Ax_i).[6]

Let us now look at some concrete examples of the less familiar patterns of (9). Constructions (9a) and (9b) are grammatical in English. Examples of (9c) are found in many Oceanic languages, for instance in Aoban (Melanesian, Keenan—Comrie 1979: 333):

---

6. Romanian, mentioned as a counterexample to this mutual exclusion of relative pronoun and personal pronoun (Downing 1978: 184), does not seem to be a real counterexample: it is true that alongside the relative pronoun, the RC may contain a coreferential clitic, but this clitic also occurs in a variety of other constructions in which some constituent is placed in initial position (Mallinson 1986: 61). In a language in which we would normally have *This book I don't like it* in a main clause, we would not count the pronominal element *it* in *this book which I don't like it* as representing an RC formation strategy.

(11) *John   lehi na toa   a   tubui   wehea*
     John   see   the chicken the woman   killed-it
     'John saw the chicken that the woman killed'

Constructions of type (9d) represent the normal relative clause type in Hebrew and many other languages. The following example is from Givón (1973):

(12) *ha-iš   še-Yoav   raa (oto)   etmol*
      the-man   that-Yoav   saw (him)   yesterday
      'the man that Yoav saw yesterday'

In the following alternative to (12), the pronoun has been attracted to the RM in initial position.[7] This exemplifies type (9e):

(13) *ha-iš   še-oto   Yoav   raa etmol*
      the man   that-him   Yoav   saw yesterday
      'the man that Yoav saw yesterday'

I believe that this type can be explained as follows: the personal pronoun tends towards the initial part of the clause on account of LIPOC (cf. *TFG1*: chapter 16). It may thus end up in clause-second position, directly after the invariable RM. One may then expect the RM and the pronoun to fuse into one constituent, which will then have the status of a relative pronoun (compare Maxwell 1979: 368).

This, however, cannot be the only source of the relative pronoun, since the fusion of a RM and a pronoun will not usually lead to a relative pronoun which has the same form as an interrogative pronoun or a demonstrative pronoun; and relative pronouns are very often formally identical to these. We return to this matter in chapter 4.

Constructions of type (9f), with a relative pronoun in P1 position, are again grammatical in English. Note that in certain cases we cannot say that the relative pronoun as such is in P1 position; rather, it may be part of a constituent which is in P1 position. This is trivially the case when the relative pronoun is part of a prepositional phrase, as in (14a), and less trivially when the relative pronoun is part of a complex term, as in (14b):

---

7. For further examples of this type of construction, see Maxwell (1979: 367-370).

(14) a. *a matter* about which *I had not thought before*
     b. *a verbal restrictor*, the predicate of which *is expressed by a finite verb*

Nevertheless, the statement holds that relative pronouns are never found in pattern position (except where pattern position accidentally coincides with initial position). In other words, we do not find constructions such as:

(15) a. **an interesting man I met whom last week*
     b. **a knife I cut the bread with which*

3.1.2. On pronominal expression of the relativized variable

We saw that the following combinations of RM, personal prounoun and Ø are quite commonly encountered:

(16) a. *the book   Ø   I   read   Ø*
     b. *the book   that I   read   Ø*
     c. *the book   Ø   I   read   it*
     d. *the book   that I   read   it*

Concerning the expression of the variable (Ax_i) by a personal pronoun, a number of generalizations can be made. Some of these statements hinge on the notion of the "Accessibility Hierarchy" as introduced by Keenan—Comrie (1977):

(17)   Subj > Obj > IndObj > Oblique > Genitive > Object of Comparison

This hierarchy was originally proposed to capture the typological distribution of relativization possibilities: from left to right through the hierarchy, relativization becomes more difficult and more constrained across languages. In chapter 16 the formulation of the Accessibility Hierarchy will be critically examined; a more composite notion of "accessibility" will be proposed there, which incorporates other types of constraints not specified in (17), such as constraints depending on intrinsic semantic properties of the terms involved, and "hierarchical" constraints, sensitive to the position of the term in the hierarchical structure of the clause (cf. Keenan 1985). In terms of such an extended notion of "accessibility", the following can be said about pronominal expression:

(18) a. If the relativized variable has Subj function, it is uncommon for it to be expressed by a personal pronoun.
   b. The less accessible the relativized variable is, the greater the chance that it will be realized by a personal pronoun.
   c. If a personal pronoun appears at a certain position in a hierarchy of accessibility, then it will appear in all lower positions on that hierarchy which are relativizable at all in the language (based on Maxwell 1979: 364).
   d. Between positions on an accessibility hierarchy where a personal pronoun is excluded and positions where a personal pronoun is required, there may be positions where a personal pronoun is optional.

Principle (18a) says that constructions of the following form are uncommon, though not excluded:

(19)   *the man that* he *kissed the girl*

Principle (18b) says that we will above all expect pronominal expression of positions if these are rather remote in terms of accessibility. This can even be observed in English (especially spoken English): although in general English does not allow pronominal expression of (Ax_i), we may find the combination of RM + personal pronoun in marginal constructions such as:

(20)   *the book* that *John claimed that Peter had considered buying* it *for Mary's birthday*

Principle (18c), applied in terms of Accessibility Hierarchy (17), says that if a language has (21a), it will also have (21b), if Genitive (or Possessor) is relativizable at all:

(21) a. *the man that I gave the book* to him
   b. *the man that I bought* his *book*

And (18d) says that the following situation is not uncommon (see Keenan—Comrie 1977, 1979 for data on particular languages):

(22) a. *the man that* (*he) *kissed the girl*   (pronoun excluded)
   b. *the man that the girl kissed* (him)   (pronoun optional)
   c. *the man that the girl gave a present* to him (pronoun obligatory)

From these different principles it is quite clear that pronominal expression of the relativized variable has the function of making the resulting construction easier to process (Keenan—Bimson 1975, Keenan 1985). Clearly, when the relativized variable is given pronominal expression, the personal pronoun provides an overt clue about how the construction is to be interpreted. This is immediately clear from a comparison of the following constructions in a supposed VSO language:

(23) a. *the man that kissed* he *the girl*
 b. *the man that kissed the girl* him
(24)   *the man that kissed the girl*

With pronominal expression, as in (23a-b), the resulting terms are unambiguous; without such expression, as in (24), ambiguity arises in a VSO language. To this we may add the observation that even in situations in which there is no danger of ambiguity, pronominal expression nevertheless helps in determining the underlying relationships. Compare:

(25) a. *the knife that I cut the bread* with it
 b. *the knife that I cut the bread* with
 c. *the knife that I cut the bread*

It seems clear that (25a) is more perspicuous than (25b), with its dangling preposition, while that construction in turn is more perspicuous than (25c), in which the relation between the "knife" and the "cutting" is left completely unexpressed.

The functionality of pronominal expression is finally also clear from the fact that languages with pronominal expression can often relativize into positions which are inaccessible to relativization in languages without such expression.[8] Thus, a construction such as (26a) is probably ungrammatical in all languages, while (26b) appears to be grammatical in quite a few:

(26) a. *the man that I saw John and in New York*
 b. *the man that I saw John and* him *in New York*
    'the man such that I saw John and him in New York'

---

8. On the basis of data from Fula, Ali and Sylla (1977) show that this is not necessarily the case.

Note that we interpret the pronominal element as it occurs in relative clauses as the manifestation of an anaphorical variable. The non-occurrence of pronominal expression may thus be compared to "zero anaphora": the non-expression of an anaphorical element in underlying clause structure. We will return to this in discussing anaphora in general in chapter 10.

3.1.3. Relative pronouns

Postnominal relative clauses may be marked by relative pronouns. We already encountered some characteristics of relative pronouns. Some other typical properties are added in the following survey.

(27)   PROPERTIES OF RELATIVE PRONOUNS
   (i)   relative pronouns are confined to postnominal relative clauses; they do not occur in prenominal VRs;
   (ii) relative pronouns occur in P1 position of the relative clause, or as part of a constituent which occurs in that position;
   (iii) relative pronouns do not co-occur with pronouns which express the anaphorical variable;
   (iv) relative pronouns are typically identical or at least similar in form to (a) demonstratives, or (b) question words, of the same language.

Relative pronouns pose an intriguing problem: when we compare the strategy of expressing relative clauses through RM+personal pronoun with that of expressing them through relative pronoun, we find that the former strategy is more effective in the sense that, in the languages that have it, it allows for a greater variety of positions to be relativized into. Notably, all sorts of constraints on extraction from relative clauses, known as "island constraints" (Ross 1967), which often hold for relative pronoun constructions, do not hold, or are less strict, in the case of RM+personal-pronoun expression. Compare:

(28) a.   *This is the man who I do not know what wants.*
     b.   *This is the man that I do not know what* he *wants.*

It is much easier to find languages in which the equivalent of (28b) is possible than languages which allow for the equivalent of (28a). And more generally, RM+personal-pronoun constructions allow for a greater variety of relative clause types than relative pronoun constructions.

One may well ask, then, why languages have relative pronouns at all, when the alternative RM+personal-pronoun strategy is apparently more flexible. Without wishing to pretend that I can answer this question, I would speculate that this has something to do with the "scenario" through which relative clauses of different types arise historically. I assume that there are several different such scenarios, and therefore several different possible historical sources feeding the language with relative clause types. It must then be assumed that when a language is involved in one of these scenarios, it does not easily switch to another scenario, even though the outcome of that alternative scenario might lead to a more flexible overall solution for construing VRs. I return to this matter in chapter 4.

3.2. Prenominal verbal restrictors

Prenominal VRs hardly ever have a finite verb. In chapter 4 we return to the question of why this should be so. Here, we consider various ways in which prenominal VRs can be expressed by means of non-finite verb forms.

3.2.1. Participial restrictors

Participial restrictors have the verbal predicate expressed in participial form, where by a participle we mean a verb-derived form which has certain adjectival properties. Participial restrictors seem to be especially connected with the prenominal occurrence of VRs, as is clear from the following facts:
 — in Postfield languages with participial VRs, at least some of these can occur in the Prefield;
 — in languages which have both postnominal and prenominal VRs, the former typically take the form of finite relative clauses, while the latter often take the form of participial VRs. Consider the following examples from German (Keenan—Comrie 1977) and Dutch:

(29) a. *der Mann, der in seinem Büro arbeitet*
 the man who in his office works
 'the man who works in his office'
 b. *der in seinem Büro arbeitende Mann*
 the in his office working man
 'the man working in his office'

(30) a. *de   leraar   die   door   velen   gehaat   werd*
       the   teacher who   by   many   hated   was
       'the teacher who was hated by many'
   b. *de   door   velen   gehate   leraar*
      the   by   many   hated   teacher
      'the teacher hated by many'

In general, the possibilities for prenominal VRs such as those in (29b) and (30b) are more restricted in Dutch than they are in German. English, too, has examples of prenominal VRs, as in:

(31) a. *hard-working man*
    b. *music-loving audience*

but these possibilities are even more restricted than in Dutch. For example, the premodifying VR in English can hardly contain any independent argument or satellite terms. Where these are present, postmodification is resorted to:

(32) a. *a man working in his office*
    b. *a teacher hated by many*

From the examples in (32) it is clear that it would be too strong a statement to say that participial restrictors only occur in the Prefield. However, since the chances for such restrictors to occur in the Postfield increase with their internal complexity, it seems fair to say that the basic position of participial restrictors is in the Prefield, and that the Postfield is resorted to only when the restrictor becomes too complex to be tolerated in the Prefield.

As intimated in some of the remarks made above, it appears that Prefield positioning of modifiers becomes more "difficult" as these modifiers increase in complexity. Prefield languages may have different degrees of "tolerance" for Prefield complexity. If the tolerance limit is crossed, measures will be taken to avoid the undesired result. Placing the VR in the Postfield rather than in the Prefield is one of those measures. On the other hand, this "solution" reduces the degree of cross-domain harmony of the language (cf. *TFG1*: 16.4.1.).

Another restriction on the participial strategy is that this strategy is typically used only in cases in which the head noun can be interpreted as the Subject or the first argument of the participle (cf. Downing 1978). Thus, we typically find the following distribution:

(33) a.   *a man reading many books*
     b.   **a book many men reading*
          'a book which many men read'
     c.   *a book read by many men*

This implies that the participial strategy can only yield a full range of VRs if the language involved has extensive Subject assignment possibilities. Where this is not the case, the participial strategy typically occurs side by side with other strategies which allow for a larger range of VR formation.

Although participles can contain aspectual and voice distinctions they typically do not make the Tense distinctions which are made in finite verbs (cf. Noonan 1985). Thus, the expressive possibilities of participial VRs are in this respect more restricted than those of relative clauses.

3.2.2. Nominalized restrictors

Another type of non-finite expression is nominalization. Nominalized restrictors, again, typically occur in the Prefield. They can be understood along the lines of:

(34)   a [*John's reading*] *paper* =
       'a paper characterized by John's reading it'

An example of this strategy is provided by Turkish.[9] If the open term position in the VR is the first argument,[10] Turkish uses a participial strategy, as in:

(35)   *Ankara'ya   gidecek   adam*
       Ankara-dat   go-fut   man
       'man who will go to Ankara'

But in all other cases Turkish uses the nominalization strategy, as in:

---

9 Cf. Van Schaaik (1983), on which the following account is based.

10. This strategy is also used when the term variable represents a Possessor WITHIN a first argument, as in "the man such that his house burnt down", which is expressed according to the schema: "his house having burnt down man".

(36) adam-ın gid-eceğ-i şehir
      man-gen go-fut-his city
      'city characterized by the man's future going to it' =
      'city that the man will go to'

The prenominal modifier in this case indeed has the properties of a nominalization, with one term, corresponding to the head noun, missing. The nominalization, in turn, uses the standard expression form of Turkish possessive constructions, which are doubly marked, according to the pattern:

(37) Hasan-ın   ev-i
      Hasan-gen   house-his
      'Hasan's his house' = 'Hasan's house'

The "open" nominalization used as VR expression in (36) corresponds to the "closed" nominalization which may be used in expressing embedded constructions, as in:

(38) Ahmet   Hasan-ın   çalış-acağ-ı-nı   söyle-di.
      Ahmet   Hasan-gen   work-fut-his-acc   say-past
      'Ahmet said Hasan's his future working.' =
      'Ahmet said that Hasan would/was going to work.'

As is the case with participles, nominalizations typically make fewer distinctions of Tense and Aspect than can be made in finite verbs. But it is to be noted that a subset of the Turkish Tense operators can be expressed within the domain of the nominalization. A further property of the Turkish nominalization strategy is that neither the term variable nor its function is coded within the VR. Thus, in the attributive nominalization in (36) there is no sign that the head noun corresponds to a directional term within the VR. This fact may help us understand why in certain cases even closed predications can act as restrictors, as discussed in the next section.

3.2.3. Closed predications as restrictors

So far we have acted on the assumption that VRs are always open predications in the term variable x_i. There are cases, however, in which closed predications seem to function as VRs. Compare the following two constructions:

(39) a. *the sound which came from the garden*
    b. *the sound of children shouting in the garden*

At first sight, these two constructions are quite different: (39a) contains a genuine relative clause, whereas (39b) contains a prepositional constituent which in some way relates "children shouting in the garden" to the head noun "sound".

The relevance of construction (39b) in the present context lies in the fact that there are quite a few languages which treat the modifier in (39b) in exactly the same way as that in (39a). Consider the following examples:

(40)   Korean (Tagashira 1972)
       aitul-i   ttetu-nun   thong
       children-Subj make-noise-RM   clamour
       'the clamour of children making noise'
(41)   Tamil (Asher 1982: 36-37)
       kaaru   varra   cattam
       car   come-RM   noise
       'the noise of a car coming'
(42)   Japanese (McCawley 1976: 297)
       piano   o   hiku   oto
       piano   Go   play   sound
       'the sound of (someone) playing the piano'
(43)   Mari (Matsumura 1983: 462)[11]
       ala-kö-n   omsa-m čot   peraltð-me
       some-who-gen   door-acc hard   knock-part
       jük-eš-ðže   pomðžaltðm.
       sound-into-poss   I awoke
       'I awoke at the sound of someone knocking hard at the door.'

In all these languages, the initial modifier of the head noun 'clamour / sound / noise' has all the properties of the relative construction in the languages in question. We could thus paraphrase these constructions asf:

(44)   *the sound such that children make noise*

---

11. Note that the first argument of the embedded clause gets possessive expression and is reflected on the head noun by a possessive suffix.

60 *Verbal restrictors 2*

The problem is, of course, that there is no obvious place for a term corresponding to the head noun within the modifying predication. For this reason, Matsumura (1983) speaks of "pseudo-relatives". Matsumura also notes, however, that these constructions are far from exceptional in the languages concerned, and that for a speaker of Japanese there is no obvious difference between such constructions as the following:

(45) sakana   o   yaku   ami
      fish   Go   fry   grill
      'a grill for frying fish'
(46) sakana   o   yaku   nioi
      fish   Go   fry   smell
      'a smell of (someone) frying fish'
(47) sakana   o   yaku   kakugo
      fish   Go   fry   willingness
      'willingness to fry fish'

whereas only in the case of (45) could the initial modifier be described in terms of a restrictor in the form of an open predication, as in:

(48) $(x_i: ami\ [N]: [Pres\ e: [yaku\ [V]\ (x_j)_{Ag}\ (sakana)_{Go}]\ (Ax_i)_{Instr}])$

Matsumura notes that, given the similarity between (45) and (46)-(47), one would wish to have a way of describing the latter without unduly differentiating them from the former.

I believe that this can be achieved by assuming that the modifiers in question are restrictors which differ from the more usual VR only in the fact that they are closed predications with no open position in x_i. This would amount to underlying term structures of the following kind:

(49) $(x_i: nioi\ [N]: [Pres\ e: yaku\ [V]\ (x_j)_{Ag}\ (sakana)_{Go}])$
        'the smell of someone frying fish'

Note that the fact that the Agent of the restricting predication is unspecified is irrelevant to the issue: all the languages concerned also have the possibility of specifying the first argument of the restricting predication, as is the case in (40), (41), and (43). Japanese, too, has this possibility, as in the following example (Matsumura: 1983):

(50)   *dareka   no   doa   o   hagesiku tataku   oto*
       someone of   door   Go   hard   knock   sound
       'the sound of someone knocking hard on the door'

which would get the representation (51), where the second restrictor modifying *oto* is a completely closed predication.[12]:

(51)   (x$_i$: *oto* [N]: [Pres e: [*tataku* [V] (*dareka*)$_{Ag}$ (*doa*)$_{Go}$] (*hagesiku*)$_{Man}$])

Note that the structures (48) and (49) are quite similar, the only difference being that in (48) there is an open position for x$_i$ in the restricting predication, whereas in (49) a complete predication restricts the term variable x$_i$.

We may now assume that this type of "closed restrictor" is also relevant to English, and can be used in representing constructions of type (39b) as follows:

(52)   (x$_i$: *sound* [N]: [Pres e: [*shout* [V] (*children*)$_{Ag}$] (*garden*)$_{Loc}$])

The way in which English and the other languages differ, then, would lie in the expression chosen for such underlying structures as (52). English usually expresses these through a prepositional phrase with *of*, while Japanese and the other languages mentioned treat them in the same way as open predications in x$_i$.

Interestingly, all the languages possessing this sort of "closed" VR appear to be rather strict Prefield languages. We can understand this fact as follows: prenominal VRs never contain relative pronouns, and pronominal expression of the term variable is rare. This means that the function of the antecedent is not coded in the VR. We thus get constructions of the form:

(53) a. [*meat cut* RM] *man*
         'meat cutting man'
     b. [*man cut* RM] *meat*
         'man-cut meat'
     c. [*man meat cut* RM] *knife*
         'knife with which man cuts meat'
     d. [*man knife with meat cut* RM] *time*
         'time at which man cuts meat with knife'

---

12 Note the possessive expression of the Agent *dareka*.

Now, constructions of type (53d) are open to different interpretations:

(54) a. 'the time such that the man cut the meat with a knife at that time'
b. 'the time characterized by the man cutting the meat with a knife'

In interpretation (54b) the relation between antecedent and modifying predication is loosened. We can now understand that this construction extends to cases in which no such relation can be reconstructed, as in:

(55)   [*man knife with meat cut* RM] *sound*
'the sound of a man cutting meat with a knife'

We thus predict that this type of construction arises in languages which have prenominal VRs which do not encode the function of the antecedent explicitly.

However, what we also see here is a gradual transition from VRs characterizing a first-order entity to closed predications characterizing a second-order entity. This can again be demonstrated with English examples:

(56) a. *a deer-hunting man*
'a man who goes hunting deer'
b. *a deer-hunting gun*
'a gun with which one goes hunting deer'
c. *a deer-hunting time*
'a time at which one goes hunting deer'
d. *a deer-hunting event*
'an event of hunting deer'

In (56a-b) *deer-hunting* clearly functions as a restrictor on first-order referents. In (56d), however, it is the nature of the event (a second-order entity) which is characterized by *deer-hunting*. The structure of this expression would have to be analyzed as:

(57)   (i1e: *event* [N]: [*hunt* [V] $(x_i)_{Ag}$ $(deer)_{Go}$])

(56c) is somewhere in between these two cases, since it is the more abstract time of the event rather than some more concrete participant in the event which is characterized by the closed predication. We thus find an area here where genuine VRs may shade off into embedded predications used to characterize second-order entities.

This is exactly what we see happen in Turkish: the construction which is otherwise used as a VR for characterizing first-order entities can also be used in such cases as:[13]

(58) Hasan   gel-me-diĝ-i   takdir-de ne   yap-alım?
      Hasan   come-not-realis-his   case-in   what do-opt.1.pl
      'What are we to do in the case characterized by Hasan's not coming?' =
      'What are we to do when Hasan doesn't show up?'

Comparing this to an English expression such as *in the event that X* we clearly see that the embedded predication is now being used in order to specify the nature of a second-order entity.

3.2.4. Appositive verbal restrictors

One way for Prefield languages to have the best of both worlds is the following. Suppose we have a prenominal relative construction of the following form:

(59)   *the chicken eat-*RM *man*
        'the chicken-eating man'

Suppose further that the head noun position can be taken by a "dummy noun":

(60)   *the chicken eat-*RM *one*
        'the chicken-eating one'

We can then use this "dummy-headed" construction as an apposition, in the following way:

(61)   *the man, the chicken eat-*RM *one ...*
        'the man, the chicken-eating one, ...'

Note that in one sense, the VR here appears in the Prefield (of the dummy head noun); in another sense, it appears in the Postfield (of the head noun *man*). This strategy could thus be understood as a way of retaining the Prefield

---

13. The example is from Van Schaaik (1983).

character of the construction, while at the same time avoiding excessive complexity in the Prefield of the lexical head noun.

A case in point is discussed in De Rijk (1972) for Basque.[14] Basque basically has prenominal VRs, but it may resort to the appositive strategy which, "if the relative clause is very long", may even be more acceptable than the prenominal VR. Compare the following examples:

(62) a. *zazpi   seme-alaba   zitu-en   errege   bat*
       seven   son-daughter   have-RM   king   a
       'a king having seven sons and daughters'
   b. *zazpi   seme-alaba   zitu-en-a*
       seven   son-daughter   have-RM-one
       'a person having seven sons and daughters'
   c. *errege   bat, zazpi   seme-alaba   zitu-en-a*
       king   a   seven   son-daughter   have-RM-one
       'a king, a person having seven sons and daughters'

Another example of the appositive relative is provided by Imbabura Quechua (Cole 1982: 51), which has prenominal or circumnominal VRs. Consider[15]:

(63) *kwitsa-ta juya-ni   Juan-wan   tushu-shka   ka-shka-ta*
      girl-acc love-I   Juan-with   dance-nr   be-nr-acc
      'I love the girl, the one who has been dancing with Juan'

Through a variety of arguments, Cole (1982: 51) demonstrates that the "head" (*kwitsa-ta*) and the VR in this case constitute two separate constituents. One of the relevant features is that both these constituents are independently marked "accusative", which is not the case when the VR precedes the head noun. Note further that an expression such as *Juan-wan tushu-shka ka-shka* can be independently used in the sense of 'the person who has been dancing with Juan' (cf. Rijkhoff 1992 and 4.3.3.2 below).

---

14. Cf. Saltarelli (1988: 36); note that Basque has a finite verb even in prenominal VRs; this verb, however, is marked by the subordinating element *-(e)n*, which makes it clear that it is not "the" finite verb of the clause.

15. The abbreviation 'nr' in the gloss means 'nominalizer'.

3.3. Circumnominal verbal restrictors

Circumnominal restrictors have not received much separate attention in typological studies of relativization (with the notable exception of Lehmann (1984)). Nevertheless, they occur in quite a few languages of different families in quite similar form, so that they can certainly not be regarded as the odd exception to an otherwise transparent pattern.

As far as I have been able to determine, all attested examples of VRs of this type are from Prefield languages. Thus, we would wish to be able to account for the special relation between this construction type and the Prefield character of the language concerned.

The following is a representative example from Yuma (Langdon 1977):

(64) John-ts   vii   uutap-in-ts   *ava-nya*   *tav-sh.*
      John-Subj   rock   throw-dem-Subj   house-dem   hit-evid
      'The rock that John threw hit the house.'

In this construction, the section in roman typeface is very similar to the main sentence meaning 'John threw a rock'. This whole clausal construction is followed by a demonstrative element -*in*, which in its turn is followed by the subject marker -*ts* (identical to the subject marker on *John*). Thus, the impression is given as if the whole embedded predication is the subject of "hit the house", as in:

(65) (*John threw a rock*)-Subj *hit the house.*

Meaningwise, however, it is clearly the rock rather than John's rock-throwing which is said to have hit the house.[16]

The identity between the VR and a complete independent or dependent

---

16. Langdon (1977) gives a general survey of the relevant phenomena in Yuman languages. For the facts of the individual languages, see Kendall (1974, 1976) on Yavapai, Munro (1973, 1976) on Mojave, Gorbet (1976) on Diegueño. Gorbet (1977) discusses the question of whether the occurrence of this type of construction must be interpreted as pointing to a genetic relation between the relevant languages.

clause is even more evident in Wappo, as described in Li—Thompson (1978). An independent sentence in Wappo has the following form:

(66) Ce kew ?ew túm-tah.
      that man fish buy-past
      'That man bought fish.'

Such a sentence can be embedded without any change as the complement of a verb like "know":

(67) ?ah ce kew ?ew túm-tah hatiskhi?.
      I that man fish buy-past know
      'I know that that man bought fish.'

However, when such a clause is embedded under a main verb which does not take a proposition but a first-order term as a second argument, we get the following result:

(68) ?ah ce kew ?ew túm-tah hakše?.
      I that man fish buy-past like
      'I like (the man bought fish).'
      =   (a) 'I like the man who bought the fish.'
          (b) 'I like the fish that the man bought.'

Thus, syntactically it is as if the whole embedded clause acts as an argument to the verb 'like'. But semantically, the second argument is to be extracted from that embedded clause, and there is no overt indication as to which term from the embedded clause is to be chosen as such (in many cases, of course, semantic and pragmatic constraints will determine the correct choice). Just as in Yuma, postpositional (or suffixal) elements relevant to the target term will be attached to the embedded clause as a whole. Consider the following examples, containing the Recipient marker -*thu*:

(69) ?ah ce kew-thu taka? mahes-ta?
      I that man-to basket give-past
      'I gave a basket to that man'

(70)   *?ah [ce kew   ?ew ṭoh-tah]-thu taka?   mahes-ta?*
       I   that man   fish catch-past-to basket   give-past
       'I gave a basket to (that man caught the fish)'
       =   (a) 'I gave a basket to the man who caught the fish'
           (b) 'I gave a basket to the fish that the man caught'

The (b)-interpretation will normally be ruled out for semantic reasons.

Consider some further examples of circumnominal restrictors, from quite divergent language groupings:[17]

(71)   Imbabura Quechua (Cole 1982)
       Ñuka   chay   punlla-pi   chaya-shka-ka   sumaj-nu
       I   that   day-in   arrive-nom-Top   beautiful-val
       ka-rka.
       be-past-3
       '(I arrived on that day) was beautiful.'
       = 'The day on which I arrived was beautiful'
(72)   Murinypata (Mallinson—Blake 1981)
       Muṱⁱiŋga   paŋanduwi   mundakŋayya-Rɛ   ŋayi   panŋbaḍ.
       woman-abs   arrive   earlier-erg   me   hit
       '(The woman arrived earlier) hit me.'
       = 'The woman who arrived earlier hit me.'

Note that in (72) the whole embedded construction is marked as ergative, the case appropriate to the transitive Subj of the verb 'hit'. On the other hand, the Subj of the embedded clause itself is marked as absolutive, in accordance with its role within the embedded clause.

(73)   Usan (Reesink 1987)
       Munon   qemi   bau-or   eng ye   me   ge-au.
       man   bow   take-3.sg.past   the I   not   see-nom
       '(The man took the bow) I did not see.'
       =   (a) 'I did not see the man who took the bow.'
           (b) 'I did not see the bow which the man took.'

---

17. In the Imbabura Quechua example, *-nu* is a validator. The Murinypata example shows that a circumnominal VR is not necessarily circumnominal in a literal sense. The crucial feature of VRs known as 'circumnominal' is that they have a structure that is identical to that of a complete clause.

68   *Verbal restrictors 2*

Note that in (73) we find precisely the same ambiguity as in the Wappo examples (68) and (70). It is usual for this type of ambiguity to arise in languages which have this kind of VR organization.

The following is a similar example from Diegueño (Gorbet 1976):

(74)   Xaṯkcok wi:m   tuc-pu-c   n^{y}iL^y
        dog   rock-with   hit-dem-Subj   black
        '(He hit the dog with a rock) was black.'
        =   (a) 'The dog that he hit with the rock was black.'
            (b) 'The rock that he hit the dog with was black.'

In Diegueño, such ambiguities are resolved by such factors as the following:
— context and situation;
— selection restrictions of the predicates involved;
— priority rules of the following kind: in (74) the potential candidates for head-status are the Goal and the Instr; the former is hierarchically "higher" in some sense (in terms of FG: on the SFH, cf. *TFG1*: 10.4.2.), and correspondingly interpretation (a) is more plausible than interpretation (b).

Where it is extremely important to avoid any ambiguity, Diegueño has some alternative constructions to which I return below.

I presume that the examples discussed so far have shown that the circumnominal restrictor is a unified type across language families, with remarkably similar recurrent properties. The most intriguing of these properties is that instead of the head term, the whole clause in which that head term is embedded acts "as if" it is an argument (or satellite) to the main verb. There thus appears to be a discrepancy between the syntactic form and the semantic content of the expression. In the next chapter we return to the question of how these circumnominal VRs could be understood in terms of FG.

3.4. Correlative relative constructions

A strategy which is also typical of Prefield languages and which is often mistaken for a circumnominal VR is the so-called "correlative relative construction" (cf. Downing 1987). This construction occurs in English as a marked option, as in:

(75)   *Whichever book I read, it bores me immediately.*

Typical features of this construction are:
- the VR occurs in clause-external, "Orientation" position;[18]
- the relative pronoun has interrogative properties;
- the relativized constituent is (optionally) resumed by a pronominal (or other anaphorical) element in the clause proper.

Consider examples (76) from Hindi[19] (Keenan—Comrie 1979) and (77) from Latin:

(76)   *Aadmii   ne   jis   caakuu   se   murgii   ko   maraa*
       man   erg   which   knife   with   chicken Obj killed
       thaa,   us   caakuu   ko   Ram   ne   dekhaa.
       have   that   knife   Obj   Ram   erg   saw
       'Which knife the man killed the chicken with, that knife Ram saw.'

(77)   *Quae   prima   nobis   navigandi   facultas   data*
       which   first   to-us   for-sailing   opportunity   given
       erit,   (ea)   utemur
       will-be   (that-one)   we-will-use
       'Whichever first opportunity for sailing will be given to us, (that one) we will use'

When we compare the properties of this construction type across languages, we find the following variant patterns:

(78) a. *Which knife John lost, that knife Peter found.*
     b. *Which knife John lost, that (one) Peter found.*
     c. *Which knife John lost, Ø Peter found.*
        'Peter found the knife that John lost'

Since, in these constructions, the "antecedent" *knife* occurs in the initial "relative clause", this construction is sometimes classed together with the circumnominal type discussed in the preceding section. The properties of this clause-external construction, however, differ markedly from the "true" circumnominal type. In chapter 4 we will try to explain the present type as derived from a dependent question, as in:

---

18. Thus, the construction has the properties of a Theme+Clause construction (cf. Lehmann 1984; section 4.3.2. and chapter 17).
19. Hindi also has a postnominal alternative to (76).

(79)   *Do you know* which knife John lost?

The occurrence of the noun *knife* within the initial "relative clauses" of (78) can then be understood in terms of this origin.

4. Verbal restrictors 3: explanations

4.0. Introduction

In the preceding two chapters I have given a survey of the typological variation among verbal restrictors and of the ways in which the various types could be interpreted in terms of FG. We saw that there is a great variety of strategies used, and that these varieties display a number of general tendencies. These general tendencies raise a number of questions at the explanatory level. In this chapter we address some of these questions, and discuss some possible answers to them. Consider the following questions:

(Q1) Do all languages have VRs? Is the VR a substantive universal of linguistic organization?

(Q2) If not, what means do languages without VRs have to achieve the effect of identifying an entity through specifying its role in some SoA?

(Q3) Why do VRs on the whole prefer the Postfield to the Prefield?

(Q4) Why do many languages nevertheless place their VRs in the Prefield?

(Q5) Why do relative pronouns only occur in postnominal VRs (cf. 3.1.3)?

(Q6) Why is it that relative pronouns are often similar to either demonstrative elements or question words of the language concerned?

(Q7) Why is pronominal expression of the relativized position incompatible with the occurrence of a relative pronoun (cf. 3.1.1)?

(Q8) Granted that relative clauses with pronominal expression of the relativized variable allow for a greater range of possible relative clauses, why is it that many languages do not use this device?

(Q9) Why do prenominal VRs typically take non-finite expression?

(Q10) Why do prenominal VRs have a greater range of varieties than postnominal ones?

(Q11) How do we understand the nature of "circumnominal" VRs?

(Q12) Why do such cirumnominal VRs typically occur in Prefield languages?

I do not pretend that I am able to answer all these questions. Rather, this chapter will offer a number of considerations and ideas which might contribute to answering some of them. First, we consider (Q1) and (Q2). We will find that the VR is (probably) not a linguistic universal, but that languages which have no VRs use alternative strategies for achieving much the same communicative effect. These alternative strategies, in turn, shed some light on the possible historical origins of VRs and on some of the other questions formulated above.

4.1. On the (non-)universality of verbal restrictors

Do VRs constitute a universal category of natural languages? The answer to this question appears to be no (cf. Comrie 1981: 137), although it is certainly unusual for a language not to have VRs of any form. In languages which do not have VRs, however, there are other means by which the communicative effect of VRs can be achieved.

For example, Hixkaryana (according to Derbyshire 1979: 26) does not have VRs in our sense of the term. There are, however "various means used to obtain the same effect as such a clause [an adjective clause]: simple nominalization; placing NPs together in a paratactic relationship, with intonational break; descriptive sentence, usually involving an equative clause; or some combination of these means." Consider the following example:[1]

(1) *Nomokye   hawana.   Horykomo   tho*
    he-came   visitor.   adult-man   devalued
         mokro   (nehxakon-i).
         that-one   (he-was)
    'There came a visitor. He was an old man.'
    = 'There came a visitor who was an old man'

Note that (1) is a paratactic combination of two independent sentences. The communicative effect, however, is quite comparable to what would be expressed in a relative clause in other languages.

It should be added here that Hixkaryana (as noted in the quotation above) does have nominalizations corresponding to

(2) a. *hunter*
    b. *deer-hunter*
    c. *big-deer-hunter*

which can be used in apposition to terms, as in:

---

1. The marker *tho* "devalued" adds negative evaluation to the description.

(3)   *The man, the big-deer-hunter, came to the village.*

Such constructions come very close to the "appositive" VR construction discussed in 3.2.4. More generally, the identity of intended referents is often established in this accumulative way, by appositionally adding more and more detail about their properties.

For another example, consider the situation in Australian languages. Most of these languages have simple adnominal participial VRs, but many of them do not have full relative clauses. Instead, they use "adjoined" subordinate clauses, which may occur at the very beginning or at the very end of the main clause, but may not occur in adnominal, clause-medial position.

Consider the following example from Warlpiri (Hale 1976):

(4)   *Ñatjulu-lu   Øna   yankiri   pantu-nu,   kutja-lpa*
        I-erg   aux   emu   spear-past,   sub-aux
            ŋapa   ŋa-ṉu.
            water   drink-past
        'I speared the emu, drinking water.'
        =   (a) 'I speared the emu while it was drinking water.'
            (b) 'I speared the emu which was drinking water.'

Such adjoined clauses were called "adjoined relative clauses" by Hale, but they have two properties which distinguish them from VRs proper:

(i) they must occur at the "periphery" (at the very end or the very beginning) of the main clause, and cannot form one constituent with the noun they are supposed to modify;

(ii) they can get a variety of interpretations (temporal, conditional, circumstantial) besides that interpretation which comes closest to that of a VR.

Later in this chapter I shall argue that such clauses should be interpreted as circumstantial satellites rather than as VRs.

From the preceding examples we may conclude that VRs are not a universal phenomenon, but that all languages have strategies of "Participant Identification" (see 2.1.), by means of which they achieve a similar communicative effect, which consists in supporting the identification of some referent through specifying its role as a participant in some SoA.

It should be added that the relation between VRs and other means of participant identification is not strictly disjunctive: languages which do have VRs will also have other means for achieving Participant Identification.

74 *Verbal restrictors 3*

4.2. Prefield versus Postfield

In 3.0. we saw that the order N-VR is typical of Postfield languages, while Prefield languages may have either VR-N or N-VR. There is thus a preference for VRs to occur in the Postfield. This preference may be understood in terms of several of the constituent ordering principles which were formulated in *TFG1*: chapter 16:
 — Principle (SP6) said that the Prefield is less hospitable to complex material than the Postfield.
 — Principle (SP7) said that complex constituents, such as VRs, tend towards a later position in the clause than less complex constructions.

These principles predict that VRs in the Prefield will be under some pressure to shift to the Postfield. There will thus be a certain skew in favour of Postfield positioning of VRs. The principles also predict that VRs may float towards the end of the clause, as is the case with so-called "extraposition-from-NP", as in the following example from Dutch:

(5)   *Ik   heb   een man   ontmoet die   gelooft dat*
      I   have   a   man   met   who   believes that
           de   aarde   plat   is.
           the earth   flat   is
      'I have met a man who believes that the earth is flat.'

In (5) it is even difficult to have the VR immediately after the head noun:

(6)   *?Ik heb een man   die   gelooft dat de   aarde*
       I   have a   man   who   believes that the earth
            plat   is ontmoet
            flat   is met
      'I have met a man who believes that the earth is flat.'

It seems correct to assume, then, that in Prefield languages there are several forces at work which push the VR towards the Postfield, while in Postfield languages there are no counter-forces which pull the VR to the Prefield. This means that if a language has VRs in the Prefield, it is either a Prefield language, or a language which is on the move from Prefield to Postfield organization, and still retains a number of Prefield properties.

If there is an overall preference for VRs to appear in the Postfield the question poses itself, of course, why many languages use the Prefield for VRs at all. The following factors would seem to be relevant to this question:

(i) *Overall Prefield character*
We saw in *TFG1*:16.4.1. that languages tend to display a varying degree of overall consistency or "harmony" in Prefield or Postfield ordering. This means that if a language has basic Prefield organisation, its starting point for placing restrictors is the Prefield. Using the Postfield for such restrictors is a departure from this principle of "field harmony".

(ii) *Mirror Principle?*
The question arises, however, whether "field harmony" is an explanatory principle itself, or an epiphenomenon of other explanatory factors. One of these more basic factors could be a preference for differentiating predicative and attributive occurrences of predicates. Consider the following example from a putative Prefield language:

(7) a. *man die*
    'the man is dying'
 b. *die man*
    'dying man'
(8) a. *man pig slaughter*
    'the man slaughters the pig'
 b. *pig slaughter man*
    'pig slaughtering man'

As these examples suggest, using VR-N ordering in a Prefield language might help to differentiate predicative and attributive constructions.

(iii) *Avoidance of centre-embedding*
Another factor, suggested by Kuno (1974), is that Prefield VRs in a Prefield language serve to reduce the degree of potential centre-embedding of VRs. Compare the following examples:

(9) a. *cat [mouse [cheese eat-ing] chase-ing] die*
    'The cat that chased the mouse that ate the cheese died.'
 b. *[cheese eat-ing [mouse chase-ing [cat]] die*

The idea is that left-branching constructions such as (9b) are easier to process than centre-embedded constructions such as (9a).

Comrie (1989) adduces this principle as of being special relevance to those languages which, contrary to expectation, have postnominal adjectives, but more complex restrictors in prenominal position. This is the case, for example, in Basque, and in Haruai, the language discussed in Comrie's paper.

It is to be noted, however, that SVO languages usually have Postfield VRs, although this may create potential centre-embeddings (see the discussion in Mallinson—Blake 1981). Consider:

(10)   *The cheese [that the mouse [that the cat chased] ate] would have pleased the lady.*

Obviously, this construction, though theoretically possible in English, will be avoided in favour of:

(11)   *The cheese that the mouse ate that the cat chased would have pleased the lady.*

But the point is that in this case the avoidance of centre-embedding is achieved in a different way than through Prefield placement of VRs. Thus, while avoidance of centre-embedding may be one factor contributing to Prefield placement of VRs, it is not a sufficient explanation for this type of ordering.

(iv) *Head Proximity*
Another related relevant factor here might be the "Principle of Head Proximity" as formulated by Rijkhoff (1986, 1992; cf. *TFG1*: 16.4.1): note that in (9a), but not in (9b), the heads of arguments (i.e. the nouns) and the predicates (i.e. the verbs) are separated by intervening material, which is non-preferred in terms of Head Proximity.

4.3. Scenarios for the creation of verbal restrictors

It is generally agreed that the VRs that a given language has at a certain point of time may have originated from a number of different diachronic sources, and that a number of VR properties can be understood in terms of how they have developed from these sources. In the following I sketch a number of different plausible historical "scenarios" which may help us understand how VRs of different types can arise in a language.

Note that if it can be made plausible that some VR type at stage B of a language has developed out of a non-VR construction at an earlier stage A, this should not be taken to imply that the language did not have any VRs at stage A: the new VR2 may have replaced an older type VR1 according to the following schema:

(12)   stage A   VR1   SOURCE

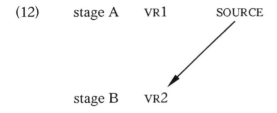

        stage B   VR2

This is in most cases more plausible than to assume that stage A had no VRs at all, since languages without some type of VR are exceptional, and the time depth into which we can reconstruct proto-languages is comparatively so shallow that it is not plausible to assume that since the time of such proto-languages there has been a qualitative mutation of one type of language into a different type.

Furthermore, developments according to schema (12), in which a construction of a certain type is replaced by some other type, which may then again be replaced in turn, are well-documented in different areas of the linguistic system.[2] Such developments should be seen as recurrent renovations of the linguistic system (like a snake periodically shedding its skin) rather than as mutations from one type of system to another.

4.3.1. From parataxis to verbal restrictor

It is an old idea that VRs with "demonstrative" relative pronouns can be historically derived from earlier paratactic clause sequences.[3] In Dutch, for example, the relative pronouns *die* and *dat* are identical in form to demonstrative pronouns. Compare the following constructions:

(13) a. *Jan   zag een man.   Die   huilde.*
         John   saw a   man   that (one) cried
         'John saw a man. He was crying.'

---

2. See the different types of "markedness shift" discussed in *TFG1*: 2.5.3.
3. For some discussion and references, see Pinkster (1988: 207-209).

b. Jan   zag een man   die   huilde.
    John   saw a   man   who   cried
    'John saw a man who was crying.'

It is clear that it is only a small step from paratactic (13a) to hypotactic (13b). And if such a development is assumed, the formal identity between relative pronoun and demonstrative is automatically accounted for. This same development could also explain why "demonstrative" relative pronouns always occur in initial position. In Dutch, at least, we have the following opposition:

(14) A: *Zie je   die   man   met   die snor?*
         see you   that   man   with   that moustache
         'Do you see that man with that moustache?'
    B: (a) *Nee,   ik   zie hem niet.*
              no   I   see him not
              'No, I don't see him.'
        (a') **Nee, hem zie ik   niet.*
              no   him see I   not
        (b) *Nee,   die   zie ik   niet.*
              no   that (one) see I   not
              'No, I don't see him.'
        (b') *?Nee, ik   zie die   niet.*
              no   I   see that (one) not

In other words: if we wish to anaphorically refer to some referent mentioned earlier in the discourse, we do so by using either the personal pronoun in pattern position, or the demonstrative pronoun in P1 position. The latter strategy is more common than the former, especially if some emphasis is placed on the anaphorical element.

Reinterpretation of an independent clause as a VR is above all to be expected if the antecedent term and the independent clause are contiguous, as in (13a). This situation does arise in VSO and SVO languages, but not in (strict) Prefield languages, as is clear from:

(15)   *John* a man *saw*. That one cried.

This might explain why the type of relative clause with an initial "demonstrative" relative pronoun is found in Postfield, but not in Prefield languages.

4.3.2. From embedded question to verbal restrictor

The scenario sketched in 4.3.1. does not explain why it is that many languages (including English) have relative pronouns similar or even identical to interrogative pronouns. I believe that we can at least understand part of this phenomenon through the following considerations. Compare the following constructions:

(16) a.   *Who started the fight?*
    b.   *Peter asked who started the fight.*
    c.   *John did not know who started the fight.*
    d.   *John knew who started the fight.*
    e.   *It was unknown who started the fight.*

Direct questions such as (16a) can be embedded under performative verbs such as *ask*, as in (16b). In many languages, embedded questions extend their domain to complements of expressions which do not immediately designate a speech act, but indicate closely related mental states such as 'know', 'not know', and 'be (un)known' in (16c-e). I believe that these latter constructions hold the key to an understanding of how an embedded question can develop into a relative clause.

As Keenan (1975) has argued, the following constructions amount to semantically very much the same thing:

(17) a.   *I do not know the answer to the question: Who started the fight?*
    b.   *I do not know the person who is such that he started the fight.*

The semantic equivalence between these two constructions is used by Keenan to explain the fact that verbs equivalent to '(not) know' in some languages take embedded questions as complements, as in (17a), in other languages terms as in (17b), and in other languages, again, either the one or the other. Given this equivalence between (17a) and (17b), however, we can also understand how an original embedded question may evolve into an expression equivalent to a term which refers to a first-order entity. Consider the following:

(18) A: *Can you tell me who started the fight?*
    B: *It is Peter who started the fight.*

In B's answer we are already close to interpreting *who started the fight* as equivalent to

(19)   *the one/the person who started the fight*

and from that point onwards, the original embedded question will function as a full-fledged relative clause.

Note that this account of the origin of "interrogative" relative pronouns assumes that free or headless VRs such as the one in (18B) form an intermediate step between embedded questions and fully headed VRs as in (19). From this one might expect that if a language has constructions such as (18B), it will also use the embedded question as a "free relative".

In this respect, the following facts about Dutch may be significant. Dutch has some "demonstrative" relative pronouns, as in (21)-(22), and some "interrogative" relative pronouns, as in (22)-(23):

(20) a. *de   man   die daar   loopt*
         the   man   that there   walks
         'the man that is walking there'
    b. *Die man   loopt   daar.*
         that man   walks   there
         'The man is walking there.'
(21) a. *het boek   dat ik   lees*
         the book   that I   read
         'The book that I am reading'
    b. *Ik   lees   dat boek.*
         I   read   that book
         'I am reading that book.'
(22) a. *de   plaats   waar   je   woont*
         the place   where   you   live
         'the place where you live'
    b. *Waar   woon   je?*
         where   live   you
         'Where do you live?'
(23) a. *de pen waar   je   mee   schrijft*
         the pen where   you   with   write
         'the pen with which you write'
    b. *Waar   schrijf   je   mee?*
         where   write   you   with?
         'What do you write with?'

Now the interesting fact is that those relatives which have an "interrogative" relative pronoun can also occur as free relatives:

(24) a. *Waar   jij   woont   is   het mooi.*
         where   you   live   is   it   beautiful
         'Where you live it is beautiful.'
    b. *Laat   eens   zien waar   je   mee   schrijft.*
         let   once   see where   you   with   write
         'Please show me what you write with.'

On the other hand, VRs with "demonstrative" relative pronouns cannot be used as free relatives. In free relatives, the "demonstrative" relative pronouns are replaced by "interrogative" ones:[4]

(25) a. **Die*   dit   leest   is   gek.*
    b. *Wie   dit   leest   is   gek.*
         who   this   reads   is   mad
         'Whoever reads this is mad.'
(26) a. **Dat*   ik   lees   is   interessant.*
    b. *Wat   ik   lees   is   interessant.*
         what   I   read   is   interesting
         'What I am reading is interesting.'

Thus, it seems correct to say that there is a correlation between "interrogative" relative pronouns (RPro) and free relatives, a correlation which is explained if the following development is assumed:

(27) (i) embedded Q-word question
     (ii) free relative with Q-word/RPro
     (iii) headed relative with "interrogative" RPro

Clauses are often preceded by a preclausal constituent, termed the Theme position in earlier writings on FG. In chapter 17, following Hannay—Vester (1987) I shall redub this position the "Orientation" position and will reserve the term "Theme" for terms with Orientation function that designate first-order entities. "Orientation" captures a wider range of (pragmatic) functions

---

4. Note that the "interrogative" relative pronouns *wie* and *wat* are also used in headed relative clauses in certain varieties in Dutch.

that this position may fulfil: it may indeed contain thematic material, but it may also define a Setting or a Condition relative to that which is presented in the ensuing clause. I will thus speak of Orientation+Clause constructions.

Free relatives derived from embedded questions, when used in Orientation position, can also form the source of the "correlative" construction discussed in 3.3. Consider:

(28) *Wie   nog nooit   in   Rome   geweest is,   die*
       who   yet never   in   Rome   been   is   that-one
       heeft   veel   gemist.
       has   much   missed
      'Anyone who has never been in Rome has missed a lot.'

It does indeed seem to be the case that we typically find "interrogative" relative pronouns in the Orientation part of such constructions, and resumptive demonstrative or personal pronouns in the main clause.

4.3.3. From circumstantial satellite to verbal restrictor[5]

4.3.3.0. Introduction. Many languages have circumstantial satellites corresponding to such English constructions as:

(29) a. *Chasing the thief, the policeman broke a leg.*
     b. *No further matters arising, the meeting was closed.*

Such circumstantial satellites come in two types: as open predications (29a), in which one term position is coreferential with a term in the main clause, and as closed predications (29b), which entertain no coreferentiality relation with the main clause. The latter are often called "absolute" constructions. It is typical of such circumstantial satellites is that they can be interpreted in different ways, e.g. temporal ('while ...'), causal ('because ...'), conditional ('if ...'), concessive ('although ...'). We assume that these are not distinct (semantic) *meanings* of the circumstantial satellite, but different (pragmatic) *interpretations*, co-dependent on contextual and situational clues, of a general semantic function "Circumstance".

---

5. For general discussion, compare Hale (1976) and Zimmermann (1985).

In certain conditions ambiguities may arise as to whether a constituent should be interpreted as a circumstantial satellite or as a restrictor. Consider:

(30) *We found the man smoking a havana.*
 = (a) 'We found the man while he was smoking a havana.'
    (b) 'We found the man who was smoking a havana.'

Such cases make us understand that circumstantial satellites may develop into verbal restrictors through constructions in which either one of these interpretations would be appropriate.

This relation between circumstantial satellites and verbal restrictors is in different ways relevant to the study of VRs. First of all we must reckon with the possibility that constructions which have been analysed as "relative clauses" in certain languages may in fact (still) be circumstantial satellites. Secondly, if it is true that circumstantial satellites have developed into verbal restrictors, this may have happened in different ways, depending on the position of the circumstantial satellite in relation to the main clause, and on other properties of the language concerned.

4.3.3.1. Circumstantial satellites. If we now reconsider the so-called "adjoined relative clauses" (Hale 1976) of certain Australian languages, we see that in many cases these are circumstantial satellites rather than verbal restrictors (Zimmermann 1985). Consider the following properties of Warlpiri clauses marked by the subordinating element *kutja* such as (4) above:

(i) they occur in clause-peripheral position (either preceding or following the clause proper), and never form one constituent with a main clause term;

(ii) depending on context and situation, they may receive the range of interpretations which is typical of circumstantial satellites;

(iii) there need not be a relation of coreference with some term position in the main clause.

The interpretation of "adjoined relative clauses" as circumstantial satellites is compatible with the view, advanced by Merlan (1982) in her description of Mangarayi (another Australian language), that these clauses should be interpreted as "generalized subordinate clauses" which are loosely added to the main clause and which, in suitable contextual circumstances, can get an interpretation which comes very close to the usual interpretation of a "real" VR.[6] Just as in Warlpiri, the Mangarayi general purpose subordinate clause

---

6. For a similar interpretation, see Comrie (1981: 137).

is attached in a "looser, more paratactic relation to the main clause than is often found in subordinate clauses cross-linguistically" (Merlan 1982: 12). It is multifunctional, in that it can get adnominal interpretations (as restricting the potential referents of a term in the main clause), but also adsentential interpretations (as specifying some circumstance or an event causally or temporally related to the SoA described in the main clause). It is marked by a subordinating verbal prefix which indicates that the clause in which it occurs "is not to be interpreted in its own right, but is to be interpreted with reference to some other constituent" (Merlan 1982: 14). The question what sort of interpretation is to be assigned depends on a number of factors (position in the clause, availability of some relevant term in the main clause, presence or absence of a relation of coreference between subordinate and main clause, semantic and pragmatic plausibility) which guide the interpreter in arriving at the intended interpretation.

Consider the following example, which is fully parallel to the Warlpiri example (4):[7]

(31) *Wurg   Ø-ga-ni   Ø-waŋgij   jaŋ?   wa-Ø-ma-ñ.*
       hide   3/3-aux-past abs-child   die   sub-3-aux-past
   =   (a) 'He hid the child that had died.'
       (b) 'He hid the child when it had died.'

The actual interpretation will be co-dependent on the setting in which the sentence is used.

I believe that all these facts are compatible with the view that the clause type in question represents a satellite to the main clause, with the semantic function Circumstance. I would thus assume (31) to have an underlying structure of the form:

(32)   Decl E: X: Past e_i: [*hide* [V] $(he)_{Ag}$ $(d1x_i: child)_{Go}$]
        (Past e_j: [*die* [V] $(Ax_i)_{Proc}$])$_{Circ}$

The circumstantial satellite will then tend to be interpreted "adnominally" when, as in (31), there is a relation of coreference between one of its arguments and some term position in the main clause. We may thus conclude:

---

7. Note that auxiliaries carry all the inflectional elements. PC = Past Continuous, PP = Past Punctual, N = Neuter.

(i) the general purpose subordinate clause as found in languages such as Warlpiri and Mangarayi is not a VR;

(ii) consequently, it has no bearing on the synchronic treatment of VRs;

(iii) however, it provides one possible source from which VRs could develop historically.

4.3.3.2. Circumstantials in Orientation position. In chapter 17 we will see that extra-clausal Orientation constituents may serve to "prepare the ground" for the information contained in the ensuing clause; Orientation constituents may themselves have term or predication status; and there is a tendency for Orientation constituents to "fuse" or integrate into the clause structure over time. Certain Participant Identification strategies may be understood in terms of Orientation+Clause sequences of the form:

(33)   *Given that the man hit the boy, he broke his leg.*
        ---> 'the man who hit the boy broke his leg'
        'the boy whom the man hit broke his leg'

This kind of Orientation+Clause construction may then, through "fusion" or "integration", lead to one type of circumnominal VR. This kind of origin is explicitly claimed for such VRs in Usan (Reesink 1983). Consider the following constructions with the orientation (Or) marker *eng*:[8]

(34)   *Munon   qemi   bau-or   eng, qemi   eng ye*
        man   bow   take-3.sg.past Or   bow   Or   I
        me   geau.
        neg   see.nom
        'Given that the man took the bow, I did not see the bow.'
        ---> 'I did not see the bow which the man took.'

This construction has the following variant:

(35)   *Munon   qemi bau-or   eng   ye me   geau.*
        man   bow take-3.sg.past   Or   I   neg   see.nom
        'Given that the man took the bow I did not see (it/him)'
        ---> 'I did not see the bow which the man took.'
             'I did not see the man who took the bow.'

---

8. FP = Far Past; the verb takes a nominalized form under negation.

This kind of development makes us understand a number of things about this type of construction:

In constructions of type (34) the relevant item from the Orientation clause is resumed in the main clause by an anaphorical element. This element may take any form which an anaphorical element may take in general in the language in question. This may be a full repetition of the relevant term, as in (34); an anaphorical pronoun, as in (33); or zero, in languages which have zero anaphora, as in (35).

Let us suppose that (35) originates from an Orientation+Clause construction with zero anaphora in the main clause. We could then suppose that the main verb, which is looking for a second argument and does not immediately find one, will have a tendency to interpret the Orientation clause "as if" it constituted the missing second argument. In that way, the Orientation would be reinterpreted as a term, and drawn into the main predication.

Another potential example of this kind of situation is provided by Navajo constructions such as the following (Platero 1974):

(36)   *Hastiin   łį́į́'   yizlohę́ę   yí'diiłid.*
        man   horse   he-roped-him he-branded-him

Note that the elements glossed as "he" and "him" cross-reference third person singular arguments, and are insensitive to animacy or other gender distinctions among these arguments. In further examples, we shall gloss these elements as "3". Constructions such as (36) can have different interpretations:

(37) a. 'The man$_i$ branded the horse that he$_i$ roped'
     b. 'The man who roped the horse$_i$ branded it$_i$'
     c. 'He branded the horse that the man roped'
     d. 'He branded the man that roped the horse'

The initial clause of (36) is commonly analysed as a circumnominal relative clause, where the head can be either "man" or "horse". Thus, that initial clause is interpreted as defining a first-order entity which can then be either the Subject or the Object of the main verb. In the latter case, the "he" included in the main verb is understood as being someone else than the "man".

I believe that there are good reasons for considering an alternative analysis of constructions of the form (36). In that analysis, the initial clause will be interpreted as a circumstantial satellite similar to what we found in Warlpiri and Mangarayi, so that we get one unified analysis of (36) along the lines of (38):

(38)   (*man horse 3-rope-3*)$_{Circ}$ *3-brand-3*
         'Given that the man roped the horse, he branded him'

We now assume that the elements 3-3 in the main verb can be anaphorically linked to different antecedents, so that the surface structure (36) can be interpreted as the expression of at least the following non-identical underlying structures:

(39) a. Given that the man$_i$ roped the horse$_j$, he$_i$ branded him$_j$
     b. Given that the man$_i$ roped the horse$_j$, he$_k$ branded him$_j$
     c. Given that the man$_i$ roped the horse$_j$, he$_k$ branded him$_i$

If our assumptions are correct, then Navajo relative constructions of this type can be analysed in terms of the following two principles:
  (i) these constructions are circumstantial satellites;
  (ii) their potential interpretations are monitored by possible antecedent-anaphor relations between circumstantial satellite and main clause.

According to this analysis the so-called relative construction would rather be a construction with a circumstantial satellite in preclausal Orientation position. This, then, is another potential source which VRs may develop from historically. Let us consider this in somewhat more detail.

In certain languages circumstantial Orientation constituents as illustrated in

(40)   *Given that the man caught the tiger, he killed it.*

will be expressed in nominalized form, as in:

(41)   *Given the man's having caught the tiger, he killed it.*

If such constituents develop into VRs, the resulting VR will have a nominalized character as well. This is relevant to the type of VR which is found in Quechua. Consider the following example from Imbabura Quechua (Cole 1982):[9]

---

9. The marker *-ka* is usually glossed "Topic", but it can also be used in marking Orientation (or) constituents. Note that the whole Orientation constituent is nominalized (nr). *-mi* is an assertive validation marker.

(42) Ñuka   chay   punlla-pi   chaya-shka-ka
      I   that   day-on   arrive-nr-or
      sumaj-mi   ka-rka.
      beautiful-val be-past
      'Given my arriving on that day, it was beautiful.'
      ---> 'The day on which I arrived was beautiful.'

There is evidence that the marker -*ka* may indeed be characterized as an Orientation marker in our sense. It can not only be used to mark first-order entities as Topic or Theme, but also to mark propositional constituents as providing the "background" or "condition" for what is stated in the main clause. Consider the following example (Cole 1982: 64):

(43) Utuvalu-man ri-shpa-ka   ruwana-ta   randi-sha.
      Otavalo-to   go-adv-or   poncho-acc   buy-fut-I
      'Given (my) going to Otavalo, I will buy a poncho.'

The adverbial constituent in this case will often get a conditional interpretation, but it can also get a temporal interpretation (Cole 1982: 64). This is typically the range of interpretations associated with the Orientation function (see chapter 17).

In the preceding paragraphs we argued that Orientation+Clause constructions with different mutual anaphorical relations may give rise to situations in which circumstantial satellites may get reinterpreted as VRs. We distinguished finite and nominalized versions of the Orientation constituent. Compare the following constructions:

(44) a. [*boy father hit*]-Given, *that boy*-acc *see*-neg-*I*.
         'Given that the boy hit his father, I didn't see the boy.'
     b. [*boy father hit*]-Given, *him*-acc *see*-neg-*I*.
         'Given that the boy hit his father, I didn't see him (= 'the boy' or 'his father').'
     c. [*boy father hit*]-Given, Ø *see*-neg-*I*.
         'Given that the boy hit his father, I didn't see.'

Especially constructions of type (44c) could be a bridge toward reinterpretation of the Orientation constituent as actually providing the second argument of the verb 'see'. Since the main clause in (44c) has zero anaphora, there is no overt second argument present in the main clause (and, *a fortiori*, no term marked by the accusative case, as would be expected with 'see'). In those conditions we could understand a development toward:

(45)   [*boy father hit*]-Given-acc *see*-neg-*I*
    =   (a) 'I didn't see the boy who hit his father'
        (b) 'I didn't see the father that the boy hit'

This scenario presupposes that this kind of construction arises above all in languages which allow zero anaphora in the relevant conditions. And indeed, Cole (1987) even states that all languages which have this construction type also have zero anaphora in conditions such as (45).

The scenario sketched above explains the type of internal head relative clause found in several Amerindian language families as illustrated with examples from Yuman languages and Wappo in 3.3. Langdon (1977) specifically states that the VR in Yuman languages can be understood as being modelled on the nominalization construction, and that the question whether a given construction must be interpreted as a nominalization or as a VR in many cases depends on semantic factors, since the constructions do not differ formally.

A typical property of internal head VRs of this kind is the occurrence of two types of potential ambiguity:

(i) there may be ambiguity between the SoA reading and the Entity-reading in constructions with higher verbs which can take either a propositional / predicational term or a first-order entity term as an argument.

(ii) in the case of the Entity-reading, there may be ambiguity as to which entity is the target of the higher verb.

The VR which can be understood as being due to the nominalization strategy typically occurs in a number of variants. Langdon (1977) mentions the following possible variants in Yuman languages:

(46) a. *father* (*son ball throw*-nom) *catch*.
    b.   *father* (*ball son throw*-nom) *catch*.
    c.   (*son ball throw*-nom) *father catch*.
    d.   (*ball son throw*-nom) *father catch*.
    e.   *father catch* (*son ball throw*-nom).
    f.   *father catch* (*ball son throw*-nom).
    g.   *father ball catch* (*son throw*-nom).
        'The father caught the ball that the son threw.'

90 *Verbal restrictors 3*

Thus:

(i) the whole nominalization may stand in the position which corresponds to its function (a.-b.), in initial position (c.-d.), or in final position (e.-g.).

(ii) in all these cases, the target term may stand in its pattern position or in initial position within the nominalization. This fronting within the domain of the nominalization can be interpreted as a means of disambiguating the construction: the fronted constituent will be the target term of the higher verb.

We must now consider the question of how the VR which can be understood as originating from the nominalization strategy can be represented in the underlying structure of the proposition / predication.

Let us start with the representation of a construction such as:

(47)   John (*boy ball hit*-nom) *believe*.
        'John believes that the boy hit the ball.'

in which the embedded proposition / predication functions as a "true" nominalization, indicating some SoA. Such a construction can be represented as follows:

(48)   Decl E_i: X_i: Pres e_i: *believe* [V] (*John*)$_{Po}$
        (X_j: Past e_j: *hit* [V] (d1x_j: *boy*)$_{Ag}$ (d1x_k: *ball*)$_{Go}$])$_{Go}$

In this construction, it is indicated that John believes something X_j, where X_j is specified by the predication "the boy hit the ball".

Let us now consider the case in which the nominalization serves as a VR:

(49)   John (*boy ball hit*-nom) *find*.
    =   (a) 'John found the boy who hit the ball.'
        (b) 'John found the ball that the boy hit.'

Let us first note that, according to the principles of FG, the representation for (49) cannot be identical to that of (47). For in (49) the main verb does not relate "John" to some SoA, but relates "John" to some entity involved in a SoA. The semantic difference between these two relations must be obvious to any speaker of the languages concerned. In other words, the difference can hardly be a matter of vagueness, such that a structure of type (49) could be assigned any of its possible interpretations, depending on context: the construction can clearly be used to formulate different, clearly distinct meanings. Secondly, on the same grounds we must assume that the two different interpretations of (49) have different underlying representations: in the first case, the verb *find* relates "John" to some "boy", in the second case it relates "John" to some "ball". Again, these are quite distinct meanings, which cannot be derived from one and the same underlying representation. In other words, we must assume that a construction of the general form of the bracketed part of (49) is in principle three-ways ambiguous, although one or more of its possible readings may be cancelled through the requirements put on the construction by the selection restrictions imposed by the main predicate. We thus need a representation through which, in the case of (49), one of the entities involved in the embedded proposition / predication is singled out as being related to "John" through the matrix verb.

On the other hand, this cannot easily be achieved on the assumption that these constructions should be analysed on the more usual (and better known) model in which the VR is seen as the expression of an open proposition / predication in x_i, which acts as a restrictor on the term variable x_i. According to that model, (49), on its first interpretation, would have a structure such as:

(50)   *find* [V] (*John*)$_{Proc}$ (d1x_i: *boy*: *hit* [V] (Ax_i)$_{Ag}$ (*the ball*)$_{Go}$)$_{Go}$
       "John found the x_i such that x_i is a boy, such that x_i hit the ball."

For on that analysis, although semantically adequate with respect to the interpretation of (49), we would need extremely complex expression rules in order to arrive at a linguistic expression which, finally, will be almost identical to that expressing the construction with the true nominalization (47). Specifically, starting from (50), the first restrictor would have to be inserted into the open position of the second restrictor, and the resulting proposition / predication would have to be nominalized so as to result in a surface form such as (49). If such "acrobatics" were involved in these VRs, it would hardly be conceivable how such different underlying proposition / predications could finally end up in much the same expression.

For these reasons, I shall assume that the constructions concerned, on their interpretation as VRs, have an underlying structure of their own, which does justice to their possible interpretations as VRs, while not being so widely different from the nominalization construction as to make it incomprehensible that VRs and nominalizations are expressed in much the same form.

I suggest the following representations for (49a) and (49b):

(51) a. *find* [V] (*John*)$_{Proc}$ (d1x_i: *hit* [V] (d1x_i: *boy*)$_{Ag}$ (d1x_j: *ball*)$_{Go}$)$_{Go}$
     b. *find* [V] (*John*)$_{Proc}$ (d1x_j: *hit* [V] (d1x_i: *boy*)$_{Ag}$ (d1x_j: *ball*)$_{Go}$)$_{Go}$

The configuration postulated in (51a) and (51b) for the second term presupposes a special type of restrictor which I will call the "half-open restrictor". Let us look at the properties of this configuration in some detail:

(52)   (d1x_i: *hit* [V]) (d1x_i: *boy*)$_{Ag}$ (d1x_j: *ball*)$_{Go}$)

In this configuration, the term variable x_i is specified by a closed predication which, however, contains an occurrence of x_i in one of its term positions. The restrictor is thus closed in the sense that all its term positions are filled in by some term. It is "half-open", however, in that one of its term positions corresponds to the term variable. In being closed, this restrictor type differs from the "open predication in x_i" which we find in a configuration such as (50). In being "half-open", it differs from restrictors discussed in 3.2.3., which have the character of a closed predication which do not contain a term corresponding to the term variable.

The half-open restrictor in configuration (52) can be interpreted as an instruction of the following form:

(53)   "pick out the term corresponding to x_i in the predication which now follows"

This instruction more or less directly captures the idea that in the constructions concerned, the matrix verb "penetrates" into the embedded predication, and selects one of the terms in that embedded predication as one of its arguments. At the same time, the underlying representations (51a-b) and (48) are sufficiently close to each other to make us understand that they can be expressed in the same surface form. In the case of the true nominalizations, the term variable is a propositional variable X_i or a SoA variable e_i which is specified by a fully closed proposition or predication specifying its content. In the case of half-open restrictors, the variable is an entity variable x_i which is specified by a closed predication, among the terms of which it has to find its target value, marked by the same variable x_i.

4.4. Conclusion

The introduction of the notion of 'verbal restrictor' has allowed us, in the preceding two chapters, to generalize across a wide range of construction types which serve the purpose of identifying participants. In this chapter we have tried to show that this notion also helps us understand the distribution of VR-types across languages and the ways in which these VR-types come about.

5. Embedded constructions 1: semantic parameters

5.0. Introduction

The argument and satellite positions in the underlying clause structure can be filled with terms, expressions which can be used to refer to entities in some real or imagined world. For a Speaker to refer means for him to help the Addressee either to establish a mental representation of some entity about which something is to be predicated (*constructive reference*), or to identify or retrieve an entity which has already been established in his mental world (*identifying reference*). Prototypical terms are used to refer to first-order entities: entities such as persons, things, and places which can be conceptualized as existing in space. Up to this point we have mainly confined our attention to such first-order terms.

We can, however, also create terms which can be used to refer to other types of entities, in fact to any of the entity types which can be designated by the different layers of underlying clause structure. Recall that we distinguished the types of entity listed in Table 1.

Table 1. Types of entities as referred to by terms

ORDER	STRUCTURE	TYPE	VARIABLE
0	predicate	Property / Relation	f
1	first order term	Spatial entity	x
2	predication	State of Affairs	e
3	proposition	Possible Fact	X
4	clause	Speech Act	E

Terms which can be used to refer to properties and relations have been discussed in *TFG1*: 6.3.1., those which can be used to refer to spatial entities have been dealt with throughout *TFG1*. In this and the following two chapters we consider terms which can be used to refer to the higher-order entities of types e, X, and E. Such terms can be formed from simplex nouns, when these designate entities of types e, X, and E, as in:

(1) a. *John watched* the match.
   (John watched an event, an entity of type e).
   b. *John knew* the facts.
   (John knew propositional contents, an entity of type X).
   c. *John answered* the question.
   (John responded to a speech act, an entity of type E).

More commonly, entities of types e, X, and E are referred to by means of *complex terms*, which contain an embedded predication, proposition, or clause. Consider the following examples:

(2) a. *John witnessed* the changing of the guards.
   — reference is made to an event, an entity of type e.
   b. *John knew* that Mary had failed to show up.
   — reference is made to a propositional content, an entity of type X
   c. *John considered* why Peter had failed to show up.
   — reference is made to a question, an entity of type E

In this chapter I consider such complex higher-order terms. For these term types I shall use the terminology and representations listed in Table 2.

Table 2. Terms for higher-order entities

TERM TYPE	STRUCTURE	EXAMPLE
predicational term	(e: [predication])	(2a)
propositional term	(X: [proposition])	(2b)
clausal term	(E: [clause])	(2c)

In general, a complex term such as (A: [Φ]) can be used to refer to an entity of type A, as specified by Φ. Φ will be said to be "embedded" in the complex term structure. We can thus speak of *embedded clauses, embedded propositions*, and *embedded predications*. In general, we shall speak of *embedded constructions*: complex terms contain embedded constructions as restrictors.

Introduction 95

Predicates may require their arguments to designate higher-order entities. For example, the predicate *believe* in the sense of 'accept as true' requires that the second argument be a higher-order term which can be used to refer to a propositional entity. We can thus set up the following predicate frame:

(3)   *believe* [V] (x: <human>)$_{Po}$ (X)$_{Go}$

Note that the second argument is selectionally restricted to terms designating a proposition. These may be simple terms such as (1), or complex terms such as (2). In the latter case, the propositional term will contain an embedded proposition. Predicates which take complex arguments of this type will be called *matrix predicates*, and the clause headed by such a predicate is the *matrix clause*.[1]

The definition of "embedded construction" covers structures embedded in argument positions (often referred to as "complements"),[2] as in:

(4) a. That Bill loves Sally *is unbelievable.* (first argument)
    b. *John believes* that Bill loves Sally. (second argument)
    c. *John convinced Peter* that Bill loved Sally. (third argument)

The definition of complex terms also covers structures embedded in satellite positions (commonly referred to as "adverbial clauses"), as in:

(5) a. Before he left the meeting, *John made some important points.* (Temporal satellite)
    b. *John is down,* because Bill loves Sally. (Cause satellite)
    c. If Bill loves Sally, *John will be down.* (Condition satellite)
    d. As long as Bill loves Sally, *John will be down.* (Duration satellite)

Adverbial clauses will not be discussed in the present context. There is no reason to assume, however, that they cannot be dealt with in terms of the parameters that will be presented in this and the next two chapters in the description of complex terms occupying argument positions.

We now consider the different types of higher-order terms one by one.

---

1. Note that (3) is only one of the frames of *believe*. In another frame, *believe* defines a relation between two human beings, as in: *John didn't believe Mary.*
2. For an excellent survey of the typology of complements, see Noonan (1985). My discussion of embedded constructions owes much to this study.

5.1. Clausal terms

Matrix predicates designating or implying speech acts require the second argument to be of type "speech act". They are thus used for reporting speech acts performed by the Agent of the matrix clause. Clausal complements come in a variety of forms, which can be thought of as constituting a spectrum ranging between the extremes of "direct speech" and "indirect speech",[3] as in:

(6) a. DIRECT SPEECH:
   John said: "Peter is feeding the cat".
   b. INDIRECT SPEECH:
   John said that Peter was feeding the cat.

A matrix predicate such as *say* takes a clausal complement for its second argument: it requires the complement to be of the type "speech act". The predicate designates a relation between a human being and a speech act which that human being performs. Both in direct and in indirect speech we may speak of a "clausal complement": although in direct speech the embedded clause retains its full independence and is in no way marked as subordinate to the matrix clause, it does occupy an argument position (here: the Goal position) of the matrix predicate. I will return to the difference between direct and indirect speech complements in 5.1.4. below.

5.1.1. Direct speech

In direct speech the embedded clause purports to be a literal quotation of what the Agent of the matrix clause says. Should this not be true, the Speaker can be taken to task for misleading or falsely informing the Addressee. A direct speech embedded clause obviously has the full internal structure of an independent clause, and may even consist of a sequence of clauses (a discourse or text), as in a (directly reported) speech or conversation.

Most importantly, direct speech preserves the orientation to the parameters of the deictic centre of the original speech act reported, whereas in indirect

---

3. See the different studies in Coulmas ed. (1986) for some evidence for the view that there is no all-or-none division between direct and indirect speech.

speech the content of the complement is presented from the point of view of the deictic centre of the reporter (cf. Coulmas 1986a).

Languages differ in their usage of direct speech complements. Adelaar (1990) shows that in Quechua the predicate *ni* 'to say' is the only predicate which takes direct complements (7); it is also a predicate which can take no other complement types. Other verbs of communication are combined with a participial form *nispa* 'saying':

(7) a. *"Z" ni-n-ku.*
        Z   say-3-pl
        '"Z", they say.'
    b. *"Z" ni-spa   kacha-rka-n.*
        Z   say-ing   order-past-3
        'They gave an order saying "Z".'

Even the predicate *ni* itself is often combined with this participial form, resulting in a somewhat redundant *nispa ni* 'say saying':

(8)   *"Z" ni-spa   ni-n-ku.*
        Z   say-ing   say-3-pl
        'They said saying "Z".'

The usage of complements with *nispa* extends beyond speech act predicates into the realm of propositional attitude predicates:

(9)   *"ñuka-kta-pas   muna-wa-nka"   ni-spa   amu-rka-n-ku.*
        me-acc-incl   want-me-fut   say-ing   come-past-3-pl
        'They came, saying "She will want (love) me as well".'
        'They came in the expectation that she would love them as well.'

There is no suggestion here that 'they' actually spoke. Thus, direct speech is here used to represent thoughts as a form of silent or inner speech. Exactly the same is demonstrated for Kombai (Papuan) in De Vries (1990).

We see in (8) how *nispa* 'saying' can be used redundantly, and in (9) how it can be used in circumstances in which no actual speech is involved. This illustrates *in vivo* how a word meaning 'saying' can develop into a generalized subordinator for clausal and propositional complements. Such subordinators are frequently found in genetically unrelated languages.

5.1.2. Indirect speech

Indirect speech complements, as in (6b), also represent what the Agent of the matrix predicate is purported to have said (asked, promised, etc.), but not necessarily in a literal sense. It is the Reporter who in this case takes responsibility for the wording of the complement, and may add his own interpretation or qualification to that which the reported Speaker has said. Correspondingly, the content of the complement now orients itself to the deictic centre of the Reporter rather than to that of the original Speaker, and a number of adjustments can be understood immediately in terms of this deictic shift (cf. Coulmas 1986a, Haberland 1986).

Indirect speech complements differ in the following respects from direct speech complements:

(i) *Subordination*
There is typically some explicit marker indicating that the complement is subordinate to the main clause. Thus, in

(10)   *John says* that *Peter is feeding the cat.*

the subordinator *that* explicitly marks the complement as a case of indirect speech. In exceptional cases such markers of subordination may be absent, so that the difference between direct and indirect speech is not segmentally marked:

(11)   *John says Peter is feeding the cat.*

In such exceptional cases where there is no segmental distinction between direct and indirect speech we may assume that there are still prosodic differences which reveal the distinction.

(ii) *Sequence of tenses*
Suppose today is Wednesday and John has said on Tuesday:

(12)   *I will arrive tomorrow.*

How are we going to report what John said? In direct speech there is no problem:

(13)   *John said (yesterday): "I will come tomorrow".*

But in indirect speech we do have a problem when the temporal reference is preserved as in the original:

(14)   *John said (yesterday) that he will come tomorrow.*

Since the complement orients to the deictic centre of the current reporting speech act, (14) will easily be mistaken as suggesting that John said he would come on Thursday. No doubt for this reason, many languages in such cases shift the original tense to the corresponding Past, while at the same time adjusting the deictic temporal satellite to the current moment of speaking:

(15)   *John said (yesterday) that he would come today.*

The adjustment of the tense is a matter of *consecutio temporum* or *sequence of tenses*: a device to avoid the tense being wrongly decoded from the current moment of speaking.

Sequence of tenses is not a necessary feature of indirect speech. Certain languages preserve the temporal reference of the original as long as it is clear in the context what is meant (Coulmas 1986a, Comrie 1985). Even in English the tense may remain unaffected if that which is reported to have been said is indeed relevant at the moment of speaking. For example:

(16) a.   *John said: "Peter is having a holiday on the Bahamas".*
    b.   *John said Peter is having a holiday on the Bahamas.*
    c.   *John said Peter was having a holiday on the Bahamas.*

If what John said implies that Peter is still having his holiday at the moment of reporting, then (16c) rather than (16b) might be misleading. Note that (16b) is another example where the difference between direct and indirect speech is not segmentally coded.

(iii) *Deictic adjustment*
In indirect speech such elements as are sensitive to the deictic centre of the reported speech act typically adjust to the deictic centre of the actual (reporting) speech act. Thus, the participants within the complement adjust to the participants of the matrix clause or, if relevant, the participants in the current speech act, in the following ways:

(17) a.   *Peter said to Mary: "I love you".*
    b.   *Peter said to Mary that he loved her.*

(18) a. *Peter said to me: "I love you".*
   b. *Peter said to me that he loved me.*
   c. *Peter said that he loved me.*
(19) a. *Peter said to you: "I love you".*
   b. *Peter said to you that he loved you.*
   c. *Peter said that he loved you.*

In general, then, the participant referents shift to third person, unless they happen to be coreferential to the current Speaker or Addressee.

It was noted above that the distinction between direct and indirect speech is not an all-or-none matter. In actual usage, we find direct speech with features of indirectness, and indirect speech with features of directness. One special type of reporting, variously called "quasi-direct" or "free indirect" speech has received special attention since it may serve clear literary purposes. As Haberland (1986) shows, however, forms of speech that fall in between direct and indirect speech are massively found in ordinary spoken conversation as well, and it is not clear that there is just one discrete in-between form: rather, there is a continuum between direct and indirect speech, defined by the combination of more and more features of one or the other style.

5.1.3. Indirect speech complements have their own illocutions

There are various reasons to assume that even in indirect reported speech the complement is a full clause structure, with its own illocutionary operator (cf. Bolkestein 1976, 1990a). These reasons are the following:

(i) embedded constructions may get different types of formal expression according as they are embedded declaratives, embedded questions, etc. Compare:

(20) a. *John said that he was tired.*
   b. *John asked whether / if Mary was tired.*

The difference between the subordinators *that* and *whether / if* can be accounted for if we assume that *say* takes a Decl, *ask* an Int complement:

(21) a. say [V] $(x_1: <hum>)_{Ag}$ (Decl $E_i)_{Go}$
   b. ask [V] $(x_1: <hum>)_{Ag}$ (Int $E_i)_{Go}$

Bolkestein (1976, 1990a) shows that similar differences serve to subcategorize Latin matrix predicates in the following way:

(22) a. matrix predicates such as *narrare* 'to tell' take a declarative complement which must be expressed in the *accusativus cum infinitivo* (AcI).
 b. matrix predicates such as *imperare* 'to order' take a directive complement which may either be expressed in the AcI or in a finite subordinate clause with subordinator *ut* 'that'.
 c. matrix predicates such as *dicere* 'to say' may either take a declarative complement in the AcI, or a directive complement expressed as an *ut*-clause.

Thus, if we want to account for the variation in formal expression of such complements, the easiest way of doing so is by assuming that they embed full clause structures which are differentiated by their illocutionary operators.

(ii) selectional constraints imposed on independent clauses of a certain illocutionary status also hold for embedded clauses of that status.

First of all, satellites such as *probably* cannot freely occur in independent interrogatives. Nor can they appear in dependent interrogatives:

(23) a. **Is Peter probably going to New York?*
 b. **Mary asked John if Peter was probably going to New York.*

The easiest way to account for this constraint is to make the satellite sensitive to the illocution of the clause in which it occurs (cf. Dik 1992). If that method is followed, the indirect embedded clause should have its own illocutionary operator.

Secondly, term operators such as *any* can freely occur in interrogatives, not in declaratives. They can also occur in indirectly embedded interrogatives:

(24) a. *Does John have any enemies?*
 b. **John has any enemies.*
(25) a. *Mary asked Peter whether John had any enemies.*
 b. **Mary told Peter that John had any enemies.*

Again, the same conclusion can be drawn from these facts.

Thirdly, imperatives impose constraints on the sorts of predications they can take in their scope.[4] In principle, these have to designate controlled SoAs. The same is true of clauses embedded under directive predicates. Compare:

(26) a. *John, go away!*
 b. **House, collapse!*
(27) a. *Mary ordered John to go away.*
 b. **Mary ordered the house to collapse.*

Again, these constraints are most easily accounted for if they can be linked to an illocutionary operator Imp, which should then be present both in the independent and in the dependent clause structures.

5.1.4. Difference between direct and indirect speech

The difference between direct and indirect speech may be accounted for by assuming that in direct speech the quoted clause immediately acts as a complement to the matrix verb, whereas in indirect speech that clause is embedded within a clausal term which functions as a complement to the matrix verb:

(28) a. *John said: "Peter is feeding the cat."*
 b. Decl E_i: X_i: Past e_i: *say* [V] (*John*)$_{Ag}$
  (Decl E_j: X_j: Pres e_j: Progr *feed* [V] (*Peter*)$_{Ag}$ (*the cat*)$_{Go}$)$_{Go}$
(29) a. *John said that Peter was feeding the cat.*
 b. Decl E_i: X_i: Past e_i: *say* [V] (*John*)$_{Ag}$
  (E_j: [Decl E_j: X_j: Pres e_j: Progr *feed* [V] (*Peter*)$_{Ag}$ (*the cat*)$_{Go}$])$_{Go}$

Now the most important difference, as we saw, is that in direct speech the speech act E_j is presented as completely independent of speech act E_i: it draws its deictic parameters from the original clause, not from the current speech act E_i in which the reporting is done. On the other hand, in indirect speech the embedded speech act loses its independent status: the deictic centre is now defined by E_i, also for the content of the embedded clause.

---

4. Following Hengeveld (1989, 1990), we assume that imperative speech acts immediately operate on predications, with no intervening propositional layer; cf. also 5.3.1. below.

5.1.5. Not all elements can be converted into indirect speech

Coulmas (1986a, 1986b) and Bolkestein (1990b, 1992) have pointed out the fact that not all types of elements which can be present in a direct speech complement can be preserved in indirect speech. Bolkestein mentions the following examples:

(i) *Exclamations*

(30) a. *What cheek she has!*
     b. **He exclaimed (that) what cheek she had.*

(ii) *Certain idiomatic imperatives*

(31) a. *Drink that and I'll kill you.*
     b. **He threatened that she should drink that and he would kill her.*
     c. *He threatened that, if she drank that, he would kill her.*

(iii) *Certain extra-clausal constituents*

(32) a. *?He said that well, he was hungry.*
     b. *?He said that ladies and gentlemen, this is a festive occasion.*
     c. *?He said that it was a festive occasion, wasn't it.*

(iv) *Certain modal particles*

(33) a. *Je   gaat   toch   zeker   niet huilen?*
         you go   toch   certainly not cry
         'You are not going to cry, are you?'
     b. **Zij vroeg of hij toch zeker niet ging huilen.*
         'She asked if he was not going to cry, was he?'

As regards these various phenomena, it must first of all be remarked that we should not all too quickly generalize within and across languages. What is impossible in one type of construction (or in one type of speech) within one language may be possible in other constructions / types of speech, and what is impossible in one language may be possible in another, and the other way around.

104   *Embedded constructions 1*

For intralinguistic variation and hesitation in this respect, consider again (33b). Although under a verb of 'asking' the relevant modal elements cannot occur, they do occur under a verb of 'suggesting', as in:

(34)   *Zij suggereerde dat hij toch zeker niet ging huilen?*
         'She suggested that he was not going to cry, was he?'

This might be interpreted as showing that the "modal" elements in question serve to convert a Question into a Suggestion, so that they can no longer be embedded under a predicate of 'asking', though they are not unembeddable *per se*.

For another example, consider the occurrence of extra-clausal Themes (see chapter 17) in Dutch indirect speech (Dik 1981). Grammatically speaking this will typically be rejected. It was found, however, that in actual spoken Dutch such embedded Themes do indeed occur rather frequently, although in a peculiar kind of construction in which the subordinator is repeated:

(35)   *Hij zei   dat die   aartsvaders en   zo,   dat   dat*
         he   said that those   patriarchs   and   so   that that
              ook niet zo'n   brave   jongens   waren.
              also not such   innocent   boys   were
         'He said that those patriarchs were not such innocent boys either.'

A second finding was, that Dutch speakers, if they want to create a Theme inside a subordinate construction, often slip back into direct speech constituent order. We then get constructions with a subordinator, but otherwise identical to a main clause. These two facts were interpreted as showing that subordination of Themes is indeed a problem, but that it can be avoided or solved in different ways.

Concerning the impossibility of using certain items in indirect speech reports, the following two principles seem to have some general validity:

(i) Extra-clausal constituents (ECCs) are in general more difficult to subordinate than intraclausal elements.

(ii) Those elements which find their *raison d'etre* in the direct address of the Addressee by the Speaker are difficult to subordinate.

These two principles often reinforce each other, since the elements relevant to (ii) often have the status of ECCs. Consider vocatives:

(36) a. *John, could you help us for a moment?*
b. **He asked whether John, could he help them for a moment?*
c. *He asked whether John could help them for a moment.*

The vocative, as a device strongly dependent on direct address (and an ECC), cannot be subordinated easily. But note that the second person which is essential for the vocative to be used at all, has shifted to third person by deictic adjustment anyway, and that there are other ways of conveying that the question was put to "John", as in (36c).

This may be compared to expressions in which Politeness distinctions are coded. In languages in which such distinctions are confined to second person address, they cannot be preserved in indirect speech:

(37) a. *Kun je   me even helpen?*
    can you.informal me moment help
    'Can you (informal) help me a moment?'
b. *Kunt U   me even helpen?*
    can   you.polite me moment help
    'Can you (polite) help me a moment?'
c. *Hij vroeg haar of ze hem even kon   helpen.*
    he asked   her   if   she him moment could help
    'He asked her if she could help him a moment'
    (no politeness variation possible)

In this connection it is interesting that certain Politeness expressions in Japanese, such as *kudasai* 'please', cannot be subordinated (Coulmas 1986a), whereas the politeness form of the verb, so pervasive in Japanese, is mainly confined to main clauses (although it does exceptionally occur in subordinate clauses, Coulmas 1986b).

If it is true that in general, independent reasons can be found for the fact that certain expressions which occur in direct speech cannot in the same way occur in indirect speech complements, this phenomenon need not be taken as indicating that direct and indirect speech complements could not both have the status of embedded speech acts.

However, as we will see in 9.3.1, those items which cannot be embedded can occur in members of a coordination. For that reason we make a distinction between "sentence" (including the ECCs) and "clause". We can then say that clauses can, but sentences cannot necessarily be embedded.

5.2. Propositional terms

5.2.1. Types of matrix predicates

Embedded propositions appear as arguments with the following types of predicates:[5]
  (i) predicates of propositional attitude
  (ii) predicates of propositional manipulation
  (iii) predicates of (acquisition / loss of) knowledge
  (iv) predicates of mental perception

(i) *Predicates of propositional attitude*
Predicates of propositional attitude specify the attitude of a person in relation to the possible fact designated by the propositional complement. These attitudes comprise intellectual attitudes, as in (38), and emotional attitudes as in (39):

(38) a. *John believed that Mary was ill.*
     b. *John presumed that Mary was ill.*
(39) a. *John feared that Mary was ill.*
     b. *John hoped that Mary was better again.*

A matrix predicate such as *believe* takes an embedded proposition for its second argument. To say that a person believes X is to say that he accepts X as a true proposition. We can thus give the following analysis:

(40) a. *John believed that Peter was feeding the cat.*
     b. Decl E: X_i: Past e_i: *believe* [V] $(John)_{Po}$
         $(X_j$: Sim e_j: Progr *feed* [V] $(Peter)_{Ag}$ $(the\ cat)_{Go})_{Go}$

In this analysis it is expressed that the content of John's belief is the proposition X_j, defined by the SoA e_j consisting of Peter's feeding the cat. In this particular example, the predication embedded within the embedded proposition is presented as simultaneous or overlapping in time with the SoA of the matrix predication, as expressed by the operator "Sim" (simultaneous).[6]

---

  5. For many of the distinctions made here and in the following sections, see Noonan (1985).
  6. For this operator, cf. Vester (1983).

Indeed, the complement in (40a) is presented as being accepted by John as true at the time of his believing it. But this is not a necessary property of complements of *believe*. Compare:

(41) a. *John believed that Peter had fed the cat.*
  b. *John believed that Peter would feed the cat.*

As is shown by these examples, the time of the predication embedded within the embedded proposition, although definable relative to the time of the "believing", need not be simultaneous with it: it may precede it, as in (41a), coincide with it, as in (40), or follow it in time, as in (41b). We can here use the relative Tense operators "Ant" (anterior), "Sim" (simultaneous), and "Post" (posterior).

(ii) *Predicates of propositional manipulation*
By predicates of propositional manipulation I understand predicates which indicate some attempt on the part of X to induce a certain propositional attitude in Y, as in:

(42) a. *John convinced Peter that Charles should be fired.*
  b. *John persuaded Peter that it was better for Charles to leave.*
  c. *John taught the students that the earth was round.*

In this case the propositional complement takes the third argument position. These predicates have alternative uses in which the third argument is a predicational rather than a propositional term. We return to this difference below, in 5.4.1.

(iii) *Predicates of knowledge and acquisition / loss of knowledge.*
Matrix predicates which designate the mental acquisition, possession, or loss of the fact designated by the propositional complement are exemplified in:

(43) a. *John learned that Mary was ill.*
  b. *John knew that Mary was ill.*
  c. *John forgot that Mary was ill.*

(iv) *Predicates of mental perception*[7]

These are predicates which designate "indirect perception" of the fact designated by the complement propositional term. We speak of indirect or mental perception when some fact is presented as being inferred from information perceived through the senses, as in:

(44) a. *Mary saw that John had been drinking.*
(she inferred this from how he looked)
    b. *Mary saw that Anna was not in the library.*
(she inferred this from the fact that she didn't see Anna in the library)
    c. *Mary heard that John was going to leave the country.*
(she inferred this from something she heard).

5.2.2. Factivity

There is a well-known semantic distinction between "factive", "non-factive", and "contra-factive" matrix predicates (cf. Kiparsky—Kiparsky 1970). These distinctions can be described as follows:

(45) a. FACTIVE:
S commits himself to the truth of the embedded proposition.
    b. CONTRA-FACTIVE:
S signals that he himself believes that the embedded proposition is false.
    c. NON-FACTIVE:
S is not committed to either the truth or the falsity of the embedded proposition.

The predicate *believe* is non-factive: the propositional content is presented as something which the believer takes to be true; as far as S is concerned, it might be true or false:

(46) a. *John believes that Mary is pregnant and indeed, she is.*
    b. *John believes that Mary is pregnant, but in fact she isn't.*

---

7. Cf. Dik—Hengeveld (1991).

Thus, *believe* by itself does not impose presuppositional constraints on the propositional complement.

Predicates such as *know* and *realize* are factive. They commit S to the truth of the embedded proposition, witness:

(47) a. **John knows that Mary is pregnant, and indeed, she is.*
 b. **John knows that Mary is pregnant, but in fact she isn't.*

(47a) is redundant and (47b) is contradictory, in contrast to (46a) and (46b).

A predicate such as *pretend* comes close to being contra-factive. A construction such as

(48) *John pretended that Mary was pregnant.*

strongly suggests that S regards the propositional content as false.

A necessarily contra-factive predicate of propositional manipulation in Dutch is *iemand iets wijsmaken*, literally 'make something wise to somebody', or 'fool someone into believing something'.[8] Thus, an expression such as:

(49) Jan   heeft   Marie   wijs-gemaakt dat de
      John   has   Mary   wise-made   that the
         aarde   plat is.
         earth   flat is
      'John has fooled Mary into believing that the earth is flat.'

signals that S himself takes the propositional complement to be false.

We can say that in choosing a factive or a contra-factive matrix predicate, S is not free to subsequently make a free choice as regards his own attitude towards the truth of the embedded proposition. This could be formally expressed by assuming that such matrix predicates have a fixed attitudinal operator which cannot be varied at will:

(50) a. *know* [V] $(x_1: <hum>)_{Po}$ (True $X_1)_{Go}$
 b. *pretend* [V] $(x_1: <hum>)_{Po}$ (False $X_1)_{Go}$

---

8. Another, more idiomatic contra-factive predicate in Dutch, with the same meaning, is *iemand iets aan zijn neus hangen* 'hang somebody something on his nose'.

110 *Embedded constructions 1*

On the other hand, a predicate such as *believe* is compatible with any choice of attitudinal operator in the complement:

(51)   *believe* [V] (x_1: <hum>)$_{Po}$ (π_3 X_1)$_{Go}$

As was shown in Dik—Hengeveld (1991), languages may have means for S to express his own opinion on the embedded propositional content secondarily in the case of non-factives. Thus, Spanish allows a choice between indicative and subjunctive mood in the complement of non-factives, where the former signals 'and I believe this too', and the latter 'but I do not commit myself to this' (see also Noonan 1985).

5.3. Predicational terms

5.3.1. Types of matrix predicates

The following types of matrix predicate take predicational terms as arguments.
   (i) directive predicates, including the imperative (Post)
   (ii) predicates of practical manipulation (Post)
   (iii) volitional predicates (Post)
   (iv) predicates of direct perception (Sim)
   (v) achievement predicates (Sim)
   (vi) phasal predicates (Sim)
   (vii) commentative predicates (Free)
   (viii) objective modal predicates (Free)
We will discuss these types one by one.

(i) *Directive predicates*
There are different ways in which it can be expressed that X did something in order to get Y to do SoA, where SoA is designated by the embedded predication. One parameter is whether or not the predicate presupposes an intervening speech act between X and Y. If that is the case we speak of directive predicates; if not, we speak of predicates of practical manipulation.
   Consider such examples as the following:

(52) a.   *John ordered Bill to leave.*
     b.   *John asked Bill to leave.*

Predicational terms 111

If we simply say that directive predicates take embedded predications as complements, we do not account for the speech act character of these matrix verbs, and for their special relation with the Imperative.

To see how this relation can be accounted for, let us first consider the status of imperatives. Imperatives are speech acts, but they do not have a propositional content, but immediately operate on the SoA which A is intended to carry out. Thus, we can give an analysis such as:

(53) a. *Leave!*
     b. Imp E: Post e: *leave* [V] (A)$_{Ag}$

in which it is expressed that S wishes A to carry out the action as specified in the predication at a moment after the moment of speaking. Requests can be given a similar analysis.

This means that we can maintain the idea that speech act predicates embed speech acts, while at the same time accounting for the fact that in (53a) there is no propositional content. This can be achieved through the following analyses:

(54) *John ordered Bill to leave.*
      Decl E$_i$: X: Past e$_i$: *order* [V] (x$_i$: *John*)$_{Ag}$
      (Imp E$_j$: Post e$_j$: *leave* [V] (x$_j$)$_{Ag}$)$_{Go}$ (x$_j$: *Bill*)$_{Rec}$
(55) *John asked Bill to leave.*
      Decl E$_i$: X: Past e$_i$: *ask* [V] (x$_i$: *John*)$_{Ag}$
      (Req E$_j$: Post e$_j$: *leave* [V] (x$_j$)$_{Ag}$)$_{Go}$ (x$_j$: *Bill*)$_{Rec}$

We may assume that a verb such as *ask* can be used in this construction only in its "requestive" sense.

(ii) *Predicates of practical manipulation*
Predicates of practical manipulation designate that X does something in order to get Y to do SoA, without an intervening speech act. Examples are:

(56) a. *John forced Bill to leave.*
     b. *John caused Bill to leave.*

Such predicates can be analysed as taking a predicational complement directly, as in:

(57)   *force* [V] (x$_1$)$_{Ag}$ (x$_j$)$_{Go}$ (Post e$_1$)$_{Ref}$

(iii) *Volitional predicates*
Volitional predicated behave in the same way as predicates of practical manipulation. That is, they require the SoA described in the subordinate clause to be posterior to the SoA described in the main clause.

(58)   *John wants Peter to go home.*

The complement of *want* has the same underlying representation as the complement of *force* in (57).

(iv) *Predicates of direct perception*
A matrix verb such as *see*, in its immediate perception sense, can take a predicational term for its second argument. We can thus give the analysis in (59b) for (59a):

(59) a.   *John saw Peter feeding the cat.*
     b.   Decl E: X: Past e_i: *see* [V] $(John)_{ProcExp}$
          (Sim e_j: Progr *feed* [V] $(Peter)_{Ag}$ $(the\ cat)_{Go})_{Go}$

This structure expresses that what John saw was of the type "State of Affairs": John witnessed the action e_j defined by Peter's feeding the cat. One property of this type of predicational complement is that the embedded SoA should be simultaneous with the time of the matrix predication. The Tense operator of the embedded predication cannot be freely selected:

(60) a.   **John saw Peter having fed the cat.*
     b.   **John saw Peter going to feed the cat.*

In the underlying structure (59b) we have captured this dependent status of the Tense of the embedded predication by using the operator Sim in the Tense position.

This analysis demonstrates two things: firstly, by analysing the complement of *see* in this "immediate perception" sense as a predicational term we account for the fact that immediate perception is a relation between a perceiver and a SoA (rather than a fact or a speech act); secondly, by imposing a "dependent" or "relative" Tense operator on the embedded predication, we account for the special requirement of simultaneity between matrix predication and embedded predication.

Predicational terms 113

(v) *Achievement predicates*
Predicates of this class too take a predicational complement describing a SoA that necessarily occurs simultaneously with the SoA described in the main clause.

(61) a.　*John managed to open the door.*
　　 b.　*John failed to open the door.*
(62) a.　**John managed to have opened the door.*
　　 b.　**John failed to have opened the door.*

This is accounted for in the following representations (but see 5.3.2 for a further refinement):

(63) a.　*manage* [V] $(x_1)_{Ag}$ $(Sim\ e_1)_{Go}$
　　 b.　*fail* [V] $(x_1)_{Ag}$ $(Sim\ e_1)_{Go}$

(vi) *Phasal predicates*
Similar representations are valid for phasal predicates, which are illustrated in (64).

(64) a.　*John began / continued to eat.*
　　 b.　*John stopped eating.*

(vii) *Commentative predicates*
Commentative predicates differ from the preceding classes of predicates taking a predicational complement in that they generally are compatible with all tense operators in their complements:

(65) a.　*It is funny that you are in Holland too.*
　　 b.　*It is funny that you have been in Holland too.*

This fact may be accounted for by assigning a free operator position π_2 to their complements:

(66)　　*funny* [A] $(\pi_2\ e_1)_{\emptyset}$

(viii) *Objective modal predicates*
Objective modal predicates are comparable to commentative predicates, in that their complements do not have a fixed temporal orientation:

(67) a. *It is (im)possible that he is in Holland right now.*
b. *It is (im)possible that he will be in Holland tomorrow.*

5.3.2. Implicatives

Among those predicates which take predicational complements a distinction can be made between:[9]

(68) a. *implicative predicates*: these imply that the complement SoA was actually realized.
b. *contra-implicative predicates*: these imply that the complement SoA was in fact not realized.
c. *non-implicative predicates*: these carry no implication as to the realization or non-realization of the embedded SoA.

The non-implicatives can simply be analysed as taking predicational complements. Most non-implicatives (e.g. *decide, want, be eager*) restrict the complement predication to posterior SoAs, but apart from that there are no limitations on the specification of the embedded predication. With implicatives and contra-implicatives this is quite different. Consider an example such as:

(69) *John managed to open the door.*
Therefore: John opened the door.

As Karttunen (1971) shows, the time and the place of the "opening" are necessarily the same as the time and the place of the "managing":

(70) a. **John managed to have opened the door.*
b. **Yesterday, John managed to open the door tomorrow.*
c. **In the garden, John managed to open the door in the house.*

Further, even if the temporal or locative satellite seems to belong to the matrix, it necessarily affects the embedded predication as well:

---

9. Karttunen (1971) was the first to describe these differences.

(71) a.   *Yesterday, John managed to open the door.*
          Therefore: John opened the door yesterday.
     b.   *In the office, John managed to open the door.*
          Therefore: John opened the door in the office.

Within our layered approach to embedding, there is a natural solution for these facts: implicative predicates do not take extended predications, but core predications for their complements.[10] Core predications have no slots for temporal operators and temporal and locative satellites of their own, so these can never be specified in a way that is incongruent with the matrix predication. This brings us to the following analysis:

(72)   *John managed to open the door.*
       Decl E: X: Past e: *manage* [V] (d1x_i: *John*)$_{Ag}$
       (*open* [V] (x_i)$_{Ag}$ (*the door*)$_{Go}$)$_{Go}$

This analysis predicts that satellites of level 1 can occur in the domain of the embedded complement, which is correct, witness:

(73)   *John managed to open the tin with a screwdriver for Mary.*

The analysis also expresses that the "managing" and the "opening" together specify one SoA rather than two. Finally, the analysis comes very close to analysing "manage to open" as a complex predicate. One step removed from (72) would be a situation in which a complex predicate {manage to open} could be formed, resulting in a structure such as:

(74)   Decl E: X: Past e: {*manage to open*} [V] (d1x_i: *John*)$_{Ag}$ (*the door*)$_{Go}$

This would explain why it is that implicative matrix verbs which take core predication complements can easily develop into complex derived predicates over time.[11]

---

10. In this respect Karttunen's remark is significant to the effect that these predicates take complements consisting of "the bare 'propositional core' ... without any illocutionary force and without any time or locative references." (1971: 349).

11. See Noonan (1985) for the claim that such predicates often take part in "clause union" processes.

5.4. Differences between types of embedded construction

The differences in the underlying structures of complement clauses may be reflected in systematic formal differences between them. We will here give just two examples of these differences. For a more elaborate treatment see Dik —Hengeveld (1991).

5.4.1. *Believe* versus *persuade* versus *force*

The verbs *believe* and *force* differ systematically with respect to the formal properties of their complement clauses. Compare:

(75) a. *John believed that turtles give milk.*
    b. **John believed to open the safe.*
(76) a. **John forced Peter that turtles give milk.*
    b. *John forced Peter to open the safe.*

We may account for these formal differences by relating them to the propositional and predicational nature, respectively, of the complement clauses that these verbs take, as represented in (77):

(77) a. *believe* [V] $(x_1:<hum>)_{Po}$ $(X)_{Go}$
    b. *force* [V] $(x_1:<hum>)_{Ag}$ $(x_2:<hum>)_{Go}$ $(Post\ e)_{Ref}$

Now compare the predicate *persuade* with the predicates *believe* and *force*:

(78) a. *John persuaded Peter that turtles give milk.*
    b. *John persuaded Peter to open the safe.*

Persuade takes both finite and non-finite complement clauses. The finite complement is interpreted as a possible fact: the propositional content that John tried to convince Peter of; the non-finite complement is interpreted as a state of affairs: the course of action John wants Peter to take. Note the fact that the two types of complements cannot be coordinated:

(79)   **John persuaded Peter that turtles give milk and to open the safe.*

Differences between types of embedded construction

We shall account for these facts in the following way: the predicate *persuade* has two predicate frames, one similar to that of *believe*, and one similar to that of *force*:[12]

(80) a. *persuade* [V] $(x_1:\text{<hum>})_{Ag}$ $(x_2:\text{<hum>})_{Go}$ $(X)_{Ref}$
 b. *persuade* [V] $(x_1:\text{<hum>})_{Ag}$ $(x_2:\text{<hum>})_{Go}$ $(e)_{Ref}$

5.4.2. Japanese complementizers

Complements of matrix predicates in Japanese can take three complementizers: *no*, *koto*, and *to* (Kuno 1973). There is a grammatical distinction between *no* / *koto* on the one hand, and *to* on the other: the former turn the complement into a nominal term, which then takes the postpositions usual for such terms. *To* does not have this nominalizing effect. Compare:

(81) *John wa nihongo ga muzukasii to itta.*
 John Top Japanese Subj difficult to said
 'John said that Japanese is difficult.'
(82) *Watakusi wa nihongo ga muzukasii koto*
 I Top Japanese Subj difficult koto
 o mananda.
 Obj learned
 'I learned that Japanese is difficult.'
(83) *Watakusi wa John ga Mary o butu*
 I Top John Subj Mary Obj hit
 no o mita.
 no Obj saw
 'I saw John hit Mary'

Thus, *to* is similar to a subordinator such as *that* in English, whereas *no* / *koto* behave like head nouns specified by the full preceding proposition or predication. (82) could be paraphrased as: 'I learned the fact defined by Japanese being difficult', and (83) as: 'I saw the event consisting of John hitting Mary'.

---

12. Subj-Obj assignment possibilities indicate that the person persuaded is the Goal of the construction; "Ref" indicates the propositional content or the State of Affairs with respect to which the Agent persuades the Goal.

118 *Embedded constructions 1*

The complementizing elements in (81)-(83) cannot be substituted for each other. In other occurrences two or even all three of them may occur, but with concomitant semantic differences. This, plus the paraphrases given above, already suggests that different semantic complementation types are involved. The basic differences in meaning and usage between the three elements are described by Kuno (1973) as follows:

— *no* is used for representing concrete events which can be perceived by the senses.

— *koto* is used for "nominalizing a proposition and forming an abstract concept out of the proposition" (Kuno 1973: 221). In most of its occurrences it is associated with a factive presupposition.

— *to* "was originally a particle for reporting someone else's statement" (Kuno 1973: 215). It is used to represent a propositional content without committing the speaker in any way to the truth of that content. In cases in which an opposition with *koto* is possible, the usage of *to* strongly suggests that the propositional content might not be / come true.

In terms of the distinctions made in this chapter, we may hypothesize that the three elements basically signal the following meanings:

(84)   *no*   (Sim e)
       koto   (True X)
       to   (E)

No and *koto* almost literally spell out the variables "e" and "X", which are then specified by the whole embedded predication and proposition, respectively.

Immediate perception verbs in Japanese take *no*-complements, as in (83) above, and in the following examples:

(85)   *Watakusi   wa   John   ga   piano   o   hiku*
       I   Top John Subj   piano   Obj   play
       no   o   kiita.
       no Obj heard
       'I heard John play(ing) the piano.'

(86)   *Watakusi   wa   sesuzi   ga   samuku   naru   no*
       I   Top spine Subj   cold   get   *no*
       o   kanzita.
       Obj   felt
       'I felt my spine getting cold.'
       =   'I felt a cold shiver running down my spine'

Kuno adds, however, that sentence (85) with *koto* "would be acceptable, but it would not longer be a statement of perception by any of the five senses: it would mean: 'I heard that John plays the piano'. Similarly, *kanziru* 'to feel' can take a *koto* clause, but then it would mean no longer 'to feel by five senses', but 'to think'" (Kuno 1973: 220). It is clear that we would interpret such cases as examples of mental perception, where the perception verb takes a propositional complement. This is fully consistent with the interpretation of the three complementizing elements given in (84) above. The three different subordinators of Japanese can thus be interpreted in terms of the three-way distinction between clausal, propositional, and predicational complements as it has been made in this chapter.

6. Embedded constructions 2: functional and formal parameters

6.0. Introduction

In the preceding chapter we developed a semantic typology of embedded constructions in terms of (i) the different types of embedded construction which can be distinguished on semantic grounds, (ii) the different types of matrix predicate which can be distinguished on the basis of their combinability with semantic types of embeddings, (iii) the additional semantic constraints which these matrix predicates may impose on their embedded complements. In this chapter we first look at the functional status of embedded constructions (6.1.), then at the formal properties which such constructions may have (6.2.). Throughout the discussion we will be on the look-out for possible correlations between meaning, function and form.

6.1. Functional parameters

The functional status of embedded constructions is determined by the functional relations which they entertain within the wider construction in which they occur. We can here distinguish the semantic functions which embedded constructions may have (6.1.1.), the perspectival functions (Subj and Obj) which may be assigned to them (6.1.2.), and the pragmatic functions which they may fulfil within the wider context in which they occur (6.1.3.).

6.1.1. Semantic functions

Embedded constructions can occupy any term position with which they are semantically compatible. We already saw examples of embedded constructions in different argument and satellite positions. Obviously, when a certain term position is intrinsically restricted to, for example, <human>, <animate> or <controlling> entities, such as term positions with the functions Agent, Positioner, Recipient, Beneficiary, and Company, then embedded constructions cannot be inserted into such positions. But that seems to be the only restriction on the insertion of embedded constructions.

(i) *Embedded constructions as arguments*
When an embedded construction serves as an argument to a higher matrix predicate (i.e. functions as a "complement"), the information it contains is essential to the integrity of the higher clause in the same way that any argument is essential to establishing the SoA intended. The following are examples of embedded constructions with different semantic functions in first, second, and third argument position:

(1)   a.   *It was quite clear that John didn't feel well.*
              (first argument, Zero function)
      b.   *It gradually became clear that John didn't feel well.*
              (first argument, Processed function)
      c.   *The defeat of the cavalry shocked the generals.*
              (first argument, Force function)
(2)   *Everyone believed that John would win.*
              (second argument, Goal function)
(3)   *John convinced Peter that he should join the navy.*
              (third argument, Reference function)

Embedded argument constructions can also have various locative and directional functions which, because of the abstract character of the content of the embedded construction, will necessarily have a somewhat metaphorical character. In certain languages, for example, such constructions as

(4)   a.   *John goes towards the solving of the riddle.*
      b.   *John is in the solving of the riddle.*
      c.   *John comes from the solving of the riddle.*

will be used for expressing aspectual distinctions (*TFG1*: 9.1.2.2.).

(ii) *Embedded constructions as satellites*
Embedded constructions may also occur as satellites to predications or propositions, as in:

(5)   a.   *John went to the station in order to meet his parents.*
      b.   *John sold his house because he couldn't afford it anymore.*
      c.   *John will only take the job if nobody else is interested.*

6.1.2. Perspectival functions

If the embedded construction occurs in second argument position, Subject assignment to it may or may not be possible. Consider again the following constructions:

(6) a. *Everyone believed that John would win.*
 b. *That John would win was believed by everyone.*
 c. *It was believed by everyone that John would win.*

Note that a passive such as (6b) is rather unnatural, and (6c) will most often be preferred. Why this is so will be discussed below.

6.1.3. Pragmatic functions

It has been suggested by different authors that the difference between main and embedded clauses can be characterized in general in terms of "foregrounded" vs. "backgrounded" information, or in terms of "asserted" versus "presupposed" information.[1] This would mean that the hierarchical status (matrix or embedded) of a construction would correlate with a difference in (discourse) pragmatic function.

Although the opposition between "foregrounded" and "backgrounded" is usually presented as scalar rather that absolute, I nevertheless believe that such general characterizations must be heavily qualified in terms of the different types of embedding which we have distinguished.

The postulated correlation can never have absolute validity, since it is easy to find examples in which it is the subordinate rather than the main clause information which is communicatively the most important:

(7) a. *John was quietly sitting in his office, when suddenly Peter came rushing in.*
 b. *I very much regret that circumstances force me to fire you.*
 c. *I honestly think you are a pompous fool.*

---

1. Grimes (1975), Reesink (1983, 1987), Mackenzie (1984). For general discussion of the issue, compare Bolkestein (1987).

These few examples show that any correlation main-foregrounded and subordinate-backgrounded can only be of a statistical nature. In general, the main or subordinate status of a construction does not prevent it from taking different pragmatic statuses.

When embedded constructions function as arguments, the information which they contain may be either new or given to A. It may well contain information which is more important than the information contained in the main clause. Consider:

(8)   *You know what? John told me that Peter has just been robbed.*

Here the important information is presumably not that John told me something, but that Peter has been robbed. Even factive complements, the truth of which is taken for granted by S, may well contain information that is new to A, as in:

(9)   *You know very well that I'm not going to stay with you forever.*

Often a subordinate construction is embedded under a predicate which mainly serves to modalize or mitigate the assertive force of its information content:

(10) A: *Where's John?*
     B: *I believe he's gone to the butcher's.*
     B: *I hope he's at the office, as he should be.*
(11) a.   *I doubt whether Arsenal will win the cup.*
     b.   *I have a feeling that you may be wrong there.*

In such cases, the matrix predication is a modal "footnote" to the content of the subordinate construction rather than a statement in itself.

When the embedded construction functions as a satellite, it is even the rule rather than the exception that the satellite present the salient, focal, foregrounded information. In general, satellites have a certain degree of "intrinsic focality" because, if the satellite information were not important, there would be no point in adding it at all. Compare in this respect:

(12) a.   *John goes to Leyden on a bicycle.*
     b.   *John doesn't go to Leyden on a bicycle.*

In (12a) *on a bicycle* will often provide the most important information. This comes out under negation, as in (12b), which, unless it carries contrastive accent of some kind, will most naturally be interpreted as signalling that John goes to Leyden, but not by bicycle (see chapter 8). The same applies to embedded satellites. Consider:

(13)   *John doesn't beat his wife because he hates her.*

Again, this will most naturally be interpreted as signalling that, although John does beat his wife, this is not because he hates her. When (13) is called ambiguous (as is sometimes done), it must be granted that the other reading to the effect that because John hates his wife, he does not beat her, is difficult to construe except with special prosody or in special preset interpretation conditions.

We may thus conclude that embedded constructions may in principle have any pragmatic function that could also be carried by first order terms. For each of the "topical" functions New Topic, Given Topic, Sub-Topic, and Resumed Topic examples with embedded constructions carrying these function can be easily given. The same applies to the different Focus types distinguished in *TFG1*: 13.4.2. Thus, embedded constructions may have Completive, Parallel, Replacing, Expanding, Restricting or Selecting Focus, just like first-order terms.

In fact, such differences in pragmatic function are important for capturing some of their formal properties, as we shall see in the next section.

6.2. Formal parameters

Embedded constructions may appear in a number of different forms, and may have different syntactic and semantic properties corresponding to these different forms. Obviously, the precise form in which embedded constructions are realized is to a certain extent a language-dependent matter. But as we shall see in this chapter, quite a few general properties of embedded constructions are invariant across languages. In this section we consider a number of general properties of the formal expression of embedded constructions:
(i) the position of the embedded construction in the matrix domain;
(ii) formal subordination markers;
(iii) internal constituent ordering within the embedded construction;
(iv) finite or non-finite realization of the embedded predicate;
(v) mood of the embedded predicate.

6.2.1. The position of the embedded construction in the matrix domain

Embedded constructions function as arguments or satellites to some main predicate. Our first expectation, therefore, is that they will be placed in the positions which are also occupied by nominal first-order terms of corresponding function.

Thus, if a language is organized on a Prefield basis, we expect embedded constructions to occur in the Prefield (before the matrix predicate); if the language is organized on a Postfield basis, we expect the embedded constructions to occur in the Postfield (after the matrix predicate). Compare the following patterns, in which "sub" represents the subordinating element:

(14) PREFIELD:
    a. *John (the story) Peter-to told*
    b. *John (Mary office-to went)-sub Peter-to told*
(15) POSTFIELD:
    a. *told John (the story) to Peter*
    b. *told John sub (went Mary to office) to Peter*

The Prefield or Postfield character of the language is certainly one factor which determines the positioning of embedded constructions. In Postfield languages we do indeed usually find embedded constructions in the Postfield, and in Prefield languages we tend to find them in the Prefield.

In fact, however, the situation is much more complicated than this. This is because several other factors of a quite different nature co-determine the positioning of embedded constructions. These factors are: (i) the categorial complexity of embedded constructions, (ii) their pragmatic function within the main predication, (iii) their semantic function within the main predication.

(i) *Categorial complexity*
In *TFG1*: 16.4.2. we saw that the ordering of constituents is co-determined by their internal structural complexity. This was formulated in Principle (SP7):

(16)   Other things being equal, constituents prefer to be placed in order of increasing complexity, where complexity is defined as follows:
(i) Clitic < Pronoun < Noun Phrase < Adpositional Phrase < Subordinate Clause;
(ii) for any category X: X < X co X;
(iii) for any categories X and Y: X < X (sub Y).

According to this principle, which I shall refer to as LIPOC, subordinate clauses will prefer to be placed at the very end of a complex clause. If embedded constructions are simply placed in pattern position, as in (14b) and (15b), the result will often be in conflict with LIPOC. Indeed, both (14b) and (15b) run counter to LIPOC. On the basis of Principle (SP7), then, we shall expect a tendency to place embedded constructions further to the end of the complex construction, preferably at the very end of that construction. And this is what we do indeed find in an overwhelming number of languages, including English. Compare the following constructions:

(17) a. *That he came surprised me.*
     b. *It surprised me that he came.*
(18) a. *?Peter proposed that Daley's should be sold to the board.*
     b. *Peter proposed to the board that Daley's should be sold.*

In (17a) the embedded construction has Subject function and is placed in initial position. More natural, however, is (17b), in which the Subject is placed at the very end, and the initial position is marked by a dummy element *it*.

Similarly, the Object embedded construction in (18a) is placed in pattern position resulting in an ambiguous construction; in (18b) it is placed at the very end, and the result is unambiguous.

Due to the influence of LIPOC, then, we may expect subordinate clauses to occur in positions later than their pattern position, and preferably at the very end of the construction in which they occur. LIPOC (as formulated in Principle (SP7)) predicts that there will preferably be no material after a subordinate clause, unless that material is of the same or greater complexity than that subordinate clause. This explains such patterns as the following:

(19) a. *That he came surprised me very much.*
     b. **It surprised me that he came very much.*
     c. *It surprised me very much that he came.*

(20) a. *That he came surprised me, since I didn't expect him.*
　　b. *It surprised me that he came, since I didn't expect him.*
　　c. *?It surprised me, since I didn't expect him, that he came.*

In (19b) the Subject clause cannot occur in non-final position, since the material which follows it (*very much*) is not of at least equal complexity; on the other hand, (20b) is correct, since the Subject clause is followed only by another subordinate clause.

A further consequence of LIPOC is the following: languages which are organized according to the Prefield pattern may nevertheless place their subordinate clauses in the Postfield; but Postfield languages will never systematically place their subordinate clauses in the Prefield.

The actual situation is again a little bit more complicated, since all languages allow some subordinate clauses to appear in the Prefield in certain conditions, which I will discuss below. The point is thus that the basic, unmarked position for subordinate clauses may be in the Postfield in Prefield languages, but not in the Prefield in Postfield languages.

The examples given in (21)-(22) illustrate two ways in which the problem posed by the complexity of embedded constructions may be solved. In (21) the pattern position of the Subject is marked by the dummy element *it*; in (22) no such dummy element is present:

(21) 　　*It surprised me that he came.*
(22) 　　*Peter proposed Ø to the board that Daley's should be sold.*

The use of a dummy element such as *it* in (21) is an elegant way to "have one's cake and eat it": the Subject clause is in its preferred, final position; nevertheless, the SVO pattern is not violated, *it* serving to mark the pattern position of the Subject. The rule introducing this dummy element can be quite generally formulated as follows:

(23) 　　If a Subject clause is placed in a position after the pattern position for the Subject, this pattern position is marked by *it*.

I thus assume that the dummy element is a means of preserving the canonical pattern of the clause, in conditions in which the Subject does not occur in its pattern position. As is evident from (22), English does not have a similar general rule for the Object position. In a language such as Hungarian (De Groot 1981b), however, any subordinate clause in final position can be "announced" in the Prefield by an appropriate demonstrative element, as in:

(24)   *Azt   nem hiszem,   hogy   Mari*
       that-acc not believe-I,   that   Mary-nom
       Chomskyt   ismeri.
       Chomsky-acc knows
       'That I do not believe, that Mary knows Chomsky'

The occurrence of such dummies in Hungarian is co-dependent on pragmatic factors.

The origin of constructions with "announcing" dummies can be explained in terms of grammaticalization of Clause+Tail constructions.[2] After all, English still has the possibility of constructions such as:

(25)   *It surprised me, that he came.*

in which *it* has its usual pronominal value, and the subordinate predication can be seen as an afterthought explication of the referent of *it*. This construction also exists for Object subordinate clauses:

(26)   *Please don't mention it to my mother, that we have lost.*

Why the dummy element has grammaticalized in Subject, but not in Object position in English is difficult to say. One reason may be that the position for Object constituents is less fixed anyway, so that constructions such as (26) do not constitute a major departure from the basic ordering pattern. Another reason may be that an apparently subjectless construction such as:

(27)   *Surprised me that he came.*

is potentially more disturbing than an apparently objectless construction such as (22). After all, almost any English construction has a Subject, but quite a few constructions lack an Object.

LIPOC correctly predicts that the favourite position of subordinate clauses is at the very end of the construction in which they occur. There is another prediction concerning the expression of embedded constructions which can be derived from LIPOC. According to the formulation in Principle (SP7) in (16) above, Noun Phrases and Adpositional Phrases count as "less complex" for

---

2 For the notion "Tail" see *TFG1*: 13.1.

the purposes of LIPOC than subordinate clauses. From this we can derive the following prediction:

(28) When embedded constructions are expressed in the form of an NP or an Adpositional Phrase, there will be less pressure for them to seek the final position in the construction.

There is some evidence in English for the correctness of this prediction. As Kuno (1973b) has shown, there are a number of structural situations in which subordinate clauses cannot occur in their pattern position, while complex NPs with almost the same content can appear in those positions. Compare:

(29) a. *Did that John showed up please you?
 b. Did it please you that John showed up?
 c. Did the fact that John showed up please you?

(29a) shows that a Subj clause cannot be placed in Subj position in an interrogative construction; it must be extraposed as in (29b). The corresponding complex NP in (29c), however, can appear in the Subject position; in fact, it cannot be extraposed:

(30) *Did it please you the fact that John showed up?

To the extent that the above principles are generalizable across languages, it follows that if a language wishes to place its embedded constructions in the Prefield (i.e. before the matrix predicate), then one way of achieving this is to give the embedded construction the form of an NP or an Adpositional Phrase. And it is a fact that many Prefield languages apply some sort of nominalization to their embedded constructions and that, once nominalized, these embedded constructions can take the postpositions which usually characterize NPs in the language.

This is true, for instance, for Japanese (Kuno 1973, 1978), at least for the elements *koto* and *no*, which turn the embedded construction into an NP, which can then take all the usual postpositions, as we saw in 5.4.2.

Another example is Tamil (Asher 1982), in which embedded constructions usually contain a nominalized verb form, followed by the appropriate case ending:

(31) *Avanka   vantate   paatteen.*
     they   come-past-nr-acc see-past-I
     'I saw their coming', 'I saw them coming.'
(32) *Avaru   vantatunaale   naanum   vanteen.*
     he   come-past-nr-instr I-also   come-past-I
     'Because of him coming, I came too.'

The greater ease with which NPs may occur in the Prefield may thus be one factor explaining the tendency for embedded constructions in the Prefield to take on the form of a nominalization. Other factors possibly contributing to such an expression will be discussed below.

(ii) *Pragmatic function*
We have postulated a universally relevant clause-initial P1 position which can be used for constituents having Topic or Focus function (see *TFG1*: 17.2.). Subordinate clauses can get Topic or Focus function just like other types of terms. Therefore, we expect subordinate clauses to be capable of appearing in P1 position. This is in apparent contradiction with LIPOC: although the favourite position for subordinate clauses according to LIPOC is at the very end of the construction, these subordinate clauses can nevertheless appear in P1 on account of their pragmatic function. We can only conclude that the tendency for Topic and Focus constituents to be placed in P1 is apparently stronger than the pressure exerted on them by LIPOC.

There is, in fact, much evidence for the rule that subordinate clauses tend to be placed either at the very end of the construction through LIPOC, or in P1 position on account of their pragmatic function.

Let us now reconsider the status of a construction such as:

(33)   *That he came surprised me.*

The ordering pattern of English relevant here is the following:

(34)   P1 S V O

This ordering pattern is such that in simple sentences such as:

(35)   *John sold his car.*

it is difficult to tell whether the Subject is in S or in P1 position: both hypotheses are compatible with the linear sequence of (35). The same question arises in the case of construction (33), but in that case various arguments go to show that the subordinate clause must be in P1 rather than in S position. If the subordinate clause were in S position we would expect it to be possible to place some other constituent in P1. But this is not possible. Consider:

(36) a. *Very often that he came surprised me.
　　 b. Very often it surprised me that he came.
(37) a. *Did that he came surprise you?
　　 b. Did it surprise you that he came?
(38) a. *Because that he came surprised me I didn't know what to say.
　　 b. Because it surprised me that he came, I didn't know what to say.

On the basis of these facts, we can formulate the following rules for English subordinate clauses:

(39) 　　Subordinate clauses which by themselves fill a term position should be either placed in P1, or at the very end of the construction (possibly followed by other subordinate clauses); when P1 is filled by some other constituent, only the latter option is available; and if that option is taken for a Subject subordinate clause, *it* is placed in S position.

Note that embedded constructions may also be in initial position if they have Orientation function, as discussed in chapter 17:

(40) 　　*If you don't stop crying, then we won't go to the movies.*

In that case, however, we assume that the Orientation constituent is an ECC, placed outside the domain of the clause proper. The P1 position of the clause proper is here occupied by the resumptive element *then*.

(iii) *Semantic function*
We have so far seen that the position of embedded constructions is a complex matter, dependent at least on the following factors: (a) the basic Prefield or Postfield character of the language; (b) the influence of LIPOC; (c) pragmatic function assignment and placement in P1.

There is evidence, however, that the positioning of embedded constructions is also dependent on the semantic function of the embedded construction within the complex clause in which it occurs. This was already made clear in Greenberg (1966: 84), where the following two universals were formulated:

Universal 14. In conditional statements, the conditional clause precedes the conclusion as the normal order in all languages.

Universal 15. In expressions of volition and purpose, a subordinate verbal form always follows the main verb as the normal order except in those languages in which the nominal object always precedes the verb.

Greenberg (1966: 103) attributed these universals to a general iconicity principle which says that "The order of elements in language parallels that in physical experience or the order of knowledge". In some sense, a condition is conceptually prior to its conclusion, and a purpose is conceptually posterior to the state of affairs that it is the purpose of. The linear order of clauses reflects these conceptual relations. Thus, Greenberg's universals predict the following markedness relations:

(41)   unmarked   marked
 a. Conditional clause   *if* X, (*then*) Y   Y, *if* X
 b. Purpose clause   X *in order that* Y *In order that* Y, X

Similar factors may be presumed to be at work in the case of temporal relationships. Psycholinguists have found that the interpretation of complex predications is co-dependent on what has been called the "Order of Mention" principle (cf. Clark—Clark 1977: 78, Clark 1971). This principle says that, other things being equal, the interpreter will expect the complex predication to be organized on a "first things first" basis: preceding events will be formulated before following events. Such a principle would explain, according to Clark (1971), why the sentences in (42) are much easier to interpret (at least for children of 3-5) than the sentences in (43):

(42) a. *The boy patted the dog before he kicked the rock.*
 b. *After the boy patted the dog, he kicked the rock.*
(43) a. *Before the boy kicked the rock, he patted the dog.*
 b. *The boy kicked the rock after he patted the dog.*

In (42), but not in (43), the sequence of clauses mirrors the sequence of the events described. The Order of Mention principle thus predicts the following markedness relations:

(44)   unmarked   marked
 a. 'after' clauses   *after* X, Y   Y, *after* X
 b. 'before' clauses   X, *before* Y   *before* Y, X

The preferences noted in (41) and (44) can now be translated into the following schema:

(45)   Preferred positions of embedded constructions according to semantic function:

Prefield   *Postfield*
Condition clauses   Purpose clauses
'after' clauses   'before' clauses

And the explanation behind this configuration can be formulated in the following Iconicity Principle:

(46)   ICONICITY PRINCIPLE
Clauses should preferably be ordered in accordance with the conceptual or temporal relations which obtain between the facts or States of Affairs which they designate.

It is to be noted that the Iconicity Principle cuts across the ordering preferences discussed earlier in this section. In certain cases, it defines preferences which run counter to the preferences defined by other factors. For example, a consistent Postfield language which, accordingly, also places its embedded constructions in the Postfield, will have to place Condition and 'after' clauses in the Prefield (at least, have the possibility of doing so). Given our earlier discussion, we shall expect placement in P2 to be overexploited in order to achieve the desired result. And indeed, this is not implausible as far as pragmatics is concerned. For in a sense Condition and 'after' clauses can be interpreted as "setting the scene" for the State of Affairs designated in the main clause; and this scene-setting is at least similar to the work which is done by Theme or Topic constituents.

On the other hand, in Prefield languages we will expect a tendency for Purpose and 'before' clauses to nevertheless occur in the Postfield (at least in those languages in which at least some constituents are admitted to the Postfield).[3]

---

3. This proviso is intended in the formulation of Greenberg's Universal 15 above.

Typological research reveals that the predictions of the Iconicity Principle are largely correct, especially in the case of Condition, 'after', and Purpose clauses. The results with respect to 'before' clauses are less convincing, in part because of the fact that quite a few languages do not appear to have any clear equivalent to a subordinate clause with *before*. All languages, of course, can save the Iconicity Principle by using a paratactic rather than a hypotactic formulation.

6.2.2. Formal subordination markers

Sometimes an embedded construction is formally expressed without any subordinator. This is optionally the case in English:

(47)   *I believe (that) John is the man for the job.*

Such embedded constructions without formal subordinators, however, are rather rare across languages. In most cases, the embedded construction is formally characterized by a subordinating element, which usually takes initial or final position. English has initial subordinators, as in:

(48)   *I gave a big party, because my brother came.*

Other languages, however, have final subordinators. The equivalent of (48) in Imbabura Quechua (Cole 1982: 64) is:

(49)   *Nuka   wawki   shamu-shka-manda-mi   jatun   fishta-ta*
       my   brother come-nr-because-val   big   party-acc
                rura-rka-ni.
                make-past-I
       'I gave a big party, because my brother came.'

Note that the embedded construction occurs in the Prefield, and that it is realized in non-finite form, marked by the nominalizer *-shka*. The subordinator *-manda* is suffixed to the nominalized verb, here followed by the validator *-mi*.

In *TFG1*: 16.3. we categorized subordinators among the class of Relators, which also contains adpositions and case markers. Relators express the relation between some constituent and the relatum with which it is construed.

We also formulated the Relator principle (Principle (SP3), *TFG1*: 16.4.2.), which says that the preferred positions of Relators are as indicated in:

(50)   (relatum (R)) Head ((R) relatum)

In other words, Relators prefer to be placed in between the two constituents which they relate to each other.

Both the English and the Quechua example above are in accordance with this principle. And in general, we can say the following:

(51)   Postfield languages have initial subordinators;
Prefield languages have final subordinators.

In this respect, subordinators do indeed behave in the same way as adpositions and case markers. In fact, subordinators will often be identical to adpositions or case markers, especially in those cases in which embedded constructions are expressed in nominalized form, or in the form of a complex noun phrase with dummy head, as in the Japanese examples in 5.4.2. above.

It will be clear, however, that the matter of preferred subordinator positions is complicated by the fact that, due to the pragmatic and semantic factors discussed above, languages which basically have their embedded constructions in the Postfield may sometimes place them in the Prefield, and conversely. Thus, alongside English (48), we can have:

(52)   *Because my brother came, I gave a big party.*

In such a case, the subordinator automatically ends up in a non-preferred position. When this concerns an incidental preposing based on pragmatic factors, the breach of the Relator Principle is not very serious, confined as it is to pragmatically marked constructions.

But when the Iconicity Principle is involved, the deviation from the Relator Principle may become a systematic matter. English subordinate clauses have their basic position in the Postfield, and are initially marked by subordinators. On the other hand, the Iconicity Principle says that conditional embedded constructions should precede the main clause, as in:

(53)   *If my brother comes, I will give a big party.*

Initial position for such conditional clauses will be more frequent and less marked than final position. This means that, if the initial subordinator is retained and nothing else is done about it, there will be a systematic violation of the Relator Principle. It is in this light that we may interpret the occurrence of alternatives to construction (53), such as:

(54) a. *If my brother comes, then I will give a big party.*
b. *Should my brother come, (then) I will give a big party.*

In such constructions, the element *then*, which anaphorically takes up the subordinate clause within the main clause, may in a sense be interpreted as a new relator which restores the preferred pattern in accordance with the Relator Principle. Note that such an element does not normally occur when the conditional clause follows the main clause:

(55) **Then I will give a big party, if my brother comes.*

In (54b) we find another construction type, in which there is no relator, and in which the subordinate clause is marked by the special dependent verb *should*.

For an example from another language type, consider the situation in Babungo, as described in Schaub (1985: 40-41). Babungo is an SVO Postfield language in which subordinate clauses normally occur in the Postfield and are initially marked. Condition clauses are the only ones which must occur in the Prefield. And precisely in this case, there are two variants:

(56) Nwə kí   ghàn   sàn   ghô,
     he   if   really beat.pf   you
     (búu)   mə táa sán   nwə.
     (then)   I   Fut beat.impf   him
     'In case he does beat you, (then) I will beat him.'

Just as in English, the optional element *búu* "then" can be interpreted as a means for restoring the preferred relator position.

Similar problems may arise in a Prefield language in the case of purposive embedded constructions which, according to the Iconicity Principle, should follow rather than precede the main clause.

6.2.3. Internal constituent ordering within the embedded construction

As for constituent ordering within the domain of subordinate clauses, there is first of all the principle which says that in general subordinate clauses never have more freedom of constituent ordering than main clauses. In other words, ordering freedom may at most be equal to that of main clauses, but will in most cases be more constrained. Thus, there is a considerable class of SOV languages in which main clause order is quite free, but subordinate order is strictly SOV.

In the second place, there are languages in which subordinate clauses systematically differ from main clauses in their ordering pattern. This is the case, for example, in Dutch and German. Compare Dutch:

(57) a. *Jan   bewondert   Marie.*
John   admires   Mary
'John admires Marie.'
  b. **Jan   Marie   bewondert.*
John   Mary   admires
'John admires Mary'
(58) a. *Ik geloof dat Jan   Marie   bewondert.*
I believe that John   Mary   admires
'I believe that John admires Mary'
  b. **Ik geloof dat Jan   bewondert   Marie.*
I believe that John   admires   Mary
'I believe that John admires Mary'

6.2.4. Finite or non-finite realization of the embedded predicate

The question whether an embedded construction is realized in finite or non-finite form is again not independent of the general constituent ordering pattern of the language involved.

By and large, Postfield subordinate clauses appear in finite form, initially marked by a subordinator, according to the pattern of English:

(59)   *Peter believed that Bill loved Sally.*

In the Prefield, however, embedded constructions typically appear in non-finite form, as in the Tamil examples (31) and (32), and in the Quechua example (49). Thus, we typically find such a pattern as:

(60)   *Peter Bill's Sally loving believed.*

We have already mentioned one fact which may underlie this difference: finite subordinate clauses are more sensitive to LIPOC than complex noun phrases and adpositional phrases; and non-finite embedded constructions typically have the form of such phrases. Thus, the non-finite form of Prefield embedded constructions may save them from being pulled to the Postfield.

It is doubtful, however, whether this is the only factor explaining this skew between Prefield and Postfield languages. Another factor may involve the chances of a Prefield subordinate clause being misinterpreted as the main clause. Suppose that we found such a construction as the following in a Prefield language:

(61)   My brother time long after country to returned when, *party big I-gave.*
         'When my brother returned to his country after a long time, I gave a big party'

Assuming that the initial part of (61) is a finite subordinate clause, and that that clause, as is usual in Prefield languages, is marked only at the very end by a subordinator, it follows that the subordinate clause could easily be mistaken for the main clause. This situation would be comparable to an English construction such as:

(62)   *The dealer offered two dollars for the painting refused to sell it.*

which psycholinguistic investigation has shown to be rather difficult to interpret. Psycholinguists have ascribed this difficulty to the fact that the initial part of (62) will at first be misinterpreted as constituting a main clause. They have concluded from this that addressees apparently apply a perceptual strategy which can be formulated as follows (cf. Bever 1970, Fodor—Bever—Garret 1974, Clark—Clark 1977):

(63)   MAIN CLAUSE PRINCIPLE
         The first sequence of constituents which can be interpreted as constituting the main clause should be so interpreted.

This principle was formulated for English, but it is not impossible that it has more general cross-linguistic validity. If that is the case, then a Prefield language with finite subordinate clauses as in (61) would be in massive trouble. In order to avoid misinterpretation, a language should either place its embedded constructions in the Postfield or, if it places them in the Prefield, it should take care that they cannot be mistaken for main clauses. From this it follows that we would expect Prefield embedded constructions to be in some way marked as being non-main clauses. Non-finite realization of the embedded construction would seem to be an effective means of doing so.

We must thus qualify our definition of subordinate clause as follows:

(64) A subordinate clause is an embedded construction which, apart from the subordinating device which signals its dependent status, could also appear as a main clause.

In subordinate clauses, the predicate can be specified for any distinctions for which it can also be specified in the main clause. In particular, it can take all the distinctions for Tense, Aspect and Mood for which a main predicate can also be specified, except where the "mood" is in fact the subordinating device: in languages in which subordinate predicates take a special subordinate form, it is customary to refer to this form as the "dependent mood". Furthermore, if the main predicate can be specified for person, number, gender etc., then the predicate in the subordinate clause must also be specifiable for these distinctions.

Finally, if the main verb shows agreement with one or more of its arguments, then the subordinate predicate must also display such agreement.

6.2.5. Mood

In many languages the verb used in embedded constructions may take either a special form which identifies the verb as an embedded one, or one of various mood-forms, the selection of which depends on the semantics of the complement-taking predicate and the complement itself. The first situation obtains, for instance, in Irish, where many verbs have special forms which only occur in dependent clauses, as shown in the following examples (Noonan 1985: 50):

(65) *Chonaic Seán   an   mhuc.*
      saw   John   the   pig
      'John saw the pig.'
(66) *Tá a   fhios   agam   go bhfaca   Seán*
      is   its knowledge   at-me   that saw   John
      an   mhuc
      the   pig
      'I know that John saw the pig.'

The second situation obtains, for instance, in Spanish, which uses indicative and subjunctive verb forms in embedded constructions:

(67) *Creo   que está   enfermo.*
      I.believe that he-is-ind   ill
      'I think that he is ill.'
(68) *Dudo   que esté   enfermo.*
      I.doubt that he-is-subj   ill
      'I doubt that he is ill.'

One of the factors triggering the use of indicative and subjunctive verb forms in Spanish concerns the factuality of the complement: in most factual complements the indicative is used, as in (67), in non-factual ones the subjunctive is used, as in (68). This is just one of the factors that may be responsible for the selection of mood-forms in languages. A systematic crosslinguistic treatment of this issue may be found in Noonan (1985).

This concludes our discussion of the formal parameters relevant to the classification of embedded constructions. The next chapter shows how the properties defined by these parameters combine to give rise to specific types of embedded construction.

7. Embedded constructions 3: types

7.0. Introduction

The different semantic and formal parameters discussed in the preceding chapter combine in different ways to produce a great variety of types of embedded constructions both within and across languages. Nevertheless, recurrent patterns can be discerned in this variety across languages. Thus, the following taxonomy of embedded constructions has quite general cross-linguistic validity:

(1)
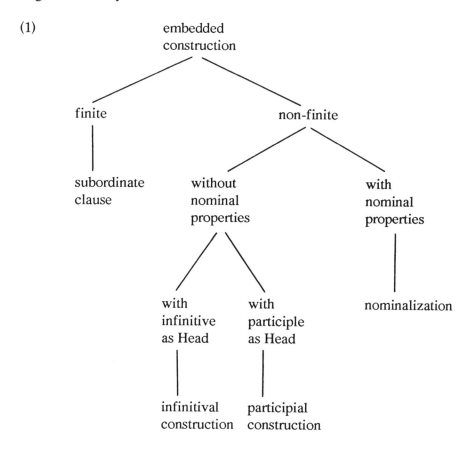

Thus, embedded constructions may be finite or non-finite. Finite embedded constructions are realized as subordinate clauses. Non-finite embedded constructions may or may not have properties in common with primary, nominal terms. If they do, they are realized as nominalizations. If not, they may have either an infinitive or a participle as their Head. This leads to infinitival and participial constructions. We shall now discuss these different types one by one.

7.1. Finite embedded constructions: subordinate clauses

Finite embedded constructions, realized as subordinate clauses, are those embedded constructions in which the predicate can be specified for the distinctions which are also characteristic of main clause predicates. This is most clearly the case when the subordinate clause, in the same form, can also appear as an independent main clause. This is generally the case in English. Compare:

(2) a. *John believes that Bill loves Sally.*
    b. *Bill loves Sally.*

We cannot simply say, however, that subordinate clauses are those embedded constructions which can in the same form also appear as main clauses, because subordinate clauses are commonly marked by some subordinating device which overtly signals their subordinate status. We can thus say that a subordinate clause is a clause which has all the properties of a main clause, apart from the device(s) which signal its subordinate status. These devices, as we saw in chapter 6, may be:
  (i) a subordinator;
  (ii) a special subordinate constituent order;
  (iii) a special "dependent mood";
  (iv) a combination of (i)-(iii)

Apart from the subordinating devices, subordinate clauses have all the properties of a main clause. In particular, arguments and satellites will be realized in the way in which they would also be expressed in main clauses. One exception to this is constructions to which some form of "Raising" has applied: Raising takes a term out of an embedded construction and places it in the domain of the matrix predicate. If Raising is applied to a finite subordinate clause, then (i) the remaining subordinate clause will contain a

Finite embedded constructions: subordinate clauses 145

gap corresponding to the raised constituent; (ii) that constituent may (but need not) be adapted in form to its host domain. Consider:

(3)   *John believed she/her that (she) had done it.*
      'John believed her to have done it'

Raising thus creates "discrepancies" between underlying clause structure and surface expression. Such discrepancies are discussed in chapter 15.

7.2. Non-finite embedded constructions

In certain circumstances embedded constructions can be realized in various non-finite forms. A non-finite embedded construction contains a non-finite verb. A non-finite verb differs from a finite verb in that it cannot (normally) be used as the main verb of a clause. Typically, the non-finite verb lacks agreement for person, number, and gender with its first argument or Subject, is unmarked or reduced with respect to distinctions of Tense, Aspect, and Mood, and has certain properties in common with adjectival or nominal predicates. The main types of non-finite verbs are infinitives, participles, and nominalized verbs. Consequently, we can speak of infinitival constructions, participial constructions, and nominalizations.

7.2.1. Infinitival constructions

Infinitival constructions are those embedded constructions which are construed around a predicate in the form of an infinitive. Infinitives typically have the following properties:

(i) the infinitive is not marked for the person-number-gender distinctions for which the finite verb is marked; there is no agreement between the infinitive and the terms with which it occurs;

(ii) the infinitive displays fewer Tense-Mood-Aspect distinctions than the finite verb; typically, the infinitive is only marked for aspectual distinctions, if at all;

(iii) the infinitive cannot, on its own, constitute the main verb of an independent clause;

(iv) the infinitive is nevertheless a verbal form; it does not display clear adjectival or nominal properties.

These properties are not absolutely valid. As for (i), there are languages in which infinitives do display some type of agreement with their Subject terms. Thus, Portuguese has an inflected infinitive which may be used to mark switch reference (difference of Subjects) between matrix clause and embedded construction. Compare (from Barker 1957: 101):

(4) a. *Passei sem os ver* (unmarked infinitive)
I-passed without them see
'I passed without seeing them'
b. *Passei sem me verem* (3rd ps pl infinitive)
I-passed without me see-they
'I passed without them seeing me'
(5) a. *Passei sem vos ver* (unmarked infinitive)
I-passed without you see
'I passed without seeing you'
b. *Passei sem me verdes* (2nd ps pl infinitive)
I-passed without me see-you
'I passed without you seeing me'

As for (iii), many languages have stylistically marked construction types in which infinitives can appear as the main verb. An example is the Latin so-called historical infinitive, which in vivid narrative can replace the finite verb in main clauses. Similar constructions are possible in Dutch:[1]

(6) a. *En jij maar tevergeefs aan die deur trekken.*
and you just in-vain at that door pull-inf
'And you pulling in vain at that door.'
b. *En hij maar lachen!*
and he just laugh-inf
'And him laughing all the time!'

These examples of inflected infinitives and infinitives-as-main-verbs, however, clearly constitute the marked exceptions to the general properties of infinitives specified in (i)-(iv).

---

1. *maar* is a modal particle which is very difficult to translate into English in this usage; it is almost obligatory in this particular construction with the infinitive.

Non-finite embedded constructions 147

7.2.1.1. Closed and open infinitival constructions. Infinitival constructions may express closed or open embedded constructions. Those embedded constructions in which all argument positions are represented by overtly specified terms are closed, and those in which at least one argument position is not overtly expressed are open.

Let us first look at some examples of closed infinitival constructions. A case in point is the English so-called *for-to* complement, as in:

(7) a. *I am longing for John to arrive in time.*
    b. *I am longing for him to arrive in time.*

A construction such as (7a) can be represented in the following way:

(8)   Decl E: X: Pres e_i: *long* [V] $(I)_{Pos}$
        (Post e_j: [*arrive* [V] $(John)_{Proc}$ $(in\ time)_{Temp}])_{Go}$

Note that the embedded construction in (8) is closed, i.e. does not contain any open argument position.

In English closed infinitival constructions of this type the embedded Subject appears in non-nominative form (*him* in (7b)). The construction is in this respect comparable to the *accusativus cum infinitivo* (AcI) construction which is more familiar from Latin:

(9)   *Cupio   te   mihi   illud   narrare.*
        I-long   you-acc   me-dat   that-acc   to-tell
        'I long for you to tell me that.'

Note that we can now interpret the inflected infinitive in Portuguese (as in (4b) and (5b)) as expressing a closed infinitival construction.

It is not impossible for a closed infinitival construction to express a proposition in which there is referential identity between the embedded Subject and some argument of the matrix predicate, as in (10) and (11):

(10)   *Se   venturum   esse   promisit.*
        himself-acc   coming-fut-acc   to-be   he-promised
        'He promised himself to come'
        = 'He promised that he would come'

The underlying structure of (10) can be specified as follows:

148 *Embedded constructions 3*

(11) Decl E: X: PresPerf e_i:
  promittere [V] $(d1x_i: p3)_{AgSubj}$(Post e_j: [*venire* [V] $(Ax_i)_{AgSubj}])_{Go}$

where (Ax_i) anaphorically relates to the Subj of the matrix verb. In (10), (Ax_i) has been mapped onto the reflexive *se* because of this relation of coreference.

More commonly, however, we find simple or "open" infinitival constructions for the expression of configurations such as (11). Compare:

(12) a. *He wanted himself to be rich.*
   b. *He wanted Ø to be rich.*
(13) a. *He was longing for himself to succeed.*
   b. *He was longing Ø to succeed.*

We can now interpret the open infinitival construction in (12b) and (13b), in which there is no overt constituent representing the embedded Subject, as an embedded construction of which the Subject is left unexpressed under the condition of coreference with the higher Subject. In other words, as an example of zero anaphora. This means that, for example, (12a) and (12b) can be given basically the same underlying structure:

(14) Decl E: X: Past e_i:
  want [V] $(d1x_i: p3m)_{PosSubj}$(Post e_j: $[rich_A(Ax_i)_{ØSubj}])_{Go}$

where the embedded Subject can be mapped either onto *himself*, as in (12a), or onto zero, as in (12b). The former is clearly the more marked construction. We may suppose that this realization of (14) is triggered when Focus is assigned to the embedded Subject, so that the coreferential relation with the higher Subject is stressed. Compare:

(15) *I don't care about everybody else being rich, I want MYSELF to be rich/ *I want Ø to be rich.*

Note that in the older transformational literature, open infinitival constructions of type (12b) were described in terms of a rule of Equi-NP Deletion. This was because a sentence such as (16a) was supposed to derive from a deep structure of the form (16b) through a rule which deleted the second occurrence of *John*:

(16) a. *John wanted to be rich.*
   b. *John$_i$ wanted John$_i$ to be rich.*

It is clear how our analysis differs from this approach: in underlying representations of type (14), the embedded Subject always has the status of an anaphorical variable (Ax), which in different conditions may be expressed in different ways. If it is expressed as zero the result is an open infinitival construction.

In certain languages, closed infinitival constructions are impossible: all infinitival constructions must be open. Dutch is a case in point. Compare:

(17) a. Ik   wil   dat Jan   weggaat.
         I   want   that John leaves
         'I want John to leave.'
   b. *Ik   wil   Jan   weg   (te) gaan.
         I   want   John   away   (to) go
   c.   Ik   wil   weggaan.
         I   want   away-go
         'I want to go away'

The general rule in Dutch is that if the embedded Subject is non-coreferential with the higher Subject, a finite subordinate clause must be chosen; if the embedded Subject is coreferential, the embedded construction must be expressed in an open infinitival construction.

We have so far restricted our attention to open infinitival constructions which contain an anaphorical Subject term. There is another usage of open infinitivals in which the embedded Subject has a generic rather than an anaphorical value. Consider such examples as:

(18) a. *It is dangerous to swim in that lake.*
   b. *It is healthy to take some rest after a hard day's work.*

It will be clear that the covert Subject of these infinitivals does not have anaphorical value: there is no antecedent to which the variable in question could be linked. (18a) rather expresses that it is dangerous for anybody, for any arbitrary person, to swim in that lake.

In order to capture the generic value of covert arguments of this type, we can make use of the generic term operator "g", introduced in *TFG1*: 7.4.3. Thus, we can specify the predication underlying (18a) as follows:

(19)   Decl E: X: Pres e_i: *dangerous*$_A$
        (e_i: [*swim* [V] $(gx_j)_{AgSubj}$ *(that lake)*$_{Loc}$])$_{\emptyset Subj}$

150   *Embedded constructions 3*

We can now stipulate that generic terms of this type, just like anaphorical terms, may be mapped onto zero under certain conditions, thus leading to open infinitival constructions with a generic interpretation. Anaphorical and generic "zero" terms may then be associated with the following interpretations:

(20) (Ax_i):   the referent of this term is identical to that of another term with the term variable x_i in the context (the antecedent).

 (gx_i):   as a referent for this term, choose any entity which fulfils the selectional requirements imposed on this argument position.

7.2.1.2. Functions of infinitival constructions. Just like embedded constructions in general, so infinitival constructions can play different roles in complex predications. In the examples which we have seen so far, the infinitival acts as first argument (as in (18a)) or as second argument (as in (16a)) to the matrix predicate. Infinitivals can also occur in satellite terms, as in:

(21)   *John went to the market in order to buy bananas.*

which will get the following representation:

(22)   Decl E: X: Past e_i: *go* [V] ($d1x_i$: *John*)$_{AgSubj}$ ($d1x_j$: *market*)$_{Dir}$
        (Post e_j:[*buy* [V] (Ax_i)$_{AgSubj}$ (imx_k: *banana*)$_{GoObj}$])$_{Purpose}$

Given that underlying structure, the semantic function Purpose will be mapped onto the prepositional phrase *in order*, and the embedded construction is expressed as the open infinitival construction *to buy bananas*. The term variable e_j symbolizes the purpose for which John went to the market, consisting of the SoA in which he buys bananas at a moment of time posterior to his going to the market.

We saw in *TFG1*: 8.5. that there is a general rule through which terms can be turned into predicates. Embedded constructions, and thus also infinitival constructions, are terms, and therefore we expect them, as well, to be capable of being used as predicates. This expectation is borne out by such constructions as:

(23)   *This picture is for you to always remember me.*

This construction is in fact rather complex. I shall assume that it can be analysed as follows: the infinitival construction is basically a Purpose term:

(24)   (e_i: [remember [V] (you) (me) (always)])$_{Purpose}$

This term is turned into a predicate through the rule of Term Predicate Formation. This results in:

(25)   {(e_i: [remember [V] (you) (me) (always)])$_{Purpose}$}(x_1)$_\emptyset$
         'the property of being for the purpose of you always remembering me applies to (x_1)'

And this complex predicate is now applied to the term *this picture*:

(26)   Decl E: X: Pres e_j:
         {(e_i: [remember [V] (you) (me) (always)])$_{Purpose}$} (this picture)$_\emptyset$

This underlying structure now correctly expresses the semantics of (23): this picture is said to have a property which consists in a purpose, where this purpose is specified as consisting in the SoA constituted by "your always remembering me". Note that, although the construction is complex, we have not used any rules or principles for construing it beyond those which have already been introduced for independent reasons.

Another situation in which infinitival constructions appear as predicates is in pseudo-cleft constructions of the following form:

(27) a. *What I would like to do is* (to) give you a good beating.
     b. *What he never did was* (to) mention his former wife's name.

Here I take the position that the infinitival constructions in roman typeface have the status of predicates similar to the one represented in (26). This position will be motivated in chapter 10 below.

It should be noted that infinitivals in predicate position in different languages tend to get modal interpretations. Consider an example such as:

(28)   *Peter is to wash the dishes.*
         = 'Peter must / is obliged to wash the dishes'

I believe that this deontic interpretation of infinitival predicates might be understood as a further development on the basis of the purposive construction exemplified in (23). More difficult to understand are cases in which the infinitival predicate does not indicate what must be done, but what can be done, as in Dutch examples such as:

(29) a. *Dit voedsel is niet te eten.*
         this food is not to eat
         'This food is impossible to eat'
     b. *Dit boek is absoluut niet te begrijpen.*
         this book is absolutely not to understand
         'This book is absolutely incomprehensible'

It is not impossible, however, that this construction can be understood in terms of another notorious usage of infinitivals, to which we turn in the next section.

7.2.1.3. Infinitivals as complements to adjectives. We here face the problem posed by such pairs as:

(30) a. *John is easy to please.*
     b. *It is easy to please John.*
(31) a. *This problem is difficult to solve.*
     b. *It is difficult to solve this problem.*

There is a long-standing tradition in the transformational literature, according to which the a-constructions should be transformationally derived from the structure underlying the b-constructions by some rule of "Object-to-Subject Raising". Such a derivation would correctly capture that *John* in (30a), though apparently the Subject of *easy to please*, is semantically the Object of *please*.

Although in principle something like a Raising operation can be formulated within FG (see chapter 15), there are semantic differences between the a- and the b-constructions which show that such a derivation cannot be correct. As Vet (1981) has argued for corresponding pairs in French, the general rule is that the truth of the a-construction implies that of the b-construction, but not the other way around. And indeed, the following are non-contradictory:

(32) *It is difficult to solve this problem, although the problem is not difficult to solve.*
(33) *Even though visas are easy to obtain, it is not easy to obtain one.*

In certain other cases, the difference is even greater, neither member of the pair implying the other:

(34) a. *She is very nice to see, but it is not nice to see her.*
     b. *It is nice to see her, though she is not nice to see.*

These semantic differences in each case stem from the same source: in the b-constructions, a property is ascribed to some SoA (e.g. the property 'difficult' is ascribed to 'solving the problem'); in the a-constructions, on the other hand, a property is assigned to some first-order entity, in relation to a certain SoA relevant to that entity (e.g. the property of being 'difficult to solve' is ascribed to 'the problem'). And the SoA may have the property in question, without that property being ascribable to the entity involved in the SoA.

For such reasons as these, we conclude, with Vet (1981), that the a- and b-constructions cannot be derived from one and the same underlying structure. Their semantic differences must be reflected in a corresponding difference of underlying structure.

The structure of the b-constructions is not problematic, and has in fact already be discussed in 7.2.1.1. above. For example, (30b) will have the following underlying structure:

(35)   Decl E: X: Pres e_i: *easy* [A] (e_j: [*please* [V] $(gx_i)_{Ag}$ $(John)_{Go}$])$_\emptyset$

The a-constructions, on the other hand, require underlying predications of the general form of:

(36)   Decl E: X: Pres e: {*easy to please*} $(John)_\emptyset$

in which *easy to please* functions as one complex predicate, formed through complementing the adjective *easy* with an infinitival construction. This requires a predicate formation rule capable of combining an adjectival predicate and an embedded construction into a complex predicate of the required type. This rule would produce complex predicates of the form:

(37)   {*easy* [A] (e_i:[*please* [V] $(gx_i)_{Ag}$ $(Ax_j)_{Go}$])$_{Ref}$} $(x_j)_\emptyset$

in which is expressed that some entity, x_j, has the property of being 'easy' in relation to the SoA of anyone pleasing x_j. From this complex predicate, the predication underlying (30a) can be construed as follows:

(38)   Decl E: X: Pres e_i:
        {*easy* [A] (e_j: [*please* [V] $(gx_i)_{Ag}$ $(Ax_j)_{Go}$])} (d1x_j: *John*)$_\emptyset$

We can now return to the question posed in the preceding section, as to how infinitival predicates can acquire a modal value which is to be paraphrased with *can* rather than with *must*. Compare the Dutch constructions:

(39) a. *Dit probleem is moeilijk op_te_lossen.*
this problem is difficult to-solve
'This problem is difficult to solve.'
b. *Dit probleem is makkelijk op_te_lossen.*
this problem is easy to-solve
'This problem is easy to solve.'
c. *Dit probleem is op_te_lossen.*
this problem is to-solve
'This problem can be solved'

The idea would be that the infinitival predicate in (39c) is, in a sense, the zero degree of those in (39a) and (39b): it simply marks the possibility of the problem being solved, without specifying anything about the ease or the difficulty involved in solving it. The situation would be comparable to what is found in another case of predicate formation, the type of valency reduction (see chapter 1) which produces:

(40) a. *This pen writes nicely.*
b. *This pen doesn't write.*

Usually, detransitivized *write* requires some extension such as *nicely*. When used without such an extension, as in (42b), it acquires the "zero degree" modal value '(im)possible to write with'. This value comes out especially in negative constructions. This is also true of the Dutch modal infinitive, which strongly favours negative contexts, as in (29a) and (29b) above.

7.2.2. Participial constructions

Participal constructions can be defined as embedded constructions construed around a participle. Participles can be defined as adjectival predicates derived from verbal predicates. Adjectival predicates are primarily used as restrictors within term structures. Participles can be used in the same way, as in:

(41)   *the dying man, the broken vase, the lost battle*

Here we are more interested in cases in which participial constructions can be used to express embedded constructions. Participial constructions are especially used for the expression of embedded constructions which function

Non-finite embedded constructions 155

as satellites, more specifically, satellites of Circumstance, serving as satellites of level 2 in relation to the core predication.

Just as in the case of infinitival constructions, participial constructions can be divided into closed and open ones. In open participial constructions, the Subject or the first argument is not overtly specified; in closed participial constructions, it is overtly specified. Consider the following examples (from Quirk et al. 1972: 762):

(42) Open participial construction:
      Reaching the river, we pitched camp for the night.
(43) Closed participial construction:
   a. *No further discussion arising, the meeting was brought to a close.*
   b. *All our savings gone, we started looking for a job.*

It is typical of participial constructions of this type that the precise semantic relationship with the core predication is not overtly specified. Depending on the context, they can receive a variety of different interpretations:

(44) temporal ('when / while')
      causal ('because / since')
      circumstantial ('in the circumstance that')
      concessive ('although')
      etc.

Rather than assume that these constructions are multiply ambiguous between these different readings, it seems proper to regard them as "vague" with respect to their semantic status; in other words, to assume that the various interpretations are a matter of pragmatic interpretation rather than of semantic content. This can be done by assuming that they always have the status of satellites of Circumstance, where "Circumstance" means that the SoA in question is in some way relevant to the SoA specified by the nuclear predication, in such a way that the particular type of relevance is left for the Addressee to infer through pragmatic interpretation. This means that the participial constructions in (42) and (43) can be represented as follows:

(45) $(e_i: [reach [V] (Ax_i)_{ProcSubj} (the\ river)_{Go}])_{Circ}$
(46) a. $(e_i: [arise [V] (no\ further\ discussion)_{ProcSubj}])_{Circ}$
   b. $(e_i: [Perf\ go [V] (all\ our\ savings)_{ProcSubj}])_{Circ}$

156 *Embedded constructions 3*

In the open construction (45), there is an anaphorical variable (Ax_i) coreferential with the Subject *we* of the main clause. In (46a-b) the Subject of the embedded circumstantial predication is overtly specified.

Closed participial constructions such as (43a-b) are not very common in English, and often have a somewhat archaic flavour about them. In Dutch they are even more unusual.

In Latin, however, this construction was particularly productive. Since the Latin closed participial construction is expressed in the ablative case, it is termed the Ablative Absolute. Consider:

(47)   *Multis   vulneribus   acceptis   strenue   pugnabat.*
        many-abl wounds-abl   received-abl vigorously he-fought
        'Many wounds having been inflicted, he fought vigorously.'

The fact that participials can be used as restrictors and as circumstantial satellites may give rise to such ambiguities as the following (cf. Quirk et al. 1972: 763, Chomsky 1965):

(48)   *I caught the boy smoking a cigar.*
        (i)   'I caught the boy who was smoking a cigar'
        (ii) 'I caught the boy while he was smoking a cigar'
        (iii) 'I caught the boy while I was smoking a cigar'

In (i), *smoking a cigar* is integrated into the Goal term as a restrictor. In (ii) and (iii) it is interpreted as a circumstantial satellite. The ambiguity between (ii) and (iii) is caused by the fact that the covert Subject of *smoking* may either have *the boy* or *I* for its antecedent.

The three interpretations of (48) may thus be analysed in the following way:

(49) (i)   Past e_i: [*catch* [V] $(d1x_i: I)_{Ag}$ $(d1x_j: boy:$
           $[e_j$: Progr *smoke* [V] $(x_j)_{Ag}$ $(i1x_k: cigar)_{Go}])_{Go}]$
           'I caught the boy who was smoking a cigar'
    (ii) Past e_i: [*catch* [V] $(d1x_i: I)_{Ag}$ $(d1x_j: boy)_{Go}]$
           $(e_j$: [Progr *smoke* [V] $(Ax_j)_{Ag}$ $(i1x_k: cigar)_{Go}])_{Circ}$
           'I caught the boy (x_j) in the circumstance e_j defined as the SoA that he (x_j) was smoking a cigar'
    (iii) Past e_i: [*catch* [V] $(d1x_i: I)_{Ag}$ $(d1x_j: boy)_{Go}]$
           $(e_j$: [Progr *smoke* [V] $(Ax_i)_{Ag}$ $(i1x_k: cigar)_{Go}])_{Circ}$
           'I (x_i) caught the boy in the circumstance e_j defined by the SoA that I (x_i) was smoking a cigar'

The structures (ii) and (iii) thus differ with respect to the antecedent that controls the anaphorical variable which takes the first argument position of the predicate *smoke*. Languages may differ in the types of antecedent-anaphor relations which are allowed in such constructions. In a language, for example, in which coreference could only exist between the anaphorical variable and the Subject of the matrix clause, a construction of the form (49)(ii) would not be well-formed, and the ambiguity between (ii) and (iii) could not arise. We return to some aspects of this problem in chapter 16.

7.2.3. Nominalizations

By a nominalization we understand an embedded construction which has one or more properties in common with a primary, nominal term. Two types of nominalization can be distinguished: headed and non-headed. In the headed type, the embedded construction is adjoined to a nominal head with a rather general meaning such as "fact", "thing", or "circumstance":

(50) a. *John deplored that Peter had to leave.*
 b. *John deplored the fact that Peter had to leave.*

The nominal properties are here provided by the head *fact*, which is specified through the finite subordinate clause *that Peter had to leave*. We saw in 5.4.2. that Japanese uses this nominalization strategy in embedded constructions headed by *koto* 'fact' and *no* 'SoA'. My general impression is that when this strategy is used in a language, the embedded construction as such appears as a finite subordinate clause.

In the case of non-headed nominalization it is the predicate itself which takes on certain nominal properties. Compare:

(51) a. *I hear* that John drinks.
 b. *Mary does not want* John to drink.
 c. *I disapprove of* John's drinking.

In each case, the constituent in roman typeface is an embedded construction specifying the same SoA. In (51a) we have a finite subordinate clause, in (51b) an infinitival construction; the latter construction is non-finite, but there is nothing particularly "nominal" about it. In (51c), however, we see the Agent constituent, *John*, appear in a genitive. Genitives are especially suited for expressing relations within nominal terms. They do not usually code Agent phrases. The fact that *John* appears in the genitive in (51c) will be interpreted as a nominal property, and therefore *John's drinking* will be described as a nominalization.

I shall say that nominalizations are embedded constructions which to some degree have adjusted to the typical expression pattern of primary, nominal terms. This is an example of the "Principle of Formal Adjustment" (Dik 1985a, see also 1.3 and *TFG1*: 17.3.1):

(52) PRINCIPLE OF FORMAL ADJUSTMENT (PFA):
Derived, secondary constructions of type X are under pressure to adjust their formal expression to the prototypical expression model of non-derived, primary constructions of type X.

I assume that the primary type of term is a nominal term which can be used to refer to some first-order entity. The typical expression model for such terms contains such constituent types as:

(53) Determiner, Quantifier, Possessor, Adjective, Noun

Embedded constructions, on the other hand, are a secondary type of term. They are used to refer to second-, third-, or fourth-order entities (i.e. SoAs, possible facts, and speech acts, respectively). The typical ingredients of embedded constructions are:

(54) π-operators, Predicate, Argument, Satellite

I now understand nominalization as due to a tendency, consonant with the PFA, to press embedded constructions into the expression format of primary, nominal terms. Many of the properties of nominalizations can indeed be understood in terms of the following types of formal adjustment:

(55) embedded construction

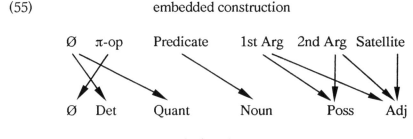

first-order term

Each arrow in (55) represents one possible adjustment of embedded constructions to the expression model of first-order terms. Every nominalization is characterized by at least one of these adjustments. Let us first look at these adjustments one by one:

(i) the predicate of the embedded construction may appear in the form of a (verbal) noun:

(56) a. *John denied the charges.*
    b. *John's denial of the charges.*

(ii) the first argument of the embedded construction may appear in the form of a Possessor:

(57)   *John's denial of the charges*

(iii) the first argument of the embedded construction may appear in the form of an Adjective:

(58) a. *The president denied the charges.*
    b. *The presidential denial of the charges.*

(iv) the second argument of the embedded construction may appear in the form of a Possessor:

(59)   *The presidential denial of the charges.*

(v) the second argument of the embedded construction may appear in the form of an Adjective:

(60) a. *The people elected a president.*
    b. *The presidential elections.*

(vi) a satellite of the embedded construction may appear in the form of an Adjective:

(61) a. *The president forcefully denied the charges.*
    b. *The president's forceful denial of the charges.*

(vii) the embedded construction may acquire a Determiner:

(62)   *the denial of the charges by the president*

(viii) it may acquire a Quantifier and/or Number distinctions:

(63)   *These charges elicited several denials on the part of the government.*

(ix) the embedded construction may lose the capacity to express π-operators. Compare the following constructions:

(64) a.   *I disapprove of John's buying the car.*
  b.   *I disapprove of John's having bought the car.*
(65) a.   *I disapprove of John's buying of the car.*
  b.   **I disapprove of John's having bought of the car.*

(64) and (65) exemplify two types of English nominalization. In the type illustrated in (64), only the first argument is adjusted to Possessor; in (65) the second argument, too, gets possessive expression. (65) is more "nominal" than (64). Concurrently, the π-operator Perfect can be expressed in (64), but not in (65). It will be clear, furthermore, that no π-operators whatsoever can be expressed in the case of verbal nouns such as *denial*.

7.2.3.1. The possessive expression of arguments. The most conspicuous and recurrent property of nominalizations is perhaps the expression of arguments of the embedded construction in the form of Possessor phrases. This phenomenon is often described in terms of assignment of genitive case to these arguments. The relevant genitives are sometimes called "subjective genitive", when the first argument is so expressed (as in (66a)), and "objective genitive", when the second argument is so expressed, as in (66b):

(66) a.   *amor patris*   'the love of a father'
  b.   *amor dei*   'the love for God'

In fact, however, this type of argument expression is not simply a matter of genitive case assignment. It is more adequate to speak, as I have done above, of expression of the argument in the form of a Possessor. This is so because it is typically the case that if a language has this type of adjustment at all, the argument in question can adjust to any type of Possessor expression available in the language, no matter whether this Possessor expression is marked by genitive case or not.

English is a case in point: Possessors can be expressed in prenominal genitives, as in (67a), in postnominal prepositional phrases with *of* if the possessor is expressed by a heavy constituent, as in (67b), and in possessive pronouns, as in (67c):

(67) a. *John's book*
 b. *the book of my old friend the brain surgeon*
 c. *his book*

Each of these Possessor expressions can also function as a target for argument adjustment within the domain of the nominalization, witness:

(68) a. *John's singing*
 b. *the singing of my old friend the brain surgeon*
 c. *his singing*

A second fact about possessive expression of arguments within nominalizations is that it is uncommon for two arguments of the nominalization to be expressed in possessive expressions of the same type. This is also true of English. Thus, we can have:

(69) a. *John's signing of the cheque*
 b. *his signing of the cheque*

because the two possessive expressions are of different types. And we can also have:

(70) a. *the singing of my old friend the brain surgeon* (first argument)
 b. *the signing of the cheque* (second argument)

because there is only one possessive argument in each case. But we cannot have:

(71) **the signing of the cheque of my old friend the brain surgeon*

because this would mean using two possessive expressions of the same type. In order to express what is intended to be conveyed by (71), we will have to use (69a) or (72):

(72)   *the signing of the cheque by John*

where only the second argument gets possessive expression, and the first argument is expressed in the normal way as an Agent phrase.

A further fact which is also exemplified by (72) is that there are often certain priority rules relevant to possessive expression. Note that it would be impossible to say:

(73) a.   **the signing of John the cheque*
     b.   **the signing the cheque of John*

In other words: when two arguments are candidates for possessive expression in a postnominal possessive phrase, then the second argument wins out. This fact can be understood in the following way. If we investigate the way in which nominalizations are actually used, we will find that it is unusual for two arguments to be expressed at the same time, and also that the following expression types account for the great majority of the actually occurring cases:

(74) a.   *the singing of the birds*
     b.   *the signing of the cheque*

In other words, in nominalizations based on transitive verbs the second argument will usually be the only one expressed; and in the case of intransitive verbs, the first argument is obviously the only one which can be expressed. In the great majority of cases, then, the following simple rule will take care of argument expression within nominalizations:

(75)   Express the single overt argument in possessive form.

This rule, together with the fact that (74a-b) are the prototypical forms in which nominalizations occur, results in an expression pattern which may be called "ergative": the transitive Object is treated in the same way as the intransitive Subject, and the transitive Subject is treated in a different way, as in (72) above. See *TFG1*: chapter 11.

7.2.3.2. *A cross-linguistic hierarchy of nominalization types.* Both within and across languages, nominalizations may display more and more of the adjustments (i)-(ix) described in 7.2.3., so that we get a range of nominalization types, ranging from almost completely verbal to completely nominal. In a cross-linguistic study of a sample of 30 languages Mackenzie (1987) found that embedded constructions can be ordered in a hierarchy between "completely verbal" and "completely nominal" in the following way:[2]

— Degree 0: The embedded construction is a completely finite, fully verbal construction:

(76)   *John saw that Peter signed the cheque.*

— Degree 1: The embedded verb is in some way characterized as dependent, non-main, non-finite; this can be seen as a form of "deverbalization":

(77)   *John saw Peter signing the cheque.*

— Degree 2: The embedded construction is externally marked in a way which is otherwise typical of nominal terms:

(78)   *John approved of Peter signing the cheque.*

— Degree 3: One or more of the arguments are given Possessor expression; there is some loss of expressibility for π-operators:

(79)   *John deplored Peter's signing of the cheque.*

— Degree 4: The nominalization acquires further properties which are characteristic of nominal terms: term operators, Gender and Number distinctions, adjectival modifiers:

(80)   *John disapproved of Peter's repeated denials of the charges.*

Mackenzie demonstrated that these "degrees of nominalization" form a hierarchy in the sense that if a language displays properties of Degree n, it will also display the properties which are characteristic of all degrees below n, but not the other way around. This can be taken as a sign that languages, in a sense, start at the verbal end, and then gradually approximate to the fully nominalized Degree 4 construction type.

---

2. Compare also Comrie (1976a); for English nominalizations, Mackenzie (1984).

Mackenzie further found that all languages have at least some degree of nominalization,[3] and that full nominalizations of Degree 4 (typically involving "verbal nouns" modified by typical nominal determiners and modifiers) are especially found in Postfield (V-initial) languages, in which their internal structure also has a Postfield organization. Thus, the following would be a characteristic Postfield nominalization:

(81) *Disapproved John of the destruction of the stadium by the hooligans.*
 "John disapproved of the destruction of the stadium by the hooligans"

For some ideas about why this should be so, see Mackenzie (1987).

7.2.3.3. The treatment of nominalizations in FG. Consider the following pair of constructions:

(82) a. *The enemy destroyed the city.*
 b. *the destruction of the city by the enemy*

There has been much discussion, especially within the framework of Transformational Grammar, about the problem posed by these constructions. The basic problem can be formulated as follows: (82a) and (82b) are clearly quite different in a number of respects: (82a) is a fully verbal construction, (82b) is almost completely nominal. On the other hand, the constructions also have a lot in common: they describe what is basically the same SoA, their predicates have identical selection restrictions, and they can be used in similar circumstances. The problem, now, is how to describe (82a) and (82b) in such a way that their basic kinship is accounted for, while at the same time the differences are duly recognized.

The early transformational solution was a derivational one (Lees 1966): nominalizations such as (82b) were supposed to be derivable from the structure underlying full sentences such as (82a) through a transformational rule of Nominalization. This type of description stressed the similarities of the two constructions, at the expense of their differences.

---

3. This presupposes that even Degree 1 is already a form of nominalization, a point of view that I do not share, since it involves no more than an indication of the non-main, non-finite status of the verbal predicate.

Since Chomsky (1970), the derivational approach has been abandoned in favour of a lexical description of nominalizations such as (82b). The idea is that both the verb *destroy* and the noun *destruction* will be entered in the lexicon as the verbal and nominal representative of a common lexical item. One implication of this is that the nominalization is no longer derived from the same underlying structure as the full sentence.

For this reason, the need arose for a mechanism for formulating regularities across syntactic categories, in order to capture the properties common to both verbal constructions of type (82a) and nominal constructions of type (82b). The solution to this problem was the theory of X-bar syntax, in which syntactic regularities can be formulated in terms of the category variable X, which can take values such as V, N or A.

Most of the problems involved in this matter also arise within the framework of FG. But given the basic assumptions of this model, there are certain important differences.

First, one principle of FG says that all contentive predicates which cannot be derived from other such predicates by productive rule must be placed in the lexicon. Since there is no productive rule of English for deriving the verbal noun *destruction* from the verb *destroy*, it follows immediately from this principle that *destruction* must have its own entry in the lexicon. Thus, the general criterion of productivity enforces the lexical solution to the problem.

In the second place, the fact that *destroy* and *destruction* must have distinct entries in the lexicon does not mean that a new theory is required to account for the similarities between these two entries. Each predicate is part of a predicate frame, and there is nothing which prevents nominal predicates from having predicate frames which are quite similar or even identical to the predicate frames of related verbs. In this particular case, we could postulate the following predicate frames for *destroy* and *destruction*:

(83) a.   *destroy* [V] $(x_1)_{Ag/Force}$ $(x_2)_{Go}$
     b.   *destruction* [N] $(x_1)_{Ag/Force}$ $(x_2)_{Go}$

The fact that *destroy* and *destruction* can appear with the same types of arguments in the same semantic functions follows immediately from these predicate frames. The semantic relationship between these two predicates can furthermore be expressed in the meaning definition of *destruction*:

(84) *destruction* [N] $(x_1)_{Ag/Force}$ $(x_2)_{Go}$
$=_{df}$
action/event defined by
destroy [V] $(x_1)_{Ag/Force}$ $(x_2)_{Go}$

The predicate frame for *destruction* can be used in term formation according to the model of an embedded construction:

(85) $(d1e_i: [destruction$ [N] $(the\ enemy)_{Ag}$ $(the\ city)_{Go}])$

which, through the expression rules determining the formal expression of arguments within the context of a nominalization, will lead to any of the following surface structures:

(86) a. *the destruction of the city by the enemy*
 b. *the enemy's destruction of the city*
 c. *the city's destruction by the enemy*

A further distinctive property of the FG model is that, alongside full syntactic derivation and pure lexical listing, it also has the device of productive predicate formation rules (see chapter 1). Thus, in a language in which verbal nouns can be productively derived from the corresponding verbs, the relevant relationship can be expressed in a predicate formation rule. Take, for example, the formation of Dutch verbal nouns with the prefix *ge-*, as in:

(87) a. *De meisjes giechel-en.*
 the girls giggle-pl-pres
 'The girls giggle.'
 b. *het ge-giechel van de meisjes*
 the nom-giggle of the girls
 'the giggling of the girls'

This rule, studied in detail by Mackenzie (1985b), is productive (given suitable input) and can be described by means of the predicate formation rule in (88):

(88) Formation of *ge*-nominalization in Dutch:
 Input : pred [V] $(x_1)_{Ag}$
 Output: *ge*-pred [N] $(x_1)_{Ag}$
 Meaning: 'repeated/continuous action of pred [V]-ing by Agent'

What we see in (88) is that the argument structure of the input verb is retained in the output predicate frame. Just as in English, the Agent will get possessive expression in the domain of the nominalization. Thus, again, the similarities between verbal and nominal structure are automatically accounted for, this time through the fact that the nominalization "inherits" a number of essential properties from the verbal predicate from which it is derived.[4]

As was demonstrated in Dik (1985c), FG thus offers three distinct ways of describing a nominalization:

(i) the nominalization is derived from a purely verbal embedded construction through appropriate expression rules;

(ii) the predicate frame underlying the nominalization is derived through productive predicate formation from the corresponding verbal predicate;

(iii) the predicate frame underlying the nominalization is separately entered in the lexicon.

The first method can be used when there is nothing particularly nominal about the predicate which acts as head of the nominalization. In one type of nominalization in Dutch, for example, the predicate is realized in the form of an infinitive:

(89) a. *De vijand verwoestte   de stad.*
       the enemy destroyed   the city
       'The enemy destroyed the city.'
   b. *het verwoesten   van de stad door   de vijand*
       the destroy-inf of the city by   the enemy
       'the destroying of the city by the enemy'

In such a case, we can simply start with an underlying structure of the following form:

(90)   (e_i: [*verwoesten* [V] (*de vijand*)$_{Ag}$ (*de stad*)$_{Go}$])

This structure can be mapped onto (89b) by expression rules which stipulate that the predicate is realized in the infinitive, and the Goal in possessive form. There is no reason to first derive a nominal predicate frame from the verbal

---

4. Note that Mackenzie (1985b) provides a somewhat different formulation for (88), with, however, the same basic property of preservation of input information.

one. A similar approach can be taken to English nominalizations of the following two types:

(91) a. *the enemy's destroying the city*
 b. *the enemy's destroying of the city*

In both cases, the expression rules stipulate that the predicate will be realized in participial form, and that the first argument will take possessive expression; in (91b), but not in (91a), the second argument also takes possessive expression.

Dutch also has a class of verbal nouns, however, which can be used in much the same conditions as the infinitive:

(92)   *de   verwoesting   van de   stad door   de   vijand*
       the   destruction   of   the   city by   the   enemy
       'the destruction of the city by the enemy'

In this construction, *verwoesting* 'destruction' is clearly a noun: it cannot possibly be regarded as a form belonging to the verbal paradigm. To the extent that this type of verbal noun can be productively formed from the corresponding verb, it can be derived through a predicate formation rule of the following form:

(93)   Verbal Noun formation in Dutch (in *-ing*)
       Input : pred [V] $(x_1)_{Ag}$ $(x_2)_{Go}$
       Output : pred-*ing* [N] $(x_1)_{Ag}$ $(x_2)_{Go}$

Again, the essential properties of the input predicate will be inherited by the nominalized output predicate. The lexical solution, finally, has been illustrated with *destruction* in (83b) above.

Note, finally, that what once was a productively derived nominalized form may at a later stage get isolated from its input and thereby lexicalized into a form which must be listed in the lexicon. This is only one instance of a quite general process of loss of productivity and subsequent lexicalization. Our discussion of nominalizations in the context of embedding has thus brought us back to several of the issues that were dealt with in chapter 1.

8. Polarity distinctions

8.0. Introduction

In *TFG1*: 9.2.2.2.3. we analysed polarity distinctions in terms of predication operators of level π_2. Positive and negative polarity were presented as the logical extremes of epistemic objective modality, as signalling that the speaker is certain about the actuality or non-actuality of the (occurrence of the) SoA. It was also noted that negative sentences with inherently negative quantifiers, such as

(1)   *John has bought* no *books.*

should not be analysed by means of a negative predication operator, to be lowered into the clause and fused with the determiner, but in terms of the notion "zero quantification" which pertains to the term operator system and is thus a term-internal matter.

When we consider the phenomenology of negation in natural languages in more detail, we find that a richer array of negation types must be distinguished on the basis of what precisely is denied or negated, of the semantic and pragmatic values of the negation, and of the various ways in which negative polarity may manifest itself in formal expression.

Most of the relevant distinctions were made in Lyons (1977: 768-777). Not counting cases of zero quantification as in (1), Lyons distinguishes three, possibly four distinct types of negation as relevant to natural languages. Interestingly, these different negation types can be interpreted in terms of the layered structure of the clause as developed in FG.

In this chapter, therefore, I consider how different types of negation could be understood in terms of the FG clause model. Within this clause model we may distinguish the following levels of analysis at which negation may be relevant:

(2) a. Clause   Speech act
     b. Proposition   Possible fact
     c. Predication   State of Affairs
     d. Predicate   Property/Relation
     e. Term   Ensemble of entities

170 *Polarity distinctions*

It will be argued that there is reason to distinguish some form of negation at each of these five levels.

8.1. Negation: operator or satellite?

So far we have talked about negation and other polarity distinctions in terms of π-operators, that is, in terms of elements that are grammatically rather than lexically expressed. This is no doubt correct for those languages in which negation is an integrated part of the expression of the verbal complex. This is most clearly the case when the negative operator is synthetically expressed in the verb, as in Japanese:

(3) a. *Taroo   wa tegami   o   kakimasu.*
       Taro   Top letter   Obj write-Pol
       'Taro writes a letter'
    b. *Taroo   wa tegami   o   kakimasen.*
       Taro   Top letter   Obj write-Pol-neg
       'Taro does not write a letter'

It is also the case if the negative element is expressed analytically, but has a clear influence on the formal expression of the verbal complex. This is the case in English, where *do*-support is triggered by negation when there is no other auxiliary in the verbal complex, as in *does not write*. It is clear that negation in English must be an integrated part of those operators which serve to trigger the formal expression of the verbal complex.

If the expression of negation is not an integrated part of the verbal complex, matters are less clear. In such a situation negation could either be captured by a π-operator or represented as a satellite of the relevant level, depending on whether we analyse negation as forming part of the grammatical or of the lexical sub-system of the language. For example, if in some language we found constructions such as

(4) a. *John accepted the proposal fully.*
    b. *John accepted the proposal hardly.*
    c. *John accepted the proposal not at all.*
    d. *John accepted the proposal not.*

there might be reason to consider the element *not* as a negative satellite on a par with the other satellites which, in one way or another, indicate the extent to which John accepted the proposal.

I do not wish to exclude the possibility, then, that in some languages negation might pattern along with lexical satellites, while in other languages it would form an integrated part of the set of grammatical operators. However, I will not try to resolve this question here, and go on talking about negative operators rather than satellites.

8.2. Negation and Focus

More often than not, when we have an expression which can be represented as neg(X), it is not the whole of X which is actually in the scope of neg. Consider:

(5)   *John didn't go to Leyden on a bicycle.*

Although the negation is best analysed here as having the whole predication ("John go to Leyden on a bicycle") in its scope, the most plausible interpretation of (5) is that in which only the satellite *on a bicycle* is negated:

(6)   *John did go to Leyden, but he didn't go on a bicycle.*

Bossuyt (1982, 1983) has explained this scope problem in terms of the following principles:[1]

(7) (i) The normal interpretation of a negative sentence is that which creates the smallest possible deviation from what is claimed in the corresponding positive sentence.
    (ii) In the absence of marked Focus assignment, that constituent "catches" the negation which is the most peripheral in the hierarchy of semantic functions.
    (iii) Otherwise, the marked Focus constituent(s) "catch" the negation.

Consider again sentence (5):

---

1. Principle (i) is based on Seuren (1976).

172 *Polarity distinctions*

(5)   *John didn't go to Leyden on a bicycle.*

Principle (i) explains why the following would be a non-standard explanation of the negation in (8):

(8)   '... for it wasn't John who went to Leyden, and the one who did go didn't go on a bicycle.'

Principle (ii) explains why (5), without Focus marking, is not used for negating that it was John who went to Leyden, or that it was to Leyden that John went (the assumption here is that *to Leyden*, as a directional argument to *go*, is more central to the predication than the instrumental satellite *on a bicycle*).

Principle (iii) explains the effect of assigning different Focus markings to (5):

(9) a. JOHN *didn't go to Leyden on a bicycle. (*PETER *did.)*
    b. *John* DIDn't *go to Leyden on a bicycle. (He* IS *going there* TOMORROW.*)*
    c. *John didn't go to* LEYDEN *on a bicycle. (He went to* HAARLEM.*)*
    d. *John didn't go to Leyden on a* BICYCLE. *(He went by* CAR.*)*
    e. *John didn't go to* LEYDEN *on a* BICYCLE. *(He went to* HAARLEM *by* CAR.*)*

Rather than assigning a different underlying position to the operator "neg" in each of the cases (9a-e), principles (i)-(iii) allow us to explain the different interpretations on the basis of the interaction between this operator (which takes the same position in all cases), the central-peripheral dimension of semantic functions, and the differential assignments of Focus to the constituents of the clause.

It should be kept in mind, then, that the different underlying positions of "neg" to be distinguished below will be multiplied by the different Focus assignment possibilities at each relevant layer.

8.3. Illocutionary negation

Lyons (1977: 769-770) first of all points to the fact that we can negate the illocutionary force of an utterance, as in:

(10)   *I don't say that John is a fool.*

By this kind of negation "... we express our refusal or inability to perform the illocutionary act of assertion, promising, or whatever it might be. But to do this is itself to perform an illocutionary act: an act of non-commitment. Acts of non-commitment are to be distinguished, on the one hand, from saying nothing and, on the other, from making descriptive statements." (Lyons 1977: 770).[2]

Searle—Vanderveken (1985) likewise argue that this kind of illocutionary negation (or "illocutionary denegation", as they call it) must be distinguished from propositional negation. Compare:

(11) a. *I promise not to come.*
 b. *I do not promise to come.*

(11a) can be used to perform an act of promising with respect to a propositional content of 'not coming'; (11b), on the other hand, is a speech act in which it is disclaimed that a promise is being made with respect to 'coming': 'an act of illocutionary denegation is one whose aim is to make explicit that the speaker does not perform a certain illocutionary act' (Searle—Vanderveken 1985: 4).

Illocutionary negation is typically achieved by negating an explicit performative verb such as *promise* in (11). It cannot be achieved by a simple modification of the basic illocutionary operators Declarative, Interrogative, or Imperative.

The way in which we account for illocutionary negation in the clause model depends, therefore, on our analysis of performative verbs such as *say* in (10) and *promise* in (11). In chapter 11 an analysis will be proposed in which such utterances as (10) and (11) have the status of grammatical declaratives which describe what the speaker is doing at the very moment of speaking, and are therefore pragmatically interpreted as signalling illocutionary acts rather than descriptive statements. This, however, has some interesting implications for the status of "illocutionary negation":

First of all, if utterances such as (10) and (11) are declaratives in which the speech act verb has the status of a matrix verb with an embedded complement, then it is to be expected that negation of the matrix should be possible. The

---

2. For the distinct status of illocutionary negation, see also Van Eemeren—Grootendorst (1982) and Hoffmann (1984).

difference between (11a) and (11b), for example, could be analysed along the lines of (12):[3]

(12) a   Decl E_i: X_i: Pres e_i: *promise* [V] $(I)_{Ag}$ [Subs Neg e_j: *come* [V] $(I)_{Ag}]_{Go}$
        'I promise not to come'
   b   Decl E_i: X_i: Pres Neg e_i: *promise* [V] $(I)_{Ag}$ [Subs e_j: *come* [V] $(I)_{Ag}]_{Go}$
        'I don't promise to come'

Secondly, this analysis predicts that in such constructions as these double negation should be possible:

(13)   Decl E_i: X_i: Pres Neg e_i: *promise* [V] $(I)_{Ag}$
       [Subs Neg e_j: *come* [V] $(I)_{Ag}]_{Go}$
       'I don't promise not to come'

Thirdly, on the assumption that illocutionary operators such as Decl are distinct from performative matrix predicates, as we will argue in chapter 11, we account for the fact that basic illocutions cannot likewise be negated so as to result in declarations of non-commitment.

Fourthly, these assumptions entail that "illocutionary negation" is not, after all, distinct from negating any other SoA; the special effect results from the fact that a declarative description of a speech act that S is performing at the very moment of speaking counts pragmatically as one way of actually doing that speech act. The negative character of the description does not affect this pragmatic inference.

The conclusion must then be that the special effect of "illocutionary negation" is mediated through the special pragmatic interpretation of negative performative statements.

8.4. Propositional negation

Compare the following two sequences:

(14)   A: *Is John rich?*
       B: *No, John is not rich.*

---

3. Assuming that *promise* takes a predicational complement, designating a SoA "subsequent" (Subs) to the reference point defined by the matrix clause.

(15)   A: *John is rich.*
        B: *NO, John is NOT rich!*

In (14A) it is an open question whether the property 'rich' applies or does not apply to John, or whether the SoA ('John is rich') does or does not obtain. There is thus an information gap with respect to the polarity of 'John is rich'. The answer (14B) fills this information gap in a neutral and objective way with a negative value. In terms of the distinctions made in *TFG1*: 13.4.2. this is a matter of Completive Focus on the polarity of the predication. A paraphrase could be: 'It is the case/true that John is not rich'.

In (15), on the other hand, A states that 'It is the case / true that John is rich', and B *denies* that this is correct: B "disagrees" with A as to the truth value of the proposition "John is rich". This is a case of Counter-Presuppositional Focus. A correct paraphrase would be: '(Contrary to what you say (imply, seem to think)) it is not the case/true that John is rich.'

Superficially, there is no difference in form between (14B) and (15B). On closer inspection, however, we see that there is a clear prosodic difference between these two expressions. Formal differences also come out when we consider the positive counterparts of (14) and (15):

(16)   A: *Is John rich?*
        B: *Yes, he is rich.*
(17)   A: *John is not rich.*
        B: *(That's not true), he IS rich!*

In other languages, such formal differences are expressed segmentally. Compare the Dutch counterparts of (16) and (17):

(18)   A: *Is Jan rijk?*
        B: *Ja, hij is rijk.*
(19)   A: *Jan is niet rijk.*
        B: *Hij is WEL rijk!*

In Dutch, the emphatic element *wel* cannot be used in (18B). It can only be used, as in (19B), in order to signal disagreement with what the other has said or is supposed to think.[4]

---

4. Houtlosser (1989) points to the importance of this type of negation within an argumentative context.

176 *Polarity distinctions*

We therefore agree with the distinction made by Lyons (1977: 768) between the assertion of a negative proposition ('it is the case that *-p*') versus the denial of the corresponding positive proposition ('it is not the case that *p*'). In the latter case Lyons speaks of "modal negation". More generally, we may deny or confirm a proposition *p* which in some sense is entertained or implied in the context, where *p* may be either positive or negative. In both cases we present our personal evaluation of the truth of *p*, which may concur with or differ from someone else's evaluation which has somehow been established in the context. Appropriate paraphrases in the case of this usage would be 'I agree that *p*' and 'I disagree that *p*'.

Within our framework, the polarities which are used to express the subjective acts of denying and confirming could be analysed in terms of propositional operators of the π_3 level (along with other subjective modalities), while the objective polarities (which concern the occurrence or non-occurrence of the SoA) might be placed at the π_2 level. Consider the following examples:

(20) *John is not rich.* (statement of fact)
Decl E: X: Pres Neg e: *rich* [A] (*John*)$_\emptyset$
(21) A: *John is rich.*
B: *John is NOT rich!* (statement of disagreement)
Decl E: Neg X: Pres e: *rich* [A] (*John*)$_\emptyset$

In this way, we make a distinction between predicational negation (= objective statement of the non-occurrence of some SoA, as in (20)), and propositional negation (= subjective denial of some pre-established proposition, as in (21)).

It must be granted that most languages do not seem to have *segmental* means for distinguishing propositional and predicational negation. But if the same segmental means are used, there will typically be clear suprasegmental differences, as we saw above. Certain segmental differences, however, can be interpreted in terms of the distinction made here. Consider the example of Mandarin Chinese: in his analysis of Mandarin Chinese negation Van den Berg (1989: chapter 15) distinguishes three negation types: negation of the predicate, negation of the predication, and negation of the message, i.e. our proposition. Negation of the predication is achieved by the negative particle *bù* 'not', or by the negative existential element *méi(yŏu)* 'there-be-not', as in:

(22) a. *Tā bù lái.*
p3 not come
'He/She does not come'

b. *Tā   méiyǒu   lái.*
    p3   there-be-not come
    "As for him/her, there is not coming."
    'He/She has not come.'

Negation of the proposition, however, is achieved by means of a construction with initial *búshì* 'it is not (the case)'. This construction can be used in denials or rejections (with Rejecting Focus in terms of *TFG1*: 13.4.2.2.), as in:

(23) *Búshì   wǒ yào   qù, shì tāmen jiào   wǒ qù.*
      not-be I   want   go   be they make   me go
      'It is not the case that I WANT to go; it is the case that they MAKE me go.'

8.5. Predicational negation

If the distinction between propositional and predicational negation as suggested in the preceding section can be maintained, we can reserve predicational negation for the type through which the non-occurrence of some SoA is objectively presented. The polarity operator in question would belong to the level of π_2 operators, alongside other operators of objective epistemic modality. This operator would thus operate on the SoA variable "e":

(24) *John is not rich.*
      Decl E: X: Pres neg e: *rich* [A] (*John*)$_\emptyset$

Note that positive predicational polarity could be analysed in a similar way. Our distinction between propositional and predicational positive polarity would now allow us to formulate the following hypotheses:

(25) a. Positive predicational polarity is not formally expressed in natural languages.
     b. Positive propositional polarity is always formally expressed in natural languages, at least through suprasegmental means.

8.6. Negation at the predicate level

8.6.0. Introduction

Negation can also be confined to the predicate as such, as in such cases as:

(26) a. *intelligent*   *unintelligent*
     b. *playing*   *non-playing*
     c. *feathered*   *featherless*

Such forms of "negation" operate locally on the predicate and, when used in a predication, do not yield negative predications or propositions, as can be seen from:

(27)   *That remark was rather unintelligent, wasn't it?*

The fact that a negative tag is attached to the clause in (27) can be taken as a sign that the clause itself is positive.

Predicates designate properties or relations. Predicate negation of this kind creates new properties/relations, the value of which can be computed on the basis of the value of the underlying "positive" property/relation, plus the kind of negation involved. In fact, therefore, this kind of negation produces new properties/relations on the basis of given ones. Grammatically speaking, such creation of new properties/relations can in most cases be described most adequately in terms of predicate formation (cf. Hoffmann 1987: 71-96).

Two types of predicate-formation-through-negation can be distinguished: complementary formation and contrary formation.

8.6.1. Complementary formation

Two properties/relations Φ and neg-Φ are each other's complementaries if, for any entity (x) of which Φ can be predicated at all, it is either the case that $\Phi(x)$ or that neg-$\Phi(x)$. For example, since any person is either married or unmarried, the formation of the derived predicate *unmarried* from *married* is a matter of complementary formation.

8.6.2. Contrary formation

Two properties/relations Φ and neg-Φ are each other's contraries if no entity (x) of which Φ can be predicated at all can be both Φ and neg-Φ at the same time, but it is not excluded that (x) is neither Φ nor neg-Φ. For example, it is in principle excluded that a person is kind and unkind at the same time, but it is not excluded that a person is neither kind nor unkind.

Contrary formation presupposes a dimension or scale on which different degrees or gradations of the property/relation in question can be distinguished. The "positive" predicate will then apply to one end of the scale, the "negative" predicate to the other end:

(28)   [+] Φ ------> neither Φ nor neg-Φ <------ neg-Φ [-]

It is well-known that in natural language contrary formation, the two ends of scales such as (28) are typically non-equivalent. For one simple illustration of this, compare the following:

(29)   English: *deep*   *shallow*
        Dutch: *diep*   *ondiep*

The equivalent of *shallow* is formed on the pattern of *un-deep* in Dutch. This type of contrary formation can be found in many languages. But we do not expect to find many languages in which the equivalent of *deep* takes a form such as *un-shallow*. In some sense, *deep* represents the positive end of the 'deepness' dimension, *shallow* the negative end. It is the negative end of such dimensions which may be formed through contrary predicate formation on the basis of the predicate which designates the positive end, but not the other way around. On the other hand, as illustrated in (29), a language may also have a separate lexical item for designating the negative end of the scale.

8.6.3. Litotes

Hoffmann (1987) presents a detailed discussion of the phenomenon of "litotes" or "negation of the contrary". This concerns expressions such as:

(30) a. *The work of Salvador Dali is not bad.*
      b. *John married a not unattractive girl.*

180 *Polarity distinctions*

Such expressions consist of the local negation of an expression (*bad, unattractive*), which is itself the contrary or polar opposite of some other expression (*good, attractive*). Such composite expressions may be used in a literal sense, as designating the complement of *bad* or *unattractive*. This could be represented as follows:

(31) [+] attractive >_____< unattractive [-]
       not unattractive -------->
                              <------------ not attractive

Very often, however, such expressions are used as an "understatement", with an intended final interpretation 'quite good', 'quite attractive'. This special stylistic effect depends on a number of semantic and pragmatic factors which are discussed in detail by Hoffmann, on the basis of Latin examples.

As for the grammatical description of expressions such as *not unattractive*, Hoffmann suggests a sequence of predicate formation rules along the following lines:

(32) 1. attractive
         CONTRARY FORMATION --->
      2. unattractive
         NEGATION OF THE CONTRARY --->
      3. not unattractive

An alternative to this treatment in terms of predicate formation has been suggested in Hengeveld (1989), as part of his ideas on the layered structure of the clause. Remember that within this layered structure we have four levels of π-operators, the lowest of which (π_1 or predicate operators) have local scope over the predicate. In such a model, while retaining the idea that the creation of *unattractive* is a matter of predicate formation, *not* in such locutions as *not unattractive* could be alternatively analysed as a π_1 operator.

8.7. Term negation or zero quantification

A quite different route for arriving at negative statements is through zero quantification. In *TFG1*: 7.4.2.1. we discussed the treatment of quantifiers in FG. Quantifiers were analysed as term operators, specifying the size "s" of ensembles (where "s" covers the cardinal number function "c" for sets, and the measure function "m" for masses). Different quantifiers were interpreted in terms of size relations between the referent ensemble R, the domain ensemble D, and the universal ensemble U.[5]

Thus, a construction such as (33a) can be analysed as (33b), and the quantifier can be semantically defined as in (33c), which expresses (33d):

(33) a. *All the children are ill.*
    b. Pres e: *ill* [A] (all dmx$_i$: *child* [N])$_\emptyset$
    c. cR = cD
    d. 'the number of children said to be ill (the number of the set R) is identical to the number of children in a previously established domain set D'

Now consider the following series of expressions:

(34) a. *John hates* all *teachers.*
    b. *John hates* five *teachers.*
    c. *John hates* some *teachers.*
    d. *John hates* no *teacher.*

All the elements in roman typeface can be interpreted as giving information on the size of the set of teachers that John hates. This means that the, admittedly marginal, expression *no teacher* can be interpreted as indicating that the set of teachers that John hates is empty, has no members or content. We can thus represent and define the element *no* as follows:

(35) a. Pres e: *hate* [V] (*John*)$_{PosExp}$ ($\emptyset$x$_i$: *teacher* [N])$_{Go}$
    b. cR = $\emptyset$
    c. 'the set of teachers that John hates is empty'

Seen in this way, the element *no* is a term quantifier representing zero quantification. The example (34d) has a non-proportional zero quantifier. We can also have a proportional zero quantifier, as in:

---

5. In this treatment of quantifiers we followed Brown (1985). This paper also —at least implicitly— contains the idea of zero quantification.

(36) a. *John hates none of the teachers.*
   b. (Ø/dmx$_i$: *teacher* [N])
   c. cR (R ⊆ D) = Ø
   d. 'the subset R of teachers that John hates, from among the previously established domain set D, is empty'

In terms of this analysis, we can immediately understand a number of properties of zero quantifier expressions:

First, there is no mystery about them being realized as part of a term, since they are term operators. The negative elements *no* and *none* need not be derived from some element "neg" that has a completely different position in the clause structure. They simply are the non-proportional and proportional zero quantifiers of English. This means that we could just as well write:

(37) a. (no x$_i$: *teacher* [N])   cR = Ø
   b. (none/dmx$_i$: *teacher* [N])   cR (R ⊆ D) = Ø

We now assume that English (like most other languages) has a limited number of synthetic or idiomatic expressions indicating frequently used zero quantified terms. These are the following:

(38) a. *nobody / no-one* = (no x$_i$: human)
   b. *nothing*   = (no x$_i$: inanim)
   c. *nowhere*   = (no x$_i$: place)
   d. *never*   = (no x$_i$: time)

Now consider the following paradigm:

(39)

	NO	SOME	ANY	Q	R	DEM
PERSON	*nobody*	*somebody*	*anybody*	*who*	*who*	
	no-one	*someone*	*anyone*			*this one/that one*
THING	*nothing*	*something*	*anything*	*what*	*which*	*this/that*
PLACE	*nowhere*	*somewhere*	*anywhere*	*where*	*where*	*here/there*
TIME	*never*	*some time*	*ever*	*when*	*when*	*now/then*
MANNER	---	*somehow*	*anyhow*	*how*	*how*	---
REASON	---	---	---	*why*	*why*	---

As this paradigm shows, there is a striking parallelism in "idiomatic" terms for the operations listed. If all these operations came from different sources, such parallelism would be a rather remarkable coincidence. In our approach, however, such parallelism is not unexpected at all, since all the terms listed are the expressions of underlying structures of basically the same form, as is clear from:

(40) a.   (no x_i:<hum>)   *nobody, no-one*
     b.   (some x_i:<hum>)   *somebody, someone*
     c.   (any x_i:<hum>)   *anybody, anyone*
     d.   (Q x_i:<hum>)   *who*
     e.   (R x_i:<hum>)   *who*
     f.   (prox x_i:<hum>)   *this one*

8.8. Term negation versus predication negation

8.8.1. Two strategies for talking about nothing

It follows from the analysis presented above that the following two constructions have quite different underlying predications:

(41) a. *John didn't buy a/any car.*
     b. X: Past neg e: *buy* [V] (*John*)$_{Ag}$ (-si1x_i: *car* [N])$_{Go}$
(42) a. *John bought no car.*
     b. X: Past e: *buy* [V] (*John*)$_{Ag}$ (no x_i: *car* [N])$_{Go}$

Example (41) is a case of predication negation, (42) of term negation. They can be taken as exemplifying two distinct strategies for constructing an empty set:

(43)   Strategy 1:   'Think of any arbitrary car; I tell you that John didn't buy it'
       Strategy 2:   'Think of the set of cars that John might have bought; I tell you that the set is empty (has no members)'

Note that for Strategy 1 it is essential that *a/any car* should be interpreted in a nonspecific rather than in a specific sense.[6] For this reason the second

---

6. For the opposition specific/non-specific see *TFG1*: 7.5.3.

argument of (41b) has been specified with the nonspecific operator "-s". The expression *any car* can only be interpreted as expressing an indefinite nonspecific term. *A car*, on the other hand, could in principle also be assigned a specific reading. This implies that a construction such as:

(44)   *John didn't buy a car.*

can in principle also be assigned the quite different reading paraphrased as 'There is a specific car which John did not buy.' In this case, the underlying representation will be rather like:

(45)   X: Past neg e: *buy* [V] (*John*)$_{Ag}$ (is1x$_i$: *car* [N])$_{Go}$

Note, finally, that if this meaning is to be unambiguously expressed, use can be made of *some* rather than *a*:

(46)   *John didn't buy some car.*

8.8.2. Typological distribution

Since the two strategies for talking about nothing mentioned in the preceding section have much the same communicative effects, we would expect a version of Keenan's (1975) principle of logical variants to determine their typological distribution. Keenan's principle can be formulated as follows:

(47)   If the semantic difference between two constructions X and Y is neutralized in a context C, so that CX and CY are semantically equivalent, then languages may be expected to vary naturally between using X or Y in context C.

And indeed we find natural variation between languages with respect to the constructions which they use to refer to empty ensembles. Thus, Dahl (1979) states that languages may have one or more of the following construction types for this purpose:

(48) a.   *John did not buy a car.*
     b.   *John did not buy any car.*
     c.   *John bought no car.*
     d.   *John did not buy no car.*

In (48a) an indefinite determiner *a* is used which, in the relevant case, can be assigned a nonspecific interpretation; (48b) has a special nonspecific indefinite determiner; (48c) is a case of zero quantification; and (48d) is a case of zero quantification with a redundant negative propositional operator.

As predicted by Keenan's principle, some languages have only one of these construction types for talking about empty ensembles, others have two or more with either specialized or (partially) overlapping meanings. Let us look at these construction types one by one.

Some languages have only constructions of type (48a); they have a general predicational operator neg, and a general indefinite determiner undifferentiated for specific and nonspecific readings. Such languages face the danger of systematic ambiguity between specific and nonspecific readings of the relevant constructions.

Hindi-Urdu (according to Davison 1978) is a case in point. There is a general negative predication operator *nah(ii)*, which combines with indefinite terms in such constructions as the following:

(49)   *Aaj   kooii   nah aayaa.*
        today   someone not came
        (a) 'Today someone didn't come.' (specific)
        (b) 'Today no-one came.' (nonspecific)

In such languages we may expect there to be certain ways of disambiguating this construction type. According to Davison, the following factors tend to disambiguate the construction one way or the other:

(i) indefinite terms intended for specific readings tend to be more specified than just 'someone'; they rather take such forms as 'some person', 'some man', etc.;

(ii) indefinite terms intended for nonspecific readings are placed as closely as possible to the negator (which itself has a fixed position in the clause);

(iii) if the indefinite term is intended to have a nonspecific interpretation, it may be marked by certain emphatic particles.

As another example, consider Usan (Reesink 1987). Usan, again, has no zero quantification (and thus also lacks terms translating as 'nobody', 'nothing', etc.). Therefore, a construction of the following form is potentially ambiguous:

(50) *Munon ger me is-au.*
man one not descend
(a) 'One man did not come down.' (specific)
(b) 'No-one came down.' (nonspecific)

However, reading (a) may be enforced by placing emphasis on *ger*, and reading (b) may be enforced by placing emphasis on *me*.

The generalization seems to be, then, that in languages which only have constructions of type (48a), with the concomitant danger of systematic ambiguity between specific and nonspecific readings, this ambiguity may be avoided or resolved through differential focusing of one or the other element in the construction.

In constructions like (48b) we find an indefinite determiner *any* which can be interpreted as having specialized nonspecific meaning. The combination of a predicate operator neg with such a nonspecific-indefinite determiner is thus unambiguous, and the construction is an effective means of talking about empty ensembles. As we saw in *TFG1*: 7.5.3., however, it is rather exceptional for a language to have specialized nonspecific indefinite determiners of this kind.

Note that although the distribution of *any* and its congeners is restricted to certain contexts, it is not correct to say that *any* is restricted to negative contexts. This is clear from such examples as:

(51) *Do you have any books on Iceland?*
(52) *Any book on Iceland will do.*

Correspondingly, *any* cannot be viewed as the expression of *some* in a negative context. Constructions of type (48b) can therefore not be analysed as the expression of such underlying structures as:

(53) neg(*John bought some car*)

Rather, we should regard *some* as having a specific-indefinite value, whereas *any* has a nonspecific-indefinite value. This explains why such oppositions as the following are possible:

(54) a. *John didn't buy some car.*
 b. *John didn't buy any car.*

In languages which have constructions of type (48c), exemplifying zero quantification, these constructions unambiguously take care of the nonspecific negative. This implies that in such languages constructions of type (48a) are in principle free to take care of the negative specific case. This situation obtains in Dutch, where we have such oppositions as the following:

(55) a. *Jan   heeft   geen   schilderij   verkocht.*
         John   has   no   painting   sold
         'John has sold no painting'
   b.   *Jan   heeft   een schilderij   niet verkocht.*
         John   has   a   painting   not sold
         'John has not sold a painting'
         = 'There is a painting that John has not sold'

In order to account for this type of opposition, Kraak (1966) distinguished two indefinite articles *een*: *een$_1$* (specific), and *een$_2$* (nonspecific). This allowed him to say that (55b) contains the specific *een$_1$*, and that this specific-indefinite article blocks neg-incorporation, which in the case of (55a) combines neg + *een$_2$* into *geen*. Our analysis is different from this, while accounting for the same semantic differences. In our view, (55a) and (55b) have quite different underlying representations, based as they are on two different strategies of talking about empty ensembles:

(56) a. *Jan heeft geen schilderij verkocht.*
   b.   X: Pres Perf e: *verkopen* [V] (*Jan*)$_{Ag}$ (Ø x$_i$: *schilderij* [N])$_{Go}$
(57) a. *Jan heeft een schilderij niet verkocht.*
   b.   X: Pres Perf neg e: *verkopen* [V] (*Jan*)$_{Ag}$ (is1x$_i$: *schilderij* [N])$_{Go}$

Construction (56a), as is the case with any type of zero quantification, unambiguously signals nonspecific meaning; (57a) is thus free to specialize in the specific reading, and this will usually be the only possible reading for this construction type.

Finally, many languages have constructions of type (48d), with double, redundant negation. Such constructions occur in certain English dialects:

(58) a. *I won't pay you nothing.*
   b.   *I don't need nobody.*
   c.   *I'm not going nowhere.*

Judging from the form of these constructions, the easiest way to account for them is to assume that they involve a sort of spurious contamination of zero quantification and predicational negation.

9. Coordination

9.0. Introduction[1]

In this chapter I give a survey of different types of *coordination* and of how these can be treated in FG. First, I give a general characterization of coordination and a survey of the different devices used for expressing coordinative relationships (9.1.). Then, I consider different methods of describing coordinated structures (9.2.), and opt for the Direct Approach to the description of coordination. In terms of this approach I then present a typology of coordinative constructions, the main distinguishing parameter being the nature of the members which are combined in the coordinative construction. For each type, the way in which it can be treated within FG is described (9.3.-9.5.).

9.1. Coordination defined

Coordination can be generally defined as follows:[2]

(1) A coordination is a construction consisting of two or more members which are functionally equivalent, bound together at the same level of structure by means of a linking device.

As a general symbolization for coordinations we can use the following schema:

(2)
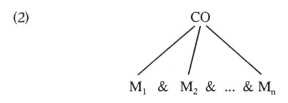

---

1. For this chapter cf. Dik (1968, 1980: chapter 9), Mallinson—Blake (1981: chapter 4), Payne (1985), Moutaouakil (1988: chapter 3).
2. Cf. Dik (1968: 25) for more detailed discussion.

where "CO" is the coordination as a whole, the "M"s are the members ($n > 1$), and "&" symbolizes the "linking device" by means of which the members are combined.

As definition (1) says, there may be two or more members to the coordination. Compare:

(3) a. *John and Peter*
 b. *John, Peter, Charles, ..., and Eugene*

These members are combined at the same structural level, i.e., none of the members M is in any way subordinate to, or dependent on any of the others. They are all on a par, and equal members of the coordination CO.

The "linking device" may be covert, in which case we speak of *juxtaposition*,[3] as in:

(4) a. *Men, women, children - all ran away in panic.*
 b. *This only takes five, six minutes.*

or the linking device may be overt. In the latter case, it will consist of one or more *coordinators* which serve to indicate the coordinative relation between the members:

(5) a. *men, women,* and *children*
 b. *five* or *six minutes*
 c. both *men* and *women*
 d. either *the one* or *the other*

Some coordinators allow for only two members (*binary coordinators*). For example, the English coordinator *for* necessarily coordinates two members:

(6) *He stayed at home,* for *he was ill.*

If more members seem to be present, there must be some hierarchical relationship between them:

---

3. Many languages predominantly use juxtaposition for the expression of coordinative relationships. See Mithun (1988).

(7)   *He stayed at home,* for (*he was ill* and *didn't think the matter was very important*).

As indicated in (7) the second member of the binary coordination consists itself of a coordination. The structural schema is thus like (8) rather than like (9):

(8)
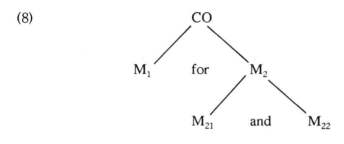

(9)
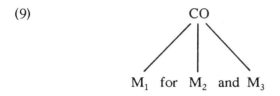

The binary coordinators of English are the causal coordinator *for* and the adversative coordinator *but*.

Other (*n-ary*) coordinators may be used to conjoin more than two members, as in (3b). The n-ary coordinators of English are the combinatory coordinator *and*, its negative counterpart *nor*, the alternative coordinator *or*, and their different correlative counterparts which may be used to signal different degrees of emphasis (*both...and, neither...nor, either...or*) (cf. Dik 1968: chapter 12; Payne 1985).

Coordinators may be *prepositive*, as in (10a), or *postpositive*, as in (10b):

(10) a1. M_1 co M_2 a2. M_1 co M_2 co M_3
     b1. M_1 M_2 co   b2. M_1 M_2 co M_3 co

When more than one coordinator is used, the coordinators may be *repetitive* (as in ...*and*...*and*...) or *correlative* (as in *both*...*and*...). For more discussion of these different expression patterns, see Dik (1968: chapter 4).

As demonstrated in Mithun (1988), coordinators may have a variety of historical sources. At the term level, the most common sources are a comitative adposition (*John with Bill*) or an adverbial element meaning 'also, as well' (*John, Bill also*). At the clausal level, the most common source is provided by discourse connectors with values such as 'and then', 'subsequently'. Once grammaticalized as coordinators, such elements may generalize either from the clausal level to subclausal constituents, or from the subclausal level to clausal constituents. Their prepositive or postpositive status may often be understood in terms of the elements from which, and the route along which they developed.

Rather important in definition (1) is that the members of the coordination should be *functionally equivalent*. Many approaches to coordination require that the members should be *categorially* equivalent (i.e. should be constituents belonging to the same category). However, the internal categorial structure of coordinated members may differ, as long as their external function is the same. For some examples, consider:

(11) Peter *and* several of his friends *left early.*
 [proper name and plural term coordinated, but both Agent and Subject of the clause]
(12) *He felt quite* happy *and* at ease *in his new office.*
 [adjective and prepositional group coordinated, but both functioning as predicative adjuncts]

As far as coordinated terms are concerned, functional equivalence means that members should have the same semantic, syntactic, and pragmatic functions. The following examples show what goes wrong when such equivalences do not hold. In (13) terms with different semantic functions have been coordinated:

(13) a. *John went to the party (Dir) *and* by car (Manner).
 b. **John cut the meat* with a knife (Instr) *and* in the kitchen (Loc).
 c. *John read the whole night (Dur) *and* a great novel (Go).

In the following examples terms which do have the same semantic function, but differ in syntactic function, have been coordinated:

(14) a. *John (AgSubj) *and* by the man (Ag) *kissed the girl.*
 b. *I gave John (RecObj) *and* to the girl (Rec) *a book.*

Coordinating Topic and Focus terms likewise leads to bad results:

(15) A: *Who did John meet at the station?*
     B: *John (Top) met the BOSS (Foc) at the station.*
     B: **John and the BOSS met at the station.*

There appears to be one systematic exception to this principle of functional equivalence: Question-words can often be coordinated even if they have different semantic functions. Compare:

(16) a. When *and* where *did you find it?*
     b. **I found it* last week *and* in the library.
(17) a. Why *and* with whom *did you go to Paris?*
     b. **I went to Paris* because I needed a break *and* with my wife.

Apparently, the assignment of Focus function in such cases overrides the functional dissimilarity of such terms.[4]

The requirement of overall functional equivalence of coordinated terms implies that the "coordination test" can yield important information on the functional (dis-)similarity of constituents.[5]

9.2. Ways of describing coordinate constructions

Coordinate constructions in which less than full clauses are coordinated have traditionally been described as reductions of coordinated full clause structures. For example, a coordination such as (18a) was described as a reduction of the coordinated full clauses in (18b):

(18) a. *John and Peter left the office.*
     b. *John left the office and Peter left the office.*

---

4. Cf. Schachter (1977) and Dik (1980: chapter 9). Moutaouakil (1988) shows that largely identical constraints hold for Arabic, including the possibility of coordinating Q-words even if they do not have the same semantic function.

5. See Pinkster (1972), Vester (1983), Pinkster (1988) for applications of this test.

We find this reductionist analysis all through the history of linguistics, under such names as Contraction and Ellipsis. It was revived in Transformational Grammar in such transformational rules as Conjunction Reduction and Gapping (cf. Dik 1968: chapters 5-6).

In Dik (1968) is was shown that for some types of coordination such a Reductionist Approach is not feasible: in all those cases in which the coordinated constituents form some kind of higher-level unit, the Reductionist Approach fails to provide an adequate analysis. Compare:

(19) a. *John and Mary form a nice pair.*
 b. **John forms a nice pair and Mary forms a nice pair.*

Such cases prove that, alongside full clause coordination we also need "local" constituent coordination. It was further argued that for those cases for which the Reductionist Approach is in principle feasible, it is not very plausible. For example, a construction such as:

(20) *John and Peter and Mary buy, repair, and sell antique toys, tools, and furniture.*

would, on the Reductionist Approach, have to be derived through conflating 27 distinct sentences, starting with (21:1) and ending with (21:27):

(21) (1) *John buys antique toys.*
 ...
 ...
 (27) *Mary sells antique furniture.*

The Reductionist Approach also seems inadequate in terms of psychological adequacy. Consider the following example:

(22) *When we consider the various implications of this law, taking into account the adverse effects it may have on family income, we are bound to conclude that it is detrimental rather than beneficial for both the rich and the poor.*

It is implausible that such a construction, given its complexity, should be created by first taking two full sentences with *the rich* and *the poor* in final position, and then conflating them into (22). Rather, what we want to account for is that S, when arriving at a certain "slot" in the construction of a clause, has the option of multiplying this slot locally so as to result in a coordinated series of items.

Such an approach to coordination may be termed the "Direct Approach". In the Direct Approach we try to define a coordination of sub-clausal constituents in terms of rules which directly multiply such constituents locally, in the position in which they occur in the clause structure.

Apart from avoiding the implausible implications of the Reductionist Approach, the Direct Approach is more compatible with the spirit of FG, which avoids structural changes and deletion of specified material wherever this is possible (cf. *TFG1*: 1.7.).

Technically speaking, the Direct Approach requires a rule through which a given item in underlying clause structure can be locally multiplied into n occurrences of the same item. Consider the following simple example:

(23)   *John, Peter, and Charles left the office.*

In order to describe this structure we start from the predicate frame for *leave*, and multiply the Agent argument into three occurrences of the same:

(24)   leave [V] $(x_1)_{Ag}$ $(x_2)_{Go}$
                  & $(x_1)_{Ag}$
                  & $(x_1)_{Ag}$

This structure can then be used to generate (23) directly through term insertion and the appropriate expression devices. When binary coordination is involved only one copy may be made of the relevant item; with n-ary coordination, n may in principle be set at any positive value although, obviously, constructions may become unwieldy if this parameter is set too high.

In order to achieve such multiplication we can make use of a simple *rule schema* of the form:

(25)   M --> M_1 & M_2 & ... & M_n (n > 1)

where M indicates the item multiplied, and "&" symbolizes the coordinative relation, without prejudging the particular form in which it will be expressed.

In the Direct Approach we assume that this rule schema may be activated at different places and various levels in underlying clause structure, and thus lead to local coordinations of quite diverse types. No doubt there will be language-dependent restrictions on the types of constituents that can be so coordinated. Some such restrictions will be mentioned below.

It has often been assumed that only *constituents* can be coordinated with each other. But the following argument shows that this restriction is impossible to maintain. Consider:

(26)   *John* washed the dishes *and* cleaned the sink.

On the hypothesis that only constituents can be coordinated, this construction would provide an argument for the assumption that the predicate plus its object form one constituent (a Verb Phrase or VP). But now consider:

(27)   John washed *and* Mary dried *the dishes.*

This construction now provides an argument for the assumption that the subject plus the predicate forms one constituent. Since no theory of grammar claims (indeed, can claim) that subject+predicate *and* predicate+object form unified constituents at the same time, the hypothesis that only constituents can be coordinated cannot be upheld without very powerful additional assumptions. In the Transformational Grammar tradition, one way out has been to claim that such constructions as (27) are ungrammatical; but such constructions can be shown to be quite normal in a variety of languages. Another way out is to assume that they are generated transformationally from coordinated full sentences; but this solution relies heavily on the Reductionist Approach which, as argued above, is in many ways implausible.

For this reason I will assume that in the Direct Approach not only single constituents, but also pairs, triples, etc. of constituents can be coordinated (i.e., multiplied locally). If only single constituents are so multiplied, I will speak of *simple coordination* (9.3.); if simple coordination applies to different constituents within the same construction, this may be called *multiple coordination* (9.4.); if coordination applies to pairs, triples (in general, n-tuples) of items, this may be called *simultaneous coordination* (9.5.).

9.3. Simple coordination

9.3.1. Coordination of sentences and clauses

At first sight, coordination of full clauses is not problematic. We simply have two or more clauses, which keep their full integrity, in a coordinate relationship of either juxtaposition or overt coordination:

(28) a. *John went out for a walk, Mary watched television.*
b. *John went out for a walk and Mary watched television.*

Nevertheless, we have a problem here. For various reasons it is necessary to distinguish between the clause proper on the one hand, and "extra-clausal constituents" (ECCs) on the other. ECCs are constituents which precede, follow, or interrupt the clause proper, and are associated with it in a loose, pragmatically definable manner. In chapter 17 the various categories of ECCs will be discussed in detail. Now the fact is that many of these ECCs can be part of one member of a coordinated construction, as in:

(29) a. *I don't believe a word of what you say and* frankly, *I don't want to believe it.*
b. John, *come here and* Peter, *stay where you are.*
c. *Finally I got a chance to give my opinion and* well, to tell you the truth, *I simply didn't know what to say.*
d. *I regard the matter as closed and*, as for the students, *we'll certainly find some other solution.*

From these facts we conclude that the units which can be coordinated in this way exceed the domain of the clause, taking certain ECCs in their scope. In 5.1.5. we saw that in the area of subordination, as well, there is a need to make a distinction between the clause proper, and the unit consisting of the clause and its associated ECCs. This was because, if clauses are embedded, the ECCs cannot (or cannot so easily) be embedded along with them (cf. Bolkestein 1990b, 1992):

(30) **John said that,* well, to tell him the truth, *he simply didn't know what to say.*

Thus, when embedded clauses are coordinated, it is difficult or downright impossible to take the ECCs along:

(31) **John said that he finally got a chance to give his opinion and that,* well, to tell him the truth, *he simply didn't know what to say.*

The unit consisting of the clause plus its associated ECCs I will call the *sentence*, as distinct from the clause proper.[6] Note that, when there are no ECCs, sentence and clause coincide. We can now say that sentences can be coordinated, but not (easily) embedded, and therefore not coordinated in embedded positions, whereas clauses can.

Clauses can obviously be coordinated both when they have independent status, as illustrated in (28), and when they are embedded under a predicate of verbal action, as in:

(32) a. *John said that he didn't feel well and that he wanted to go home.*
     b. *John asked whether Mary felt all right and whether she wanted to come along to the party.*

In chapter 5 we argued (following Bolkestein 1976, 1990a) that the embedded constituents in (32a-b) indeed contain full clauses, including their illocutionary operator(s).

Coordination of (independent or dependent) clauses in general requires that the coordinated members have the same illocution (cf. Moutaouakil 1988). But there are certain conditions in which coordination of clauses with different illocutions is not fully excluded. Consider:

(33) a. *Everybody seems to have gone and where is Mary?*
     b. *Everybody seems to be there but where is Mary?*
     c. *I don't feel like going there and why should I?*

Thus, interrogative clauses can be coordinated with preceding declarative clauses. More idiomatic are such examples as the following:

(34) a. *Come here and I'll hit you on the head!*
     b. *Stop or I shoot!*

In these cases an imperative clause is coordinated with a declarative one. The overall meaning is idiomatic, however, in the sense that these examples cannot be simply paraphrased as in (35); rather, they require a conditional paraphrase:

---

6. Moutaouakil (1988) makes a similar distinction between coordination of sentences and coordination of predications. In Arabic, as in the English examples given above, constructions consisting of Theme+Clause can be coordinated, even though Themes can presumably not (or not easily) be embedded.

(35) a. *Do X and Y is the case.*
     b. *Do X or Y is the case.*
(36) a. *If you do X then Y is the case.*
     b. *If you don't do X then Y is the case.*

We can say that such coordinations are heterogeneous as to illocution. A general principle seems to be that such heterogenous coordinations cannot be embedded (cf. Bolkestein 1990b, 1992):

(37)   **He said that come here and he should hit him on the head.*

The following factors might explain this fact. Embedding requires a higher speech act verb which is consonant with the illocution of the clause to be embedded. However, it is difficult to find higher speech act verbs which are compatible with both illocutions. Note the difference between:

(38) a. *He said that everybody seemed to be there but where was Mary?*
     b. *He said that everybody seemed to be there but where - he asked - was Mary?*

According to the pattern of (38b) even the more idiomatic cases are marginally embeddable:

(39)   *He told him to stop or else - he said - he would shoot.*

Moutaouakil (1988) argues that coordinated sentences or clauses should be pragmatically congruent in the sense that they must carry the same type of Focus function or must have the same kind of internal Focus distribution. This is rather clear in Arabic, in which there are clear formal and positional differences between New Focus and Contrastive Focus. But the constraint can also be seen to be operative in English examples such as:

(40) a. *JOHN is nice, and BILL is nice, too.*
     b. **JOHN is nice, and Bill is NICE, too.*
(41)   *What happened?*
     a. *JOHN fell off his bike, and BILL started SCREAMing.*
     b. **JOHN fell off his bike, and Bill started SCREAMing.*

In both cases, when *Bill* is not focalized in a way parallel to *John* in the first conjunct, the result is hardly acceptable.

9.3.2. Coordination of propositions and predications

Predicates such as *believe* take propositional terms for their second argument: terms specified by a propositional structure which designates the possible fact believed. Such propositional terms can be coordinated, as is clear from:

(42)   *John believes that ants lay eggs and that turtles give milk.*

Predicates such as *force* take predicational terms for their second argument. These terms specify the SoA that a person is forced to implement. Such predicational terms can be coordinated, as in:

(43)   *The burglar forced Peter to open the safe and to hand over the money.*

That the difference between propositional and predicational terms is relevant also to coordination patterns can be seen through the following arguments. Compare:

(44) a.   *John saw Peter come down the stairs.*
b.   *John saw that Peter was sad.*

In chapter 5 we saw that the predicate *see* in (44a) takes a predicational complement, designating a SoA which John is said to have directly perceived, while in (44b) it takes a propositional complement, designating mental perception, i.e. a mental inference on the basis of something perceived. This difference can be used to explain the fact that these two distinct complement types cannot be coordinated:

(45)   **John saw Peter come down the stairs and that he was sad.*

This is immediately accounted for if we assume that *see*, on these two readings, has two distinct predicate frames, roughly

(46) a.   *see* [V] (x: <hum>)$_{ProcExp}$ (X: <proposition>)$_{Go}$
b.   *see* [V] (x: <hum>)$_{ProcExp}$ (e: <predication>)$_{Go}$

and if it is further assumed that coordination of propositional and predicational terms comes about by direct multiplication of the second argument positions of (46a-b). It then follows that either propositional complements or predicational complements can be so multiplied, but no mixtures of propositional and predicational terms.

For a similar argument compare the predicate *persuade* with the predicates *believe* and *force*, the differences in complementation patterns between which were discussed in 5.4.1. *Believe* can only take propositional complements ("X believed that Y"); *force* can only take predicational complements ("X forced Y to Z"). *Persuade*, however, can take either propositional or predicational complements, as in:

(47) a.   *John persuaded Peter that turtles give milk.*
           (propositional: possible fact)
     b.   *John persuaded Peter to open the safe.*
           (predicational: state of affairs)

Now note the fact that the two types of complement cannot be coordinated:

(48)   **John persuaded Peter that turtles give milk and to open the safe.*

We shall account for these facts in the following way: the predicate *persuade* has two predicate frames, one similar to *believe*, and one similar to *force*:[7]

(49) a.   *persuade* [V] $(x_1:<\text{hum}>)_{Ag}$ $(x_2:<\text{hum}>)_{Go}$ $(X:<\text{proposition}>)_{Ref}$
     b.   *persuade* [V] $(x_1:<\text{hum}>)_{Ag}$ $(x_2:<\text{hum}>)_{Go}$ $(e:<\text{predication}>)_{Ref}$

Again, when local multiplication is applied to the third arguments of these frames, the unwanted "mixed" coordination of type (48) is excluded.

9.3.3. Coordination of terms

It seems that in most languages single terms (arguments and satellites) can be coordinated with each other, as in:

---

7. The Subject and Object assignment possibilities are consistent with the Goal status of the person persuaded; "Ref" indicates the propositional content or the state of affairs with respect to which the Agent persuades the Goal.

(50) a. *John and Mary left.*
b. *I saw John and Mary leave.*
c. *I arrived with John and with Mary.*

As long as such terms each entertain an independent relation with the predicate, this type of coordination can easily be captured by direct multiplication, as was shown above (see 9.2.). However, there is one quite complex problem concerning term coordination. To begin with, many languages have differences such as those between:

(51) a. *I bought a present for John and for Mary.*
b. *I bought a present for John and Mary.*

In (51a) the semantic function is expressed on each coordinated term, in (51b) it is only expressed once for the whole series. If (51b) can still be taken to mean that I bought a present for each of John and Mary taken separately, then the difference can be seen as being due to alternative applications of the expression rules; if, on the other hand, (51b) necessarily means that I bought a present for the pair of John and Mary taken together, then it requires a solution to a second aspect of our problem.

This concerns the difference between such coordinated terms as those in:

(52) a. *The king and the queen are intelligent.*
b. *The king and the queen are a happy couple.*

The most usual interpretation of (52a) is that the king and the queen are each said to be intelligent. It is a straightforward case of term coordination, which can be accounted for by means of the rule schema given above. In the case of (52b), however, the predicate *(be) a happy couple* is necessarily predicated of the pair constituted by the king and the queen. For this, the separate multiplication of term positions is not adequate, since the terms do not entertain a separate relation to the predicate, as in (52a), but form a higher-level unit which as a whole constitutes a single argument to the predicate: in (52b) the expression *the king and the queen* represents one unified single argument of which 'being a happy couple' is predicated. We thus have coordination inside a term rather than coordination of terms. How can this be captured by the Direct Approach?

What we want to be able to express is that, starting from the separate terms *the king* and *the queen*, a higher level unit can be formed which can be used to refer to the entity constituted by the pair formed by the entities designated by the two terms:

(53)   (x_i: {(*the king*) *and* (*the queen*)})

It is to this complex term that the predicate is applied:[8]

(54)   {(*a happy couple*)} (x_i: {(*the king*) *and* (*the queen*)})

The combination {(*the king*) *and* (*the queen*)} in fact has the status of a compound term predicate, which is used as a restrictor in (53). We can thus solve this problem by assuming that two or more terms can be input to a rule of "coordinated term predicate formation" which may output compound expressions which can be used as restrictors within terms.

9.3.4. Coordination of predicates

A rather more difficult case is formed by constructions in which only the predicates are coordinated, as in:

(55) a.   *John* buys and sells *second hand cars.*
     b.   *John* opened and closed *the window several times.*

These constructions provide a difficulty for the FG model as so far developed, because, given the nature of predicate frames, such predicates as *buy* and *sell* each have their own predicate frame, and there is no open predicate slot which could be easily multiplied into a coordinated series of predicates as we did with terms.

In order to solve this problem we can make use of the "predicate variable" introduced in *TFG1*: 3.1., following Hengeveld (1992) and Keizer (1992a). With the predicate variable made explicit, the predicate frame of *buy*, for example, takes the following form:

(56)   (f_i: *buy* [V]) (x_1: <hum>)$_{Ag}$ (x_2)$_{Go}$

---

8. Note that, at least in English, the whole term behaves like a plural term. One might expect other languages to have singular agreement here.

In (56) the variable f_i represents the relation that is specified by the predicate *buy*. More generally, predicate variables can be seen as designators of the properties and relations that can be specified by predicates. At a level more abstract than the predicate frame we can thus envisage a *predicate schema* of the following form:

(57) $(f_i) (x_1) (x_2) \ldots (x_n)$

As an abstract template for nuclear predications, this schema may be compared to the term schema. We can now say that the predicate frames in the lexicon instantiate the predicate schema.

The predicate variable in the predicate schema can be used as a target for coordinative multiplication, in order to arrive at such constructions as (55):

(58) $(f_i) (x_1: <\text{hum}>)_{Ag} (x_2)_{Go}$
        & (f_j)

We may now take (58) as signalling that in the positions (f_i) and (f_j) we may select two predicates from the lexicon which have the same quantitative and qualitative valency. *Buy* and *sell* are such predicates, and can thus be applied in the coordinated structure given in (59):

(59) $(f_i: buy\ [V])$ & $(f_j: sell\ [V]) (x_i: John)_{Ag} (x_j: second\text{-}hand\ cars)_{Go}$

Note that this type of predicate coordination should be distinguished from cases such as:

(60)   *John buys cars and repairs them.*

As the pronoun *them* shows, in such cases there is a second argument position to the second predicate, and therefore it is a case of coordination of predicate + term rather than of just the predicate. Should we find a construction such as (60) in a language which allows zero anaphora in this case, the difference between direct coordination of predicates and simultaneous coordination of predicates + terms may be harder to tell, as in (61a). This is especially the case in Prefield languages, as in (61b):

(61) a. *John buys cars and repairs Ø.*
     b. *John cars buys and Ø repairs.*

Coordinations of predicates + terms will be discussed below.

In all examples of predicate coordination given so far I have assumed that the coordinated predicates retain their independent status, and that the arguments entertain separate relationships with these predicates. We should also envisage the possibility, however, that such conjoined predicates fuse into a single semantic or conceptual unit, as when 'buy and sell' were interpreted as designating one, compound activity. In such a case we would rather analyse such compound predicates by means of a predicate formation rule with the effect shown in:

(62)   Input: $(f_i: buy$ [V]$)$ $(x_1: $<hum>$)_{Ag}$ $(x_2)_{Go}$
        $(f_j: sell$ [V]$)$ $(x_1: $<hum>$)_{Ag}$ $(x_2)_{Go}$
        Output: $(f_k: buy$ [V] $and\ sell$ [V]$)$ $(x_1: $<hum>$)_{Ag}$ $(x_2)_{Go}$

Given the device of the predicate variable, actual predicates can be seen as restrictors on this variable. In the output of (62) we have a case of coordination of such predicate restrictors: the coordinated combination specifies one relation, f_k, *buy 'n sell*. In the next section we take a closer look at coordination of, or inside restrictors.

9.3.5. Coordination of or inside restrictors

We have already encountered two examples of coordination in relation to restrictors. We do indeed need this type of coordination for a variety of construction types. However, we have to distinguish between coordination of term restrictors (= coordination of properties and relations) and coordination inside term restrictors. Let us start with coordination of term restrictors. Consider, for example, the following pair (see *TFG1*: 6.2.):

(63) a.   *They have a beautiful old house.*
     b.   *They have a beautiful, old house.*

While in (63a) the restrictor *beautiful* is stacked onto the restrictor *old*, in (63b), with appropriate prosodic contour, these restrictors are rather coordinated by juxtaposition. In the latter case there is no hierarchical difference implied among the specified properties. The difference between (63a) and (63b) comes out in the following representations, in which, for reasons to be clarified below, we now write the predicate variables as well:

(64) a.   (i 1 x_i: *house* [N]: (f_i: *beautiful* [A]): (f_j: *old* [A]))
   b.   (i 1 x_i: *house* [N]: (f_i: *beautiful* [A]) & (f_j: *old* [A]))

In (64a) we thus have a case of stacking of restrictor properties (f_i) and (f_j), in (64b) a case of coordination of these properties. The coordination of term restrictors thus in effect comes out as a coordination of predicates in attributive position.

In terms of the difference between coordination of terms and coordination of term restrictors we can now also consider the famous problem of the difference between disjunctive questions such as:[9]

(65) a.   *Do you want COFFEE or TEA?*
         presupposition: you want either coffee or tea.
         question: tell me which of the two you want.
   b.   *Do you want coffee or tea?*
         presupposition: you want something.
         question: is the something you want correctly described as 'coffee or tea'?

Note that there is a prosodic difference between (65a) and (65b). Possible answers to (65a) are *Coffee*, or *Tea*. Possible answers to (65b), on the other hand, are *Yes* or *No*. (65b) is a Yes-No question which contains an internal disjunction of the description of 'that which you want'. The difference can be made clear in the following representations:

(66) a.   Int E: X: Pres e: [*want* [V] (*you*) (x_i: (f_i: *coffee*))$_{Go}$ *or* (x_j: (f_j: *tea*))$_{Go}$]
   b.   Int E: X: Pres e: [*want* [V] (*you*) (x_i: (f_i: *coffee*) *or* (f_j: *tea*))$_{Go}$]

In other words, we analyse (65a) as a form of term disjunction, (65b) as a form of restrictor disjunction. (66b) now appropriately expresses that the question is whether you want something x_i such that x_i has either the property 'coffee' or the property 'tea'.

However, coordination of independent restrictors should be distinguished from compound restrictor formation (a form of predicate formation). In the latter, but not in the former case, the coordinated items constitute a unit which designates one, complex property. Compare:

---

9. Disjunctive questions will be more fully discussed in 12.2.

(67) a. *In the shop we saw black and white dresses.*
b. *In the shop we saw black-and-white dresses.*

In (67a) it is expressed that we saw black dresses and white dresses. In (67b), on the other hand, we saw only one type of dress with the property 'black-and-white'. In the latter case, a compound derived adjectival predicate *black-and-white* has been formed on the basis of the input adjectives *black* and *white*. The difference can be brought out as follows:

(68) a. (i m x_i: *dress* [N]: (f_i: *black* [A]) *and* (f_j: *white* [A]))
b. (i m x_i: *dress* [N]: (f_i: *black* [A] *and white* [A]))

If we take a predicate to be an instantiation of a predicate variable, then in (68a) we have coordinated two distinct predicates, while in (68b) we have used two predicates to create a compound new predicate, in the manner specified in (62) above. The first is then a matter of predicate coordination, the latter of compound predicate formation.

9.3.6. Coordination of operators and functions

To a limited extent, coordination can also apply to minor, non-lexical categories such as operators and functions. The possibility of having such types of coordination is more strongly language-dependent,[10] and often leads to rather "bookish" construction types. It seems to be more freely possible to the extent that the relevant operators or functions are expressed in independent words, and combine with the same kinds of constituents. To the extent that this kind of coordination is possible at all, it can be captured in the Direct Approach by direct multiplication of the relevant operator or function slot.

In considering this possibility care should be taken that the examples are cases of *use* rather than *mention* of linguistic material. In cases of mention, almost any two items can be coordinated, as in:

(69) a. *Did you say "re-" or "deceive"?*
b. *Did you say "in-" or "onto"?*

---

10. Cf. Mallinson—Blake (1981: 197-201). Much in this section, including some of the examples, is due to these authors.

This kind of metalinguistic coordination is left out of account here.

Among the *term operators*, numerals and demonstratives can usually be freely coordinated with each other:

(70) a. *Could you lend me* three or four *dollars?*
b. *Do you want* this or that *book?*

Coordination of definiteness/indefiniteness operators becomes more difficult:

(71) *Do you want* a or the *record by Elvis Presley?*

Semantic functions can be directly coordinated if they are expressed by independent adpositions which, if they govern any case at all, govern the same case:

(72) a. *They gave their lives* to and for *God and their country.*
b. *They ran* into and out of *the house.*

If the prepositions do not govern the same case forms, coordination becomes difficult or even impossible:

(73) *Romani in   et   ex   Asia(m)   transierunt.
     Romans into and out-of   Asia   cross-over
     'The Romans crossed over into and out of Asia.'

(73) was probably ungrammatical in Latin because *in* (with a directional sense) governs the accusative, while *ex* governs the ablative case.

Even certain π-*operators* can be directly coordinated if they are expressed by independent words taking the same type of complement and operate at the same level:

(74) *John* may but won't *ask his friends for help.*

But with distinct complement types this becomes impossible:

(75) *Bill has and will *underestimate the opposition.*

See Mallinson and Blake (1981: 197-201) for further discussion of the (im)possibility of coordinating minor constituents.

9.4. Multiple coordination

If several slots in the underlying clause structure are multiplied independently we may speak of *multiple coordination*. The following is an example of coordination in the Subj and Obj positions:

(76)   *John and Bill bought a book and a newspaper.*

In such cases of multiple coordination the number of items in the independently coordinated slots need not be the same. Thus, we can also get:

(77) a.   *John and Bill and Charles bought a book.*
 b.   *John and Bill bought a book, a newspaper, and some envelopes.*

Since multiple coordination involves independent coordinative multiplication of positions which may be so multiplied, a great variety of types of multiple coordination may be distinguished, but the phenomenon as such does not add qualitatively to the notion of simple coordination.

It is useful, however, to have a look at certain cases involving coordination of predicates and terms, since these provide certain special problems. Consider a construction such as:

(78)   *John took a plane and went to New York.*

In approaches in which the combination of Verb + Complement is considered to constitute one constituent (a VP) one will simply say that this is a matter of VP-coordination. However, FG, does not recognize a constituent of the VP type, and therefore (78) cannot be described as resulting from a coordination of VPs. However, neither can it be handled as a matter of multiple coordination of predicates and terms, since the argument structures of the two conjuncts need not be the same. Suppose we tried to get this kind of construction by means of a schema such as:

(79) $(f_i) (x_i)$ (x_j)
      & (f_j) & (x_j^*)

The asterisk here indicates that the term position has been copied but that the term to be inserted should be different from the one inserted in the original position. Then we could get some such output as:

(80)   *John (buys and sells) (cars and motor bikes).*

But from this type of coordination we do not immediately get a construction such as:

(81)   *John buys cars and sells motor bikes.*

which, obviously, is not only formally, but also semantically different from (80).

How, then, can we describe constructions such as (78) and (81)? In Dik (1980) I argued that the most appropriate way of handling this type of construction within FG is to regard them as being due to zero anaphora in the second conjunct, so that we get an underlying structure along the lines of (82) for both (83a) and (83b):

(82)   *John (x_i) took a plane and (Ax_i) went to New York.*
(83) a. *John took a plane and he went to New York.*
    b. *John took a plane and Ø went to New York.*

This method can then also be used for such cases in which an intransitive predicate is coordinated with a transitive predicate + second argument, as in:

(84)   *John (x_i) stopped and (Ax_i) looked at the scenery.*
(85) a. *John stopped and he looked at the scenery.*
    b. *John stopped and Ø looked at the scenery.*

This means that in fact these apparent cases of "VP-coordination" come out as a form of clause-coordination, with zero expression of the first argument of the second clause. In chapter 18 I will present some arguments which support this analysis.

In certain cases, however, there seems to be a closer bond between the two coordinated units in constructions such as (85b). This is the case in such combinations as:

(86) a. *I'll* go and get *you something to eat.*
    b. *I'll* try and explain *the rules to you.*

These constructions (in English) have several properties which point to the fact that the conjunctions of predicates in roman typeface have coalesced into one complex predicate [V1 and V2]. These properties are the following (Ross 1967: 93-94; Quirk et al. 1972: 616-617):

(87)   There are restrictions on the choice of V_1 and V_2:
    (i) V_1 is drawn from a restricted set of verbs:
        (a)   verbs of movement and refraining from movement: *go (to X), come, run, hurry up, stop*
        (b)   verbs of position: *stand, sit, lie*
        (c)   *try* (only in infinitive)
        (d)   *be certain, be sure, be nice* (mostly in imperative)
    (ii) V_2 cannot designate a state
    (iii) V_2 cannot be negated
    (iv)   The tenses of V_1 and V_2 cannot be independently chosen

These sorts of restrictions are typical of "serial verb constructions" and in the case of such constructions, in general, there are reasons to assume that they are single complex predicates rather than independently conjoined clause structures. Thus, a construction such as (88) would not be represented as (89), but rather as (90):

(88)   *John* ran and fetched *his shirt.*
(89)   Past e_i: (f_i: *run* [V]) (*John*)$_{Ag}$ and
        Past e_j: (f_j: *fetch* [V]) $(Ax_i)_{Ag}$ (*his shirt*)$_{Go}$
(90)   Past e_i: (f_i: *run* [V] *and fetch* [V]) (*John*)$_{Ag}$ (*his shirt*)$_{Go}$

In (90) the complex predicate {*run and fetch*} designates a single relation, specifying a single action e_i. Such an analysis immediately accounts for the fact that the two predicates cannot be independently tensed and negated.

Note that this type of construction is one way for a language to develop a kind of semi-grammaticalized expression form for aspectual distinctions. Compare, in this respect, the following three construction types:

(91) a.   English: *John is writing a letter.*
     b.   Dutch : *Jan   zit   een brief   te   schrijven.*
                       John   sits   a   letter   to   write
                       'John sits writing a letter.'
     c.   Danish : *Jan   sidder   og   skriver   et   brev.*
                       John   sits   and writes   a   letter
                       'John sits writing a letter.'

In English we have a fully grammaticalized expression for the Progressive. Such constructions as (91b) and (91c) are only semi-grammaticalized. In Dutch and in Danish these expressions can generally not be used unless "Jan" is actually in a sitting position (otherwise, verbs such as 'stand' or 'lie' should be used). On the other hand, the construction is one way of expressing what comes close to Progressive aspect. While in Dutch this construction is formed on the pattern Position verb + Infinitival complement, Danish has exploited the coordination strategy. Constructions such as (91c) might well be described as being due to a form of predicate formation which combines two predicates into one complex predicate, as exemplified in (62).

9.5. Simultaneous coordination

When two or more term positions are multiplied simultaneously within the same clause structure, we get such constructions as:[11]

(92)   *John bought a book and Peter a newspaper.*

In the Reductionist Approach such constructions are usually described as being due to "Gapping",[12] the idea being that they should basically be seen as conjoined sentences or clauses, with a verb having been removed from the second conjunct:

(93)   *John bought a book and Peter (bought) a newspaper.*

Given our present theoretical apparatus we have two distinct ways in which this construction could be described. The first one would assume that there is zero predicate anaphora in the second conjunct; the second method would assume that pairs, triples, etc. of terms can undergo multiplication.

In the first approach it would be assumed that the structure of (92) is as follows:[13]

(94)   *John (f_i: buy [V]) book and Peter (Af_i) newspaper.*

---

11. Certain languages, such as Mandarin and Thai, do not allow this type of construction (Mallinson—Blake 1981: 218).
12. The term is due to Ross (1970).
13. See Keizer (1991) for this anaphorical usage of the predicate variable.

and that the anaphorical predicate (Af_i) is expressed by zero. This analysis would come closest to "Gapping", with this difference that the second, "understood" predicate is never overtly present in underlying structure.

I do not believe, however, that this analysis is plausible, for the following reason: anaphorical reference to predicates is a rather marked phenomenon, and *cataphora*, where the anaphorical element precedes the "antecedent", is a marked phenomenon as well (cf. Maes 1987). Therefore, cataphorical reference to predicates should be doubly marked. Such cataphorical reference would occur in constructions of the form:

(95) *John book* (Af_i) *and Peter newspaper* (f_i: *buy* [V])
'John a book and Peter a newspaper bought'

However, we have known since Ross (1970) that such constructions are quite common in Prefield (SOV) languages, and do not appear to be more marked in such languages than constructions corresponding to (94). This can be illustrated with the situation in Dutch, where we find (96) in main clauses, but (97) in subordinate clauses:

(96) *Jan   koopt   een boek   en Piet   een krant.*
       John   buys   a   book   and Peter   a   newspaper
      'John buys a book and Peter a newspaper.'
(97) *Ik   geloof   dat Jan   een boek   en Piet*
       I   believe that John   a   book   and Peter
      een krant   koopt.
       a   newspaper   buys
      'I think that John buys a book and Peter a newspaper.'

There is nothing more marked about (97) than there is about (96).

For this reason I assume that the second method of describing this construction is more appropriate. In this method, we assume that pairs, triples, in general n-tuples of slots can be multiplied simultaneously:

(98) *buy* [V] $\{(x_1: \text{<hum>})_{Ag} \quad (x_2)_{Go}\}$
               & $\{(x_1^*: \text{<hum>})_{Ag} \quad (x_2^*)_{Go}\}$

In such a case we could say that the pair:

(99) $\{(x_1: \text{<hum>})_{Ag}, (x_2)_{Go}\}$

is the relevant value for "M" in the rule schema (2). This method has the additional advantage that it immediately explains why in this form of coordination the number of members coordinated in each slot must be the same. Compare:

(100) a. *John bought a book and Bill a newspaper.*
       b. **John bought a book and Bill.*

This Direct Approach to "Gapping" has a further advantage. Since Ross (1970) a distinction has been made between "Forward Gapping", as in (96), and "Backward Gapping", as in Dutch subordinate clauses such as (97) above. On a Gapping analysis the "direction of Gapping" does not immediately follow from the description: it requires some separate principle. On the present analysis, however, it follows from the constituent ordering rules of the language in question. In an SOV language, S and O must in principle precede the V. Here, we have two {S,O} pairs. We would thus expect the ordering {S, O}, {S, O} V, which is indeed what we get in such constructions as (97). It should be noted, however, that in Dutch subordinate clauses (and in other SOV languages of the liberal type) we may also find an alternative of the form:

(101) ... *dat   Jan   een boek   koopt en   Piet*
           that John   a   book   buys   and Peter
           een krant.
           a   newspaper
       '... that John buys a book and Peter a newspaper.'

In our approach we could understand this alternative as being due to the principle which says that the Prefield should not be overloaded with complex material, if this can be avoided.

10. Anaphora

10.0. Introduction

In this chapter I discuss the way in which anaphorical relationships can be approached within the framework of FG.[1] 10.1. defines some basic notions, and 10.2. formulates some crucial questions concerning anaphora. 10.3. then concentrates on anaphorical reference to first-order entities and discusses which relations can exist in underlying clause structure between an anaphorical element and its antecedent. 10.4. describes the different ways in which anaphorical elements can be formally expressed. 10.5. discusses anaphorical reference to different types of (non-first-order) entities as distinguished in the typology of entities.

Some distinctive features of the present approach are the following:

(i) the notion 'anaphorical relation' is given a wide interpretation, including anaphorical reference to different types of entities, and encompassing different formal expressions of anaphorical elements. The underlying anaphorical relation is thus abstracted from its formal expression.

(ii) we concentrate on attempts to define the well-formedness conditions for anaphora in functional terms.

(iii) the relativized variable in verbal restrictors is seen as one type of anaphorical element.[2]

10.1. Definitions

I speak of *anaphora* when an element of underlying clause structure refers to an entity which has already been established, directly or indirectly, in the preceding discourse (*discourse anaphora*) or is being established in the same clause (*sentence anaphora*). The element which so refers will be called an *anaphorical element* (*anaphorical term* if the anaphorical element has term

---

1. For many of the points made in this chapter see Cornish (1986).
2. To my surprise I learnt from Cornish (1986: 6) that *relativum* as in *pronomen relativum* was intended as a Latin translation of *anaphorikos* and that, therefore, a link between relativization and anaphora has been there from the very beginning.

status). The expression with which the entity in question has been or is being established in the discourse is the *antecedent* of the anaphorical element. Notwithstanding its etymology, the antecedent may in certain cases follow the anaphorical element in the linear order of the sentence.[3] The relation between anaphorical element and antecedent will be called an *anaphorical relation*.

When the anaphorical element and the antecedent are used to refer to the same entity they are said to be *coreferential*. There are several cases, however, in which an anaphorical element is not, or not strictly coreferential with its antecedent:

(i) *The antecedent introduces a variable*
There are cases in which the anaphorical element refers to a member of the set defined in the antecedent, as in the following example:

(1) *Every mother likes* her *children.*

In (1) the anaphorical element *her* refers to any individual member of the set defined by *every mother*. The anaphorical element *her* is thus not strictly coreferential with its antecedent *every mother*.

(ii) *The anaphorical element refers to a Sub-Topic*
In many cases the anaphorical element does not strictly refer to the entity referred to by the antecedent, but to a Sub-Topic which can be inferred from that entity; such a Sub-Topic may be a part of the entity introduced by the antecedent:

(2) a. *On a bench in the park he saw an elderly couple.* The man ... the woman ...
     b. *John bought a book, but after reading* the first few pages *he threw it away.*

Or the Sub-Topic may be inferentially related to the entity introduced by the antecedent in some other way (cf. *TFG1*: 13.3.3):

---

3. Cases in which the anaphorical element precedes its antecedent are sometimes termed "cataphora" rather than "anaphora". I will not use this terminology, since it disrupts the fundamental unity of the anaphorical relationship.

(3) a. *The party was tolerable, but* the music *was awful.*
    b. *A lady was attacked in High Street yesterday.* The attacker ... the victim...

In each of these cases the constituents in roman typeface can be said to be anaphorically used according to the definition given above, although they are not strictly coreferential with the antecedent.

(iii) *The antecedent does not refer*
Anaphorical reference is possible to entities which have been established by antecedents which themselves are not used referentially. For one example, consider anaphorical reference to properties:

(4) *Jan   is   intelligent   maar   Piet   is   het niet.*
     John   is   intelligent   but   Peter   is   it   not
     'John is intelligent but Peter isn't'

The pronoun *het* is used anaphorically since it refers back to the entity which has been established by the predicate *intelligent*, namely the property f_i of being intelligent. Again, the pronoun is used anaphorically, though strictly speaking it is not coreferential with the antecedent. A similar relation is involved in:

(5)   *The car was orange and John hated* that colour.

The two sources of non-coreferential anaphora mentioned under (ii) and (iii) may combine, as in:

(6)   *John liked the car, but he hated* the colour.

In this case *the colour* anaphorically refers to a property which may be inferentially derived as a Sub-Topic from the entity established by the antecedent *the car*.
 Our definition of anaphora has the following implications:
 (i) expressions such as "the anaphorical element refers to the antecedent" are to be avoided. First, expressions do not refer, but speakers refer by means of expressions (Lyons 1977). Second, speakers do not usually refer anaphorically to antecedents, but to entities which have been established by antecedents. We do have a case of anaphorical reference to an antecedent in expressions such as:

(7)   A man big *is wrong*. It *is ungrammatical.*

(ii) all anaphorical elements have an antecedent in the discourse; the antecedent itself is not used anaphorically, but serves to establish some entity in the discourse.

(iii) although anaphorical elements are generally definite (since they presuppose the availability of the intended referent as established by the antecedent), not all definite terms are anaphorical: definite terms are used non-anaphorically (according to this definition) when the basis for their presumed identifiability lies in general or situational information rather than in contextual information:

(8)   *When John left,* the sun *was shining, though* it *was less bright than the previous day.*

The sun, though definite, is not anaphorical, since there has been no previous mention of 'the sun' in the discourse. The term's definiteness is warranted by presumed general knowledge. The pronoun *it* is anaphorically used to refer to the entity which has been established by *the sun*.

(9)   That man with the brown jacket *is the new science teacher.* He *has just started teaching.*

In this case the term's definiteness is warranted by presumed situational information. Again, it is not used anaphorically. *He* is used anaphorically to refer to the entity which has been introduced by *that man with the brown jacket*.

(iv) Anaphorical elements may form "chains" through the discourse. Such chains are variously called "topic chains" (Dixon 1972), "identification spans" (Grimes 1975), or "anaphorical chains" (Chastain 1975). I will here use the term "anaphorical chain". An anaphorical chain consists of the antecedent and all subsequent anaphorical references to the entity established by the antecedent.

10.2. Accessibility

Within the structure of the clause it is in certain conditions impossible to establish an anaphorical relationship between some term position and a certain potential antecedent. Consider the following examples:

(10) a.   *John_i saw himself_i in the mirror.*
      b.   **John*_i* saw John_i in the mirror.*

The anaphorical element *himself* can relate to the antecedent *John* when *John* has Subject function and *himself* has Object function, but not the other way around. An Object antecedent is not "accessible" from the Subject position in the same clause.

(11) a.   *When he_i entered the room, John_i saw an enormous mess.*
      b.   **He_i entered the room and John_i saw an enormous mess.*

The anaphorical element *he* can relate to the antecedent *John* when it is in a preceding subordinate clause, but not when it is in a preceding coordinate clause. The antecedent *John* is accessible from the former, but not from the latter position. Obviously, sentence (11b) does have a possible interpretation, but on that interpretation *he* and *John* are necessarily non-coreferential. In that case *he* is either used deictically (to point to an entity available in the communicative situation), or discourse-anaphorically (coreferential to some antecedent in the preceding context). The question is thus: what factors determine whether a given antecedent is accessible to an anaphorical element? In chapter 16 this issue will be dealt with in more general terms.

10.3. Expression

10.3.0. Introduction

We have defined the notion "anaphorical relation" in a wide sense, disregarding for the moment the way in which the anaphorical element is to be expressed. This wide usage of anaphora is expedient from a functional point of view, since the primary functional question is whether or not it is possible, from a given position in the structure of the clause, to anaphorically refer to an entity that has been or is being defined by some antecedent. This is the kind of relationship that has to be established in the underlying clause structure. A second question is then: given this anaphorical element, how can or should it be expressed?

The expression of anaphorical elements is determined by two main factors. First, the expression varies with the type of entity that the anaphorical element refers to. Compare:

220 *Anaphora*

(12) a. *John saw Bill$_i$ and Peter saw him$_i$ too.*
   b. *John saw [Bill win]$_i$ and Peter saw it$_i$ / that$_i$ too.*
   c. *John thought that [Bill would win]$_i$ and Peter thought so$_i$ too.*

Thus, the form of the anaphorical element varies according as the antecedent entity is a first-order entity (12a), a second-order SoA (12b), or a propositional content (12c). Such differences will be discussed in 10.3.2.

Secondly, if the anaphorical element refers to a first-order entity, the expression may vary with the type of anaphorical relation. Certain types of anaphorical element will be expressed by nominal terms:

(13) a. *When the suspect$_i$ was brought in, the lady recognized the man$_i$ immediately.*
   b. *When John$_i$ entered the room, the idiot$_i$ didn't say a word to anyone.*

When the anaphorical element and the antecedent are relatively close in underlying clause structure, expression by a reflexive pronoun is often mandatory; when they are more remote, the anaphorical element may be expressed by a personal pronoun. In other circumstances, again, the anaphorical element may be expressed by zero:

(14) a. *John$_i$ saw himself$_i$ / *him$_i$.*
   b. *John$_i$ wanted Mary to see him$_i$ / *himself$_i$.*
   c. *John$_i$ wanted Ø$_i$ / *himself$_i$ / *him$_i$ to see Mary.*

Apart from the structural factors determining expression differences, there are pragmatic factors involved. These will be discussed in section 10.3.1.

10.3.1. Pragmatic factors

Even when we restrict our attention to anaphorical reference to first-order entities, anaphorical terms may take many different forms, as indicated in the following survey:

(15)   FORMS OF ANAPHORICAL TERMS
Nominal: a term with nominal head, with
      Operators   Nominal head
      a. Definite   a. Identical to that of antecedent
      b. Demonstrative b. Hyperonym of that of antecedent
                             c. "Epithet" of entity referred to
Pronominal
    Reflexive pronoun
    Relative pronoun
    Possessive pronoun
        Plain
        Reflexive
    Demonstrative pronoun
    Personal pronoun
        Strong
        Weak
Inflectional
Zero

These forms can be ordered on a scale of explicitness in the following way:

(16)   Nominal term > Demonstrative > Strong personal pronoun > Weak personal pronoun > Zero

Givón (1983) advanced the idea that the explicitness of coding of anaphorical elements correlates inversely with the degree of continuity of their intended referents in the ongoing discourse. Continuity was supposed to be quantitatively measurable in terms of Referential Distance (number of clauses intervening between anaphorical element and antecedent), Persistence (of the referent in question in the following context), and Potential Ambiguity (number of alternative antecedents available). Such correlations can indeed be established, but it has also become clear that a variety of more qualitative distinctions may be relevant for the choice of expression of the anaphorical element.

Van de Grift (1987) and Bolkestein—Van de Grift (1994) studied the pragmatic factors which in Latin discourse influence the choice between the following anaphorical Subject expressions:

(17) NP   full nominal term
      ille remote demonstrative
      hic   proximate demonstrative
      is   discourse demonstrative
      Ø   inflectional and real zero anaphora

They found that the following factors at least partially explain the choice between these expressions.

(i) *Topic continuity*
Relation to Topic continuity in the sense of Givón (1983):

(18)
		Ref Distance	Persistence	Ambiguity
Preference	1	Ø	*ille*	*ille*
	2	*hic*	Ø	NP
	3	*ille*	NP	Ø

(ii) *Position in the anaphorical chain*
We have to distinguish three distinct positions in the anaphorical chain: chain-1, the antecedent (or a term resuming an earlier Topic), chain-2, the first anaphorical term in the chain, and chain-n, any later position in the chain. The preferred usage can then be described as follows:

(19)
		chain-1	chain-2	chain-n
Preference	1	NP	*hic*	Ø
	2	*is*	*is*	*ille*
	3	*hic*	*ille*	NP

These data show that there are not two, but three functionally different positions in the chain: chain-1 is used to introduce a New Topic (typically by an NP), or to re-introduce (resume) a Topic; chain-2 is used to reconfirm that this NewTop is now the Given Topic for the rest of the chain; chain-n carries on the chain about this GivTop. In the latter case, Ø is used when there is a smooth flow from one anaphorical element to the next; *ille* is preferably used when confusion might arise through intervening candidate Topics.

(iii) *Continuation of Subject*
Does the Subject expression continue the Subject of the preceding clause (same Subject, SS) or not (different Subject, DS)?

(20)   SS   DS
    Preference 1   Ø   NP
                2   *hic*   *ille*
                3   *is* / *ille* *is*

(iv) *Pragmatic status of antecedent*
Is the antecedent NewTop, Focus, or (already) GivTop?

(21)   NewTop   Focus   GivTop
    Preference 1   *hic*   *ille* Ø
                2   *is*   *hic*   *ille*
                3   Ø   NP   NP

These various preferences may be roughly summarized as follows (for details see the original publications):

(22)   NP   especially used for introducing NewTops into the discourse or for later anaphorical reference when there is a change of Subject or Topic and / or a danger of ambiguity
        ille   especially used for later anaphorical reference, especially when there is change of Subject and / or danger of ambiguity; signals longer distance in preceding, and persistence in the following discourse.
        hic   especially used for reconfirming NewTops at short distance in preceding context
        is   especially used for reconfirming NewTops
        Ø   especially used in short-range highly continuous anaphorical reference with no change of Subject or danger of ambiguity

We may conclude that not only the question whether there may be an anaphorical element at all at a certain point, but also the question of how it is expressed is heavily dependent on a variety of pragmatic properties of the discourse. We also see that anaphorical chains make an important contribution to the continuity, the coherence, and the structuring of the discourse.

10.3.2. Types of entities

10.3.2.0. Introduction. Prototypically, terms are used to refer to first-order spatial entities. Anaphorical terms often refer to first-order entities as well.

224 *Anaphora*

That is why we have so far restricted our attention to anaphorical reference to first-order entities. However, anaphorical reference can also be made to other types of entities, in particular the types of entities that we have distinguished in the layered structure of the clause. We can thus make anaphorical reference to any of the entity types distinguished in Table 3:

Table 3. Types of entities which can be anaphorically referred to.

order	type	variable
0	Property / Relation	f
1	Spatial entity	x
2	State of Affairs	e
3	Possible Fact	X
4	Speech Act	E

Let us consider the ways in which anaphorical reference can be made to any of the non-first-order entities distinguished in Table 3.

10.3.2.1. Anaphorical reference to properties and relations. Zero-order entities (properties and relations) can be anaphorically referred to both in predicative and in attributive position. In attributive position we can have such relations as:

(23)   John has a red car *and Peter has a blue* one.

Note that *one* must here be interpreted as referring back to *car*. However, *car* in *a fast car* designates a property rather than an entity. Thus, *one* is used to anaphorically refer to the property designated by *car* (cf. Hengeveld 1992; Keizer 1992a). This can be captured by means of a representation such as:

(24)   *have (John)* (i1x_i: (f$_j$: *car*): (f$_j$: *red*)) *and*
        have (Peter) (i1x_j: (Af$_i$): (f$_k$: *blue*))

This representation makes it clear that Peter is said to have a blue instance of an entity with the same property ('car') as the one of which John is said to have a red instance.

Anaphorical reference can als be made to entities designated by secondary (adjectival) restrictors. Compare:

(25)   *John has a* fast *car and Peter has* such a *car too.*

It is difficult in English to simultaneously refer to both the properties 'fast' and 'car' in a construction such as (25). But this can be done explicitly in Dutch:

(26)   *Jan   heeft   een snelle$_i$ auto$_j$ en Piet   heeft*
        John   has   a   fast   car   and Peter has   he
        er   ook zo$_i$ een$_j$.
        there   also such   one
       'John has a fast car and Peter has one too'

As is clear from (26), the two restrictors 'fast' and 'car' are separately referred to in Dutch. The underlying representation could be roughly as follows:

(27)   *hebben (Jan) (i1x$_i$: (f$_i$: auto): (f$_j$: snel)) en ook*
        hebben (Peter) (i1x$_j$: (Af$_i$): (Af$_j$))

In English, judging from the paraphrase of (26), it would seem at first sight that *one* refers back to the whole term *a fast car*. This, however, cannot be the case, since the sentence does not mean that John and Peter own the same car (there is no coreferentiality between *a fast car* and *one*). Rather, the English construction has the same paraphrase as the corresponding Dutch one, viz. that Peter has another entity x_j with the same properties as the entity x_i which John has. Thus, structure (27) would be appropriate for the English construction as well.

This means that we now have a way of capturing the difference between what is often called "identity of sense" as against "identity of reference". Compare the following constructions:

(28) a. *John has seen* a monkey$_i$ *in the zoo and Peter has seen* it$_i$ *too.*
     b. *John has seen a* monkey$_i$ *in the zoo and Peter has seen* one$_i$ *too.*

In (28a) we have identity of reference: Peter is said to have seen the same monkey as John. In (28b), however, there is "identity of sense": Peter is said to have seen another entity with the same property as the entity John has seen. The difference can be represented as follows:

(29) a. $(i1x_i: (f_i: monkey))$ ..... (Ax_i) --> *it*
     b. $(i1x_i: (f_i: monkey))$ ..... $(i1x_j: (Af_i))$ --> *one*

We thus reconstruct "identity of sense" in terms of anaphorical reference to properties rather than to first-order entities.

10.3.2.2. Anaphorical reference to States of Affairs. Chastain (1975: 205) discusses the following passage about an ARVN officer interrogating a prisoner (slightly adapted):

(30)   *... when the prisoner failed to answer, the officer beat him repeatedly. An American observer who saw* the beating *reported that the officer "really worked him over". After* the beating *the prisoner was forced to remain standing against the wall for several hours.*

The two occurrences of *the beating* form part of an anaphorical chain. Usually, an anaphorical chain starts with an indefinite antecedent, through which the entity in question is introduced into the discourse. Such an antecedent is not overtly present in (30). But, Chastain adds, it is clear that the beating in question is the one first mentioned in the first sentence: "... we can therefore think of the first link (of the chain) as being an indefinite description — perhaps a beating of the young prisoner by the ARVN officer — which would appear after a deeper analysis of the first sentence" (Chastain 1975: 205-206).

This is exactly what we can achieve in terms of the underlying clause structures of these sentences. The crucial structures would look as follows:

(31)   Past e_i: [*beat (the officer)(him)*]....
          An American observer who saw (Ae_i) *reported* ....
          After (Ae_i) *the prisoner was forced* ...

In our terminology the predication *the officer beat him* does not REFER to the State of Affairs e_i, but it does establish that State of Affairs as a potential referent to which later anaphorical reference can be made. Such anaphorical reference is then made twice, as expressed by the definite anaphorical terms *the beating*. Thus, these anaphorical terms refer back to an entity (the SoA e_i) which has been established by the antecedent consisting of the predication *the officer beat him*. That the antecedent entity is indeed the SoA of the officer beating the prisoner (rather than, for example, the beating-relation as such) is further established by two facts: the observer is said to have seen the entity, and we cannot see relations; and the entity is used in the temporal satellite expressed as *after X*, in which we expect X to represent an SoA rather than anything else. Note further that this type of anaphorical reference to SoAs helps to create coherence in discourse. See chapter 18 for further discussion.

10.3.2.3. Anaphorical reference to Possible Facts. Similar things can be said about anaphorical reference to Possible Facts. First consider the following examples:

(32)   *John thought that [Bill would win]$_i$ and Peter thought so$_i$ too.*

In (32) the anaphorical pronoun *so* anaphorically refers to the Possible Fact described in the complement proposition of the first instance of the verb *think*. This may be represented roughly as in (33):

(33)   *think (John) (X_i: [Bill would win]) and*
         think (Peter) (AX_i) too

Particularly interesting are (seeming) relative constructions such as those illustrated in the following example from Spanish and in its English translation:

(34)   *Juan   creía   [que   Pedro   iba   a   ganar]$_i$,*
         Juan   believed that   Pedro   went   to   win
         [lo que]$_i$ no   era   verdad.
         which   not   was   true
         'Juan thought that Pedro was going to win, which wasn't true'

The Spanish neuter relative pronoun *lo_que* 'which' is exclusively used in contexts in which reference is made to a non-nominal antecedent not referring to a first order entity. In all other cases either the masculine or the feminine forms have to be used, which agree with the inherent gender of the antecedent noun. Here the antecedent is a full proposition, so the neuter form of the relative pronoun is selected.

(35)   creer (Juan) (X_i: Pedro iba a ganar), Neg verdad (AX_i)

10.3.2.4. Anaphorical reference to Speech Acts. Anaphorical reference to speech acts is illustrated in the following examples:

(36)   *And he concluded by saying: ["Let's not overreact"]$_i$. After making [this statement]$_i$, he left the room.*
(37)   *This$_i$ is my conclusion: ["We should not overreact"]$_i$.*
(38)   *[Stay away from me!]$_i$ [That]$_i$'s a warning!*

In all these cases the anaphoric element refers to an antecedent which is a full speech act. Underlying structures such as the one in (39), which represents (38), may capture this fact:

(39)   (Imp E_i: [stay away from me]). (Decl E_j: [Warning$_N$ (AE_i)$_\emptyset$]).

10.3.2.5. Conclusion. In the preceding sections it has been shown that the hierarchical model of the underlying structure of the clause advocated in FG allows us to distinguish between anaphora referring to entities of different orders. Since the nature of the entity referred to is in several cases reflected in the form of the anaphorical elements, such an approach has been shown to be directly relevant to a general model of natural languages.

11. The illocutionary layer

11.0. Introduction[1]

In *TFG1*: 3.1. I briefly discussed the way in which illocutionary distinctions can be treated in FG. Formally, the full structure of the clause at the illocutionary level can be represented as follows:

(1) π_4 E: [proposition] σ_4

where π_4 indicates a (possibly complex) *illocutionary operator*, E the *speech act variable*, and σ_4 one or more *illocutionary satellites*. Illocutionary operators represent grammatical means for specifying or modifying the illocutionary force of the clause, illocutionary satellites represent lexical means for achieving similar purposes. Together, π_4 and σ_4 specify the illocution to the extent that it is coded in the linguistic expression. As is the case with any (feature of a) linguistic expression, the illocution as coded in the expression may receive further specification in the pragmatic interpretation. The illocutionary features coded in the expression (including prosodic features) will have to be accounted for in the grammar; the further pragmatic interpretation is a subject for a wider theory of verbal interaction which explains how linguistic expressions with given properties can be used to achieve different communicative ends.

The operandum of the illocutionary elements in the clause is typically the proposition (that part of the clause structure which may be evaluated in terms of truth value). There is reason to assume, however, that imperatives (more generally, "directives") operate directly on the extended predication which specifies the SoA of which the realization is desired by S (cf. Hengeveld 1989). On that view, imperatives have no propositional content: they are used to get another person to do something, not to get him to contemplate or

---

1. For various suggestions concerning the treatment of illocutionary distinctions in FG, compare De Jong (1981), Peres (1984), Moutaouakil (1984a), Hengeveld (1989), Risselada (1990), and Bolkestein (1992). My presentation in this chapter uses certain ideas from these authors, but also differs from some of their proposals. The most important of these differences will be mentioned in the text.

otherwise respond to a proposition. In 5.3. we saw that this corresponds with the fact that "directive" matrix-predicates take embedded predications rather than embedded propositions as complements. In this way, illocutionary operators can also be differentiated according to the type of complement they take.

11.1. The status of "illocution"

Since Austin (1962) and Searle (1969) it has generally been accepted that linguistic expressions should not only be regarded as having a certain (propositional) content, but also as being capable of being used as a certain type of speech act, an act by which S establishes some kind of communicative relation with A. Every linguistic expression has a *performative* aspect: it can be used to perform certain kinds of communicative acts.

The value of a linguistic expression qua speech act has been called the *illocutionary force* of the expression. There is some equivocation, however, as to the precise interpretation of the notion "illocutionary force". In discussing this notion, Austin and Searle in principle thought of the final interpretation qua speech act of a given linguistic expression, used in a given context. If illocutionary force is taken in this way, each of the following expressions can be said to have the illocutionary force of a warning (if used in appropriate circumstances):

(2) a. *I warn you that there is a bull in the field.*
     b. *There's a bull in the field.*

If both these expressions are said to be warnings, however, how do we account for the rather considerable differences between the two? In (2a), the semantic aspect of "warning" is explicitly coded in the lexical verb *warn*. In (2b), on the other hand, there is no such explicit coding: if anything is coded at all, it is that (2b) is a declarative statement or an assertion rather than a warning.

In later work, Searle (1976) tried to solve this problem by calling "warning" the *primary* illocution of an expression such as (2b), and "statement" the *secondary* (literal) illocution. An utterance in which the primary illocution is different from the secondary one (in this sense) was called an *indirect speech act*. This, however, leads to two quite different interpretations of the notion "illocutionary force" (or illocution, for short): illocution-1 refers to the final value of the expression qua speech act, illocution-2 to what is coded in the expression as such, where illocution-1 may be distinct from illocution-2.

I believe that the notion of illocution can be clarified if we think of it in terms of the model of verbal interaction sketched in *TFG1*: 1.3.1. Just as in general we can distinguish between the communicative intention of S, the semantic content coded in the linguistic expression, and the interpretation arrived at by A, so we can distinguish between the intended illocution on the part of S, the illocution as coded in the linguistic expression, and the illocution as interpreted by A. And just as intention, semantic content, and interpretation need not be identical, so there may be differences between these three types of illocution. We can thus make the following distinctions:[2]

(3) a. the illocution-as-intended-by-S Ill_S
    b. the illocution-as-coded-in-the-expression Ill_E
    c. the illocution-as-interpreted-by-A Ill_A

We can now say that the task of A is to reconstruct Ill_S in Ill_A. In other words, an act of communication will be fully achieved with respect to illocution if Ill_A = Ill_S. If Ill_E does not code Ill_S very explicitly, the reconstruction of Ill_S may be difficult for A. Consider (2b). On the most probable interpretation, (2b) will function according to the following constellation:

(4) Ill_S = warning
     Ill_E = assertion
     Ill_A = warning

However, the interpretation of (2b) as a warning depends, in a crucial way, on the interpretative work that A does on the basis of the information which is provided in the expression as such. In such a case, there is a chance that A may come to an interpretation which was not intended by S (i.e. in which Ill_A is different from Ill_S). If that happens, there will be a misunderstanding between A and S concerning the intended illocution. In the case of (2b), for instance, the following constellation might be established:

(5) Ill_S = assertion
     Ill_E = assertion
     Ill_A = warning

---

2. See Weijdema et al. (1982: 47-49) for these distinctions.

This might be the case if (2b) is a simple remark on the part of S, which A, however, interprets as a warning. The context might be as follows:

(6)   S: *Hey John, there's a bull in the field!*
       A: *I know there is — I didn't intend to go into the field.*
       S: *I didn't think you were. I just mentioned it.*

What this example of a mismatch between Ill_A and Ill_S makes clear is that here, as in any area of linguistic communication, it is useful to think in terms of S developing a certain communicative intention and coding it (to a certain degree of explicitness) in a linguistic expression; and of A reconstructing S's presumed intention on the basis of what is coded in the linguistic expression plus whatever pragmatic information may be relevant to the final interpretation of the expression. The coding may be rather explicit (much of S's intention is coded in the expression; little is left to A's pragmatic information), or very implicit (S just gives a hint in the expression, and much is left to A's use of the relevant pragmatic information).

Given these distinctions, we can now say that from the point of view of grammar we are primarily interested in Ill_E: the illocution to the extent that it is coded in linguistic expressions. Ill_E will on the one hand have some kind of reflection in the formal (including the prosodic) structure of the linguistic expression (if not, it could not be said to be coded in that expression); on the other hand, it is an integrated part of the semantic structure of the expression. For these two reasons, Ill_E is a property of linguistic expressions that a grammar will have to account for. The relations between Ill_E, Ill_S, and Ill_A are then a matter for a pragmatic theory which specifies how expressions with given linguistic properties can be used in various communicative patterns.

11.2. Explicit and implicit performatives

11.2.1. Explicit performatives

Explicit performative expressions were given pride of place in the earliest discussions of speech act theory. They are exemplified in (7):

(7)   a.   I hereby ask you *to leave immediately.*
        b.   I promise you *that I'll do my best.*
        c.   I warn you *that this game may be dangerous.*

Austin (1962) specified the conditions under which an expression can count as an explicit performative of this type:

(i) it must contain a matrix verb such as *ask, promise, warn,* indicating some type of communicative act,
(ii) with the S as Subject,
(iii) the A as Recipient, and
(iv) a proposition as Goal or Object. Furthermore,
(v) the speech act verb must be in the present tense indicative.

As a practical criterion for distinguishing English explicit performatives, one can use the possibility of adding *hereby* to the construction (as in example (7a)).[3]

It is to be noted that, outside overtly institutional contexts (in which explicit performatives may be required in order for some procedure to be legally valid), explicit performative expressions are extremely rare. In a study of natural, spontaneous Dutch conversation (Weijdema et al. 1982) we had difficulty in finding even a single genuine example. In the second place, where explicit performatives do occur in natural conversation, they often show up in pragmatically marked contexts, for instance in sequences of the following type:

(8) A: *Did you enjoy the party?*
     B: ---
     A: *John, did you like the party?*
     B: *ehmm, sorry?*
     A: *I AM ASKING YOU WHETHER YOU ENJOYED THE PARTY!!!*

In general, when explicit performatives are used in spontaneous conversation, they often constitute emphatic repetitions of earlier speech acts, when S has reason to assume that A has either not heard or not understood the earlier

---

3. These criteria are not watertight. They rather define the "prototypical case" of an explicit performative expression. Where one or the other of these criteria is not fulfilled, the result may still be a performative, be it of a less prototypical type. For example, a passive construction such as:
(i) *Passengers are warned to cross the track by the bridge only.*
can be called a performative (Austin 1962: 57; Lyons 1977: 729), although the Speaker is not explicitly mentioned and the performative verb is in the passive. But this type of performative is obviously less "prototypical" than active expressions which do have an overt S mentioned.

speech act, or is unwilling to communicate at all. The general conclusion must be that we normally do not speak in explicit performative expressions.

11.2.2. Implicit performatives

Usually, then, we speak in implicit performatives such as (9a-c) rather than in their explicit counterparts (7a-c):

(9) a. *Leave immediately!*
    b. *I'll do my best.*
    c. *This game may be dangerous!*

There has been a tendency among speech act theorists to take these implicit performatives as somehow derivative or secondary with respect to "true", that is, explicit performative constructions. Thus, Austin (1962: 32) says that "...we can *on occasion* [my emphasis, SCD] use the utterance 'go' to achieve practically the same as we achieve by the utterance 'I order you to go'", and comments that in such cases one might say that "the ritual was incompletely carried out by the original speaker".

Searle (1969: 19) even elevated the presumed priority of explicit performatives to the status of a general "principle of expressibility":

> Wherever the illocutionary force of an utterance is not explicit it can always be made explicit. This is an instance of the principle of expressibility, stating that whatever can be meant can be said. (Searle 1969: 68).

This principle, according to Searle, allows us:

> ...to equate rules for performing certain speech acts with rules for uttering certain linguistic elements, since for any possible speech act there is a possible element the meaning of which (given the context of the utterance) is sufficient to determine that its literal utterance is a performance of precisely that speech act. To study the speech acts of promising or apologizing we need only study sentences whose literal and correct utterance would constitute making a promise or issuing an apology. (Searle 1969: 21).

A similarly reductionist view, now in a syntactic framework, was proposed by Ross (1970) in his "performative analysis". According to this proposal, any implicit performative expression is derived from an underlying structure more closely corresponding to the explicit performative. Thus, the structure underlying (10a) would be of the form (10b):

(10) a. *Prices slumped.*
 b. *I tell you that (prices slumped).*

Implicit performatives such as (10a) would be derived from structures such as (10b) through a rule of "performative deletion", which deletes the whole performative matrix structure *I tell you that*, and only leaves the bare proposition to be actually expressed.

I shall not follow such a reductionist course, for a variety of reasons:

(i) it is rather counterintuitive to take an expression type (the explicit performative), which hardly ever occurs in natural verbal interaction, as the norm for the expression type (the implicit performative) which is used in unmarked conditions.

(ii) in the opposition between explicit and implicit performative expressions, it is the former which constitutes the pragmatically marked type, as we saw above. Again, the pragmatically marked type should not be taken as the norm for the pragmatically unmarked expression type.

(iii) Ross's performative analysis boils down to postulating an underlying performative superstructure for any sentence type, only to be deleted in the great majority of actual sentences. This is very close to a situation of "absolute neutralization": the postulation of elements of underlying structure which never come to the surface. It is in the interest of any theory to avoid such cases of near-absolute neutralization wherever this is possible.

(iv) the idea that every implicit performative expression should be analysed in terms of a corresponding explicit performative expression faces a variety of semantic and syntactic problems (extensively discussed in Levinson 1983: 251-263), each of which goes to show that there is no full equivalence between the implicit performative and its presumed explicit underlying structure.

(v) finally, the reductionist approach is not open to FG on general methodological grounds. First, FG wishes to describe a natural language as an instrument which can only be understood correctly as functioning in a wider, pragmatic setting. There is no reason for such a theory to try and code the pragmatic setting in the syntactic structure of the instrument as such, unless the parameters of the pragmatic setting have a systematic reflection in the form (including the prosody) of linguistic expressions. Secondly, FG does not allow for the type of (quite complex) transformational operations required by a theory which in one way or another incorporates the performative analysis.[4]

Some (not all) of these arguments also militate against the idea, advanced within the context of FG by Hengeveld (1989), of capturing the illocution by means of an "illocutionary frame", consisting of an abstract illocutionary predicate, taking S, A, and the proposition for its arguments:

(11)   ILL (S) (A) (Proposition)

It is evident that such a structure can be used to capture all Ross's phenomena without leading to the undesirable consequence of deletion of specific lexical material; and certainly S and A are "understood" as being relevant to any speech act. But this is precisely why they need not be explicitly mentioned in the STRUCTURE of each particular utterance. If they are always there, one default principle is sufficient to make them available. Note that the same omnipresence holds for "utterance time" (t_0) and "utterance location" (l_0). These elements can be taken to be contained in the specification of the "deictic centre" relevant to any utterance (cf. *TFG1*, 2.4.3.). All those elements in the structure of the clause which crucially depend on parameters of the deictic centre can then take their cues from the deictic centre as relevant for this particular utterance.

For these various reasons, then, I will not describe the implicit performative in terms of the structure underlying the corresponding explicit performative. Nor will I treat the implicit performative as being in any way derivative or secondary with respect to the explicit performative. On the contrary, in order to account for the marked character of explicit performatives, I will rather treat them as more complex structures which receive their performative interpretation in a special, derived way. I return to this problem in 11.6.

11.3. Sentence types as carriers of basic illocutions

Speech act theory has so far paid little attention to the codification of illocutionary distinctions in distinct sentence types across languages. A typical statement is that by Searle—Vanderveken (1985: 2):

---

4. The performative analysis requires deletion of specified elements, an operation avoided in FG. See *TFG1*: 1.7.1.

... illocutionary logic studies the properties of illocutionary forces ... without worrying about the various ways that these are realized in the syntax of English ... and without worrying whether these features translate into other languages.

Such an approach would not seem advisable from a linguistic point of view. It runs the danger of disregarding the very facts which have occasioned the recognition of the notion "speech act" in the first place, and of leaving typological universals in the illocutionary domain unexplained.

It would seem preferable, then, to take some general facts concerning the different sentence types distinguished in natural languages as a point of departure for developing a general illocutionary theory. All languages have a restricted number of basic sentence types such as Declarative, Interrogative, Imperative, and perhaps some others (cf. Sadock—Zwicky 1985). I will interpret these sentence types as grammaticalized carriers of basic illocutions of linguistic expressions.[5] Once these basic illocutions have been established in this way, we can consider how they can be "modified" or "converted"[6] so as to lead to different, typically more specific illocutionary values.

This is based on the following reasoning: Ss can perform a wide variety of types and sub-types of speech acts with respect to As. Apparently, some of these types are functionally more important than others. Those speech act types which are functionally most important have been codified by distinct grammatical means (sentence types) in the grammar of a language. The most basic speech act types are those which have been so codified in all languages. We can thus consider Illocution as a grammatical category with a limited number of possible articulations.

---

5. Compare Levinson (1983: 244) for the view that the basic sentence-types of a language may be regarded as "grammaticalized conventional indicators of illocutionary force". Levinson also notes that one would expect a theory of speech acts to explain why it is precisely these sentence-types which are prevalent among the languages in the world (Levinson 1983: 242).

6. I speak of "modification" when a given illocution is further specified while otherwise remaining the same, and of "conversion" when a given illocution is changed into some other, derived illocution. The borderline is not always easy to draw (cf. Risselada 1990). For example, does *please* as in *Please, go away!* turn the Imperative into a mitigated Imperative (modification) or into a Request (conversion)?

Some impression of these articulations can be gleaned from Table 4, which summarizes the information contained in the first seven volumes of *Lingua Descriptive Studies*.

Table 4. Sentence types in seven languages.[7]

Language	Decl	Int	Imp	Excl	Other
Abkhaz	+	+	+	+	curse wish
Egyptian Arabic	+	+	+	+	hortative
Hixkaryana	+	+	+	+	rhetorical question counterfactual ideophone
Kobon	+	+	+	+	prescriptive counterfactual vocative
Mangarayi	+	+	+		compassionate
Quechua	+	+	+	+	
Tamil	+	+	+	+	desperate question

From this table we may induce that:
— all languages have the three basic sentence-types Declarative, Interrogative, and Imperative;
— most of them have a distinct exclamatory type;
— nearly all of them have some further (minor) types, with a variety of different functions.

Even on the basis of such a limited survey, there can be no doubt that the three-way division into declarative-interrogative-imperative forms the core of grammaticalized illocutionary systems in natural languages (cf. Sadock—

---

7. Sources: Abkhaz: Hewitt (1979), Egyptian Arabic: Gary—Gamal-Eldin (1982), Hixkaryana: Derbyshire (1979), Kobon: Davies (1981), Mangarayi: Merlan (1982), Quechua: Cole (1982), Tamil: Asher (1982).

Zwicky 1985). These sentence types can be interpreted in terms of the following basic illocutionary functions:[8]

(12) Declarative: S wishes A to add the content of the linguistic expression to his pragmatic information.
Interrogative: S wishes A to provide him with the verbal information as requested in the linguistic expression.
Imperative: S wishes A to perform the controlled SoA as specified in the linguistic expression.

And, for the many languages which have special Exclamative constructions:

(13) Exclamative: S wishes A to know that the content of the linguistic expression impresses S as surprising, unexpected, or otherwise worthy of notice.

11.4. Illocutionary operators

The basic illocutions as encapsulated in distinct sentence types can be formalized in FG in the form of illocutionary operators, which take the proposition or, in the case of the Imperative, the predication in their scope.[9] These illocutionary operators can be semantically and pragmatically defined along the lines of (12) and (13). Formally, they will trigger those rules which map the underlying clause structure onto the appropriate sentence type. This will provide us with analyses such as:[10]

---

8. Note that these distinctions are closely reflected in Bühler's (1934) typology of basic communicative functions: *Darstellung* (representation), *Kundgabe* (expression), and *Appell* (elicitation). However, the widespread distinction between Interrogative and Imperative suggests a further basic bifurcation into elicitation of verbal vs. non-verbal action on the part of the A. Compare also Jakobson's (1960) elaboration of Bühler's distinctions.

9. Cf. De Jong (1981), Moutaouakil (1984a).

10. The operator Post(erior) is taken to mean that the SoA coded in the predication is posterior to the time of the matrix structure under which it occurs. In this case, that matrix structure is the speech act E, and therefore the reference time is t_0 as retrievable from the deictic centre associated with the speech act.

(14) a. Decl E: X: Pres e: *polite* [A] (*you*)$_\varnothing$
'You are polite.'
b. Int E: X: Pres e: *polite* [A] (*you*)$_\varnothing$
'Are you polite?'
c. Imp E: Post e: *polite* [A] (*you*)$_\varnothing$
'Be polite!'

At this point it is useful to note the following property of our analysis. Take an example such as (15a), with the underlying structure given in (15b):

(15) a. *Prices slumped.*
b. Decl E: X: Past e: *slump* [V] (*prices*)$_{Proc}$

The illocutionary operator Decl is an element of the grammatical (as opposed to the lexical) vocabulary of the language. It is provided with some such definition as (12). Through this definition, (15) can be paraphrased along the lines of (16):

(16) S wishes A to add the content of the proposition 'prices slumped' to his pragmatic information.

Indirectly, then, our analysis achieves that which Ross's performative analysis was designed to capture in a more direct way: that the expression implies a performative act of some S with respect to some A. The analysis does not, however, involve the less attractive implications of the Performative Hypothesis.

11.5. Illocutionary conversion

11.5.1. Derived illocutions

We saw above that a linguistic expression with a given illocution Ill_E may be used to convey a different intended illocution Ill_S, and may be interpreted as such in Ill_A, where Ill_A is meant to be a reconstruction of the intended illocution Ill_S. This process, in which a given illocution is converted into another illocution, will be termed "illocutionary conversion".

This formulation might suggest that illocutionary conversion is purely a matter of pragmatics. However, the notion of illocutionary conversion is also relevant at the level of the linguistic expression as such. Consider the following example:

(17)   *She is a nice girl, isn't she?*

This expression consists of two parts. The first part, *she is a nice girl*, has all the properties of a declarative clause and would thus, at first sight, be an appropriate means for conveying an assertion. The second part, the tag *isn't she*, however, defines the whole expression as a question rather than an assertion. What, then, is the Ill_E of this expression? If we say that it is a declarative, we do not account for its interrogative character. But if we simply say that it is an Interrogative expression, we do not account for its special formal and semantic properties, as compared to a straightforward interrogative such as:

(18)   *Is she a nice girl?*

Formally, it will be very difficult to formulate expression rules for "interrogatives" in such a way that they sometimes produce declarative constituent order; semantically, expressions such as (17) differ from straight interrogatives in that they count as requests for confirmation rather than as requests for information.

I believe that this problem can be solved by assuming that the Ill_E of (17) is composite: the basic Ill_E of the first part of this construction is declarative, but this illocution is converted into Interrogative by the tag. The tag can thus be seen as implementing an operation which converts a basically declarative illocution into an interrogative one. This could be represented as follows:

(19)   [Tag [Decl] > Int] E: X: Pres e: {*a nice girl*} (*she*)$_\emptyset$

in which the composite illocutionary operator indicates that we have a basic Decl which is converted into Int by a "Tag" operation.

We can thus distinguish two forms of illocutionary conversion:

(i) *grammatical* illocutionary conversion, through which an illocution Ill_E is converted into an illocution Ill_E* through means which are in some way or other coded in the linguistic expression itself.

(ii) *pragmatic* illocutionary conversion, through which a linguistic expression with a given illocution Ill_E is understood in terms of a converted illocution Ill_A, such that $Ill_A \neq Ill_E$, although there is no information pertaining to this conversion to be found in the linguistic expression as such.

The possible interactions between these two types of conversion can be symbolized in the following schema:

(20) Ill_E ---(grammatical conv)---> $Ill_E{*}$ ---(pragmatic conv)---> Ill_A

The brackets indicate that neither grammatical nor pragmatic conversion is necessarily applied to the basic illocution as coded in the expression. On the other hand, grammatical and pragmatic conversion may well be both relevant to the same expression, as in the following example:

(21) *You're not oversensitive, are you?*

Here a basic Declarative is grammatically converted into an Interrogative through the tag. But the resulting Interrogative may be intended / interpreted as a Warning (e.g., when said by a dentist to a patient), or as a Threat (e.g., when said by a bully to his victim). In such cases we can say that Ill_E = Declarative, $Ill_E{*}$ = Interrogative, and Ill_A = Warning, Threat.

We shall say that in such cases as these, Ill_E is the *basic illocution of the expression* and $Ill_E{*}$ is the *derived illocution of the expression*. The grammatical conversion of Ill_E into $Ill_E{*}$ must by definition be coded by some overt means in the linguistic expression. These means, whatever they are, will be termed "illocutionary converters". Tags of the type which occur in (17) and (21) are thus illocutionary converters which map a basic declarative illocution into a derived interrogative one. In terms of these distinctions we can now try to set up a typology of illocutionary conversion. Two main questions are to be asked here:

(i) What types of grammatical illocutionary conversion can be distinguished across languages?

(ii) What means are used by languages to effect these grammatical conversions?

In the following sections I present some first suggestions relevant to these questions.

11.5.2. Types of grammatical conversion

Even on the basis of English alone, we must recognize at least the following forms of grammatical conversion:

(43) a. Decl > Interrogative
　　　 Decl > Request
　　b. Int > Request
　　　 Int > Rhetorical question
　　　 Int > Exclamation
　　c. Imp > Request
　　　 Imp > Exclamation

The following are examples of each of these conversion types:

(22) Decl > Int
　　a. *She is a nice girl.*
　　b. *She is a nice girl, isn't she?*

(23) Decl > Req
　　a. *Johnny, I hate this music!*
　　b. *Please, Johnny, I hate this music!*

(24) Int > Req
　　a. *Can you pass me the salt?*
　　b. *Please can you pass me the salt?*

(25) Int > Rhet
　　a. *What difference does it make?*
　　　 (Tell me the difference)
　　b. *What DIFference does it make?*
　　　 (It surely makes no difference)

(26) Int > Excl
　　a. *Has she grown?* (please tell me)
　　b. *Has she GROWN!*

(27) Imp > Req
　　a. *Give me the scalpel.*
　　b. *Please give me the scalpel.*
　　　 Give me the scalpel, will you?

(28) Imp > Excl
　　a. *Look who is there.* (Go and have a look to see who is there)
　　b. *Look who's THERE!!*

Some comments on these examples are in order.

I have in (25) used the traditional label "rhetorical question". There is reason to assume, however, that rhetorical questions in fact function as forceful statements (Quirk et al. 1972: 401), so that a conversion from Int to Decl or Excl would be involved. It is difficult, for example, to embed rhetorical questions under verbs of questioning, as in (29), in which the embedded clause cannot be interpreted as a rhetorical question:

(29)   *He asked who in the world would want to do such a thing.*

The idea that a grammatical conversion from Int to Rhet is involved at all is based on the assumption (which is debatable) that (25b) crucially differs from (25a) in prosodic contour. Quirk et al. (1972: 402) say that "...the intonation is that of an ordinary wh-question, except that a rise-fall tone is likely". For rhetorical Yes-No questions, the authors say that these are phonologically distinguished only by the unusually low or high starting-point of the rise. It is clear that, if these intonational differences are not sufficient to be considered a form of linguistic coding, then the conversion given in (25) is not a grammatical, but a pragmatic conversion.

There are certainly languages, however, which do have the type of grammatical conversion intended here. We may cite the following example from Dutch:

(30) a. *Wie   wil   er   voorzitter   worden?*
         who   wants   there   chairman   become
         'Who wants to be chairman?'
     b. *Wie   wil   er   nou   VOORzitter   worden???*
         who   wants   there   now   chairman   become
         'Who on earth would want to be CHAIRman?!'

(30a) is a normal question, which would be difficult to use, in this form, as a rhetorical question. (30b), with unstressed *nou* (a "modal" particle distinct from stressed *nou* 'now'), can only function as a rhetorical question. Thus, unstressed *nou* converts Int into Rhet. There is an accompanying prosodic difference between (30a) and (30b).

11.5.3. Types of illocutionary converters

Those linguistic elements and devices through which the basic illocution of a clause may be grammatically converted into some other illocution may be termed "illocutionary converters". I shall here briefly discuss the following types of illocutionary converter: (i) intonation; (ii) elements such as *please*; (iii) so-called "modal" particles; (iv) tags.

(i) *Intonation*
Compare the following two constructions:

(31) a. *Don't you like the soup?*
     b. *You don't like the soup?*

The difference between these two types of interrogative can be captured by assuming that (31a) has a basic Int illocution, whereas (31b) has a basic Decl illocution, which is converted into Int through the intonation pattern. The structure of (31b) would then be like:

(32)   [Inton [Decl] > Int] [*you don't like the soup*]

where Decl will trigger the rules leading to a declarative expression of the segmental part of the clause, and Inton will trigger the interrogative intonation superimposed on this basic declarative structure.

Such an analysis would seem to be semantically appropriate as well, since what S does in uttering (31b) can be described as confronting A with a statement, and signalling that he wishes A to confirm or disconfirm that statement. (31b) is a request for confirmation rather than a request for information.

The presence of a Decl operator in (32) is also useful for the following reason. There are certain elements which cannot occur in straightforward interrogatives, but which do occur in declaratives; an example is the adverb *probably*. Such elements, however, do occur in declarative interrogatives of type (31b). Compare:

(33) a. **Don't you probably like the soup?*
     b. *You probably don't like the soup.*
     c. *You probably don't like the soup?*

The possibility of adding *probably* to (33c) can be taken care of in terms of the Decl operator present in that construction. This is an indication that (31b) is correctly described as a declarative converted into an interrogative.

Several authors have done empirical research on these "questioned declaratives" (Geluykens 1987a). Their main question was: how can a sentence with declarative form be recognized as carrying a (derived) interrogative illocution? The results of this work, very briefly summarized, are as follows:

(a) In about half of the relevant cases, the prosodic pattern of the sentence clearly reveals its interrogative intention.

(b) In a part of the remaining cases, there are segmental elements which give away the interrogative character of the sentence.

(c) In the remaining cases, the expression can only be decoded as having interrogative intention through features of the context and the situation.

In our terminology we would say that (a) and (b) exemplify grammatical conversion, (a) by prosodic and (b) by segmental converters, whereas in (c) we are dealing with pragmatic conversion.

(ii) *Elements such as* please
As we saw in 11.5.2. above, *please* can be interpreted as an element converting Interrogatives, Imperatives, and Declaratives into Requests:

(34) a. *Can you pass me the salt, please?*   Int   >   REQ
     b. *Please, John, stop tickling me!*   Imp   >   REQ
     c. *Please, John, it's broad daylight!*   Decl >   REQ

Such constructions can be described according to the schemas:

(35) a. [*please* [Int] > REQ]
     b. [*please* [Imp] > REQ]
     c. [*please* [Decl] > REQ]

in which *please* is represented as operating on any of the basic illocutions Int, Imp, and Decl, yielding the value of a requestive illocution for the expression as a whole.

(iii) *So-called "modal" particles*
Many languages have particles through which one illocution can be grammatically converted into another. Consider the following examples from Dutch:

(36) Kun jij   deze   koffer   optillen?
      can you   this   trunk   lift
      'Can you lift this trunk?'
(37) a. *Kun jij deze koffer* even(tjes) *optillen?*
     b. *Kun jij deze koffer* soms even(tjes) *optillen?*
     c. *Kun jij deze koffer* misschien even(tjes) *optillen?*

(36) can be interpreted as a genuine request for information, although it could also be used for conveying a Request. Usually, however, when a Request is intended, the interrogative will be expanded by any of the elements in roman typeface in (37a-c); these elements can also be combined in various ways. Literally, these elements have such meanings as: 'a (very) short while' (*even(tjes)*), 'perhaps' (*misschien*), 'sometimes' (*soms*). These literal meanings, however, are hardly relevant in such constructions as (37a-c). In these constructions, the only function of these elements is to convert the basic interrogative illocution of the expression into a Request. We can thus describe the structure of (37a) according to the schema:

(38)   [*even(tjes)* [Int] > REQ]

A similar function can be assigned to the German particle *mal*, literally 'once', in a pair such as:

(39) a. *Kannst   du   das   Fenster   aufmachen?*
         can   you   the   window   open
         'Can you open the window?'
     b. *Kannst du das Fenster* mal *aufmachen?*
         'Could you open the window, please?'

(iv) *Tags*
We shall here interpret "tags" as illocutionary converters which are added at the end of the clause, not forming an integrated part of it (that is, as Extra-Clausal Constituents, see chapter 17). Tags may have the form of invariable particles, or they may contain verbal forms "mirroring" material in the clause, as in the rich tag system of English. Compare Dutch and English:

(40) a. *Het   is   warm   hier,   hè?*
         it   is   warm   here,   eh
     b. *It's warm here, isn't it?*

248   *The illocutionary layer*

Another difference is that tags may or may not be sensitive to the polarity of the clause. Thus, Dutch *hè* can without formal adaptation be added to negative clauses, but negative clauses in English require a positive tag (at least in the usage intended here). Compare:

(41) a.   *Het is hier niet warm, hè?*
     b.   *It's not warm here, is it?*

Tags of the type exemplified in (40)-(41) can now be interpreted as illocutionary converters with the effect of turning Decl into Int. English also has other types of tags,[11] which convert imperative sentences into requests, as in:

(42) a.   *Open the door, will you?*   Imp > REQ
     b.   *Don't close the door, will you?* Imp > REQ

By defining Tags as illocutionary converters we clearly interpret them in functional rather than formal terms. The examples in (40) and (41) go to show that Tags may have quite different forms. Specifically, on our interpretation they need not contain any finite verb.

Conversely, not just any post-clausal constituent containing a finite verb can be functionally classified as an illocutionary converter. Consider the following examples:

(43) a.   *He's a nice chap, John is.*
     b.   *He made a lot of money, John did.*

In neither of these cases does the post-clausal constituent modify the basic illocution of the clause: the illocution is Declarative with or without the appendix. In fact, these appendices fully conform to our definition of Tail (to be discussed in chapter 17): they have precisely the same function as the corresponding constituents without the verbal form added. We may thus conclude that there is a functional difference between Tag and Tail, and that this functional difference does not necessarily correlate with the formal difference residing in absence vs. presence of a verbal element.

---

11. See Quirk et al. (1972: 390-392) and Lyons (1977: 749, 766) for more detailed accounts of the English tag system.

11.5.4. The borderline between grammatical and pragmatic conversion

In practice the borderline between grammatical and pragmatic illocutionary conversion is not always easy to draw. Consider the following example, due to Gordon—Lakoff (1975), and also discussed in Levinson (1983: 267).

(44) a. *Why don't you paint your house purple?*
 b. *Why not paint your house purple?*

(44a) is an interrogative construction which, in suitable settings, can also be interpreted as a suggestion by S to A to perform a certain action. In this case we can say that the Ill_E Interrogative can be pragmatically converted into a piece of Advice. There is nothing in the structure of (44a), however, which forces this interpretation. (44b), on the other hand, can only be interpreted as a piece of Advice from S to A, not as a genuine request for information, no matter in which setting it is used. In other words, the illocution Advice, which is reached through pragmatic conversion in the case of (44a), has become part of the linguistic properties of (44b).

Since (44b) also has a number of properties typical of interrogative constructions we can say that it is an interrogative converted into a piece of Advice:

(45) [Int > Adv] [*you paint your house purple*]

Another, less clearcut example is the following. Consider:

(46) *Could you open that door?*

There can be no doubt that a construction of this type is predominantly used for conveying a request to A to open the door, rather than as a genuine question about A's ability to do so. However, (46) CAN be used to ask the latter type of question, as in:

(47) *You claim that you are very strong. Well, could you open that door, for instance?*

This means that the illocution Request is not actually coded in the linguistic expression as such, but is a matter of pragmatic conversion, even if that form of pragmatic conversion is the rule rather than the exception for this expression type. As soon as a construction such as (46) has specialized to such an extent that it can ONLY be used to convey a Request, we will have to say that the illocution Request has become part of the semantic structure of the construction as such.[12]

For a final example, consider the following Arabic construction, discussed in Moutaouakil (1986a) in this connection:

(48) *Hal tusaʕiduni*
      Int help.you.me

which, literally speaking, could be paraphrased as 'Do you help me?', but in fact is used by convention as a Request for help: 'Could you help me?'. If it is true that (48) can only be used as such a Request, then again we could analyse the construction in terms of a schema such as:

(49) [Int > Req] [*you help me*]

This representation is based on the assumption that the illocution Request, originally associated with the interrogative through pragmatic conversion, has been absorbed into the semantic structure of (48).[13]

11.5.5. Embedded converted illocutions

Bolkestein (1992)[14] points to the interesting fact that at least in Latin there is reason to assume that even certain converted illocutions can be embedded, and then lead to different formal expression types. The evidence is as follows: a question such as (50) may get different illocutionary interpretations, either Int or Int converted to Rhet (this would be a matter of grammatical conversion if the two readings were differentiated prosodically).

---

12. Cf. Risselada (1988).
13. This is indeed the analysis proposed in Moutaouakil (1984a). See also Haverkate (1979: 103), who speaks of "multiple illocutionary function" in cases such as these, and Risselada (1988).
14. Using data from Orlandini (1980).

(50) Quid   est   turpius?
     what   is   more.shameful
     (a) Int 'What is more shameful? Tell me.'
     (b) Rhet 'Surely nothing can be more shameful!'

Now when (50) is embedded on reading (a) we get a normal dependent question (a finite subordinate clause in the subjunctive). But embeddings corresponding to reading (b) have a different, infinitival form:

(51) (clamabat ...)   quid   esse turpius
      he.exclaimed   what   be   more.shameful
      'What could be more shameful?!, he exclaimed.'

Another relevant fact is that rhetorical questions do not embed under verbs of "asking", a clear sign that their illocutionary value has been converted.
   Another example is the following:

(52) a. Vide   quot   sint. (subjunctive)
         look   how.many   they-are
         'Look how many there are'
     b. Vide quot sunt! (indicative)
         'Look how many there are!!'

Dependent questions in Latin normally have the predicate in the subjunctive. In (52b), however, we find the indicative, which is a clear sign that the embedded construction is not a dependent question (S is in no doubt about their number). Thus, the embedded construction in (52b) can be interpreted as a rhetorical question. A similar opposition between subjunctive and indicative is found in some other pairs of non-converted and converted illocutions in Latin.
   These different facts require us to assume that even converted illocutions of embedded clauses must be available if we are to correctly account for their behaviour in the grammar.

11.5.6. Indirect speech acts

In terms of the terminological distinctions made in this chapter, we can now define *indirect speech acts* as speech acts in which there is a difference between Ill_E on the one hand, and Ill_S / Ill_A on the other, that is, in which the illocutionary force of the expression is pragmatically converted into some other illocutionary force. Let us take an extreme example:

(53)   *The door is open.*
        Ill_E = Decl
        Ill_S / Ill_A = REQ 'Please, close the door'.

In this case, there is no indication whatsoever in the linguistic expression signalling that (53) is used as a Request rather that a statement. In other words, the requestive use of (53) is purely a matter of pragmatics, and outside the scope of a FG. This does not mean that pragmatic conversion is not determined by rules and strategies. But these are not rules and strategies governing the language system, but rules and principles governing the use of the system.[15]

11.6. Explicit performatives again

We can now return to the problem posed by explicit performatives. The following points are elevant to our approach to this problem:
— In chapter 5 it was argued that Indirect Speech complements have their own illocutionary operators.
— Explicit performatives are formed with higher speech act verbs. Such verbs do not pertain to the grammatical, but to the lexical domain. The relevant predicates are to be found in the lexicon, languages may differ in their degree of lexical articulation in the illocutionary domain, and when S wishes to create an explicit performative, he will choose an appropriate matrix verb from the lexicon.

The problem is thus: how can a construction which looks like a normal complex sentence with a clause embedded under a speech act verb acquire its peculiar performative character for which it was originally singled out by Austin for special philosophical reflection? In other words: how can we account for the differences between:

(54) a.   *John told Peter that he would fail.*
     b.   *I tell (you) that you will fail.*

---

15. For a description of the factors that determine the pragmatic interpretation of expressions with given grammatical properties, see Haverkate (1979).

Why does (54a) count as a description of what John did in a particular speech act, while (54b) counts as an act of telling? Our strategy will here be to assign to (54a-b) basically the same structure, and to explain the peculiar effect of (54b) in terms of the distribution of deictic parameters across embedded clause and main clause.

Let us look at the structure of (54b) in more detail. I will assume that the embedded clause has its own Decl operator, and that the matrix clause also has a Decl operator, since the construction as a whole takes the form of a declarative rather than, say, an interrogative. The Decl operator of the embedded clause will be interpreted in terms of the S and A of the higher clause, 'I' and 'you'. These, however, are identical to the S and A which are relevant to the interpretation of the higher Decl operator. Further, the main verb *tell* is evaluated in terms of the current moment of speaking, in contrast to otherwise similar constructions which would contain a verb such as *told* or *will tell*.

The whole construction, then, can be interpreted as reporting a speech act which S is currently carrying out with respect to A. Such reporting of a current act is interpreted as a reinforcement of that act.

The structure of (54) will thus be as follows:

(55)   Decl E_i: X_i: Pres e_i: *tell* [V] (S) (A)
       (Decl E_j: X_j: Post e_j: *fail* [V] (A))

When we apply the definitions of (12) to this construction, the result is the following:

(56)   S wishes A to add the content of 'I tell you that you will fail' to his/her pragmatic information;
       S wishes A to add the content of 'You will fail' to his / her pragmatic information.

In itself, the assertion 'You will fail' would be sufficient to achieve the desired result. The fact that S reports that he is telling that assertion counts as a reinforcement of the assertion. Note that this analysis does not claim that implicit and explicit performatives such as the following pair are synonymous:

(57) a.   *You will fail.*
     b.   *I tell you that you will fail.*

For one thing, the lexical verb *tell* does not occur in the definition of the illocutionary operator Decl. For another thing, a construction of type (57b) comes out as a more forceful or emphatic way of doing what one can also do by means of constructions of type (57a). This correctly accounts for (i) the fact that the properties of (57a) cannot be derived from those of (57b), and (ii) the fact that (57b) rather than (57a) is the pragmatically marked member of the opposition.

Let us now compare the following pair:

(58) a. *I will marry you.*
  b. *I promise that I will marry you.*

(58a) is obviously a Decl construction. If it is interpreted as a Promise, this is a matter of purely pragmatic conversion: there is nothing in (58a) which marks it as containing a promise. Therefore, if S wishes to make it unmistakably clear that he is doing a promise, the explicitly performative construction (58b) can serve the purpose. This construction explicitly adds the element of promising which in (58a) is not linguistically coded. Again, the properties of (58a) cannot be reduced to those of (58b), and (58b) rather than (58a) is the marked member of the opposition.

11.7. Conclusion

What emerges from our discussion is the following picture of the illocutionary component of the grammar.

In order to code his illocutionary intention S can choose between a grammatical and a lexical strategy. In the grammatical strategy, a choice is made among the basic sentence types of the languages. All languages have a restricted number of such sentence types. These can be interpreted as encoding a restricted number of global or basic illocutions, such as Declarative, Interrogative, Imperative, etc. These global illocutions can be captured by means of illocutionary operators such as Decl, Int, Imp etc. In most cases these basic, global illocutions will be sufficient to achieve the desired communicative effect.

Most languages have certain forms of grammatical illocutionary conversion, through which an expression with basic illocution Ill_E can be converted into an expression with derived illocution Ill_E^*. The derived illocution may constitute a modification or a conversion of the basic illocution. Constructions characterized by basic or derived illocutionary operators can be used, through pragmatic conversion of the illocution, for a variety of communicative purposes. Thus, a Declarative, which basically signals only that S wishes A to add the content of the clause to his pragmatic information, can be used to convey a statement, a promise, a warning, a threat, a suggestion, a request, etc. In all these cases, that which is conveyed is not a matter of linguistic information (not part of the semantic content of the linguistic expression), but a matter of pragmatic intention and corresponding interpretation.

For many purposes the basic and derived illocutions, presented in the appropriate setting, are sufficient to achieve the desired communicative effect. The non-explicit nature of these illocutions may even be exploited in specific circumstances, in which it is expedient for S not to commit himself too much to any one particular illocutionary intention.

In the situation in which there is some pressure on the communication, however, it may be necessary for S to make his intentions more explicit. "Pressure" can be taken in terms of difficulty of getting through to A, or in terms of the importance of some speech act being interpreted in precisely the way in which it is intended. In such situations, S can opt for the lexical strategy. This strategy involves the choice of a speech act verb from the lexicon, which is then used in order to comment on what precisely S is doing in issuing an expression with a given basic or derived illocution. This is what is done in explicit performative constructions. Thus, we take an expression such as (58b) to be paraphrasable along the lines of:

(59)   *What I am doing in saying I will marry you is promising you that I will marry you.*

Thus, the performative preface does not "spell out" what is already coded in a simple statement of the form (58a). Rather, it codes in the linguistic expression some element of information which, in other circumstances, could be left to the pragmatic interpretation of A. Other means of achieving the same result are such expressions as:

(60) a.   *I will,* I promise, *marry you.*
     b.   *I will marry you,* I promise.
     c.   *I will marry you.* This is a promise.

In each of these constructions, the expression in roman typeface makes it explicit how S wishes A to interpret his statement *I will marry you.*

All languages encode a limited number of basic illocutions in their grammatically relevant illocutionary operators. And all languages can specify an in principle unlimited number of more specific illocutions by using lexical performative verbs contained in the lexicon. Such lexical verbs describe, in various degrees of specificity, what Ss are doing when issuing a linguistic expression of a given type.

12. Interrogative clauses

12.0. Introduction

In this chapter I discuss the way in which various types of questions can be treated in FG. I start with some preliminary remarks on the function of questions, their illocutionary force, and how this illocutionary force can be represented in underlying clause structures. I discuss the various types of responses which may be given to questions, and the various types of question which may be distinguished in terms of (i) what type of information is questioned, and (ii) what types of possible answer can be given to the question.

After a brief discussion of Yes-No questions and disjunctive questions, I go into more detail with respect to Q-word questions. This is because Q-word questions display the most interesting typological properties, specifically in their interrelations with verbal restrictors (VRs)[1] on the one hand (see Lehmann 1984), and Cleft constructions on the other. Q-word questions relate to VRs in that, just like the most widespread type of VR, they can be understood in terms of an operation (in this case, the questioning operation symbolized by the operator Q) applied to the vacant position of some open (extended) predication. This is reflected in many similarities with respect to accessibility and expression between Q-word questions and VRs. There is also a more direct connection between Q-word questions and VRs if it is true, as was argued in chapter 4, that the former provide one historical source of one type of the latter.

Q-word questions relate to Cleft constructions in that they are a particular type of Focus construction: the Q-constituent in a Q-word question intrinsically carries the Focus function. Furthermore, many languages have Q-word questions which take the form of Cleft constructions, as in:

(1)   *What was it that Peter found in the garden?*

In certain languages such constructions even constitute the only possible form that Q-word questions can take (in general, or in certain conditions). An

---

1. For the notion "verbal restrictor", see chapters 2-4.

example such as (1) vividly illustrates the interrelations between Q-word question, Cleft construction, and VR, since, according to the analysis of Cleft constructions to be defended in chapter 13, (1) contains a VR as a proper subpart. Since the analysis of Cleft questions, on this view, presupposes a theory of Cleft constructions in general as well as a general idea on the structure of VRs, a discussion of Cleft interrogatives is postponed until chapter 14.

12.1. The illocutionary force of questions

In the preceding chapter we characterized questions as linguistic expressions through which S can signal that he wishes to receive a relevant verbal response from A: they are sentence types with interrogative illocutionary force as their basic illocution. The general structure of questions can thus be represented as follows:

(2)   Int E: X: [Extended Predication]

where the illocutionary operator Int is pragmatically interpreted along the lines of:

(3)   S wishes A to provide him with a true proposition X with a content as specified in the Extended Predication.

Just as is the case with any illocutionary operator, Int can be grammatically and pragmatically converted into other illocutions such as Request, Exclamation, or Rhetorical Question. For such conversions, see chapter 11.

Questions are requests for answers. An answer to a question is a linguistic expression which provides the information which was requested in the question. A distinction must be made between "answer" and "response": all answers are responses, but not all responses are answers. Non-answer responses include indications on A's part that he is not able or unwilling to provide an answer, or that the question is based on incorrect presuppositions on the part of S, and counter-questions in which A asks S for further information necessary for A to be able to provide an answer. They are, in other words, all those reactions on the part of A which do not provide S with the true proposition X as requested in the question. For example:

(4) S: *Where is Peter's office?*
    A: *I don't know.*
       I can't tell you.
       That's none of your business.
(5) S: *Where is Peter's office?*
    A: *Peter doesn't HAVE any office.*
(6) S: *Where is Peter's office?*
    A: *Which Peter do you mean?*
       Why do you want to know?

All these non-answer responses have to a certain extent a meta-communicative character, since they concern the appropriateness, the answerability, or certain conditions for the answerability of the question. None of them provides the information which S's question signals he wishes to receive.

Once answers have been restricted to verbal responses in which A provides S with the true proposition as requested in the question, question types can be equivalently distinguished either in terms of "type of information requested" or of "type of possible answer".

One interesting typological fact should be mentioned immediately: all languages have specific interrogative sentence types (linguistic expressions specialized for interrogative function), but hardly any language has a special sentence type for answering questions. In other words, an answer usually takes the form of (a fragment of) a declarative statement not overtly coded for its functioning as an answer.

This typological fact can be explained in the following way: questions are typically "initiative speech acts": they are used to open up an exchange between S and A; answers are necessarily "reactive speech acts": they can only be used in response to a question.[2] Questions may come "out of the blue" and set the scene for the further course of communication: answers are typically "second members" of adjacency pairs of question-answer type.

Since questions can be used without previous conditions having been established, it is essential for them to be marked for their interrogative character. Answers, however, fill a slot in a previously established communicative pattern. Therefore, they need not be overtly marked as being answers.

---

2. For this distinction, compare Franck (1980).

12.2. Different types of interrogative construction

I shall discuss the different types of interrogative constructions in terms of the following schema:

(7)
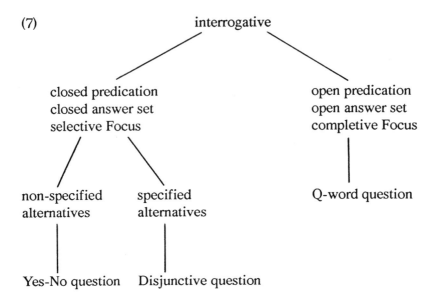

Q-word questions are formed on the basis of an open (extended) predication, in the sense of a predication in which at least one constituent is left unspecified. Usually the unspecified constituent is a term position, but it may also be part of a term structure or, in exceptional cases, the predicate itself. Any Q-word question can thus be likened to a fill-in form with certain blanks in which one is to add the relevant information. A's task is to complete the predication in such a way that it results in a true proposition X. Compare:

(8) Int E: X: Past e: [*kiss* [V] (*you*)$_{Ag}$ (*???*)$_{Go}$] (*the park*)$_{Loc}$
'Who did you kiss in the park?'

(9) Int E: X: Past e: [*kiss* [V] (*you*)$_{Ag}$ (*Peter*)$_{Go}$] (*???*)$_{Loc}$
'Where did you kiss Peter?'

(10) Int E: X: Pres e: [*have* [V] (*you*)$_\varnothing$ (i *???* x_i: *child* [N])]
'How many children do you have?'

Q-word questions relate to an open answer set in the sense that the number of possible answers is just as unlimited as the number of possible constituents which can appropriately take the place of the blank so as to result in a well-formed predication. Q-word questions signal "Completive Focus" as discussed in *TFG1*: 13.4. S indicates that he wishes a blank in his pragmatic information to be filled in by A, and an appropriate answer to a Q-word question does fill in such a blank, and thus completes the pragmatic information of S in the relevant sense. I return in detail to the typological properties of Q-word questions below.

Other question types can be analysed as being based on closed extended predications, and as being associated with a limited set of possible answers.

In disjunctive questions, S provides A with two or more alternative propositions, on the assumption that one of these is true, and requests A to tell him which of them is. An appropriate answer to a disjunctive question indicates which one of the presented alternatives is true; usually the answer consists of a repetition of (the relevant part of) the question. Consider:

(11) S: *Is Peter going to London or is he going to Paris?*
     A: *He is going to Paris.*

The number of possible answers to a disjunctive question is limited in the sense that it never exceeds the number of alternatives presented in the question. Disjunctive questions are associated with "Selective Focus" in the sense that S asks A to choose the correct alternative, and that A, in answering the question, does just that. Note that this is only true on the assumption that in an exchange such as:

(12) S: *Is Peter going to London or is he going to Paris?*
     A: *He is going to New YORK!*

A's response is not considered an answer to the question. And indeed, a response of this type implicitly signals that the question was wrongly put. Note that a response of this type requires a special intonation. The response exemplifies one form of "Corrective Focus".

A disjunctive question of type (11) can be represented according to the following format:

(13)   Int E: X: [(Predication-1) or (Predication-2)]

where the combination of Int and *or* suffices to indicate the disjunctive nature of the question.

262   *Interrogative clauses*

In many cases, of course, it is not full predications which are presented as alternatives in the disjunctive question. (11) would more usually be phrased in the following way:

(14) S: *Is Peter going to London or to Paris?*
     A: *To Paris.*

An analysis of such local disjunctions in questions was suggested in 9.2.above.

Yes-No questions present a single closed extended predication and question whether this predication represents a true proposition or not. Consider:

(15)   *Is Peter going to London?*
       — representation:
       Int E: X: Pres e: [Progr *go* [V] (*Peter*)$_{Ag}$ (*London*)$_{Dir}$]
       — interpretation:
       'Tell me whether the predication *Peter is going to London* represents a true proposition or not'

The number of possible answers to a Yes-No question is limited to 'yes' (true) and 'no' (not true) and various modalizations of these, as in:

(16) a.   *Yes, I believe he is.*
     b.   *No, it appears he isn't.*
     c.   *He probably is.*

There are obvious connections between Yes-No questions and disjunctive questions. Usually, a disjunctive question offers two alternatives from which A is to select the correct one. A Yes-No question implicitly does the same, since it is taken as presenting the alternative 'true or not true?'. In principle, therefore, the same effect may be achieved through a disjunctive question of the form:

(17) a.   *Is Peter going to London or is he not going to London?*
     b.   *Is Peter going to London or is he not?*

Since such disjunctive questions would always consist of the positive and the negative version of the same predication and since, therefore, the second alternative can always be reconstructed on the basis of the first, it is clearly more economical to just present one predication in interrogative format, and interpret this by convention as bearing on the choice whether that predication represents a true proposition or not.

The disjunction implicit in Yes-No questions explains, however, why it is that many languages mark their Yes-No questions with elements which are reminiscent of disjunction, such as:

(18) a. *Is Peter going to London, or not?*
     b. *Is Peter going to London, or?*

If, on the basis of these facts, one wishes to see Yes-No questions as a particular subtype of disjunctive questions, this is semantically no doubt correct: a Yes-No question offers a selection from two alternatives which, however, consist in the polar values True/Not True.

Formally, however, Yes-No questions are quite easily distinguished from disjunctive questions in most languages; and they can most easily be characterized as consisting of a single predication presented with some sort of signal of interrogative illocution.

In 5.1.3. we argued that not only independent clauses, but also embedded constructions may be provided with their own illocutionary operator. This is certainly true in the case of questions. In fact, each of the question types discussed above has an indirect, embedded counterpart:

(19) a. *John asked where Peter was going.*
         (embedded Q-word question)
     b. *John asked whether Peter wanted coffee or tea.*
         (embedded disjunctive question)
     c. *John asked whether Peter was going to London.*
         (embedded Yes-No question)

12.3. Q-word questions

12.3.1. The nature of Q-word questions

We saw that a Q-word question can be likened to an open form presented by S to A with the request to fill in the missing information. Consider an example such as:

(20)   *Where is Peter going?*

264   *Interrogative clauses*

The communicative value of such a question can be analysed as follows:

(21) (i) S presents A with the open predication: 'Peter is going to ? '
 (ii) S assumes that there is a correct value L such that, if L is filled in in the position of the blank, the resulting predication yields a true proposition.
 (iii) S assumes that A knows L.
 (iv) S requests A to provide him with L.

If all these presuppositions on the part of S are fulfilled, and if A is willing to comply, A may come up with some such answer as:

(22)   *To London.*

which effectively fills in the gap in S's information.

An important property of Q-word questions is their association with the presupposition on the part of S that there must be a correct value L for filling the gap. A question such as (20) can be properly asked only if S assumes that Peter is going to some place L. Contrast this with a Yes-No question such as:

(23)   *Is Peter going somewhere?*

which can appropriately be answered by 'No, he's just strolling around'. Note that our view of the presuppositionality of Q-word questions implies that in a sequence such as:

(24) S: *Where is Peter going?*
 A: *He isn't going anywhere!*

A's reaction is a non-answer response, indicating that the question was wrongly put or inappropriately used.

Much of the typology of Q-word questions can be understood on the basis of the view that Q-words, or constituents containing Q-words, have intrinsic Focus function. We know that the most common expression devices for Focus constituents (FocC) are the following:
  (i) assign emphatic accent to FocC;
  (ii) mark FocC by means of some Focus marker;

(iii) place FocC in a special position for pragmatically important constituents. Such positions, in order of decreasing frequency, are the following: (a) clause-initial position P1; (b) preverbal position Pb; (c) other positions (rare).

(iv) place FocC in the Focus position of a Cleft construction.

When Q-word terms are inherently Focus constituents, we expect similar devices to be used for the expression of Q-word questions. And this expectation is correct. In many languages, the treatment of Q-word terms is identical to that of Focus constituents; in many other languages, it is quite similar; and in probably all languages, Q-word questions are treated by some of the devices (i)-(iv) characteristic of Focus constituents.

Q-word questions can either take the form of questioned simplex predications or of Cleft constructions. Questioned simplex predications either have the Q-word term in pattern position (= the position occupied by non-questioned constituents of the same functional status), or in Focus position, where Focus position is most usually the clause-initial position P1. This means that the following three construction types exemplify the most common strategies for forming Q-word questions:

(25) a. Q-pattern
John went to the dance with whom?
b. Q-focus
With whom did John go to the dance?
c. Q-cleft
Who was it that John went to the dance with?
With whom was it that John went to the dance?

In the following sections I shall discuss the properties of the first two types in more detail. Q-cleft constructions will be discussed in chapter 14. I start with some remarks on the status of Q-word questions and Q-words in general. Then I discuss the status of simplex questions of types (25a) and (25b). The chapter ends with a discussion of some special topics concerning Q-word questions: constructions with more than one questioned term and constructions in which the predicate rather than a term is questioned.

12.3.2. The operators Int and Q

In our representation of Q-word questions we use the interrogative operator Int to symbolize the interrogative character of the construction as a whole (Int is the operator which all questions have in common), and the operator Q to indicate which particular part of the predication is questioned in Q-word questions. The underlying structure of (26a) is thus (26b):

(26) a. *Where is Peter going?*
   b. Int E: X: Pres e: Progr *go* [V] *(Peter)*$_{Ag}$ (Q x$_i$)$_{Dir}$

It is indeed useful to have both Int and Q represented in the underlying structure: Int indicates that the whole predication is a question, Q indicates which part of the predication is being questioned. It will be clear, however, that Int is redundantly specified in any predication which contains at least one occurrence of Q. In other words, all predications containing an occurrence of Q also have the operator Int, though the converse is not true.

We can thus say, in general, that the structure of any Q-word question can be represented by means of the following schema:

(27)   Int E: X: [...... Qx$_i$ ......]

where Int is the interrogative illocutionary operator, Q is the question operator, and x$_i$ is the operand of Q, i.e. the constituent of which the identity is requested in the Q-word question.

The idea that a Q-word question can be understood in terms of a question operator operating on a gap in an open predication is at least as old as Carnap (1937: 296):

> Suppose I want someone to make an assertion of the form "Charles was — in Berlin", where a time-determination of which I am ignorant but which I wish to learn from the assertion is to take the place of the dash. Now the question must indicate by some means that the missing expression is to be a time-determination. If symbols are used this can be effected by giving a sentential function in which in the place of the argument a variable "*t*", which is established as a temporal variable, occurs. To symbolize the question, the variable whose argument is requested must be bound by means of a question-operator, e.g. "(?*t*) (Charles was *t* in Berlin)".

Our analysis of Q-word questions is in principle the same, except for one difference of more general relevance: the questioning operator Q is not treated as a sentential or predication operator, as in Carnap's logical analysis, but as a term operator working locally on its operand (which is usually a term position). We saw in *TFG1*: chapter 7 that FG differs from most logical calculi in distinguishing a set of term operators corresponding to what logical calculi usually express through sentential operators. The reason for this difference is that natural languages do not usually organize their expressions according to the logical model.

In the case of Q-word questions, the reasoning is entirely parallel: if the semantic structure of such questions were like that postulated by Carnap, then one would expect many languages to have Q-word questions of such a form as:

(28) *At what time did Charles go to Berlin at that time?*

Such question types, however, do not in fact seem to occur in natural languages. Q-word questions as they occur in natural languages are much more easily understood if it is assumed that they have an interrogative operator at work in precisely the spot about which missing information is requested. Thus, questions equivalent to (28) can be understood in terms of underlying structures of the form:

(29) a. *Charles went to Berlin (when)?*
     b. *Charles went to Berlin (at what time)?*

For this reason we analyse Q-word questions by means of the locally active question operator Q. Our analysis of (29a) and (29b) will then take the following form:

(30) a. Int E: X: Past e: [*go* [V] (*Charles*)$_{Ag}$ (*Berlin*)$_{Dir}$] (Qx$_i$: <time>)$_{Temp}$
     b. Int E: X: Past e: [*go* [V] (*Charles*)$_{Ag}$ (*Berlin*)$_{Dir}$] (Qx$_i$: *time*)$_{Temp}$

In both cases, Q takes the position of a term operator, indicating that the identity of the item filling the relevant term position is to be revealed. The difference between the questioned terms in (29a) and (29b) will be dealt with below.

12.3.3. Types of Q-constituents

The questioned item in the underlying predication will be expressed in the final structure of the clause by some constituent which consists of or contains a Q-word. Such constituents may be called Q-constituents. Q-constituents come in different types, according to what information they express, and how they express this information.

The information expressed by a Q-constituent may potentially consist of the following components:

(i) the information that a questioned constituent is involved;
(ii) the information about the type of entity that is being questioned;
(iii) information about the functional status of the questioned constituent within the predication.

These various bits of information may be expressed either synthetically or analytically. Compare in this respect the following Q-constituents:

(31) Synthetic   Analytic
      who   *what person*
      what   *what thing*
      when   *at what time*
      where   *at what place*
      why   *for what reason*
      how   *in what way*

It is to be noted that two distinct types of synthetic expression may be involved in Q-constituents: either the operand type or the functional relation may lack overt expression; and in some cases these two may combine into one unanalysable portmanteau form. This can be illustrated as follows:

(32)   Function   Q   Type
    a.   *at*   *what*   *time*
    b.   ∅   *what*   *time*
    c.   *at*   *what*   ∅
    d.   *when*   ∅

Obviously we can speak of non-expression of the functional status of the Q-constituent only in those cases in which the corresponding non-questioned constituent would be overtly marked for its semantic or syntactic function.

The synthetically expressed Q-constituents in a language clearly concern the basic conceptual "categories" in terms of which we organize our experience. And when we paraphrase these synthetic Q-constituents by means of their analytic correspondents, we get a set of nouns indicating those basic categories: *person, thing, time, place, reason, manner, quality, quantity*. Interestingly, Aristotle indicated five of his ten categories by means of question words (*Categories* 4,1):

Q-word questions 269

Every simplex word designates either a *substance* or a *how much* or a *what kind of* or a *in relation to what* or a *where* or a *when* or a *position* or a *having* or a *doing* or an *undergoing*.[3]

It would be interesting to study the occurrence of synthetic Q-words across languages, to find out whether any typological hierarchy could be established between these basic categories.

12.3.4. The representation of Q-constituents

There are various possibilities for representing Q-constituents in the structure of underlying predications. I have opted for a representation which spells out the operand type even if it is not overtly expressed; but in that case the operand type predicate is placed between angled brackets, as a kind of selection restriction incorporated in the Q-word term. The correct form of the Q-constituent will then be determined by the expression rules. We thus arrive at such representations as the following:

(33) a. $(Qx_i: <person>)$ 'who / whom'
  b. $(Qx_i: person)$ 'which person'
(34) a. $(Qx_i: <thing>)$ 'what'
  b. $(Qx_i: thing)$ 'which thing'
(35) a. $(Qx_i: <time>)_{Temp}$ 'when'
  b. $(Qx_i: time)_{Temp}$ 'at what time'
(36) a. $(Qx_i: <place>)_{Loc}$ 'where'
  b. $(Qx_i: place)_{Loc}$ 'at what place'
(37) a. $(Qx_i: <reason>)_{Reason}$ 'why'
  b. $(Qx_i: reason)_{Reason}$ 'for what reason'
(38) a. $(Qx_i: <way>)_{Manner}$ 'how'
  b. $(Qx_i: way)_{Manner}$ 'in what way'

This type of representation is somewhat redundant in the case of *when*, *where*, *why* and *how*: in each of these cases, the semantic function alone would be sufficient to trigger the expression rules. In the case of *who* vs. *what*, on the other hand, the selection restrictions are required to properly differentiate

---

3. "Substance" was later indicated by an expression which could be paraphrased as "being (an answer to the question) 'what was it?'"

between the two. And in all the analytic b-constructions we need the basic nominal predicate as a restrictor in order to get the correct output. A further reason for having these nominal restrictors in the analytic construction is that further modification of these predicates is possible, as in:

(39) a. *for what particular reason*
    b. *at what precise place*
    c. *in what devilish way*

It would be difficult to account for these structures if the head noun were not present in the underlying structure of these Q-word terms.

12.3.5. Accessibility to Q

What constituents of the predication are accessible to Q? I.e., what constituent types can be questioned? There are two distinct aspects to the accessibility question:
   (i) which types of constituents are accessible to Q in principle?
   (ii) under which conditions are these constituents accessible to Q?
Distinguishing these two sub-problems is necessary since constituents which are in principle accessible to Q may not be so when they occur in certain positions within the predication. Constraints on accessibility are in such cases definable, not in terms of intrinsic properties of the operand of Q, but in terms of its position within the hierarchical network of the predication.

In English, for example, Subject terms are in principle accessible to Q, but they are inaccessible to Q when they occur, for instance, within restrictors or within embedded questions, as in:

(40) a. *He found the book that my brother lost.*
    b. **Who did he find the book that lost?*
(41) a. *He wondered whether my brother had lost the book.*
    b. **Who did he wonder whether had lost the book?*

Such "hierarchical" constraints on accessibility will be separately discussed in chapter 16, in the context of a more general discussion on accessibility. Here, I concentrate on question (i), concerning the types of constituents which are in principle accessible to Q. It should be understood that if a constituent type is in general accessible to Q, it will usually not be so in all conditions of occurrence.

The accessibility problem may be discussed under three headings:
(i) Questioning of term positions;
(ii) Questioning of constituents within terms;
(iii) Questioning of predicates.
These three types of questioning are discussed in separate sections below.

12.3.5.1. Questioning of terms. As a general rule, any type of term position within the extended predication can in principle be questioned in a Q-word question. Q can usually be applied to both argument and satellite terms, and the application of Q does not appear to be restricted in terms of the semantic and syntactic functions of these terms. Accessibility to Q does not seem to be sensitive to some hierarchy of constraints comparable to the Accessibility Hierarchy which governs accessibility to Relativization.

12.3.5.2. Questioning of constituents within terms. Most languages allow certain constituents within terms to be questioned. The following constructions represent the most common cases:

(42) A: *Which book do you want?*
    B: *This book.*
(43) A: *How many books do you want?*
    B: *Three books.*
(44) A: *What kind of book do you want?*
    B: *A book about flowers.*
(45) A: *Whose book do you want?*
    B: *John's book.*

We shall say that Q applies to the demonstrative operator in (42), to the quantifier in (43), to a restrictor in (44), and to a Possessor restrictor in (45).
   (i) Questioned demonstratives. Consider the following constructions:

(46) a. *Which book do you want?*
    b. *Which of the books do you want?*

In both expressions, S asks A to choose one item from a pre-established set of books. In answering such a question it is sufficient for A to identify the particular book that he wants. This can be done by using a demonstrative, as in *This book* or *That book*. Even pointing at the desired item may be a sufficient reaction.

272 *Interrogative clauses*

For this reason *which* may be called a questioned demonstrative *Qdem*. Using the conventions introduced in *TFG1*: chapter 7, we can then represent the constructions in (46a-b) as follows:

(47) a.   Int E: X: Pres e: *want* [V] (*you*) (Qdem 1 x_i: *book* [N])
     b.   Int E: X: Pres e: *want* [V] (*you*) (Qdem / d m x_i: *book* [N])

Note the difference between:

(48) a.   *Which books do you want?*
          (presupposition: you want more than one book)
     b.   *Which of the books do you want?*
          (presupposition: you may want one or more of the books)

Note further that in English it is impossible to answer a partitive construction such as (48b) by:

(49)   **This of the books.*

Usually, the answer will be simply:

(50) a.   *This book.*
     b.   *This one.*

(ii) Questioned quantifiers. We saw in *TFG1*: 7.4. that quantifiers concern the size of the ensemble defined in a term, where size equals number in the case of sets, and measure in the case of masses. Questioning of quantifiers may thus be represented as follows:

(51)

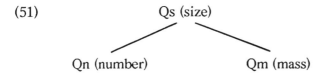

In English there is no neutral expression for Qs. Questioned quantifiers must be specified as either Qn or Qm, as in:

(52)   *How many books do you want?*
          (Qn i m x_i: *book* [N])

(53)   *How much sugar do you want?*
         (Qm i x_i: *sugar* [N])

In other langages we find neutral expressions for Qs, such as *hoeveel* in Dutch:

(54) a. *Hoeveel boeken wil je?*
     b. *Hoeveel suiker wil je?*

(iii) Questioned restrictor predicates. Consider the following constructions:

(55) a. *What kind of book do you want?*
     b. *What books do you read?*

In both constructions A is requested to specify a subtype of books. Specifying a subtype of a given ensemble is the work of restrictors. Therefore, both *what* and *what kind of* in (55a-b) can be regarded as questioned restrictors asking for a property. Using the predicate variable f we can analyse (55a-b) as follows:

(56) a. Int E: X: Pres e: *want* [V] (*you*) (i 1 x_i: *book* [N]: Qf)
     b. Int E: X: Gen e: *read* [V] (*you*) (i m x_i: *book* [N]: Qf)

Note that the Qf has the status of a predicate.

(iv) Questioning Possessors. In *TFG1*: 8.6. we analysed a Possessor expression such as *John's* as a possessive term predicate which may be used in either attributive or predicative function. When the possessive predicate is used as an attributive restrictor, we get the following construction type:

(57)   *John's book*
         (d1x_i: *book* [N]: {(d1x_j: *John* [N])$_{Poss}$})

When the Possessor term is questioned, we get the following:

(58)   *whose book*
         (d1x_i: *book* [N]: {(Qx_j)$_{Poss}$})

It is clear, then, that *whose* in this case also represents application of Q within a restrictor. But the fact that a term predicate is involved makes it clear that the question does not bear on just any quality of the item in question, but on the

274   *Interrogative clauses*

quality defined by the relation of the item to whoever is the possessor of the item.

12.3.5.3. On questioning the predicate. We have seen that Q can operate on just about any term position within the extended predication: any term position can in principle be questioned. An interesting fact about natural languages is that questioning the predicate is a much more difficult matter. Let us first consider the matter in an abstract way. Take a construction such as:

(59)   *John kissed Mary.*

In such a construction we can question the Subject, the Object, or even both of them at the same time:

(60) a. *(Q x_i) kissed Mary?*   'Who kissed Mary?'
     b. *John kissed (Q x_j)?*   'Who did John kiss?'
     c. *(Q x_i) kissed (Q x_j)?*   'Who kissed whom?'

But it is not at all that easy to question the predicate. The closest one could get to expressing a construction such as (61a) would be (61b):

(61) a. *John (???) Mary?*
     b. *What did John do to / with Mary?*

But note that (61b), strictly speaking, is again a construction in which some term position rather than the predicate is questioned. Rather than to (61a), it corresponds to (62):

(62)   *John do (Q e_i) to / with Mary?*

If one should want to maintain that 'do what' is simply the standard form for a questioned predicate, then one has to explain why, instead of (61b), we do not get a construction such as:

(63) a. *(What do) John Mary?*
     b. *What did John do Mary?*

The appearance of *to / with* on *Mary* in (61b) demonstrates that *Mary* does not function as an Object, as in (60), but rather has some non-Object function.

It seems clear, then, that in English there is a strategy which says that if one wants to know the identity of some property or relation, one builds up a predication by means of which the required information can be obtained through questioning a term position. This proves that, for some reason or other, it is not possible to directly question the predicate position.

In the context of FG we may understand this situation as follows: all linguistic expressions are built up from predicate-frames; these are structures in which a specified predicate is combined with a number of open term positions. Questioning the identity of the terms which could fill the open positions is a straightforward matter. Questioning the identity of a specified predicate, on the other hand, would be contradictory. This is why in most languages, if one wishes to know the identity of some predicate, one has to resort to the roundabout strategy of choosing some very general predicate such as *do*, *be*, or *happen*, and combine this with some term position which, when questioned, will make clear that one wishes to know something more about the identity of that predicate.

If this account is satisfactory, however, we must have some special explanation for those languages which do have interrogative predicates. This is rare, but it does occur. Thus, Dyirbal has intransitive *wiyamay* and transitive *wiyamal*, both meaning 'do what?', and functioning like any other verbal predicate (Dixon 1972: 55):

(64)   *bayi   yaRa   wiyaman^{y}u?*
       that   man   do.what
       'What was the man doing?'
(65)   *ŋinda   bayi   yaRa   wiyaman?*
       you   that   man   do.what
       'What did you do (to) that man?'

These interrogative verbs can also be used adverbially, and then mean 'do-how' ('in what way' or 'by what means').

Similar interrogative predicates occur in some other Australian languages (Yallop 1982: 129). Thus, Ngaanyatjara (Western Desert) has a verb *nyaarri-*, formed by adding the verbalizer (vr) *-rri* to the question word *nyaa* 'what', as in:

(66)   *Nyaa-rri-ngkula-yan?*
       what-vr-pres-you all
       'What are you all doing?'

276   *Interrogative clauses*

And Bahasa Indonesia has a verb *meN-apa* 'do what', formed from *apa*, which can undergo the same processes as any other verb, witness a passive construction such as (67), based on the derived active verb *meN-apa-kan* 'do what to (somebody)' (Sie Ing Djinang, pers. comm.):

(67)   *Di-apa-kan   adik-mu,   hingga*
        Pass-do.what-to   younger.sibling-your,   so-that
            ia   menangis?
            he   cry
        'What was done to your younger sibling, that he / she is crying?'

In order to explain these cases, we will not assume that these languages in some way possess "open" predicates which can be freely questioned just like open term positions. Rather, we will assume that they have lexicalized an interrogative predicate which can be chosen from the lexicon whenever one wishes to question the identity of some predicate. Given the infrequent occurrence of such interrogative predicates, this form of lexicalization must be regarded as a marked option for a language to take.

12.4. The placement of Q-constituents

Q-constituents can take different positions in the final structure of the clause, the most obvious difference being that between placement in initial position, as in (68a), and placement in pattern position, that is, the position that the corresponding non-questioned term would take, as in (68b):

(68) a.   *What did John see in the zoo?*
     b.   *John saw what in the zoo?*

Note that both positions are possible in English, but that the construction with the Q-constituent in pattern position has a special pragmatic status, in that it can only be used as an echo question: a question by someone who did not hear or understand precisely what the other said, or cannot believe what he thinks he has understood:

(69) A: *John said he saw a platypus in the zoo.*
     B: *He saw (a) WHAT in the zoo??*

In many languages, however, placing the Q-constituent in pattern position is the normal way of forming Q-word questions.

Several attempts have been made to predict the choice between pattern position and initial position in terms of more general principles.[4] Thus, Bach (1971) formulated the following rules:

(70) (i) movement of Q-constituents will always be to the left;
    (ii) such movements will occur only in VSO and SVO languages, not in SOV languages.

Neither of these rules, however, can be maintained in the light of current typological data: though Q-constituents, if they are not placed in pattern position, are usually placed in some earlier position in the clause, there are also cases (to be discussed below) in which they appear in a position later than their pattern position. As for principle (ii), there are many SOV languages which place their Q-constituents in initial position (cf. e.g. Frantz (1973); Scott—Frantz (1974)).

Baker (1970) formulated similar generalizations in terms of an abstract morpheme Q, which would take initial position in VSO and SVO languages and final position in SOV languages:

(71) (i) Q V S O, Q S V O
    (ii) S O V Q

For Q-word questions, the general rule would be that Q-constituents can only go to the left and will replace the Q-morpheme. Again, this generalization cannot be upheld in the light of the typological data: as we saw earlier, there are quite a few SOV languages which place their Q-constituents in initial position.

Finally, Bresnan (1970) formulated a principle of "complementizer replacement", according to which the correct generalization would be that Q-constituents can only go to the COMP (or subordinator) position of the language concerned. Languages with a final COMP position will thus have no initial Q-constituents. Again, this generalization breaks down on the fact that there are quite a few SOV (Prefield) languages in which subordinate clauses are finally marked (thus having a final COMP position), which nevertheless bring their Q-constituents to initial position.

---

4. For critical discussion of these attempts see Sasse (1977).

278 *Interrogative clauses*

Let us now consider how we can arrive at a better characterization of the typology of Q-constituent placement. In order to do so, we first have to give a more general characterization of the possible positions of Q-constituents. As far as I have been able to ascertain, the following is the correct generalization:

(72)   Q-constituents are placed:
  (i) in pattern position (Q-Pattern strategy)
  (ii) in that special position (those special positions) which is / are available for Focus constituents in the language concerned (Q-Focus strategy)

Note that this generalization is entirely natural and congruent with our interpretation of Q-constituents as having intrinsic Focus function. It is also consonant with the fact that, if a language has special segmental Focus markers, Q-constituents will often be marked by such markers. The general principle is thus that Q-constituents will tend to be expressed, qua form and position, according to the rules for expressing Focus constituents.

In *TFG1*: 17.2. I discussed the typology of "special positions". The conclusion was that all languages have the clause-initial special position P1; that some languages have more than one special position, and that these may then have specialized in accommodating either Topic or Focus constituents. We also saw that the various possibilities for special positions can be characterized in terms of the following schema:

(73)   P1 ..... PØ V Pa .....

where P1 is the clause-initial position, PØ the position immediately before the Verb, and Pa the position immediately after the Verb. P1 was claimed to be universally valid; PØ is not uncommon; Pa is rare. Our principle (72ii) predicts that whatever the position for Focus constituents, that position will also be used for Q-constituents, unless these remain in pattern position.

This prediction appears to be correct. Consider Aghem, as described in Watters (1979). This language has the rare Pa position, used for placing Focus constituents. Consider the following examples:[5]

---

5. DP = Distant Past, DS = dummy subject marker.

(74) Éná?   mÒ ñĭŋ nô.
      Inah   DP run Foc
      'Inah ran.'
(75) À   mÒ ñĭŋ ndúghÓ?
      DS DP run who
      'WHO ran?'
(76) À   mÒ ñĭŋ éná.
      DS DP run Inah
      'INAH ran.'

(74) is a neutral statement, in which no constituent receives special emphasis. In that condition, the immediately postverbal position must be marked by *nô*, glossed as a Focus marker. Note that a Q-word is placed in Pa, as in (75), and that in an answer to a Q-word question, the Focus constituent is also placed in Pa, as in (76). Since Aghem basically has SVO order, the focussed Subject ends up in a position after its pattern position; in that (and only that) condition, the pattern position corresponding to the Q-word is marked by the dummy *à*.

In view of the rarity of a postverbal Focus position it could be that (75) and (76) should be analysed, at least historically, as going back to Cleft interrogatives corresponding to 'the one who ran was who?' and 'the one who ran was Inah'. See chapter 14 for this type of construction.

For another example, consider Turkish, which has a Focus position immediately before the verb (Van Schaaik 1983). Again, this is also the position used for Q-words. Compare:

(77) A: *Plak-lar-ın-ı   kim-e   sat-tı-n?*
        record-plur-your-acc who-dat sell-past-you
        'To whom did you sell your records?'
     B: *Plak-lar-ım-ı   Hasan-a   sat-tı-m.*
        record-plur-my-acc   Hasan-dat sell-past-I
        'I sold my records to HASAN.'

Again, in Turkish there are situations in which a Q-word is placed in a position to the right of its usual pattern position. This is the case when the first

280 *Interrogative clauses*

argument (A¹) is questioned, since according to Van Schaaik's analysis the ordering pattern for Turkish is:[6]

(78)   P1 A¹ X Y Foc V

Similar placement rules for Q-words hold in Hungarian (cf. De Groot 1981) and Basque (Ortiz de Urbina 1989). All these example languages are in accordance with generalization (72ii). They are thus Q-Focus languages.

12.4.1. Q-Pattern versus Q-Focus

Assuming the correctness of this generalization, the next question is: what factors determine the choice between the Q-Pattern and the Q-Focus strategy? For a Q-Pattern language consider Tamil, as described in Asher (1982):

(79)   *Raaman kriṣnyanukku oru peenaa kuṭuttaan.*
        Raman Krishnan-dat one pen   give-past-3sgmasc
        'Raman gave a pen to Krishnan.'
(80)   *Raaman yaarukku ori peenaa kuṭuttaan.*
        Raman who-dat   one pen   give-past-3sgmasc
        'To whom did Raman give a pen?'
(81)   *Raaman kriṣnyanukku enna kuṭuttaan.*
        Raman Krishna-dat what give-past-3sgmasc
        'What did Raman give to Krishnan?'

As a general rule, then, Tamil Q-constituents go to the position of their corresponding non-questioned counterparts. This also applies to complex constructions:

(82)   *Raaman vantapoo   lakṣmi veliyee*
        Raman come-past-rp-when   Lakshmi outside
           poonaa.
           go-past-3sgfem
        'When Raman came, Lakshmi went out'

---

6. In Van Schaaik's analysis, the syntactic functions Subject and Object are not judged to be relevant for Turkish.

(83) *Yaaru   vantapoo   laksmi   veliyee*
      who   come-past-rp-when   Lakshmi outside
         poona?
         go-past-3sgfem
      'When who came did Lakshmi go out?'

It has been shown by Keenan—Bimson (1975) that in languages which apply Q-Pattern, a greater variety of positions are accessible to questioning than in languages which apply Q-Focus. The Tamil example (83) is suggestive in this respect. Compare the English constructions:

(84) a. *Mary left the room when Peter entered*
     b. *Mary left the room when WHO entered??*
     c. **Who did Mary leave the room when entered?*

Note that the relevant position can be questioned through Q-Pattern in English as well but, as we saw above, the resulting construction can only be used in "echo" conditions; it cannot be interpreted as a pragmatically neutral question. And (84c) is ungrammatical in English. Thus, Tamil has wider possibilities of forming Q-word questions than English.

Note that the correct statement is that languages using Q-Pattern can question a wider variety of positions than languages using Q-Focus. This does not imply that there will be no constraints on accessibility to questioning in Q-Pattern languages. Such constraints are simply less restrictive than in Q-Focus languages. The fact that similar constraints may obtain in the two types of languages proves that such constraints cannot be formulated in terms of restrictions on "movement" or on "displacement" of constituents.

The situation is similar to what we found to be the case in relative clause formation (see chapters 2-4): in languages which have relative clauses with personal pronouns in pattern position, a greater variety of positions can be relativized than in languages without such pronominal expression.

Underlying these facts there thus appears to be a principle to the effect that some operation O has easier access to a term (t) when the expression rules for O-constructions are such that they place some overt element in the pattern position of (t). I return to this principle in chapter 16.

In order to understand what factors determine the choice between Q-Pattern and Q-Focus, it is useful to consider some advantages and disadvantages of these two placements strategies:

Q-PATTERN
advantages:
(i) the structure of the question is in no way different from the corresponding declarative;
(ii) therefore, given the structure of declaratives, no special rules are required for forming questions;
(iii) since the relational structure of the question is easily recoverable, a wide variety of term positions can be questioned.
disadvantages:
(i) the questioned constituent does not get much special prominence, and thus the interrogative status of the sentence is not very clearly signalled;
(ii) when the questioned constituent occurs "late" in the structure of the clause, that a question is involved may only become apparent when the sentence is well under way.

As for disadvantage (ii), consider a ("pseudo-English") construction of the following type:

(85) *After Jim had managed to steer his canoe all the way down the rapid stream without incurring any damage to speak of, he suddenly realized that he had forgotten what?*

If we assume, as seems natural, that it is important for A to pay extra attention when a question is put to him (since he will be expected to give an appropriate answer), then a construction such as (85) will certainly not appear to be a very effective means for securing that attention: A can mistakenly take (85) to be a statement, until the very last word tells him that it is, in fact, a question. Compare this with:

(86) *What did Jim suddenly realize that he had forgotten, after he had managed to steer his canoe all the way down the rapid stream without incurring any damage to speak of?*

It appears that the advantages of Q-Pattern do not outweigh its disadvantages: Q-Pattern is used in only about 30% of all languages.

The advantages and disadvantages of Q-Focus are more or less the reverse of those involved in Q-Pattern:

Q-FOCUS
advantages:
   (i) because the Q-word takes the special Focus position, it gets the special prominence conveyed by that position to any Focus constituent;
   (ii) because the Focus position is usually the initial P1 position, and otherwise most often a special position before the verb, the interrogative character of the sentence is overtly marked at an early point in the linear sequence.
disadvantages:
   (i) the Q-word question will be rather different in structure from the corresponding declarative. This may make it more difficult to reconstruct the underlying structure of the question.
   (ii) there may be a rather long distance between the Q-word and the pattern position of the term which it questions (the "gap" in the question), especially in complex sentences in which some constituent of an embedded clause is questioned.
   (iii) as a result of (i) and (ii), Q-Focus allows a smaller variety of term positions to be questioned than Q-Pattern.

For disadvantage (ii), compare the following two hypothetical constructions:

(87) a.   Q-Focus
         What did Peter think that Mary would be happy with the outcome of ...?
     b.   Q-Pattern
         Peter thought that Mary would be happy with the outcome of what?

As for disadvantage (iii), compare Q-Pattern advantage (iii). The accessibility difference can also be illustrated with (87). Note that (87a) is ungrammatical in English; (87b), however, would be grammatical in many a language using the Q-Pattern strategy.

In this case, the advantages appear to win the day: Q-Focus is found in roughly 70% of all languages.

12.4.2. A question about pronoun retention

When we reconsider the balance of advantages and disadvantages of the two strategies for positioning Q-constituents, then it is not difficult to think of an alternative strategy which would have the advantages and lack the dis-

284 *Interrogative clauses*

advantages of both of them. This would be a strategy in which the question would be initially marked by some particle indicating its interrogative character, and in which the pattern position of the questioned term would be marked by some overt element. Each of the following hypothetical constructions would have that effect:

(88) a. *QP did John believe the rumour that Mary went there?*
 b. *QP did John believe the rumour that Mary went where?*
 c. *Where did John believe the rumour that Mary went there?*

where QP is some invariable sentence-initial question particle.

Such structures, however, do not commonly occur in natural languages. This is all the more remarkable for the following reasons:

(i) many languages do have invariable question particles, but these are typically used in Yes-No questions rather than in Q-word questions.

(ii) many languages do have a pattern comparable to (88a) in relative clauses (see chapters 2-4); thus, the following would be a typical relative clause in such languages:

(89) *This is the place that John believed the rumour that Mary went there.*

Note, finally, that constructions of type (88a-c) come very close to the logical structure of questions as postulated by Carnap (see 12.3.2. above). The fact that natural languages hardly use these construction types, even though it would seem to be functionally advantageous to do so, is a further indication that such logical structures do not correctly represent the underlying structure of Q-word questions. This fact also presents a problem for the functional approach to language itself.

12.4.3. The distribution of Q-Pattern and Q-Focus

Many languages have either Q-Pattern or Q-Focus, but some have both these strategies side by side. In that case, the two strategies may stand in a relation of:

(i) *contrast*, when the one and the other placement of Q-constituents results in constructions with different pragmatic properties (as in English Echo vs. non-Echo questions);

(ii) *free variation*, when application of the one or the other strategy is optional.

As Greenberg (1966) has already noted, it is not an arbitrary question whether a language applies Q-Pattern or Q-Focus. At least the initial placement of Q-constituents (which is the most common implementation of Q-Focus) vs. the non-initial placement correlates heavily with the basic constituent order typology of the language. This can be seen from the following table, based on the data in Greenberg (1966) plus those of Ultan (1969):

(90)

	VSO	SVO	SOV	total
Q-Initial	15	25	8	48
Q-Pattern	3	6	16	25
total	18	31	24	73

It is clear that the great majority of VSO and SVO languages place Q-constituents in initial position, whereas two-thirds of the SOV languages place their Q-constituents in pattern position.

Using our terminology of Prefield vs. Postfield languages (see *TFG1*: chapter 16), there thus appears to be a strong correlation between:

(91)   Prefield: Q-Pattern
       Postfield: Q-Initial

From this it follows that the tendency to place Q-constituents in initial position does not represent a universal preference, but is co-dependent on the position of the predicate. Apparently the essential point is that the Q-word should appear before the verb. Consider the following figures, based on the same data:

(92)   YES   NO
  (a) all Q-constituents occur before the V   87.7%   12.3%
  (b) all Q-Subjects occur before the V   95.9%   4.1%

We can reformulate these facts more simply in the following form:

(93)   Q-constituents strongly prefer the Prefield.

Why this principle should hold is difficult to say. I have the following speculations to offer:

(i) The predicate is the central pivot of the predication. Once the predicate has been reached in the linear sequence of the linguistic expression, the major parameters for interpreting the expression are fixed. It would be difficult to switch from a declarative to an interrogative interpretation on the basis of information which is received only after the predicate has been decoded.

(ii) The Prefield is the "light" area, the Postfield the "shaded" area in the linear sequence of a clause. The Prefield is therefore eminently suited for constituents which are to receive extra relief in the linear sequence.

Note that the latter explanation, although rather metaphorically phrased, is compatible with some other relevant phenomena:

(i) all Postfield languages make use of special positions in the Prefield (P1, Theme position) for giving special relief to pragmatically important constituents;

(ii) special positions for placing focussed constituents are almost exclusively found in the Prefield (i.e. either P1 or Pb in terms of schema (78)); a special postverbal position for focussed constituents (Pa in schema (78)), exemplified in Aghem (74)-(76) is the exception to this rule.

12.5. Multiple Q-word questions

So far we have restricted our discussion to Q-word questions in which just one term position is questioned. There are, however, also cases in which more term positions are simultaneously questioned. Such multiple Q-word questions have been discussed by Kuno—Robinson (1972) and Wachowicz (1974), especially in view of the fact that they appear to provide counterexamples to various generalizations which have been proposed concerning Q-word questions in the literature.

I shall split the problem of multiple Q-word questions into two separate questions:

(i) can more than one term position be questioned in one and the same clause?

(ii) if so, where will the corresponding Q-constituents be placed?

The answer to (i) is clearly "yes" for many (though not all) languages. Consider Dutch:

(94) *Wie   kocht   wat?*
      who   bought   what
      'Who bought what?'

Multiple Q-word questions 287

The answer to (ii), however, is a more complicated matter. First, consider languages which have only one special initial position P1, which can accommodate just one constituent. Dutch is clearly such a language, as is evident from the fact that no more than one Q-word can be placed in initial position:

(95) *Wie wat kocht?
 who what bought
 'Who bought what?'

For such languages we need some sort of "priority rule" which will tell us which one of several Q-words will go to P1: some choices will lead to decidedly marked constructions, such as:

(96) What did who buy where?

Kuno—Robinson (1972) even formulated a constraint which would rule out (96) as ungrammatical. On the other hand, Hankamer (1974) argued that there are multiple questions with the questioned Object in P1 which appear to be reasonably acceptable, for instance:

(97) Which girl did which boy kiss?

I believe that the priority rule for Q-constituents might be reduced to the rule which regulates P1-placement of non-questioned terms. In English, placing an Object in P1 leads to quite marked constructions:

(98) This book John does not want to read.

In Dutch, on the other hand, such Object preposing is much less marked:

(99) Dit boek wil Jan niet lezen.
 this book want Jan not read

Correspondingly, the following multiple question in Dutch would seem to be much less marked than its English counterpart:

(100) Wat wil wie niet lezen?
 what wants who not read?
 'What does who not want to read?'

288 *Interrogative clauses*

There are also languages, however, in which not only more than one term per simple predicate can be questioned, but in which the questioned constituents can all be placed in initial position. Wachowicz (1974, 1978) mentions Russian, Polish, and Hungarian. And Toman (1982) adds Czech as an example of multiple Q-constituent preposing. The following examples are from Polish:

(101) *Kto   kogo   budzi?*
      who   who   wakes.up
      'Who wakes up whom?'
(102) *Kto   co   powiedział?*
      who   what   said
      'Who said what?'

As we saw in *TFG1*: 17.2.2., we must assume that certain languages have more than one special position in the Prefield, so that several Topic and Focus constituents can be preposed in the same clause. These are also languages in which the ordering of constituents in general is strongly determined by pragmatic factors. We may now presume that the languages which allow constructions such as (101)-(102) are just those languages which also have multiple preposing possibilities in non-interrogative constructions. This is precisely what Wachowicz (1978: 155) assumes to be the case. As the following example shows, Polish allows more than one constituent in the Prefield in declarative constructions, even though its most frequent surface pattern is SVO:

(103) *Marek jeszcze namioty Dance   nie zwrócił.*
      Marek yet   tent   to-Danka not returned
      'Marek did not return the tent to Danka yet.'

Note that a problem remains for such languages as Hungarian. We saw in *TFG1*: 17.2.2 that the ordering pattern of Hungarian can be represented as (see De Groot 1987b):

(104) P1 PØ V X ...

where P1 can accommodate one or more Topic constituents, and PØ just one Focus constituent. If it is true, as Wachowicz (1978: 154) claims, that multiple preposing of Q-constituents is possible in Hungarian, as in:

(105) Ki   mit   mondott?
       who   what   brought
       'Who brought what?'

then somehow the PØ position must be assumed to be more hospitable to questioned than to non-questioned constituents.

In Arabic, according to Moutaouakil (1990), the rules for the formation of multiple questions are as follows:

(i) if only one term is questioned, this may be any argument or satellite;

(ii) two or three, but no more than three terms may be questioned in the same predication; this multiple questioning, however, can only be applied to arguments.

(iii) only one questioned term may be placed in the special preverbal PØ position.

(iv) priority for being placed in that position is according to Subj > Obj > Other terms.

As for (ii), consider the following contrasts:

(106) a. *man*   *jā?a*
         who   has.come
      b. *matā*   *ji?ta*
         when   have.come.you
      c. *man*   *qābala*   *man*
         who   has.met   who
      d. **man*   *jā?a*   *matā*
         who   has.come   when

As for (iii): Moutaouakil postulates the following ordering pattern for Arabic:

(107)   P2, P1 PØ V S O X , P3

where P1 is the position for subordinating elements, and PØ the position for Q-words, Topics, or (contrastive) Focus constituents. However, PØ can only harbour one constituent at the time. Thus Arabic seems to confirm the idea that two Q-words can only be preposed if the language in question more generally allows more than one focussed constituent to be fronted.

13. Focus constructions: basic patterns

13.0. Introduction

In *TFG1*: chapter 13 it was shown that constituents which carry Focus function can be expressed in a variety of ways:
   (i) they can get special prosodic prominence;
   (ii) they may be placed in special positions;
   (iii) they may be marked by special particles;
   (iv) they may occur in special construction types.
In this chapter I shall be concerned with (iv): special construction types which specifically have the function of bringing some Focus constituent into prominence. Such constructions will, in general, be called *Focus constructions*. Within the class of Focus constructions, pride of place is taken by so-called "Cleft" and "Pseudocleft" constructions. Therefore, most attention will be paid to these. But as we shall see, once we have defined Cleft and Pseudocleft constructions in a coherent way, we will also have to recognize some other types of Focus construction.

Cleft and Pseudocleft constructions themselves appear in different forms, and may be used in different pragmatic and textual functions. In dealing with the complexities of form-function correlations in this area, I will start out with what may be regarded as the "prototypical" form of Cleft constructions, taking these in what I consider to be their prototypical pragmatic function. After that, I will treat other forms and uses of Cleft constructions in terms of how they differ from the prototypical case.

13.1. A note on terminology

According to established terminology, (1) is an example of a Cleft construction, and (2) an example of a Pseudocleft construction:

(1)   *It was John's watch that Peter found in the garden.*
(2)   *What Peter found in the garden was John's watch.*

This terminology is, in different respects, rather unfortunate. Consider the following points:

(i) The term "Cleft" construction suggests that (1) should be considered as derived from the structure underlying a non-Cleft construction such as:

(3)   *Peter found John's watch in the garden.*

by some operation of "cleaving", through which the structure of (3) is mapped onto the more complex, bi-clausal expression of (1). In our analysis, however, there will be no such direct derivational relation between the structure of (3) and that of its Cleft counterpart (1). The Cleft construction will be argued to have an underlying structure of its own, distinct from the structure of non-Cleft constructions such as (3).

(ii) The term "Pseudocleft construction" suggests that (2) is in some sense to be considered as a secondary or derived variant of (1). In our analysis, however, the Pseudocleft construction (2) will be treated as more "prototypical" than the Cleft construction (1), that is, as more faithfully expressing the underlying structure which will be postulated for both the Cleft and the Pseudocleft construction. Thus, the Cleft construction will be regarded as a secondary variant of the Pseudocleft construction rather than the other way around.

(iii) This can also be established on typological grounds. Very many languages have construction types which more or less directly correspond to the Pseudocleft construction (2). But only few languages also have a construction corresponding to the Cleft construction (1), especially if the presence of some such dummy element as *it* is considered to be an essential property of the Cleft construction.

(iv) Finally, the term Cleft construction is usually taken to comprise construction types such as:

(4)   *It was with much effort that John managed to open the coffin.*

which, in our analysis, will come out as fundamentally different from the type of construction exemplified in (1).

In order to circumvent some of this unfortunate terminology will I use the term Cleft construction as a general term comprising both (1) and (2). Only when it is required to distinguish between these two construction types, I will use the term "Dummy-Cleft" to specifically refer to constructions of type (1), or to their counterparts in other languages.

As a general term covering constructions which typically serve to bring some particular constituent into Focus, I will use the term *Focus construction*. Thus, Cleft constructions can be considered a specific subtype of Focus constructions. But there are also Focus constructions which are not Cleft constructions. Thus, in our final analysis (4) will come out as a Focus construction which is distinct from the Cleft construction.

In the examples (1)-(2) a nominal term, *John's watch*, is brought into Focus. This property I will also regard as being characteristic of the prototypical Cleft. In (4), the Focus-construction, which is distinct from a Cleft, an adpositional term is brought into Focus.

Many languages also have so-called "predicate Cleft" constructions, which very often are quite similar to prototypical Clefts. Thus a language might have the following ("pseudo-English") constructions side by side:

(5)   *It was the DOUGHNUT that John ate.*
(6)   *It was EAT that John ate the doughnut.*

where (6) is used to Focus on the identity of the predicate. This type of predicate focusing construction will be regarded as at least one step removed from the prototypical Cleft exemplified in (1)-(2). Predicate Cleft constructions will be further discussed in 14.1.

13.2. The prototypical Cleft construction

As prototypical examples of the Cleft construction I consider such cases as:

(7) a. *The thing that Peter found in the garden was John's watch.*
     b. *That which Peter found in the garden was John's watch.*
     c. *What Peter found in the garden was John's watch.*
(8) a. *John's watch was the thing that Peter found in the garden.*
     b. *John's watch was that which Peter found in the garden.*
     c. *John's watch was what Peter found in the garden.*

The prototypical Cleft has the following properties:
 (i) It is an identifying construction, in which some entity, described by means of expressions such as *the thing that Peter found in the garden* is

identified as being nothing else than another entity, described by such expressions as *John's watch*.[1]

(ii) As is required for identifying constructions, the identifying expression (in this case: *John's watch*) is, in the prototypical case, definite rather than indefinite. This implies that constructions of the form:

(9) *What Peter found in the garden was a watch of John's.*

will be treated as at least one step removed from the prototypical Cleft.

(iii) The identifying expression (*John's watch*) constitutes the Focus of the Cleft predication; the other term (*what Peter found in the garden*) is the Given Topic of the construction.

(iv) The Given Topic presents an entity presupposed to be available to the Addressee; the Focus presents the most salient information, usually that which is supposed to be new to the Addressee. Thus, in the prototypical case, the pragmatic import of the Cleft construction can be represented as follows:

(10) 'I assume you already know that Peter found something in the garden. Well, I can now inform you that the something was nothing else than John's watch.'

(v) The Topic is presented in the form of either a free relative clause, such as *what Peter found in the garden*, or of a complex term containing a general, classificatory, almost dummy-like head nominal (such as *thing, that, person, one*), followed by a restrictive relative clause. This implies that a construction such as:

(11) *The watch that John found in the garden was John's watch.*

in which the head noun of the first term is lexically specified, is again regarded as falling outside the domain of the prototypical Cleft.

---

1. "Cleft sentences ... are equational sentences which establish an identity between a known or presupposed entity and a focussed entity which represents the new information". Harries-Delisle (1978: 422).

13.2.1. The prototypical Cleft in FG

The prototypical Cleft is an identifying construction comparable to such constructions as:

(12)   *The winner of this game is John.*

Identifying constructions are analysed according to the schema:

(13)   {(*John*)} (*the winner of this game*)$_\varnothing$

in which *John*, itself a term, is applied as a predicate to another term. We saw in *TFG1*: 8.4. that this type of structure can be formed by a rule of Term-Predicate formation, through which any term can be transformed into a one-place predicate. With a little more detail, the structure underlying (12) will have the following form:

(14)   {(d1x_j: *John*)} (d1x_i: *winner of this game*)$_\varnothing$

in which it is expressed that the entity described as being the winner of this game has the property of being (no one else than) John.

When π-operators are specified for (14), these will, in English, trigger *be*-support, so that we get:

(15)   Pres e: *be*$_V$ {(d1x_j: *John*)} (d1x_i: *the winner of this game*)$_\varnothing$

The argument term will receive Subject function, and the most natural distribution of pragmatic functions is that GivenTopic is assigned to the Subject, and Focus to the predicate term, so that we arrive at:

(16)   Pres e: *be*$_V$ {d1x_j: *John*)}$_{Foc}$ (d1x_i: *winner of this game*)$_{\varnothing SubjGivTop}$

This configuration will then be mapped onto one of the following expressions:

(17)   *The winner of this game is JOHN.*
(18)   *JOHN is the winner of this game.*

In (17) the Subj-GivTop has been placed in initial P1 position; in (18) the predicate term in Focus has been placed in that position.

296   *Focus constructions: basic patterns*

The only difference between constructions such as (17)-(18) and the prototypical Cleft is that in the latter construction the GivTop constituent consists of, or contains, a relative clause:

(19) a. *The one who won this game is* JOHN.
   b. *The person who won this game is* JOHN.
   c. JOHN *is the one/person who won this game.*
   d. *It is* JOHN *who won this game.*

As a first approximation, we can thus give the following underlying representation for these constructions:

(20)   Pres e_i: be_V {(d1x_j: *John*)}$_{Foc}$
   (d1x_i: [Past e_j: win_V (Ax_i)$_{Ag}$(*this game*)$_{Go}$])$_{\emptyset SubjGivTop}$

In this structure, the GivTop term more or less directly reflects the formal expressions *who won this game* and *the one who won this game*.

13.2.2. Dummy head nouns

We must now ask the question of how dummy head nominals such as *person*, *thing*, etc. are to be treated in the underlying clause structure. One view would be that these nominals simply spell out configurations such as (20) in an alternative, slightly more explicit way. Another view is that they are present in underlying term structure as head nouns in their own right, so that the structure underlying the GivTop term in (19b) would be as follows:

(21)   (d1x_i: *person*$_N$: [Past e: win_V (Ax_i)$_{Ag}$ (*this game*)$_{Go}$])

Mackenzie—Hannay (1982) argue that the second view is to be preferred. One argument is that nominals such as *person* can be modified by further restrictors, as in:

(22)   *The most unexpected person who won this game is* JOHN.

which should be described in terms of the following underlying structure:

(23)   (d1x_i: *person*$_N$: *most unexpected*: [Past e: win_V (Ax_i)$_{Ag}$(*this game*)$_{Go}$])

Another, more general argument is that the expression rules become rather complicated if such expressions as (19a) and (19b) are to be derived from the same underlying structure.

This treatment of head nouns such as *person*, *thing*, etc. raises a problem, however, with respect to the interpretation of the notion "Cleft construction". Consider the following series:

(24) a. *What I found is John's watch.*
     b. *The thing I found is John's watch.*
     c. *The watch I found is John's watch.*

There is a tendency for the notion of "Cleft construction" to be restricted to constructions of type (24a), in which the GivTop term is represented by a headless relative construction. However, there is not much semantic difference between (24a) and (24b): these two constructions may alternate in one language or between languages. However, if we include (24b) in the notion of Cleft, why not include (24c) as well? In that case, however, the Cleft construction will gradually shade off into construction types which can be analysed as "normal" identifying constructions, no different in any special way from constructions such as:

(25)   *The silver watch is John's watch.*

which are not usually described as Clefts.

As we saw in chapter 4, however, there are certain reasons for assigning a somewhat different status to nouns such as *thing* than to nouns such as *watch*. *Thing* belongs to a small group of quite general "classificatory" nouns, which also includes *person*, *time*, *place*, *reason*, and *way* (cf. 12.3.3.). These classificatory nouns are also needed in the analysis of synthetic question words such as:

(26) a. *who*   =   *what person*
     b. *what*   =   *what thing*
     c. *where* =   *at what place*
     d. *when*   =   *at what time*
     e. *why*   =   *for what reason*
     f. *how*   =   *in what way*

Because of the special status of these classificatory nouns I shall regard constructions of type (24b), but not those of type (24c), as falling under the

298 *Focus constructions: basic patterns*

notion of Cleft construction, although maybe one step removed from the empty-headed "prototypical Cleft" exemplified in (24a).

13.2.3. On expressing Cleft constructions

On this interpretation of Cleft constructions, the GivTop term of such constructions can be expressed in a variety of ways:

(27)

	HEAD	REL			
	the person	who	won this game	)	
	the person	that	won this game	)	headed
	the one	who	won this game	)	
	the one	that	won this game	)___	
	---	who	won this game	)	headless

(28)

	Head	Rel			
	the thing	which	John read	)	
	the thing	that	John read	)	
	the thing	---	John read	)	headed
	that	which	John read	)	
		what	John read	)___	
	---	which	John read	)	
	---	what	John read	)	headless
	---	---	John read	)	

As indicated in schemas (27) and (28), these possible realizations of the GivTop term divide into headed and headless realizations. In making this division, I assume that *what* in *what John read* can be regarded as a fused expression of head + relative element, so that the construction falls in the "headed" class. It can now be shown that the difference between headed and headless realizations of the GivTop constituent in the Cleft construction can be held responsible for the traditional distinction between Cleft and Pseudo-cleft.

Let us first recapitulate the ordering patterns for English declarative clauses (29) and Q-word questions (as well as some minor sentence types) (30):

(29)

	P1	S	Vf	Vi	O	X
	Perhaps	John	has	seen	an ostrich	in the zoo.

(30)   P1   Vf   S   Vi   O   X
       Where   did John   see an ostrich yesterday?

These patterns, however, are not quite sufficient for non-verbal predications (copular constructions). Consider the following:

(31)   *Not so successful   has been his attempt at breaking the record*
       P1------------------ Vf   Vi   S--------------------------------

For this (marked) construction type, then, we need a further pattern of the form:

(32)   P1 Vf Vi S X

which can then also be used for such constructions as:

(33)   P1   Vf   Vi   S   X
       There have   been three men at the door.

which would otherwise be difficult to account for in terms of patterns (29)-(30).

We can now account for the possible realization of a construction such as (28) in terms of the following rules:

(34) (i) if the GivTop term is given a headed realization, then
         (a) pattern (32) is relevant,
         (b) either the GivTop or the Focus can be placed in P1.
    (ii) if the GivTop is given a headless realization, then
         (a) pattern (29) is relevant,
         (b) the GivTop can only be placed in X,
         (c) the dummy *it* is inserted into S position.

Rule (i) will give us the following realizations of (28)

(35) a. *The thing which/that/Ø John read*)
     b. *That which   John read*) *is THIS PAPER.*
     c. *What   John read*)
(36) a.   (*the thing which/that/Ø John read.*
     b. *THIS PAPER is*   (*that which John read.*
     c.   (*what John read.*

Rule (ii) will yield the following further realizations:

(37)   *It is* THIS PAPER *which/that/Ø John read.*

The fact that a headless realization of the Topic constituent cannot be placed in P1 position can be understood in terms of ordering principle SP7 (also called LIPOC, see *TFG1*: 16.4.2.). Note that a headed realization has the properties of a complex NP; a headless realization has the form of a bare subordinate clause. The fact that the former is less sensitive to LIPOC than the latter is paralleled by such differences as between:

(38)   *Because the fact that John didn't show up irritated Peter, he decided to quit.*
(39)   **Because that John didn't show up irritated Peter ...*
(40)   *Because it irritated Peter that John didn't show up ...*

where the placement of the "bare" subordinate clause, as distinct from the complex NP, parallels what we saw in the Cleft construction, including the conditions under which *it* is inserted into the Subject slot.

The above account of the structure and the expression of Cleft constructions is of course partly dependent on factors particular to English grammar. This account, however, contains a number of points which we find reflected in many other languages as well, namely:

(i) alternative expression possibilities for the GivTop constituent;

(ii) restrictions on placement of the GivTop constituent, depending on the choice made in (i);

(iii) otherwise, the general possibility that either the GivTop (argument) term or the Focus (predicate) term is placed in P1.

13.2.4. Selection restrictions

In early versions of Transformational Grammar it was usually assumed that a Cleft construction such as (41) should be transformationally derived from the structure underlying the corresponding non-Cleft (42):

(41)   *What John counted was the pigeons.*
(42)   *John counted the pigeons.*

One argument for such a derivation was based on the selection restrictions between the embedded verb (*count*) in (41) and its object (*the pigeons*). Compare:

(43)   *What John counted was the soup.
(44)   *John counted the soup.

In general terms, one could say that the Focus term in the Cleft construction must be compatible with the selection restrictions imposed by the embedded verb on its arguments. In a transformational description, this selectional relationship is automatically accounted for in terms of the identical underlying structure for Cleft and non-Cleft.

I have assumed that the Cleft construction has an underlying structure which is fundamentally different from the corresponding simplex sentence. The question thus arises as to how the correct selectional relations will be established in terms of such structures.

Let us consider the structure assigned to (43) according to our analysis:

(45)   Past e_i: {(dmx$_j$: *pigeon*)}$_{Foc}$
       (dx$_i$: [Past e_j: *count* [V] (*John*)$_{Ag}$ (Ax$_i$)$_{Go}$])$_{\emptyset SubjGivTop}$

We can now formulate the relevant relationship as follows:

(46)   The term in the Focus predicate must be compatible with the selection restrictions imposed on the (Ax$_i$) position.

This means that the predicate term must be chosen so as to conform to the restrictions imposed on the relativized position in the GivTop. The integration of a rule such as (46) into the grammar does not appear to provide any particular difficulty. Moreover, there are other situations in which a quite similar rule must be assumed to operate. Consider the following constructions, with their underlying representations:

(47) a.   *the pigeons that John counted*
     b.   **the soup that John counted*
     c.   (dmx$_i$: *pigeon*: [Past e: *count* [V] (*John*)$_{Ag}$ (Ax$_i$)$_{Go}$])
(48) a.   *As for the pigeons, John counted them.*
     b.   **As for the soup, John counted it.*
     c.   (dmx$_i$: *pigeon*)$_{Theme}$, Decl E: X: Past e: *count* [V] (*John*)$_{Ag}$ (Ax$_i$)$_{Go}$

302 *Focus constructions: basic patterns*

In the relative construction, the position (Ax$_i$) must be such that the material in the earlier restrictor(s) fits its selectional restrictions (*TFG1*: 6.4.1.). In the Theme+Clause construction likewise, if the Clause contains an anaphorical term coreferential to the Theme, the Theme is such that it fits the selectional restrictions imposed on (Ax$_i$) by the predicate.

There are thus several different situations in which some term and some open predication must be chosen in such a way that the term would fit the open position in the open predication.

13.2.5. The form of the Focus term and agreement patterns in the Cleft construction

Given the underlying representation which we have postulated for the prototypical Cleft construction, we would expect the copular verb to agree with the Subject-GivTop. As to the form that the Focus term will take, no specific prediction can be drawn from this underlying structure, since the Focus term is neither the Subject nor the Object, but the predicate of the Cleft construction.

In this light, consider the notorious variation in English between *it is I* and *it is me*. Akmajian (1970) distinguishes three dialects with respect to this variation. In Dialect I we find the following configuration:

(49) a. *The one who is responsible is* ME.
     b. *It is* ME *who is responsible.*
     c. *I am the one who is responsible.*

As far as (49a-b) are concerned, we could formulate the following rules, which are compatible with the underlying structure which we have postulated for the Cleft construction:

(50)   (i) the copula agrees with the Subject;
        (ii) the Focus term takes oblique case.

This, however, does not account for (49c). Rather, we would expect:

(51)   *ME *is the one who is responsible.*

The question arises, then, whether (49c) has the same, or rather a different underlying structure than (49a). Compare the following pairs:

(52) a. *The one who is responsible is JOHN.*
b. *JOHN is the one who is responsible.*
(53) a. *The one who is responsible is ME.*
b. *I am the one who is responsible.*

Just as (52a-b) can be regarded as variant expressions of the same underlying structure, so it would seem that (53a-b) can also be treated as variant expressions of the same structure. If this is done, however, we must assume that both the form of the Focus term and the agreement pattern of the copular verb are sensitive to the position in which the Focus term is placed. The rule could be formulated as follows:

(54) If the Focus term is placed in P1, then
(i) it takes nominative case,
(ii) it triggers agreement on the copula.
Otherwise,
(i) it takes oblique case, and
(ii) does not trigger agreement.

Note that, unless we are prepared to postulate different underlying structures for (53a-b), for which there seems to be little reason from a semantic and pragmatic point of view, we can only account for the pattern found in (53b) in terms of an exceptional rule such as (54). Similar problems present themselves in less complex types of non-verbal predication:

(55) A: *Who is the winner?*
B: (a) *The winner is ME.*
(b) *I am the winner.*

Again, since both (a) and (b) can be used in the context of (55A), there seems to be no reason to assume that these two answers differ in their underlying structure. We may thus conclude that (53b) must be accounted for in terms of an exceptional rule such as (54). This rule can be understood as due to a tendency for the Focus term in the Cleft construction (and more generally in identifying constructions) to start behaving as if it were the Subject of the construction, which, in our analysis, it is not.

304 *Focus constructions: basic patterns*

In a second dialect of English (Dialect II of Akmajian (1970)), we find the following distinction:

(56) a.   *It is I who is responsible.*
     b.   *It is ME who(m) John is after.*

In this dialect, then, we find the Focus term in the nominative in one more condition, which can be formulated as:

(57)   Express the Focus term in the nominative if it corresponds to an (Ax_i) with Subject function.

Since the underlying structure of (56a) would be:

(58)   Pres e_i: $\{(I)\}_{Foc}$ $(d1x_i$: [Pres e_j: $responsible_A(Ax_i)_{\emptyset Subj}])_{\emptyset SubjGivTop}$

rule (57) will choose *I* rather than *me* to express the Focus term in (56a) in Dialect II. Again, our only way to account for this is to say that the Focus term starts behaving "as if" it were a Subject — in this case because, in some derivative sense, it is indeed a Subject, or at least corresponds to a Subject position in the relative clause structure.

In Dialect III, finally, we find, instead of (56a), the following construction:

(59)   *It is I who am responsible.*

This can be interpreted as one further step towards treating the Focus term as the Subject of the construction. Just as in the case of placement in P1 the agreement is now triggered by the Focus term rather than by the "real" Subject of the Cleft construction.

Akmajian's explanation of (59) is that this type of agreement is brought about by some low-level adjustment rule which may have arisen on the analogy of constructions with non-restrictive relative clauses such as:

(60)   *I, who am responsible, ...*

Our account is similarly based on the assumption that the nominative form and the agreement with the Focus term are brought about by some relatively superficial rule, based on a certain tendency to "mistake" the Focus term for the Subject of the Cleft construction in certain conditions.

The prototypical Cleft construction 305

One might say, more generally, that speakers tend to be a bit hesitant as to the precise functional relations obtaining within the Cleft construction. In different languages, different sorts of patterns arise from this hesitancy. In Dutch, for example, the general rule is that if the Focus term is a pronoun, it is always realized in nominative form, and it always triggers agreement on the copula. Compare the following examples:

(61) a. *Degene die verantwoordelijk is ben IK.*
 the one who responsible is am I
 'The one who is responsible am I.'
 b. *IK ben degene die verantwoordelijk is.*
 I am the.one who responsible is
 'I am the one who is responsible.'

However, another rule says that first and second person pronouns cannot appear in the Dutch equivalent of the Dummy-Cleft. Compare:

(62) a. *Het is JAN die verantwoordelijk is.*
 it is John who responsible is
 'It is John who is responsible.'
 b. *Het is HIJ die verantwoordelijk is.*
 it is he who responsible is
 'It is he who is responsible.'
 c. **Het ben/is IK die verantwoordelijk ben/is.*
 it am/is I who resposible am/is
 'It am/is I who am/is responsible.'
 d. **Het ben/is JIJ die verantwoordelijk bent/is.*
 it are/is you who responsible are/is
 'It are/is you who are/is responsible.'

One might say, perhaps, that constructions of type (62c-d) are avoided because of the difficulty of choosing the correct agreement pattern for the two occurrences of the copula.

Just as problems may arise concerning Person agreement, so there may also be problems with respect to Number agreement in the Cleft construction. Consider the following Dutch examples and their English equivalents:

(63) *Wat ik het.meest betreur is/zijn de BOEKEN.*
 what I most regret is/are the BOOKS
 'What I regret most is/are the books.'

(64)   *De* BOEKEN *is/zijn   wat   ik   het.meest   betreur.*
         the BOOKS   is/are   what   I   most   regret
         'The books is/are what I regret most.'

In both languages there appears to be some hesitancy as to whether the copula should take singular or plural form in such constructions as these. In Dutch, this hesitancy is also apparent from the fact that, when constructions such as (63) are subordinated, the result is not very acceptable, either with a singular or with a plural copula:

(65)   ?*Ik denk dat wat ik het meest betreur de* BOEKEN *is/zijn.*
         'I think that what I most regret is/are the books'

For similar examples from another language consider the following data from Portuguese (Peres 1984: 161-164). In Portuguese, agreement with the Focus term is sometimes required (note that the personal pronoun in Focus position takes nominative form):

(66) A: *Quem   é   o   próximo?*
         who   is   the next?
         'Who is the next one?'
     B: *O   próximo   és   TU.*
         the next   are   you
         'The next one are YOU.'
     B: **O próximo   é   TU.*
         the next   is   you
         'The next one is you.'

In other cases, such agreement with the Focus term is strongly preferred:

(67) A: *Qual   é   a   tua   distraccão?*
         which is   the your   hobby
         'What is your hobby?'
     B: *A   minha   distraccão   são   os   livros.*
         the my   hobby   are   the books
         'My hobby are books.'
     B: ?*A   minha   distraccão   é   os   livros.*
         the my   hobby   is   the books
         'My hobby is books.'

These agreement and expression phenomena constitute one of the arguments which lead Peres (1984) to reject the analysis advocated here at least for Portuguese identificational constructions, for which he prefers the analysis with a two-place identificational predicate corresponding to *be* in English.[2] But as we saw in the preceding, hesitancy with respect to case expression and agreement seem to be a general phenomenon with this construction type, which can also be understood as due to the fact that both the predicate and the argument of the construction are constituted by terms.

13.2.6. Typological predictions

Following up the discussion of the preceding sections, I submit that the prototypical Cleft construction is a construction with an underlying structure conforming to the following schema:

(68) $\{(\text{definite term})\}_{Foc} \, (dx_i: \ldots (Ax_i) \ldots)_{\emptyset GivTop}$

where the GivTop is a definite term, restricted by some type of relative construction, and the Focus also a definite term, applied to the GivTop as a predicate.

I now assume that this representation for the prototypical Cleft is cross-linguistically valid. That is, that in any language which has prototypical Clefts at all, these constructions will have underlying representations conforming to (68). If this is correct, then we can formulate a number of general predictions concerning the form which Cleft constructions will assume in different languages. More specifically:

(i) the Cleft construction will conform to the rules for expressing non-verbal predications, especially with respect to (a) constituent ordering, (b) the presence or absence of copula support.

(ii) the argument of the Cleft construction will behave as a GivTop constituent, and the predicate term will behave as a Focus constituent, and these constituents will thus conform to the rules for the treatment of GivTop and Focus constituents in the language concerned.

(iii) the GivTop constituent in the Cleft construction will have the properties of a verbal restrictor, more specifically, the properties of a headless or dummy-headed relative construction.

---

2. Cf. the argument to the same effect in Keizer (1992b).

For some confirmation of these predictions, let us consider two examples.

(i) *Mojave*
Mojave (like other Yuman languages) has two peculiarities relevant to the present discussion:
    (a) VRs are formed on the pattern of the circumnominal type (see 3.3);
    (b) Constructions with non-verbal predicates are expressed according to the following pattern:

(69)   argument-term$_1$ predicate-term$_2$-č BE-tense

in which -č, which otherwise functions as a Subject marker, appears unexpectedly on that term which represents the predicate rather than the Subject. Thus, we get (Munro 1977: 445):

(70)   *John   k^{w}aθ?ide:-č   ido-pč.*
            John   doctor-Subj   be-tense
            'John is a doctor.'

Munro (1977) explains the latter phenomenon on the plausible assumption that the original structure of the non-verbal predication had a form which could be paraphrased as:

(71)   *(John - doctor) is the case.*
            'It is the case that John is a doctor.'

in which a predication, verbless by itself, is embedded under a higher existential verb.

What is significant in the present context, however, is that precisely these same two properties (a) and (b) characterize the Mojave Cleft construction (cf. Munro 1973: 54):

(72)   *?in^{y}ep   ?-u:a:r-n^y ?ahat-č   ido-pč.*
            I   I-want-nom-dem   horse-č   be-tense
            'What I want is a horse.'

This construction therefore confirms two of the typological predictions formulated above.

(ii) *Tagalog*
Tagalog has the following two relevant properties:
  (a) non-verbal predications do not take copula support;
  (b) only Subjects can be relativized.
Precisely these two properties are found in the Cleft construction. Thus, a construction such as:

(73)   *Ang ISDA   ang   kinain   ni   Juan.*
        Foc fish   Subj   be.eaten by   John
        'It is the FISH that is eaten by John'

can be given the following underlying representation:

(74)   Pres e_i: {$(dx_j$: *isda*)}$_{Foc}$
        $(dx_i$: [Pres e_j: *kain* [V] $(Juan)_{Ag}$ $(Ax_i)_{GoSubj}$])$_{ØSubjGivTop}$

Note that within the GivTop, Subject function has been assigned to the Goal term (which is the term relativized). This is the only possibility for expressing a restrictor with relativized Goal in Tagalog. In other words, there is no direct equivalent to the English construction:

(75)   *It is the FISH that John has eaten.*

13.3. Focus constructions with adpositional predicates

Alongside prototypical Clefts such as (76a-b), constructions of type (77) are often also treated as Clefts:

(76) a. *It was JOHN with whom I went to New York.*
     b. *It was JOHN that I went to New York with.*
(77)   *It was WITH JOHN that I went to New York.*

In fact, however, I shall argue that the structure of (77) is rather different from the Cleft construction, even though (76) and (77) may be used to describe much the same event.[3]

Note that in (77) only *that* (or Ø) can appear, not the relative pronoun *who(m)*. This suggests that the embedded clause in (77) is not a relative construction, but a general subordinate *that*-clause. This is confirmed by languages such as Dutch, German, and French, in which the general subordinator for complement clauses (*dat, daß, que*) cannot be used in relative clauses (for French: not in clauses with relativized Subjects). In each of these languages, the equivalent of (77) takes the general subordinator rather than the relative pronoun. Compare Dutch:

(78) a. *Het is Jan met wie ik naar New York gegaan ben.*
it is John with whom I to New York gone am
b. *Het is met Jan dat ik naar New York gegaan ben.*
it is with John that I to New York gone am

In each of these languages, again, the construction (78b) is similar to constructions such as:

(79) a. *It is good that I have gone to New York.*
b. *Het is goed dat ik naar New York gegaan ben.*

in which *good/goed* clearly is a one-place adjectival predicate predicated over a predicational term.

Just as in (79) no identity is established between 'that I went to New York' and 'good', so in (77) no identity is established between 'that I went to New

---

3. Schachter (1973: 27-28) used constructions of type (77) as an argument that the Topic constituent of the Cleft construction cannot have the form of a (free) relative clause. Harries-Delisle (1978: 474) provides evidence for the fundamental difference between (76) and (77). See also Pinkham—Hankamer (1975) and Gundel (1977) for the differences between these constructions.

York' and 'with John'. In other words, (77) and (79) are not identifying constructions, but property-assigning ones.

This provides the key to an understanding of constructions of this type. Consider the structure of (79):

(80)   Pres e_i: *good* [A] (PresPerf e_j: *go* [V] (I)$_{Ag}$ (*New York*)$_{Dir}$)$_\emptyset$

In this structure, we recognize the representation for predicational terms discussed in 5.3.

We may now assume this same type of structure for (77). This can be done by using the possibility of an adpositional term acting as a term predicate (see *TFG1*: 8.5.), as it does in:

(81) a. *Mary is with John.*
   b. Pres e: {(*John*)$_{Comp}$} (*Mary*)$_\emptyset$

We take it that in (77), similarly, the property of 'being with John' is assigned to the State of Affairs of 'my going to New York': 'My going to New York was in the company of John':

(82) a. *It is with John that I went to New York.*
   b. Pres e_i: {(*John*)$_{Comp}$} (Past e_j: *go* [V] (I)$_{Ag}$(*New York*)$_{Dir}$)$_\emptyset$

Once it has been established that constructions of type (76) and (77) have different structures, and are also semantically different types of predications (identifying vs. property assigning, respectively), we can also understand why it is that the conditions of occurrence for these two constructions are different. Specifically, construction (77) may be used in conditions in which (76) is excluded:[4]

(83) a. *It was with much pleasure that I received your letter.*
   b. **It was much pleasure with which I received your letter.*
(84) a. *It is for fun that he studies archaeology.*
   b. **It is fun for which he studies archaeology.*
(85) a. *It was at dawn that they attacked.*
   b. **It was dawn at which they attacked.*

---

4. The examples (83)-(85) are from Jacobsen (1977: 370).

In semantic terms, this difference can be understood as follows. The Cleft construction requires a Focus term specifying some entity which can be identified with some other entity. Expressions such as *with much pleasure, for fun, at dawn* do not specify such identifiable entities. Rather they present conditions which can be taken to modify a whole State of Affairs. It is no coincidence, then, that almost any satellite which can appear in a simplex predication as modifying the nuclear State of Affairs, can also appear in constructions of type (77). Further, it is to be noted that as soon as an expression of the type found in predicate position in (83)-(85) is definitized so as to refer to some specific entity, the use of the resulting expression in the Cleft construction also becomes possible:

(86) a. *It was for that kind of pleasure that he went to the Moulin Rouge.*
 b. *It was that kind of pleasure for which he went to the Moulin Rouge.*
(87) a. *It was in that election that he had his highest hopes of success.*
 b. *It was that election in which he had his highest hopes of success.*

As to the formal expression of constructions of type (77), we may assume that this is governed by much the same principles as in the case of the Cleft construction: the argument term is expressed as a subordinate clause which, on account of LIPOC, will be placed in final position. In that condition, *it* will be inserted into the vacant Subject position. The only thing which is not predicted by this analysis, and for which I have no immediate solution, is the following difference:

(88) a. *That I went to New York was fortunate.*
 b. *It was fortunate that I went to New York.*
(89) a. **That I went to New York was with John.*
 b. *It was with John that I went to New York.*

In other words, for reasons unclear to me, the subordinate predication can be placed in P1 position in the case of adjectival predicates as in (88), but not in the case of adpositional predicates as in (89).

After this general discussion of cleft and pseudo-cleft constructions, we will look at a number of more specific focus constructions in the next chapter.

14. Predicate focus; cleft interrogatives; demarking of Focus constructions

14.0. Introduction

In this chapter I discuss three more specific phenomena concerning Focus constructions.

First, although Focus constructions are typically used for focusing on terms, some languages have special construction types for focusing on the predicate. These constructions are discussed in 14.1.

Second, it appears that Focus constructions are especially suitable for expressing Q-word questions. And indeed, many languages have Q-word Focus constructions, either as a variant alongside "straight" Q-word questions, or even as the only strategy for the formation of such questions. Such interrogative Focus constructions are discussed in 14.2.

Third, many phenomena in different languages can be understood if it is assumed that Focus constructions (declarative and interrogative alike) may undergo a process of "markedness shift" through which their degree of markedness diminishes, often with concomitant formal simplifications, such that finally they may end up as the unmarked (declarative or interrogative) sentence type of the language in question. This process of "demarking" of Focus constructions is discussed in 14.3.

14.1. Focusing on the predicate

So far we have concentrated on constructions which serve to bring some TERM into Focus: either a bare nominal term, as in (1a), or an adpositionally marked one, as in (1b):

(1) a. *It is THIS MAN who kissed Mary.*
    b. *It is WITH MARY that John went home.*

Most languages also have certain special constructions which can be used to focus on the predicate. These constructions may have certain similarities to those of (1), but they typically also differ from these in certain respects. Compare the following constructions:

(2) a. *John wore his best suit to the dance tonight.*
b. *It was HIS BEST SUIT that John wore to the dance tonight.*
c. **It is WORE that John his best suit to the dance tonight.*

From these examples (from Quirk et al. 1972: 951-952) it is clear that the verbal predicate cannot simply be "clefted out" of a predication in the same way as a term can. If we want to focus on the predicate by means of a Dummy-Cleft in English, we must form such structures as:

(3) a. *It is TEACH(ING) that he does for a living.*
b. *What he does for a living is TEACH.*

in which the focused predicate takes a non-finite form, and the support verb *do* appears in the GivTop constituent. This means that the relation between a predicate-focused construction and its neutral counterpart is more complex than in the case of clefted terms.

The differences come out quite clearly in constructions in which Focus is placed on a transitive predicate. Consider:

(4) a. *John kissed Mary.*
b. *What John did was KISS MARY.*
c. *What John did to Mary was KISS her.*

In (4b) the Focus is on the whole phrase *kiss Mary* rather than on just the predicate. In (4c) the predicate itself is focused on, but there is a pronominal object *her* added to the predicate, while what is semantically the Goal of *kiss* appears in a prepositional form *to Mary*.

All these phenomena are difficult to account for in any theory which derives Cleft constructions from the corresponding non-Cleft ones. They are more easily understood in terms of our analysis, in which we regard Cleft constructions as identifying constructions in which a term-predicate is applied to some other term, signifying that the referent of the latter is identical to that of the former. For a Cleft construction, then, we need two terms to be related to each other, rather than predicates. And this is exactly what we find in the predicate-focusing constructions mentioned so far. Consider again a construction such as:

(5) *What John did was kiss Mary.*

Here the GivTop constituent *what John did* is a term referring to some Action of John's; and *kiss Mary* is not a predicate, but a predicational term realized in the form of an infinitival construction. We can thus analyse (5) as follows:

(6)   Past e_i: {(e_j: *kiss* [V] (Ø)$_{Ag}$ (*Mary*)$_{Go}$)}$_{Foc}$
   (e_k: *do* [V] (*John*)$_{Ag}$ (e_k)$_{Pat}$)$_{ØSubjGivTop}$

in which it is expressed that the entity e_k defined as 'what John did' is nothing else than the entity e_j, defined as the act of 'kissing Mary'.

We can thus say, in general, that a Cleft construction (in English) can only be used to place Focus on the predicate if that predicate is placed within an embedded predication within a predicational term, which is then applied as a predicate to the GivTop constituent. This admittedly complex analysis of predicate-Cleft constructions explains quite a few properties of these constructions which would otherwise be difficult to explain: the GivTop must be some term referring to some predicate; in English this can only be done by means of *do*. And the predicate is a predicational term rather than a simple predicate. This explains why terms belonging to the predicational term (such as *Mary* in (6)) can come along with the predicate in the Focus term.

The analysis is also able to explain the difference between such constructions as:

(7) a. *What John did was disappointing.*
    b. *What John did was disappoint.*

In (7a), the predicate *disappointing* is simply applied to the term *what John did*. 'What John did' is said to have the property of 'being disappointing'. (7a) is therefore a property-assigning construction. In (7b), on the other hand, *disappoint* expresses a predicational term which is applied as a predicate to *what John did*. 'What John did' is there identified as being nothing else than 'disappoint'. (7b) is therefore an identifying construction. The difference comes out in the following representations:

(8) a. Past e_i: *disappointing* [A] (e_j: *do* [V] (*John*)$_{Ag}$ (e_j)$_{Pat}$)$_{ØSubjGivTop}$
    b. Past e_i: {(e_j: *disappoint* [V] (Ø)$_{Ag}$ (Ø)$_{Go}$)}$_{Foc}$
        (e_k: *do*$_V$ (*John*)$_{Ag}$ (e_k)$_{Pat}$)$_{ØSubjGivTop}$

We can thus say that in English, Cleft constructions can be used to focus on the predicate, but only through embedding that predicate in a term which is

316 *Focus constructions 2*

then converted into a predicate again. As in other cases, the Cleft construction here again consists in a Focus term being applied to a GivTop term.

In certain languages, we find special constructions used for focusing on the predicate, containing a repetition of the predicate in what otherwise looks very much like a Cleft construction. Such constructions take such forms as illustrated in the following "pseudo-English" example:

(9)   (*It's*) KISS (*that*) *John kissed Mary.*

Constructions of this type are especially common in West-African languages, and also occur, probably as a syntactic borrowing from these languages, in a number of Creole languages.

Koopman (1984: chapter 6) describes the properties of the so-called "Predicate-Cleft" construction as it occurs in Vata, a West-African language of the Kru family. Compare the following constructions:

(10)   *N   wà   nā ǹ   kà   ngÓnÙ   à.*
       you want   that you Fut sleep   Q
       'Do you want to sleep?'
(11)   *NgÓnÙ ǹ   wà   nā ǹ   kà   ngÓnÙ   à.*
       sleep you want   that you Fut sleep   Q
       'Is it SLEEP that you want to sleep?' =
       'Do you want to SLEEP?'

As far as this construction type goes, this focusing strategy might be described as consisting in placing a copy of the verb in clause-initial position. Koopman shows that this process of "V-fronting" is sensitive to similar, though not identical constraints to the process of "Wh-fronting" in Vata. There are thus certain constraints on the accessibility of verbs to this kind of focusing by repetition. Certain relevant properties of this construction type are:

(i) it is the bare form of the verb, without any tonal specification, which is placed in initial position;

(ii) this verb can in no way be modified or be part of some more complex constituent;

(iii) there must be a fully specific verb in the construction for the fronted verb to correspond to.

Thus, we get a distribution pattern as illustrated in the following "pseudo-English" example:

Focusing on the predicate 317

(12) a. *John will kiss Mary.*
   b. *Kiss John will kiss Mary.*
   c. **Kiss Mary John will.*
   d. **Kiss John will (do) Mary.*

The Vata predicate-focusing construction can (in our terminology) be described in terms of an expression rule placing a copy of the (bare) verbal predicate in P1 position when Focus is assigned to that predicate. There does not appear to be any special reason to speak of a "Cleft" construction in the case of Vata: first, the construction simply does not have the properties of a Cleft construction; second, there is a "real" Cleft construction which can be used to focus on the predicate, as in:

(13) NgÓnÚl mÍ ṅ wà à.
      sleeping it you want Q
      'Is it SLEEPING that you want?'

In that case, however, the preposed predicate is nominalized and there is a pronominal element, here glossed 'it', which does not appear in constructions of type (11) (Koopman 1984: 154). Furthermore, there is no repetition of the verb involved in this construction.

In some languages focusing on the predicate does have properties of a Cleft construction. This can be seen from Muysken's (1978) account of the relevant constructions in Papiamentu. Compare the following constructions:

(14) a. M'a   duna   e   buki.
         I-Asp   give   the book
         'I gave the book.'
   b. (Ta)   e   buki   m'a   duna.
       (be)   the book   I-Asp give
       'It's the BOOK I gave.'
   c. (Ta)   duna   m'a   duna   e   buki.
       be   give   I-Asp give   the book
       'I really GAVE the book.'

(14a) is a neutral construction. (14b) places Focus on the Object. Without *ta*, that construction could simply be described in terms of a rule of Object fronting. With *ta*, it rather has the properties of a Cleft construction (note that *ta* in other constructions clearly functions as a copula). (14c), without *ta*, is completely comparable to the Vata construction (11), especially since it also obeys conditions similar to those of (i)-(iii) above. It would then be a simple case of placing a copy of the verb in initial position. Given these circumstances, it seems better to analyse elements such as *ta* in constructions such as (14c) as a focus marker rather than as a copula. If this analysis is correct, there seems to be room for the view that there is no such thing as a genuine predicate cleft construction. Special constructions used to focus on the predicate are then either regular cleft constructions which involve some kind of embedding or nominalization of the predicate focused on; or they come about by repeating the predicate in conspicuous (typically: P1) position. In that case the original predicate is either left intact, or represented by a dummy predicate comparable to English *do*.

14.2. Interrogative Focus constructions

In many languages Q-word questions can be formed on the pattern of the Cleft construction. Compare:

(15) a. *John bought the book.*
  b. *Who bought the book?*
(16) a. *John is the one who bought the book.*
  b. *Who is the one who bought the book?*

Such questions may be called "Cleft questions". The fact that Cleft questions can be formed is readily understood when we realize that Cleft constructions prototypically have the function of focusing on some constituent, and that Q-words have intrinsic Focus function. From this it follows that the Cleft constructions should be particularly appropriate for forming Q-word questions, with the constituent marked by the Q-word in the Focus position of the Cleft construction.

This, however, also implies that there is a certain skew between the simplex and the Cleft interrogative in (15b) and (16b), and their declarative counterparts in (15a) and (16a). A better picture of their relationship would be the following:

(17) declarative   interrogative
  a. *John bought the book.*   ---
  b. *JOHN bought the book.*   *WHO bought the book?*
  c. *JOHN is the one who bought the book.* *WHO is the one who bought the book?*

The point is that in the declarative (17a) there is no necessary Focus on any of the constituents. The construction can be used in a setting in which there is no presupposition involved that someone bought the book. Such a presupposition is involved, however, in the declarative constructions (17b-c), and in their interrogative counterparts. And just as the declaratives (17b-c) are pragmatically equivalent, so are their interrogative counterparts.

In each case, the presupposition is 'some person x_i bought the book', and the question is: 'give me the identity of x_i'. Only the strategy through which the questions are formed is different, just as in the case of the declaratives (17b-c). Consider the clause structures underlying (17b-c):

(18)   Int E: X: Past e: *buy* [V] $(Qx_i:<hum>)_{Ag}$ $(d1x_j: book)_{Go}$
        'Who bought the book?'

(19)   Int E: X: Pres e_i: *be* [V] {$(Qx_k:<hum>)$}
        $(d1x_i: [Past\ e_j: buy\ [V]\ (Ax_i)_{Ag}\ (d1x_j:book)_{Go}])_\emptyset$
        'Who is the one who bought the book?'

In (18) the Agent position of the simplex predication is directly questioned. In (19) a description is formed of the presupposed entity 'the one who bought the book', and then the identity of this entity is questioned through a questioned term-predicate. In both cases the result is pragmatically equivalent, at least in the sense that simplex and Cleft questions have the same presuppositions.

Just as we did in the case of Q-Pattern and Q-Focus constructions in chapter 12, we may compare the advantages and disadvantages of the Cleft question strategy:

Advantage: Highlighting is guaranteed no matter what other devices (marking, position, prosody) are used. This is because the Cleft construction intrinsically highlights the Focus constituent.
Drawback: The construction of the question is inherently more complex than that of a straight question, both in underlying structure and in actual expression.

Languages vary in their usage of Cleft questions. Some languages have only simplex questions, some have simplex and Cleft questions in free variation, some have the two types in complementary or overlapping distribution, and some have obligatory Cleft questions across the board. The existence of this type of variation may be explained in terms of Keenan's principle of "logical variants". Keenan (1975) developed this principle on the basis of a similar situation of the occurrence of two distinct constructions being "logically" equivalent in certain conditions. Consider a construction such as:

(20)   *John did not understand what Peter was saying.*

The complement *what Peter was saying* could here be interpreted as either a free relative construction, equivalent to (21a), or as a dependent question, equivalent to the indirect version of (21b):

(21) a. *that which Peter was saying*
     b. *What was Peter saying?*

Keenan demonstrates, however, that in the complement of a verb such as *understand* the semantic import of these two distinct constructions is equivalent, as can be seen from the two paraphrases:

(22) a. 'John didn't know the identity of that which Peter was saying'
     b. 'John didn't know the answer to the question: What was Peter saying?'

On this equivalence Keenan bases a typological principle called the "Principle of Logical Variants". This principle says the following:

(23)   If the semantic difference between two constructions X and Y is neutralized in a context C, so that CX and CY are semantically equivalent, then languages may be expected to vary naturally between using X or Y in the context C.

"Varying naturally" between X and Y may be understood as follows: some languages will only have CX, some only CY, and some may have CX and CY side by side as optional alternatives to each other. This is more or less what we find in the case of the opposition between simplex and Cleft Q-word questions.

There is one phenomenon, however, which cannot be so easily understood in terms of Keenan's principle. This is the fact that a number of languages have the following property:

(24) For all types of terms simplex questions can be formed (usually by the side of optional Cleft variants), except for cases in which the Subject is questioned. If one wishes to question a Subject, one must use a Cleft question (or, in some languages, a Cleft question is strongly preferred in that condition).

This type of organization obviously asks for an explanation: why should the choice between two in principle equivalent constructions be enforced in favour of one of them precisely in the condition of Subject questioning?

I will illustrate this phenomenon with data from Lango, a Western Nilotic language of Uganda, described in Noonan (1981). I have chosen this language because Noonan not only describes the phenomenon, but also provides an answer to the question of why this particular patterning should exist.

The basic functional pattern of Lango can be represented as follows:

(25)   P1 S V O X

Thus, a neutral sentence type would be as follows:

(26)   Lócà   òmÌyò   búk   bòt   dákô.
       man   he-give-perf book   to   woman
       'The man gave the book to the woman.'

The initial P1 position can be used for constituents with Topic function, corresponding to a variety of distinct functions within the predication:

(27)   Àpwó   àtÍn   ònÈnò.
       hare   child   he-saw-perf
       'I tell you about the hare (Topic): the child saw it.'

The Topic, and also the Subject (thus, any constituent in preverbal position) will be interpreted as definite, unless it is explicitly marked as indefinite. The P1 position in Lango can thus be said to have specialized as a position for Topic constituents.

The strategy followed in Lango for the formation of Q-word questions is Q-pattern:

(28)   Lócà   òmÌò   pàlà   bòt   ngà?
       man   he-give-perf knife   to   who?
       'To whom did the man give the knife?'

This strategy, however, will come into conflict with the Topic-specialization of the P1 position in the case of Subject questioning:

(29) Ngà   ònÈnò   òpíò?
      who   he-saw-perf   Opio?
      'Who saw Opio?'

This construction is in accordance with the Q-Pattern strategy, but it has a constituent in initial position which has Focus, not Topic function. This explains, in Noonan's view, why it is precisely in this case that the Q-Cleft construction is preferred, as illustrated in (30), in which *àmÉ* is a relative marker (rm):

(30) Ngà   Én àmÉ   ònÈnò   òpíò?
      who   it rm   he-see-perf   Opio?
      'Who (is) it that saw Opio?'

Although this construction still has the Focus constituent in initial position, this is not the initial position of the neutral sentence structure, but the initial position of the special Cleft construction, which specifically signals that the constituent in initial position is a Focus constituent.

If Noonan's explanation is correct, we may specify some properties of languages in which Q-Cleft is preferred specifically in Subject questioning:

(i) these languages will otherwise apply Q-Pattern. For if they used "Q-Front", then obviously the P1 position could not have specialized for Topic terms and thereby be incompatible with Focus constituents;

(ii) their P1 position will have strongly, or even exclusively specialized in hosting Topic constituents.

Given these properties, however, we can derive a further prediction concerning declaratives in such languages:

(iii) focusing the Subject in declaratives by simply stressing it will be non-preferred.

Clearly, such focusing would lead to precisely the same clash between the Focus constituent and the Topic-expectation associated with the initial P1 position as in the case of question type (29). This prediction is borne out in Lango (Noonan 1981: 171-172). A question such as (31) can in principle be answered by (32), with emphatic stress on the Subject:

(31) *Ngà   òjwàtò   òkélò?*
     who   he-hit-perf   Okelo?
     'Who hit Okelo?'
(32) *Òpíò   òjwàtò   òkélò.*
     Opio   he-hit-perf   Okelo
     'Opio hit Okelo.'

But, just as a Cleft question is preferred to (31), so a Cleft answer is preferred to (32):

(33) *Òpíò   Énn àmÉ   òjwátò   òkélò.*
     Opio   it   rm   he-hit-perf   Okelo
     'It (was) Opio that hit Okelo.'

We may thus conclude that preferential Q-Clefting of the Subject may be expected to occur in languages in which the P1 position has specialized as a Topic position, and may be interpreted as a measure for avoiding the positioning of Focus constituents in the P1 position of simplex predications.

The organization discussed here is very common in Bantu languages. Swahili (Ashton 1947) has the same patterning as Lango in this respect. The same applies to Dzamba (Bokamba 1974). In this language, there is one point of special interest, in that the Q-word can appear at the very end of the clause, so that at first sight it seems as if "movement to the right" is involved, something excluded by different transformational theories of wh-question formation (such as Bach 1971). Compare:[1]

(34) *O-Musa   a-tom-áki   i-bondoki.*
     the-Musa   he-send-ta   the-gun
     'Musa sent the gun.'
(35) *Ó-tom-áki   i-bondoki   nzanyi?*
     R-he-send-ta   the-gun   who
     'Who sent the gun?'

There are several reasons, however, for regarding (35) as a Cleft rather than as a simplex question. First, the pronominal prefix *ó-* in (35), glossed by 'R', is characteristic of relative clauses. Second, alongside (35) we find an alternative with an explicit head:

---

1. ta = marker for Tense/Aspect; R = pronominal prefix.

(36) O-moto   ó-tom-áki   i-bondoki   nzanyi?
      the-person R-he-send-ta the-gun   who?
      'Who is the person who sent the gun?'

And third, there is also a Cleft question of similar type, but with explicit copula. Compare the following declarative and interrogative sentences:

(37) (Embaka) é-e-kp-áki   Musa e-báki   zikongo.
      thing   R-it-it-take-ta Musa it-was   spear
      '(The thing) which Musa took was a spear.'
(38) (Embaka) é-e-kp-áki   Musa e-báki   binde?
      thing   R-it-it-take-ta Musa it-was   what
      'What was the thing that Musa took?'

From this last pair we see that the Q-word in the Cleft question takes precisely the same position as the Focus term in the corresponding declarative. There is thus no reason to postulate any special placement rules for Q-words, different from those determining the placement of Focus terms in declarative constructions.

An interesting variant of the above pattern is found in Babungo (Schaub 1985: 9), a P1 S V O language in which Q-constituents may either go to pattern position or to Focus position, which in Babungo is a postverbal position. Questioned Subjects, however, may not remain in pattern position, but MUST go to Focus position. Thus, Q-constituents never appear in clause-initial position. Schaub's explanation is the same as Noonan's: since P1 has specialized as a Topic position, it does not accept Focus constituents. Babungo has an interesting alternative strategy for Subject questioning: a construction in which the verb is repeated in initial position, so that we get a pattern of the form: V Subj V Obj. Note that this is not a predicate-focusing, but a Subj-focusing construction. The initial V may, again, be understood as a device for keeping the focused Subj off the clause-initial P1 position, which has specialized in harbouring Topic terms.

14.3. Demarking processes

14.3.1. Demarking of Focus constructions

Certain grammatical phenomena in mutually unrelated languages can be interpreted as being due to a historical process of markedness shift, through which an originally marked Focus construction is increasingly used in conditions in which no special focusing is called for, and finally ends up as the pragmatically neutral, unmarked clause type of the language involved. This process of markedness shift (see *TFG1*: 2.5.3.), which seems to be especially common in languages with P1 V S O ordering, can be illustrated as follows:

(39)   UNMARKED   FOCUSED

Stage 1: *Kissed John Mary.*   *(Be) JOHN who kissed Mary.*
Stage 2: a.   *Kissed John Mary.*
         b.   *(Be) John who kissed Mary.*   *(Be) JOHN who kissed Mary.*
Stage 3: *(Be) John (who) kissed Mary.*   (new Focus construction)

At Stage 1 there is a marked Focus construction; at Stage 2 this construction is also used when no special Focus is involved; at Stage 3 it has ousted the original unmarked construction and lost its marked character completely. At that stage we may expect some innovative Focus construction to emerge.

There is also evidence that in the course of the demarking process, the original marked Focus construction may lose some of its special formal features, so that it comes closer and closer to the expression form of the neutral sentence type. The logical limit of this process is a construction which has lost any trace of its earlier existence as a marked Focus construction, except that the ordering of constituents may be different from what it was before. In fact, the demarking of an original Cleft construction may be one route through which an original P1 V S O language may end up as a P1 S V O language.[2] This process can be illustrated as follows:

---

2. Another such route is through a demarking of the construction in which the Subj-GivTop is placed in P1. See *TFG1*: 16.4.2.

(40) Stage 1: *Kissed John Mary.* (neutral)
Be JOHN who kissed Mary. (marked)

Stage 2: *Kissed John Mary.* (neutral)
Be John who kissed Mary. (alternative neutral)

Stage 3: *Be John kissed Mary.* (neutral)

Stage 4: *John kissed Mary.* (neutral)

At Stage 1 we have the original P1 V S O order, with the original marked Focus construction; at Stage 2 this construction is also used outside Focus conditions; at Stage 3 it loses its relative marker, and at Stage 4 it loses its copula. At that Stage, the result is a simple SVO clause stemming from an earlier P1 V S O stage.

Note that (40) is meant to illustrate one possible route that the "erosion" of the original Focus construction might take; several other such routes do probably occur in the history of different languages. Note further that many languages have no copula, and only few use dummy elements corresponding to English *it*. Cleft constructions may therefore take any of the following forms:

(41) a. *It be JOHN who kissed Mary.*
b. *Be JOHN who kissed Mary.*
c. *JOHN who kissed Mary.*

It is clear that, especially starting from constructions of type (41c), the step toward the completely unmarked construction *John kissed Mary* is small indeed.

Another feature of this demarking process is that elements which originate as the equivalents of English *it* and/or *be* may lose something of their original status and develop into unanalysable particles which, when the Focus construction has shifted to the position of the neutral sentence type, may then acquire the function of marking the declarative or the interrogative clause type.

Thus, a putative demarking process applied to French Cleft constructions might have such effects as the following:

(42) Stage 1: *C'est   JEAN   qui   a   embrassé   Marie.*
             that.is John   who   has   kissed   Mary
             'It is John who has kissed Mary.'

    Stage 4: *Sè   Jean   a   embrassé   Marie.*
             particle   John   has   kissed   Mary
             'John has kissed Marie.'

(43) Stage 1: *Qu'est   ce   que   Jean   a   fait?*
             what.is   that which   John   has   done
             'What is that which John has done?'

    Stage 4: *Kèsk   Jean   a   fait?*
             Q-word   John   has   done
             'What has John done?'

Note that in the case of (43), the original combination *qu'est ce que* 'what is that which' ends up as a new unanalysable Q-word *kèsk*.

Similarly, an original copula deriving from the Cleft construction may, in the course of the demarking process, end up as a simple particle marking the neutral declarative or interrogative construction.

In Dik (1980: 160-166) it was argued that some variant of this demarking of original Focus constructions may explain the development from the P1 V S O pattern which is common in Celtic languages towards the SVO pattern which is found in Breton. Thus, the following are neutral sentence types of Breton which, however, may be interpreted as deriving from earlier constructions corresponding to the glosses in English:[3]

(44) *Krampouezh   a   zebro   Yannig   e   Kemper   hiziv.*
     crêpes   which   will-eat   John   in   Quimper   today
     'John will eat crêpes in Quimper today.'

(45) *E   Kemper   e   tebro   Yannig   krampouezh   hiziv.*
     in   Quimper   that   will-eat   John   crêpes   today
     'In Quimper John will eat crêpes today.'

---

3. The data are from Anderson—Chung (1977).

Note that *a* corresponds to the relative marker *a* of Welsh, whereas *e* corresponds to the general subordinator *y* of Welsh. (45) thus goes back to the type of Focus construction discussed in 13.3, which can be paraphrased by English:

(46)   It is in Quimper that John will eat crêpes today.

A situation which can be interpreted as an incipient stage of the demarking of Cleft constructions is found in Tamazight (Moroccan Berber), as described in Penchoen (1973). Tamazight is a P1 V S O language with a rather strong tendency to use cleft constructions:

> Clefting is very frequent in Berber languages in general. In Tamazight, it is very often used under conditions where no particular stress or emphasis is intended - particularly in sentences with the verb *g* 'be': *aryaz ag-ga* 'He's a man' (lit. '(It's) a man that he is'). (Penchoen 1973: 77).

The fact that clefting is used even where no special Focus is involved is a clear sign of markedness shift.

Cleft constructions in Tamazight are formed on the pattern:

(47)   The MEN that going to the house.
       'It's the MEN that are going to the house'

where the Focus constituent is in initial P1 position, and the GivTop is introduced by the demonstrative element *ay* 'that', 'that one', followed by a construction which has all the properties of a verbal restrictor, with the Verb in participial form. Compare:

(48) a.   Ddan   irəyzən   γər-taddart.
          went   men   to-house
          'The men went to the house.'
     b.   Irəyzən ag-gəddan γər-taddart.
          men   that-going to-house
          'It's the MEN who went to the house.'

Significantly, almost all types of Q-word question have the form of Cleft Questions:

(49)   M-ag-gəddan   γər-ṭaddarṭ.
         who-that-going   to-house
         'Who is it that has gone to the house?'

It would be interesting to know whether there is any correlation between these facts. I.e., does demarking in declarative cleft constructions occur above all in languages with Cleft Q-word questions?

14.3.2. Demarking of pragmatically marked construction types

We can now generalize the demarking process described in the preceding section into a more general principle which says that any pragmatically marked construction type is liable to undergo markedness shift, finally leading to a pragmatically unmarked, neutral construction type. In various sections of this work we encounter the following examples of this process:

(i) Theme+Clause constructions may lead to neutral constructions through integration of the Theme into the clause. This process, which will be described in 17.2.3., can be exemplified as follows:

(50)   Stage 1. *My brother, he doesn't like you.*

         Stage 2. *My brother he-doesn't like you.*

         Stage 3. *My brother doesn't like you.*

At Stage 2 the original Theme is integrated into the Clause; at Stage 3 the pronominal cross-referencing element, now redundant, disappears.

(ii) Clause+Tail constructions may lead to neutral constructions through integration of the Tail into the clause. For this process, see 17.2.3. It can be exemplified as follows:

(51)   Stage 1. *He doesn't like you, my brother.*

         Stage 2. *He-doesn't like you my brother.*

         Stage 3. *Doesn't like you my brother.*

The Stages are similar in (i).[4]

(iii) The special initial P1 position, when frequently used for GivTop Subjects, may be reinterpreted as the pattern position for the Subject. For this process, see *TFG1*: 16.4.2. It can be illustrated as follows:

(52)   Stage 1. basic order: *Kissed John Mary.* (VSO)
                 marked   : *John kissed Mary.* (GivTopVO)

       Stage 2. basic order: *John kissed Mary.* (SVO)

(iv) Focus constructions may be demarked to result in neutral declarative or interrogative constructions. This process has been described in the preceding section.

Pragmatically marked constructions are constructions with a high degree of "expressiveness"; in the process of markedness shift, they lose their special expressive quality. The process described here thus exemplifies an even more general tendency for expressions with high expressiveness to get demarked and develop into neutral expressions. If it is true that neutral construction types may historically arise through demarking of pragmatically marked constructions, then the latter may be viewed as providing a constant source of innovation for the linguistic system.

---

4. For detailed discussion of these two processes, see De Groot—Limburg (1986).

15. Discrepancies between underlying clause structure and surface expression

15.0. Introduction

Most languages have certain construction types the surface form of which seems to be at variance with the network of semantic relations which must be postulated in underlying clause structure in order to understand their semantic content. Let us illustrate such construction types with some examples. Compare:

(1)   a.   *I believe that John/he is a fool.*
      b.   *I believe John/him to be a fool.*

A predicate like *believe* takes a propositional complement, and (1a) can be rather straightforwardly analysed as:

(2)   Decl E: X_i: Pres e_i: *believe* [V] $(I)_{Pos}$
            (X_j: Pres e_j: [{*a fool*}(*John*)$_{\emptyset Subj}$])

The propositional term in this structure is directly mapped onto the subordinate clause *that John is a fool*. There is no discrepancy between underlying clause structure and surface realization.

In the case of (1b), however, *John/him* seems to behave "as if" it were the Object of *believe* rather than the Subject of *a fool*, whereas the semantic relations seem to be the same as in the case of (1a). There is no reason to assume that in (1b), contrary to (1a), there is a direct semantic relation between *believe* and *John*. Of course, one might find reasons to assume that (1b) has an underlying clause structure different from (1a), a clause structure which is close to its surface realization. But if no such reasons are found, and (1b) is given the same underlying clause structure as (1a), then there is a discrepancy between that clause structure and its surface realization (1b).

For a second example consider the following Danish construction (Falster Jakobsen 1978):

332   *Underlying structure and expression*

(3)   *Det tror   jeg ikke hun ved.*
      that think   I   not she knows
      'That I do not think she knows.'
      =   'That is something I do not think she knows.'

Semantically, *det* is the Goal of *ved* in the subordinate clause. At the surface, however, it takes the P1 position of the matrix clause. Again, there is no reason to assume that *det* belongs to the matrix in underlying structure.

For a third example, consider the following Latin construction:[1]

(4)   *Orator   occisus   facinus   pessimum   videbatur.*
      orator   killed   crime   most-terrible was-considered
      'The killing of the orator was considered a most terrible crime.'

Translated literally, this construction would come out as: 'The killed orator was considered to be a most terrible crime'. But this, of course, is nonsense: it was not the orator, but the killing of the orator that was considered a most terrible crime, and this is indeed the meaning of (4). Thus, the expression *orator occisus*, which would normally be used to refer to a person having the property of having been killed, must here be interpreted as designating an act, perpetrated with respect to a person. There is thus a discrepancy between underlying structure (which must contain a representation of the act of killing the orator) and surface expression, which looks exactly like the first-order entity term *the killed orator*.

In such cases as those exemplified above we speak of a "discrepancy" between underlying clause structure and surface expression.[2]

15.1. Types of discrepancies

As the examples in 15.0. have already shown, there may be different kinds of discrepancies between the surface form of a linguistic expression and its most plausible underlying clause structure:

(i) formal discrepancy: the surface form of some constituent is not as would be expected on the basis of its functional status in underlying clause structure.

---

1. Cf. the detailed discussion of this construction in Bolkestein (1981b).
2. For earlier discussion of such discrepancies in the context of FG see Bolkestein et al. (1981).

(ii) positional discrepancy: some constituent from the underlying clause structure is placed in a position outside its proper domain. This phenomenon will be called "displacement".

(iii) formal and positional discrepancy: a combination of (i) and (ii): a constituent is displaced *and* gets a form different from what would be expected on the basis of its underlying status.

(iv) structural discrepancy: there is a wholesale discrepancy between underlying structure and surface form, so that, for example, an underlying predicational term is expressed in a form more appropriate for a first-order entity (as in (4) above).

In the following sections we consider these different types of discrepancy in the order mentioned. In each case, we shall also consider the question of how the discrepancy in question could be explained.

15.2. Formal discrepancy

By formal discrepancy we understand the phenomenon whereby some constituent gets a form which is not expected on the basis of its function(s).

15.2.1. Non-nominative first arguments or Subjects

In various types of embedding the first argument of a predication is not realized in the "nominative" form which it would get in a main clause.

(i) First Argument or Subject in Object form. In Latin the Subject of an embedded predication appears in the accusative (rather than the nominative) in the so-called "accusativus-cum-infinitivo" construction:

(5) a. *Claudius   ridet.*
       Claudius-nom   laughs
    b. *Marcus   [Claudium   ridere]   vult.*
       Marcus-nom   Claudius-acc   to-laugh   he-wants
       'Marcus wants Claudius to laugh.'

In (5b) the Subj of the embedded infinitival verb *ridere* 'to laugh' is expressed in the accusative (more appropriate for Goal/Obj terms) rather than in the nominative, as in (5a).

In interpreting this construction we must first of all determine whether it is only a matter of formal discrepancy, or whether positional discrepancy is also involved. It is only a matter of formal discrepancy if the structure is as suggested in (5b): the Subj of the embedded construction remains within its proper domain, and only its form is different from what one would expect on the basis of its function. It would ALSO be a matter of positional discrepancy if the structure were as in:

(6)   *Marcus Claudium [ridere] vult.*

In that case the embedded Subj would have been displaced into the main clause domain (and its accusative form might perhaps be ascribed to the influence of the main verb). Arguing against (6), which has been suggested by Pepicello (1977), Bolkestein (1979) has proposed structure (5b). One of her arguments can be exemplified with:

(7)   [*Claudium   ridere*]   *necesse   est.*
        Claudius-acc to-laugh   necessary   is
        'It is necessary for Claudius to laugh.'

If it were assumed that in such a construction the constituent *Claudium* has been displaced to the main clause domain (an assumption for which there is otherwise little evidence), then, if anything, one would expect nominative rather than accusative case in relation to *necesse est*.

Formal adjustment of this type is the rule rather than the exception for embedded constructions which are expressed in non-finite form. It is, in other words, exceptional to find nominative Subjects in infinitival, participial, or nominalized constructions. The typical expression of Subjects within infinitival constructions would seem to be the language's most unmarked non-nominative case, which will often be the accusative. The same applies to Subjects of participial constructions, unless these are adjusted to the case of the construction as a whole, as in so-called "absolute" ablative or genitive constructions exemplified in Latin:

(8)   *his   verbis   dictis*
        these-abl   words-abl   having-been-said-abl
        'these words having been said'

(ii) First Argument/Subject or Second Argument/Object in Possessor form. Within the domain of nominalized constructions we typically find Possessor expression of the Subject (or A^1) and/or the Object (or A^2), as in:

(9) *John's drinking*
(10) *the destruction of the city*

In 7.2.3. I have explained this type of formal discrepancy in terms of the Principle of Formal Adjustment, according to which there is pressure on a predication designating a second-order entity (SoA), which appears in a term position, to adjust to the prototypical expression format for first-order terms. Possessor expression is typical of terms associated with a head noun within the domain of a first-order term.

15.2.2. Relative attraction

By "relative attraction" we understand the phenomenon whereby the form of a relative pronoun adjusts to the case appropriate to the antecedent head noun rather than to its own function within the relative clause. Consider the following example from Ancient Greek (Rijksbaron 1981):

(11) *Periestaúrosan   autous   tois   déndresin*
     fence-around-3pl   them   the-dat   trees-dat
     ha   ékopsan.
     which-acc   cut-3pl
     'They fenced them around with the trees which they had cut.'
(12) *Periestaúrosan   autous   tois   déndresin*
     fence-around-3pl   them   the-dat   trees-dat
     hois   ékopsan.
     which-dat   cut-3pl
     'They fenced them around with the trees which they had cut.'

In (11) the relative has the accusative form (*ha*) expected on the basis of its Goal function within the relative clause. In (12), however, it takes an unexpected dative case (*hois*), in congruence with the head noun.

The converse of Relative attraction also occurs in this case the antecedent noun takes a case form which is appropriate to the function of the relativized variable within the relative clause rather than to its function in the matrix clause. This is called "inverted attraction" in classical grammar.[3] The following is an example from Persian (Comrie 1989: 153):

(13) a. *Zan-i*   [*ke didid*]   *injā-st.*
      woman-nom   that you-saw   here-is
      'The woman that you saw is here.'
   b. *Zan-i-rā*   [*ke didid*]   *injā-st.*
      woman-acc   that you-saw   here-is

In (13b) the head noun is marked accusative, as if it were the Goal of the verb 'see' within the relative clause rather than the Subj of the main verb *injā-st* 'is here'.

Rijksbaron (1981) assumes that relative attraction can be understood in terms of alternative systems of expression rules applied to underlying term structures of the form:

(14) $(dmx_i: tree$ [N]: R [Past e: Pf *cut* [V] $(they)_{Ag}(Ax_i)_{Go}])_{Instr}$

Note that when no attraction is involved, the expression of (Ax_i) should be sensitive to the function Go, and that of 'tree' to the function Instr. Relative attraction would involve "mistaken" sensitivity of (Ax_i) to Instr. Inverted attraction could then be understood as due to "mistaken" sensitivity of 'tree' to the function Go. The former would be a matter of "perseverance" of the antecedent case into the relative pronoun; the latter a matter of "anticipation" of the relative pronoun case in the head noun.

Cases of relative attraction such as (12) have been explained by Lehmann (1984: 307) as originating in constructions with headless relatives as exemplified in:

(15)   *Periestaúrosan*   *autous*   *(toutois)*   *ha*
          fence-around-3pl   them   (those-dat)   which-acc
          ékopsan.
          cut-3pl
          'They fenced them around with those which they had cut.'

When the antecedent demonstrative pronoun *toutois* is left out we get a headless relative clause, the function of which in the main clause is left

---

3. See Pinkster (1988: 127) for a Latin example.

unspecified. Such constructions do indeed occur in Ancient Greek. Lehmann's hypothesis is that this construction is the natural source for relative attraction, which is then "secondarily" extended to constructions with overt head nouns such as (12). It is not clear whether there is positive historical evidence for such a scenario.

In this context it is interesting to consider the properties of relative clauses in Arabic, as described in Moutaouakil (1988). Consider the following example:

(16)   *qabaltu   l-fatatayni   l-latayni   najahata.*
       met-I   the-girl-dual-acc who-fem-dual-acc   succeeded-they
       'I met the two girls who succeeded.'

Moutaouakil analyses the element *l-latayni* as a relative pronoun, sensitive to Gender, Number, Case, and Definiteness. Since the relative clause, as is clear from the gloss, also has pronominal expression of the relativized variable, this would then constitute a rare case of co-occurrence of a relative pronoun and a personal pronoun within the domain of the relative clause (see 3.1.1.). Clearly, *l-latayni* cannot be regarded as an invariable relative marker, which would be more compatible with pronominal expression.

Note, however, that the case form of the "relative pronoun" (accusative) is appropriate to the head noun rather than to the restrictor predicate (which would require a nominative). This is a general property of these "relative pronouns": they always take the case form corresponding to the head noun rather than the form fitting their role within the restrictor. If these elements are analysed as relative pronouns, this would be a case of massive and systematic relative attraction.

In view of these various facts, which would constitute various exceptions to well-established typological generalizations, it seems appropriate to consider the following alternative analysis. Let us suppose that the "relative pronoun" is in fact a dummy head nominal, and that the relationship between head noun and relative clause is "appositional" in the way discussed in 3.2.4. We would then analyse (16) according to the pattern:

(17)   *We met the two girls - the two female ones who succeeded.*

This analysis would have the following advantages:
— the case of the dummy head is as expected (since it is an appositional repetition of the head noun).

338 *Underlying structure and expression*

— the construction, on this analysis, is no exception to the typological generalization that relative and personal pronoun do not co-occur.
— we do not need a rule of (systematic and obligatory) relative attraction.
— on this analysis we expect the relative clause to be able to occur on its own, without lexical head noun. This is correct, witness:

(18)   qabaltu   l-latayni   najahata.
       met-I   who-fem-dual-acc   succeeded-they
       'I met the two females who succeeded.'

A possible counter-argument to this analysis would be that the construction in question can also be used as a non-restrictive relative:

(19)   qabaltu   l-fatatayni,   l-latayni   najahata.
       met-I   the-girl-dual-acc   who-fem-dual-acc   succeeded-they
       'I met the two girls, the ones who succeeded.'

For this non-restrictive usage one would surely wish to propose an appositional analysis. How, then, could it be distinguished from the restrictive use if the latter is also analysed as appositional? However, quite apart from the present problem, we do need two distinct types of apposition anyway, witness the difference between such constructions as:

(20) a.   *my friend John*
     b.   *my friend, John, ...*
(21) a.   *my brother the lawyer*
     b.   *my brother, the lawyer, ...*

In "restrictive" appositions such as exemplified in (20a) and (21a) the appositional item does indeed restrict the potential reference of the term. These terms suggest that I have other friends than John, or other brothers who are not lawyers. The non-restrictive appositions in the (20b) and (21b) do not restrict the reference of the term, but provide additional information.

Thus, if we analyse the relative clauses of Arabic as dummy-headed appositional terms, we must assume that these can be used both in "restrictive" and in "non-restrictive" apposition.

15.3. Positional discrepancy

Principle (GP4) of *TFG1*: chapter 16 (the Principle of Domain Integrity) said that constituents prefer to be placed within their proper domain, and that domains prefer not to be interrupted by constituents from other domains (cf. Rijkhoff 1992). Both within and across languages, however, we find a number of systematic exceptions to this principle. Constructions, that is, in which a constituent or part of a constituent is "displaced" outside its proper domain.

15.3.1. Types of displacement

Displacement occurs in different circumstances.

(i) *Displacement of Q-word terms*
Consider the following examples:

(22) a. *John believed [that Qx_i had blown up the bridge]*.
    b. *Who did John believe [that had blown up the bridge]?*
(23) a. *John believed [that the enemy had blown up Qx_i]*.
    b. *What did John believe [that the enemy had blown up]?*

Displacement of Q-word terms is probably the most common form of displacement, typically found in languages in which:
    — Q-word terms (in non-echo questions) are obligatorily placed in P1;
    — terms within embedded constructions are accessible to the operator Q.
In such languages the embedded Q-word term is typically placed in the P1 position of the main clause rather than in P1 of the embedded construction, as would be the case in:

(24)   *John believed [what the enemy had blown up]?*
    'What did John believe the enemy had blown up?'

In this type of construction, the preference for having the Q-word term in the prominent sentence-initial position (a matter of "pragmatic highlighting") is apparently stronger than the Principle of Domain Integrity.

(ii) *Displacement of non-questioned terms*
Displacement of non-questioned terms is exemplified in the following construction type:

(25) a. John believed [that the enemy-nom had blown up the bridge-acc].
     b. The enemy-nom John believed [that had blown up the bridge-acc].

Such displacement without formal discrepancy (that is, in which the displaced constituent retains the form appropriate to its proper domain) and with finite realization of the "remaining" complement occurs in many languages. The phenomenon is sometimes called "prolepsis" in classical grammar. For detailed studies of this phenomenon see Bolkestein (1981a) on Latin, De Groot (1981a) on Hungarian, and Gvozdanović (1981) on Serbo-Croatian. Consider the following examples:

(26) Latin (Bolkestein 1981a)
      Scio   iam   filius   quod   amet   meus
      know-I already son-nom   that   loves-he my-nom
        hanc meretricem.
        this whore
      'I already know that my son loves this whore.'

Note that in this case *filius meus* must be interpreted as underlyingly forming one constituent. Only the head noun of this constituent has been displaced into a position preceding the subordinator.

(27) Hungarian (De Groot 1981a)
      Mari   nem hiszem,   hogy   ismeri   Chomskyt.
      Mary-nom   not believe-I   that   knows-she   Chomsky-acc
      'Mary I do not believe that she knows Chomsky.'
      = 'I do not believe that Mary knows Chomsky.'

(28) Serbo-Croatian (Gvozdanović 1981)
      Dečko   sam   mislio   da je   vidio   most.
      boy-nom   I-am   thought   that he-is   seen   bridge-acc
      'The boy I thought that had seen the bridge.'
      = 'I thought that the boy had seen the bridge.'

These are clearly examples of displacement unaccompanied by any form of formal adjustment to the matrix domain.

(iii) *Extraposition from NP*
Another type of displacement is involved in "Extraposition from NP", as in:

(29) a.   *John met [a man who tried to sell him a second-hand car] yesterday.*
     b.   *John met [a man] yesterday [who tried to sell him a second-hand car].*

In this case we find a relative clause, separated from its Head noun, in clause-final position.

15.3.2. On explaining displacement

Displacement, in its various guises, may be attributed to a defeat of the principle of Domain Integrity (GP4) by certain other principles, the most important of which would seem to be the principle of Pragmatic Highlighting (GP7) and the principle of Increasing Complexity (GP9), (SP7).

Pragmatic Highlighting is involved when the displaced constituent is placed in some special position of the host domain on account of its pragmatic functionality. This factor is especially clear in cases of displacement of Q-word terms (as in (30a)), a widespread phenomenon in languages which place Q-word terms in special positions, especially if the special position is P1. This kind of displacement of Q-words is so widespread that it might well be taken as the source of displacement phenomena in non-interrogative clauses. The reason why it should spread to non-interrogative constructions might be a preference for using the same format for Q-word questions and their corresponding answers:

(30) a.   *What did John believe [the enemy had blown up]?*
     b.   *THE BRIDGE John believed [the enemy had blown up].*

The strategy should thus be to find out what pragmatic factors might explain the displacement phenomena in these cases. Indeed, all authors mentioned above agree that for this kind of displacement to be possible, the constituent in question must have special pragmatic significance (e.g., must have Topic or Focus function),⁴ whereas sometimes further pragmatic conditions must be fulfilled as well.

We may thus assume that this kind of displacement is triggered by a wish to "highlight" pragmatically important material even in embedded constructions; the price to be paid for this is an entanglement or "intertwining" (De Groot 1981a) of the structure of main and subordinate clause.

Increasing Complexity is involved when the displacement can be interpreted as a means of reducing the complexity of constituents in the position in which these occur. The clearest case is provided by so-called "Extraposition from NP", as illustrated in (29b). The displacement of the relative clause from the complex term relieves that term of the excessive complexity which creates difficulties in the non-final position in which it occurs in (29a). Another factor favouring displacement might be the preference for avoiding "centre-embedding" (cf. the discussion in 4.2.). This, too, is exemplified in (29b), since the relative clause in (29a) is in centre-embedded position.

Note that displacement for pragmatic reasons will bring constituents to "special positions" which are typically found towards the front end of the clause, whereas displacement for complexity reasons will typically bring constituents towards the end of the clause. Even in the latter case, however, pragmatic factors may also be involved: thus, Guéron (1980) argued that Extraposition from NP is restricted to presentative constructions in which (in our terminology) the NP has NewTopic function, and both the NP as such and the extraposed constituent contain focal information.⁵

15.4. Formal and positional discrepancy

When formal discrepancy and positional discrepancy (displacement) combine we find a constituent outside its proper domain, in a form which conforms to the host domain rather than to the embedded domain from which the constituent originates. Consider the following Latin example (Bolkestein 1981a):

---

4. For example, De Groot (1981a) analysed displacement phenomena in Hungarian in terms of the rule that a Topic term may be displaced out of a Topic embedded construction, and a Focus term out of a Focus embedded construction; in each case, the displaced constituent will be placed in the Topic or Focus position of the higher clause.

5. See Siewierska (1988: 41) for some further evidence to this effect.

(31)   *Haec   me   ut   confidam   faciunt.*
       these   me-acc   that I-trust   they-make
       'These things make me that I have confidence.'
    = 'These things make me have confidence.'

In this construction the pronoun *me* is semantically the argument of the embedded verb *confidam*. In relation to that verb it should appear in the nominative, but in displaced position it now appears in the accusative, as would be proper if it were a real argument of the main verb *faciunt*. That it is not a real argument of this matrix verb is clear from the meaning: there is no sense in which 'these things' can be said to 'make me'. We can thus understand this type of construction as follows:

(i) a term from the embedded domain is displaced to a position in the matrix domain;

(ii) having arrived there, it comes under the influence of the matrix verb, and adjusts to the form which would be required if it were a (second) argument of that verb.

We can say that the term in question acts "as if" it were an argument of the matrix verb. Such terms may be called "pseudo-arguments" (cf. Bolkestein et al. 1981).

For another example compare the Danish construction (Falster Jakobsen 1978):

(32)   *Ham   tror   jeg   for evigt   har forladt*
       him-acc   believe   I   for ever   has left
           sin   kone.
           his   wife
       'Him I believe has for ever left his wife.'
    = 'I believe him to have left his wife forever.'

The accusative form *ham* 'him' can be interpreted as formally governed by *tror* 'believe'; but semantically the term belongs to the subordinate clause.

As long as the resulting constructions can be described in terms of the two operations of displacement and formal adjustment and the overall structure is not further affected, the formal adjustment can be described at the level of the expression rules: there is no need to assume that the term in question entertains any "real" functional relation with the matrix verb.

Note that, contrary to what is commonly believed, displacement plus formal adjustment can occur without the (remainder of the) embedded construction being realized in non-finite form.

15.5. On "Raising"

When a term which semantically belongs to an embedded domain appears in the matrix domain this phenomenon is often described in terms of "Raising".

15.5.1. Forms of Raising

In considering Raising phenomena we must distinguish the following cases:
  (i) Raising-1. We speak of Raising-1 when the process can be described as a form of pure displacement: the term in question appears in the matrix domain, but further remains unaffected: it retains the form appropriate to its function in the embedded domain. This is the case in the construction exemplified in (3) above.
  (ii) Raising-2. Raising-2 is involved when the term in question is displaced into the matrix domain and is formally adjusted to suit the requirements of the matrix predicate: it acts as a pseudo-argument of the matrix predicate. This is the case in (5b) above.
  (iii) Raising-3. We have a case of Raising-3 when there is more to the discrepancy than just displacement and formal adjustment. Consider the following English constructions:

(33) a. *The police believed them to have stolen the apples.*
 b. *They were believed by the police to have stolen the apples.*

(33a) could in principle be described in terms of Raising-2: the term *them* could be said to be the result of displacement and formal adjustment. This is not sufficient for (33b), however. Suppose that we try to arrive at (33b) starting from the structure underlying (34):

(34) *That they had stolen the apples was believed by the police.*

If (33b) were only a matter of Raising-2, then we would expect an output such as:

(35) **They was believed by the police to have stolen the apples.*

In that construction, *they* would have been displaced to the matrix domain; formal adjustment would apply vacuously, since the passive matrix predicate requires a nominative pseudo-argument anyway. In (33b), however, the matrix verb, in turn, agrees in number with the presumed pseudo-argument.

This means that the displaced term in (33b) in all respects behaves as the Subject of the matrix verb *believe*. On the other hand, it also entertains a Subject relation with the embedded verb, as can be seen most clearly in a construction of the form:

(36)   *The apples were believed to have been stolen by them.*

In this construction the passive form of the embedded verb must be due to Subj assignment to its Goal term *the apples*; but at the same time, the passive form and the number agreement of the main verb suggests that *the apples* is the Subj of *believe*. For this reason, (33b) has been described (Dik 1979) in terms of an underlying clause structure of the following form:

(37)   Decl E: X_i: Past e_i: *believe* [V] $(x_i)_{Pos}$
          $(X_j$: Past e_j: *steal* [V] $(they)_{Ag}$ $(the\ apples)_{GoSubjSubj})_{Go}$

The idea is that the inner Subj function on the Goal term (*the apples*) pertains to the embedded verb *steal* ('the apples were stolen by them'), while the outer Subj function pertains to the matrix verb *believe* ('the apples were believed ...').[6] This presupposes that, under certain circumstances, the Subj function relevant to the matrix verb can "penetrate" into the embedded domain and be assigned to a term within that domain rather than to the embedded Goal constituent as a whole. The latter is also possible, as in (38a), which would be expressed as in (38b):

(38) a. Decl E: X_i: Past e_i: *believe* [V] $(x_i)_{Pos}$
          $(X_j$: Past e_j: *steal* [V] $(they)_{Ag}$ $(the\ apples)_{GoSubj})_{GoSubj}$
     b. *It was believed that the apples had been stolen by them.*

The term "Raising" is also used for the relationship between such constructions as:

---

6. For an application of this type of analysis to Arabic, see Moutaouakil (1988). Constructions of the type "X is said to (be) Y" are discussed in this framework in Goossens (1991).

(39) a. *It is easy to please John.*
     b. *John is easy to please.*

In 7.2.1.3., however, we argued that there do seem to be semantic (rather than just pragmatic) differences between these two construction types, and that these differences can be accounted for by assuming that (39b) is the outcome of a rule of predicate formation rather than just a matter of alternative expression of the structure which also underlies (39a). If this is correct, the term Raising is less appropriate for such cases as these.

15.5.2. Constraints on Raising

Any type of Raising lifts an embedded term out of its embedded domain and places it in the matrix domain. However, not all embedded terms are "accessible" to Raising: there are constraints on which terms can be raised from the embedded domain. Usually, such constraints have been formulated in terms of syntactic functions or grammatical relations. One strong formulation of such constraints is:

(40)   Only Subjects of embedded domains can be raised.

In language-particular circumstances, there may be some truth in such a constraint. Thus, the type of Raising-3 which we find in English *believe*-constructions can only apply to constituents which have Subject function with respect to the embedded domain. Compare the examples given so far with:

(41) a. *John believed Peter had stolen the bike.*
     b. *John believed Peter to have stolen the bike.*
     c. **John believed the bike Peter to have stolen.*
(42) a. *John believed the bike had been stolen by Peter.*
     b. *John believed the bike to have been stolen by Peter.*
     c. **John believed by Peter the bike to have been stolen.*

Some authors tend to assign absolute cross-linguistic validity to constraint (40). Counterexamples to (40) are then considered to be in need of special explanation. Consider the following argument.

In Niuean (Polynesian, Chung—Seiter 1980), Raising can exceptionally be applied to embedded Objects as well as to embedded Subjects. Niuean is an ergative language, and Chung and Seiter attribute this exceptional behaviour to a presumed shift within the Polynesian languages from accusative to ergative organization, part of which is the reinterpretation of an originally passive construction of accusative languages as a new active transitive construction in ergative languages. This reinterpretation can be symbolized as a shift from (43a) to (43b):

(43) a. *cut down*-pass *tree* (GoSubj) *by boy* (Ag)
     b. *cut down*-act *by boy* (AgSubj) *tree* (GoObj)

Note that in this process the original GoSubj is reinterpreted as the new GoObj. Niuean can now be interpreted as a language in which this reinterpretation has not been completely achieved, so that in the ergative construction not only the new AgSubj, but also the original GoSubj display Subj-like properties, for example with respect to Raising.

The shift from accusative to ergative in Polynesian languages is certainly a well-established phenomenon, but it is questionable if the Raising argument can be used in this way. This would only be the case if constraint (40) had general validity for Raising processes, at least in the Polynesian languages. However, there is independent evidence that this supposition is incorrect. Thus, Besnier (1988) shows that in Tuvaluan not only Subjects, but also Objects and certain "obliques" can be raised.[7] An example of oblique Raising is (44b), with its non-raised counterpart (44a):

(44) a. *Koo   ttau   [o faipati   au   kiaa   Niu]*.
         Inch   must   sub speak   I   to   Niu
         'It is necessary that I have a word with Niu.'
     b. *Koo   ttau   iaa Niu [o faipati   au   ki   ei]*.
         Inch   must   at Niu sub speak   I   to   him
         'It is necessary to Niu that I have a word with him.'

In the oblique case of Raising there must be a pronominal copy of the raised term in the subordinate clause (this is optional with Subj/Obj). The case marking of the raised term in the superordinate clause is either the same as in the subordinate clause (no formal adjustment, thus Raising-1), or determined somewhat idiosyncratically by the higher predicate (Raising-2). Besnier (1988), however, also gives some information on the circumstances in which

---

7. I am grateful to Niko Besnier for some additional explanation of the relevant phenomena.

Raising can and does in fact apply: although Raising of obliques is in principle possible in Tuvaluan, it is a highly constrained process in several respects:

(i) Raising applies to the most responsible entity in the subordinate clause. In a case such as (44b) the suggestion is that Niu must have done something which has created a situation such that I need to talk to him.

(ii) Being the most responsible entity in the subordinate clause correlates with both semantic functions and clause perspective: responsibility will decrease along the Semantic Function Hierarchy, and Subjects will normally be more responsible than Objects, and the latter more responsible than obliques. This implies that in actual usage the chance that a non-Subj, non-Obj term will be raised is very slight indeed.

(iii) This is underpinned by Besnier (1988) with the following text frequency data: in a corpus of 150,000 words there were 1,059 cases in which a term might have been raised.

	N	%
Of these there had in fact undergone Raising:	306	20
with the following distribution of functions:		
Intransitive Subject (absolutive)	161	53
Transitive Subject (ergative)	129	42
Total Subject	290	95
Direct Object (absolutive)	15	4
Oblique	1	<1

Note that out of 1,059 constructions where Raising could have occurred, only one (0.01 %) occurrence of oblique raising was found.

These data show that although Subjects are not the only potential "raisees", they appear to represent the initial position in a hierarchy of "Accessibility to Raising". This is confirmed by what we find in other languages. Indeed, many cases can be found in which Raising applies to terms with other than Subj function in the embedded domain. This seems to be especially common with Raising-1 and Raising-2 constructions. In fact, we already cited some examples in which non-Subjects had been "raised" into the matrix domain. This is the case, for example, in (44) above. Other examples can easily be added to this. Consider the following examples:

(45) Hungarian (De Groot 1981a)
Az egyetemet husz eves volt
the university-acc 20 years was-he
amikor elkezdte.
when started-he
'The university 20 years was he when he started.'
= 'He was twenty years when he started university.'

(46) Serbo-Croatian (Gvozdanović 1981)
Most sam mislio da je vidio dečko.
bridge-acc I-am thought that he-is seen boy-nom
'The bridge I thought that had seen the boy.'
= 'I thought that the boy had seen the bridge.'

(47) Danish (Falster Jakobsen 1978)
Den plan kan du godt opgive at få udført.
that plan can you well give-up that get realized
'That plan can you as well give up that (you) get realized.'
= 'You better give up the idea of getting that plan realized.'

In fact, Falster Jakobsen states that the raisee can have any possible relation within the embedded construction.

What these various data show is the following:

(i) cross-linguistically, Raising is not absolutely constrained to Subjects.

(ii) the Raising potential of a term in a subordinate construction is indeed monitored by its "prominence" as a participant in the subordinate clause SoA: "responsibility" is one factor which loads this prominence.

(iii) even though Raising of obliques is in principle possible (as is clear from grammaticality judgements), it is hardly ever realized in actual texts: oblique terms are usually "out-prominenced" by Subjects and (sometimes) Objects.

(iv) what is an absolute grammatical constraint in one language may be reflected by a text frequency constraint in another language (for this correlation, cf. *TFG1*: 2.3.).

15.5.3. The pragmatic motivation of Raising

The facts discussed above suggest that constraints on Raising should not be directly described in terms of grammatical relations, but in terms of pragmatic factors which indirectly favour Subjects over Objects, and these over other term types.

In order to understand this pragmatic effect, let us start from the following diagram:

(48)   believe—(John)-_ _ _
           ＼responsible (Peter)

This configuration can be expressed as either of the following:

(49) a. *John believes that Peter is responsible.*
     b. *John believes Peter to be responsible.*

In (49a) the complement is presented in a "detached", objective way; no further involvement on the part of John is suggested than that he happens to have this opinion. In (49b), however, it is suggested that in some way there is a more direct involvement of John with Peter (cf. Steever 1977). This more direct involvement, symbolized by the dotted line in (48), serves to "upgrade" the term *Peter* from its embedded position into the matrix clause. We may thus assume that (49a) and (49b) have the same underlying semantic structure, but differ in the pragmatic status of the embedded term which is the potential target of the Raising operation.

Borkin (1974) mentioned the following factors as being conducive to Raising in English:

— the embedded proposition expresses a subjective opinion rather than an objective judgement on the part of the matrix Subject.

— the embedded predication assigns a characteristic property rather than a contingent event to the raisee (concomitantly, the SoA is a static situation rather than a dynamic event);

— definite-specific terms allow Raising more freely than indefinite or generic ones.

Steever (1977) formulated the condition that for a term to be raised the Subject of the matrix must have "direct access" (in a cognitive sense) to the entity involved.

Bolkestein (1981a) argues that the form of Raising which in Latin leads to the "nominativus-cum-infinitivo" construction can be used only when the raisee rather than the complement as a whole carries Topic or Focus function. In such a case, the complement is "pragmatically split up"; if the complement constitutes a unified whole pragmatically, raising of constituents out of the complement is impossible.

De Groot (1981a) showed that displacement out of complements is possible when the displacee has Topic function within a topical complement, or Focus function within a focal complement. Again, it is the pragmatic function distribution within the complement which makes displacement possible.

Many of these factors are compatible with the idea that the displaced constituent must have a highly topical or focal status against the background of the rest of the complement. However the special pragmatic function is formulated precisely, it would seem that the assignment of this pragmatic function is what allows an embedded term to be raised into the matrix domain.

15.6. Other forms of structural discrepancy

We saw in 15.5.1 above that Raising-3 is a phenomenon which cannot be simply described in terms of superficial operations of displacement and formal adjustment: there is a more "structural" discrepancy between underlying clause structure and surface form. In the case of Raising-3 we tried to account for this structural discrepancy by means of a rule of exceptional Subject assignment (for details, cf. Dik 1979).

There are other cases of structural discrepancy in which it is whole constructions rather than individual constituents which seem to take a form which is not consonant with their underlying semantics. I shall here concentrate on two types of such discrepancies, which we have encountered in various guises in the preceding chapters. In the first type an expression which must be semantically interpreted as designating a SoA (a second-order entity) appears in a form more appropriate for designating first-order entities (see example (4) above). The second type is the reverse of this: a second-order expression must be interpreted as designating a first-order entity. This is the case with certain "circumnominal" verbal restrictors as discussed in chapter 3.

15.6.1. First-order expression designates second-order entity

A constituent which must semantically be interpreted as a second-order entity (SoA) appears in the form of a first-order entity expression:

(50)   [*The killed orator*] *stupefied everybody.*
       'The killing of the orator stupefied everybody.'

How could this phenomenon be understood? I believe the following considerations may be of some relevance.

Most languages have a class of predicates which can take either first-order or second-order entities for their second argument. This is typically the case with perception verbs.[8] Compare:

(51) a. *John saw the orator.*
 b. *John saw the killing of the orator.*

These two constructions are clearly distinct: there is no mistake as to whether the second argument designates a first-order or a second-order entity. In many languages, however, we find constructions in which the difference is less clear-cut. Let us see how these more ambiguous construction types may come about.

First-order terms such as *the orator* in (51a) can obviously be modified by adjectival, participial, and other types of attributive restrictors:

(52) a. *I saw the nervous orator.*
 b. *I saw the laughing orator.*

More interestingly, many languages also allow constructions of the form:

(53) a. *I saw the orator nervous.*
 b. *I saw the orator laughing.*

Such constructions raise the problem of how precisely they should be interpreted. The first question to be posed is whether, given such constructions, the following entailment holds:

(54) *I saw the orator laughing.*
 Therefore, I saw the orator.

Let us suppose that this entailment does indeed hold in the given language. We then have reason to still regard [the orator] as the first-order argument of *see*, and of interpreting [laughing] as a "predicative adjunct" to this argument. In such conditions, the analysis should be along the lines of (55a) rather than (55b):

---

8. For the section now following, cf. Dik—Hengeveld (1991).

(55) a. *I saw [the orator]*$_{Go}$ *[laughing]*$_{PredAdjunct}$
b. *I saw [the orator laughing]*$_{Go}$

The predicative adjunct may be interpreted as a circumstantial satellite to the predication. We can thus give the following analysis of (55a):

(56)   [Past e_i: [see_V (I)$_{Exp}$ (d1x_i: $orator_N$)$_{Go}$]] (Sim e_j: [$laugh_V(x_i)_\emptyset$])$_{Circ}$

Note, however, that the difference between seeing an orator while in the act of laughing and seeing the laughing of an orator, although important in principle, may become very subtle in practice. We are here in a borderline area in which reinterpretation of construction (56) in terms of a second-order entity designating second argument could easily occur. Compare, for example:

(57) a. *We saw [a man] [falling off a ladder].*
b. *We saw [a man falling off a ladder].*

In (57a) we have represented the entity reading, in (57b) the SoA reading (cf. Hannay 1985), but the message is not that different in the two readings. This might explain how a construction such as (57a) could develop into a construction such as (57b), through a loosening of the entailment condition illustrated in (54).

Consider, in this connection, the following English examples, adduced by Kirsner—Thompson (1976) and Noonan (1985):[9]

(58)   *I smelled Hank spreading the muck.*
[I didn't necessarily smell Hank]
(59)   *We heard the farmer slaughtering the pig.*
[We didn't necessarily hear the farmer]
(60)   *We heard it thundering.*
[We didn't hear "it" in the circumstance that it was thundering]

These examples show that the English construction with participle has, at least in these cases, already been reinterpreted in terms of a second-order Goal. Note that there is still the possibility that English has the two constructions side by side:

---

9. For this kind of argument cf. also De Geest (1970, 1973).

(61) a. *I heard [the children singing a song].*
b. *I heard [the children] [singing a song].*

The Latin construction exemplified in (4) could be understood in a similar way. Compare:

(62) a. *[Orator] visus est.*
'The orator has been seen.'
b. *[Orator] [occisus] visus est.*
'The orator has been seen in the state of having been killed.'
c. *[Orator occisus] facinus est.*
'The orator having been killed is a crime.'

In this way we may understand a shift from first-order to second-order expression across the bridge formed by first-order expressions extended by predicative adjuncts. Such adjuncts commonly take the form of adjectives, participles, or gerunds. In this way we do not immediately arrive at the construction with an infinitive, as in:

(63) *I heard Sally sing a song.*

since infinitives do not commonly occur as predicative adjuncts. Perhaps the infinitive can be understood as a further development which may occur once the construction in question has been reinterpreted as designating an SoA. It does seem to be the case, at least for English, that the entailment condition does not hold for constructions with infinitival complements:

(64) *I smelled Hank spread the muck.*
[I didn't necessarily smell Hank]
(65) *We heard the farmer slaughter the pig.*
[We didn't necessarily hear the farmer]
(66) *We heard it thunder.*
[We didn't hear "it" in the circumstance that it was thundering]

The difference between such constructions as:

(67) a. *We smelled Hank spreading the muck.*
b. *We smelled Hank spread the muck.*

may in English be described in terms of an aspectual difference (Kirsner—Thompson 1976, Comrie 1976, Dik—Hengeveld 1991): in (67a) the complement has Imperfective, in (67b) it has Perfective aspect.

The various steps from purely first-order towards second-order interpretation of such complements as these could thus be understood as follows:

(68) a. *We saw [the orator].*
 b. *We saw [the orator] [laughing].*
 c. *We saw [the orator laughing].*
 d. *We saw [the orator laugh].*

Once the complements of (68c-d) are interpreted as SoA-designating complements, they could, from there on, extend their domain to third-order complements, as in:

(69) a. *We believed [the orator laughing/laugh].*
 b. *We said [the orator laughing/laugh].*

In this way, then, we might arrive at an "accusativus-cum-infinitivo" construction characterized by the wide domain of application which we find in Latin.

15.6.2. Second-order expression designates first-order entity

This is the reverse of the discrepancy discussed in the preceding section: a constituent which must be semantically interpreted as designating a first-order entity appears in the form of an expression appropriate for a second-order entity:

(70) [*The soldier the general killed*] *jailed was.*
 'The soldier who killed the general was jailed'

This is the kind of construction which we find in certain Prefield languages with "circumnominal" verbal restrictors. In 4.3.3. we explained this construction type as follows:

(71) a. [*The soldier the general killed*]-Given, *he jailed was.*
 b. [*The soldier the general killed*]-Given, Ø *jailed was.*
 c. [*The soldier the general killed*]-Given *jailed was.*
 d. [*The soldier the general killed*] *jailed was.*

If this type of development has proceeded to such an extent that there is no longer a discernible anaphorical relation between some element in the main clause and some entity-designating term in the circumstantial predication, we have arrived at a situation in which it seems as if an SoA-designating predication must in fact be interpreted as referring to a first-order entity rather than to a second-order (SoA) entity.

16. Accessibility

16.0. Introduction

In the course of our discussion of various construction types as treated in FG we have come across a number of different processes which can all be thought of in terms of some operation being applied to some term position. Thus, Subject assignment can be applied to certain term positions and not to others, and relativization can be applied to certain anaphorical term positions within restrictor predications and not to others. Using the terminology introduced by Keenan (1972) and Keenan—Comrie (1977) we shall say that some term positions are "accessible" to the operation involved, and others "inaccessible" to that operation. Where certain term positions are inaccessible to a given operation, there can be said to be certain constraints on the accessibility of those term positions to that operation. Accessibility can thus be defined as the capacity of a term position to be the target of some grammatical operation. A term position T to which an operation O can be applied is accessible to O; otherwise it is inaccessible to O. If T is inaccessible to O, there is apparently some accessibility constraint which prevents O from applying to T.

There are different types of constraints on accessibility:

— *Intrinsic constraints* on accessibility crucially involve intrinsic properties of the target term (T).

— *Hierarchical constraints* on accessibility crucially involve the hierarchical position of the target term (T) within the clause structure in which it occurs.

— *Functional constraints* on accessibility crucially involve the functional status of the target term (T).

In the following sections we will discuss each of these types of constraints separately. Intrinsic constraints will be discussed in 16.2, hierarchical constraints in 16.3, and functional constraints in 16.4. Given their relevance to a functionally oriented theory such as FG, the emphasis in the discussion will be on the latter type of constraints. Before turning to the various types of constraints, however, we will give an overview of the types of operation sensitive to accessibility constraints in 16.1.

16.1. Operations

The following are the most important grammatical operations subject to accessibility constraints. All these operations are such that for any given language, they can be applied to certain term positions, and not to others. In each case I give an example of an English construction which is ungrammatical because the operation in question has been applied to a term which is inaccessible to that operation.

(i) Subject assignment. Sentence (1) is ungrammatical because Subject function is assigned to a term with the semantic function External Location:

(1)   *The garden is being eaten in by many people.

(ii) Object assignment. The following example is ungrammatical because Object function is assigned to a term with the semantic function Instrument:

(2)   *John cut the knife the meat.

(iii) Relativization. Relativization leads to ungrammaticality if it is applied to a term with Possessor function within a complex term within a dependent question:

(3)   *the man who I wonder if John knows the answer to the question of
        (Relativization is applied to a term with Possessor function within
        a complex term within a dependent question)

(iv) Q-word questioning. Under the same conditions, Q-word questioning is ungrammatical:

(4)   *Who do you wonder if John knows the answer to the question of?

(v) Anaphora. Sentence (5) is ungrammatical because the term which is expressed anaphorically precedes and is not commanded by its antecedent.

(5)   *He_i is ill and $John_i$ cannot come.

(vi) Raising. Example (6) is ungrammatical since the raised term is not the subject of the complement clause:

(6)   *John believed the bike Peter to have stolen.

16.2. Intrinsic constraints

As we saw in *TFG1*: 2.4., the accessibility of some term to some operation may be co-determined by intrinsic properties of the target term. Suppose that in a certain language only definite terms can be assigned Subject function. In that case it is the definiteness which determines accessibility. Definiteness is neither a hierarchical nor a functional property of a term. It is a property intrinsic to the term as such. Constraints of the type illustrated here may thus be called *intrinsic constraints*. They may be represented as in (7):

(7)   O (T: <P>)
        'the operation (O) may only be applied to terms (T) with the intrinsic property P'

Very often intrinsic constraints cannot be defined in absolute terms. In *TFG1*: 2.4. we showed that various semantic and pragmatic factors rather defined priority relations between terms. Such priorities can be interpreted in terms of accessibility: for example, if term t_1 has priority over term t_2 in receiving Subject function, this amounts to the same thing as saying that t_1 is more accessible to Subject function than t_2.

The most relevant intrinsic factors presented in *TFG1*: 2.4. were the following:

(8) The Person Hierarchy
    $\{1, 2\} > 3$ or:
    Speech Act Participant > Non-Participant

(9) The Animacy Hierarchy
    human > other animate > inanimate force > other inanimate

(10) The Gender Hierarchy
    Masculine > Feminine > Other

(11) The Definiteness Hierarchy
    definite > other specific > non-specific

It was noted that these different hierarchies are not completely independent of one another and can be conflated in various ways.

As an example of the operation of an intrinsic constraint consider the phenomenon of Dative Clitic Doubling in Spanish, as illustrated in the following example, adapted from Solé—Solé (1977: 32):

(12) Les   quitó   a   los Pérez
      3pl-dat he-took-away from   the Pérez
         todo lo   que   tenían.
         all   that which   they-had
      'He took away from the Pérez family all they had.'

The dative clitic pronoun *les* 'them' doubles the nominal term *los Pérez* 'the Pérez family'. The lexical term may be suppressed, but the pronoun may not:

(13) a. Les   quitó   todo lo   que   tenían.
         3pl-dat he-took-away all   that which they-had
         'He took away from them all they had'
     b. *Quitó   a   los Pérez todo
         he-took-away   from the Pérez all
            lo   que   tenían.
            that which   they-had
         'He took away from the Pérez family all they had.'

In this sense the pronominal clitic functions much the same way as the subject marker on the verb, which also allows for the absence of a subject term, as examples (12) and (13) illustrate.

Dative Clitic Doubling is obligatory in Spanish when the argument term refers to a specific human being. It is not used with argument terms that refer to non-humans or to non-specific humans, as shown in examples (14) and (15), respectively (adapted from Solé & Solé 1977: 33):

(14) a. Hará   Usted   un servicio al   mundo
         will-do   you-polite   a   service   to-the world
            civilizado.
            civilized
         'You will perform a service to the civilized world.'
     b. *Le   hará   Usted   un servicio al   mundo
         3sg-dat   will-do   you-polite   a   service   to-the world
            civilizado
            civilized
         'You will perform a service to the civilized world.'

(15) a. *Envió   los documentos   a   los abogados.*
he-sent   the documents   to   the lawyers
'He sent the documents to the lawyers.'
b. *Les   envió   los documentos   a   los abogados.*
3pl-dat   he-sent   the documents   to   the lawyers
'He sent the documents to his lawyers.'

Note that examples (15a) and (15b) are both grammatical, but that they have a different reading: in (15a) reference is made to *los abogados* as an institution, e.g. as a party in a legal conflict; in (15b) reference is made to the individual lawyers.

From these facts we may conclude that only specific terms designating human beings are accessible to Dative Clitic Doubling in Spanish, i.e. there is an *intrinsic constraint* on accessibility within which both the Animacy Hierarchy in (9) and the Definiteness Hierarchy in (11) play a role. This intrinsic constraint may be formalized as in (16):

(16)   Dative_Clitic_Doubling (T: <+human, +specific>)

16.3. Hierarchical constraints

Hierarchical constraints on accessibility have received much attention within the theory of Transformational Grammar. An early example of such a constraint was the A-over-A principle, as formulated in Chomsky (1964). Important progress was achieved in Ross (1967), in which a typology of constraints of different types was developed, which came to be known as Island Constraints, where an Island was conceived of as a structural domain from which a given type of constituent may not be moved. Some examples of such Island Constraints are the Complex Noun Phrase Constraint, the Coordinate Structure Constraint, and the Sentential Subject Constraint. In Chomsky (1973) an attempt was made to derive the different Island Constraints from more general underlying principles such as the Tensed-S, Specified Subject, and Subjacency conditions. Various variant formulations of such constraints were proposed in later work in the Extended Standard Theory. Special attention was paid to conditions on anaphora and coreference relations, formulated in terms of Command (in different versions, since Langacker (1966)), and C-Command (also in different versions, since Reinhart (1976), compare also Reinhart (1983)).

Initially, the various hierarchical constraints and principles mentioned above were discussed mainly as constraints on transformational operations of movement and deletion. In the meantime, it has become clear that this is inadequate, for the following reason: if these constraints were intrinsically tied up with movement or deletion, then they should not hold in cases in which no movement or deletion is involved. More generally, when some constraint C is interpreted as a constraint on some transformation T, then one would expect a language which does not have T not to be sensitive to C. This expectation, however, is not borne out by the facts. Consider the following two constructions:

(17)   *What do you deplore the fact that I did?
(18)   You deplore the fact that I did what?

Constructions equivalent to (18) are ungrammatical in many languages, except as an echo question, due to the Complex Noun Phrase Constraint (CNPC). In languages observing this constraint, it is impossible to question (or otherwise operate on) a term position X which is part of a complex NP such as *the fact [that I did X]*. If the CNPC were a condition on the transformation which fronts the question word, then we would expect languages which place their question words in pattern position not to be sensitive to the CNPC. Thus, constructions such as (18) would be expected to be grammatical in languages which form their questions in this manner. But this is not, in general, the case. Though it is probably true that languages having constructions such as (17) are generally less sensitive to the CNPC, constructions of type (18) are nevertheless excluded in many of these languages. Since the CNPC is therefore relevant to languages which neither move nor delete the target constituent in question, the CNPC, in its most general formulation, cannot be stated as a constraint on transformations. It must be formulated as a constraint on the accessibility of certain term positions to certain operations.

This argument, first presented in Keenan (1972), was further developed in Cole et al. (1977), and was shown to be relevant to Navajo relativization in Platero (1974). Navajo relativization is sensitive to both the Coordinate Structure Constraint and the CNPC. These constraints cannot be formulated in terms of deletion, since Navajo deletion operations are not in general sensitive to these constraints. Platero's conclusion is that these constraints are relevant to the question which pairs of NPs can be linked by a "relative connection", given the configuration in which they occur with respect to their antecedent NP.[1] This view thus leads to a "configurational" rather than a "transformational" view of such constraints.

Such a configurational view was adopted within Transformational Grammar from Chomsky (1973) onwards. From this point of view, constraints are defined on configurations such as (19a) by means of formulations such as (19b):

(19) a. X ... [$_c$ ... Y ...]
   b. No rule can relate X and Y in a configuration such as (19a), where C = some specified category.

Categories such as C, which define an island for rules which might otherwise relate some X outside it to some Y inside it, came to be known as Bounding Nodes or Bounding Categories. This type of formulation comes closer to our definition of hierarchical constraint on accessibility, which is given in (20):

(20)   A hierarchical constraint on accessibility crucially involves the hierarchical position of the target term (T) within the clause structure in which it occurs.

Using the abbreviations introduced earlier in this chapter, the general representation for hierarchical constraints is then as follows:

(21)   O [$_X$ ... (T) ...]
   'the operation (O) may only be applied to terms (T) which form part of a constituent of type X'

For an example of a hierarchical constraint consider the restrictions on the use of the AcI-construction in Dutch illustrated in the following examples:

(22)   *Ik   zag   hem weggaan*
        I   saw   him go.away
        'I saw him leave.'
(23)   **Ik   geloofde hem ziek zijn /   ziek te   zijn.*
        I   believed him ill be   ill   to   be
        'I believed him to be ill.'

---

1. A similar argument is given in Foley and Van Valin (1984) in relation to questioning into relative constructions in Lakhota.

(24) *Ik wil hem weggaan / weg te gaan
I want him go.away away to go
'I want him to leave.'

(25) *Ik betreur hem ziek zijn / ziek te zijn
I regret him ill be / ill to be
'I am sorry he is ill.'

The AcI-construction is allowed with complement clauses that designate States of Affairs which are necessarily simultaneous with the main clause state of Affairs, as in (22). Here the immediate perception sense of the verb *zien* 'see' forces a simultaneity interpretation upon the complement clause. Since the main clause State of Affairs is situated in the past, the embedded State of Affairs is interpreted as taking place in the past, too. Complement clauses of this type may be said to have 'dependent time reference' (Noonan 1985), in this case simultaneous dependent time reference. Within FG such complement clauses may be represented as embedded predications (e) provided with a simultaneity (Sim) operator (cf. Dik—Hengeveld 1991), as in the following partial underlying representation of (22)

(26) (Past e_i: [zien [V] (x_i: 1.sg)$_{ProcExp}$
      (Sim e_j: [vertrekken [V] (x_j: 3.sg)])$_{Go}$])

When the complement clause designates a propositional content instead of a State of Affairs, as in (23), the AcI-construction is not allowed, neither with nor without the infinitival complementizer *te* 'to', even though in this example the State of Affairs designated in the complement clause occurs simultaneously with the main clause State of Affairs. Neither is the AcI-construction allowed when the complement clause designates a State of Affairs but has independent time reference, as in (25), nor when it designates a State of Affairs but has posterior dependent time reference, as in (24).

This hierarchical constraint on AcI-formation in Dutch may be captured by the formula given in (27):

(27) AcI [$_{(Sim\ e)}$ ... (T) ...]

Note that many hierarchical constraints may be captured by making reference to one of the layers of structure distinguished within the underlying clause representation in FG.

16.4. Functional constraints

16.4.0. Introduction

The approach to accessibility in which the functions of terms are taken into account was introduced by Keenan (1972) and Keenan—Comrie (1977), who described constraints on the accessibility of term positions to relativization in terms of grammatical functions such as Subject, Object, Indirect Object, etc. These *functional constraints* can be represented as in (28):

(28)   O (T)$_F$
'the operation (O) may only be applied to terms (T) with the function F'

Within FG three types of function are distinguished: Semantic, Syntactic, and Pragmatic Functions. In what follows I intend to demonstrate that all three types of function are relevant to the description of accessibility phenomena. More in particular, I will argue that within the framework of FG functional constraints on accessibility can be partially reconstructed in terms of three distinct hierarchies, which interact with each other:

(29) (i)   *the Semantic Function Hierarchy*
           Arg-1 > Go > Rec > Ben > Instr > Loc
     (ii) *the Syntactic Function Hierarchy*
           Subj > Obj > non-Subj, non-Obj
     (iii) *the Pragmatic Function Hierarchy*
           Topical > Non-topical
           Focal > Non-focal

In 16.4.1. I will discuss the role of Semantic and Syntactic Functions in relation to accessibility phenomena. This discussion will take the form of a critical reinterpretation of Keenan—Comrie's pioneering work, in which no clear distinction was made between semantic and syntactic functions. In 16.4.2. I will then discuss some accessibility phenomena which are related to the Pragmatic Functions of the target term.

16.4.1. Semantic and Syntactic Functions

16.4.1.1. Keenan and Comrie's Accessibility Hierarchy. Keenan (1972) and Keenan—Comrie (1977) argue that relativization possibilities across languages can be defined in terms of an Accessibility Hierarchy, formulated in terms of the grammatical functions or relations of target terms:

(30)   Accessibility Hierarchy
       SU > DO > IO > OBL > GEN > OCOMP

where SU = Subject, DO = Direct Object, IO = Indirect Object, OBL = Oblique term, GEN = Genitive or Possessor, and OCOMP = Object of Comparison.

The Accessibility Hierarchy thus concerns the following series of construction types:

(31) a. *the man who* (SU) *killed the chicken*
     b. *the chicken which* (DO) *the man killed*
     c. *the man to whom* (IO) *the boy gave the chicken*
     d. *the knife with which* (OBL) *the man killed the chicken*
     e. *the man whose* (GEN) *chicken the boy killed*
     f. *the man taller than whom* (OCOMP) *nobody in the village was.*

In terms of the Accessibility Hierarchy, Keenan and Comrie formulated the following constraints on relativization (relative to different strategies of relativization):[2]

(32) (i)   all languages have a primary relativization strategy which can at least be applied to SU.
     (ii) strategies other than the primary strategy may begin to apply at any point in the Accessibility Hierarchy.

---

2. Various refinements and modifications of these constraints have been proposed in later publications by the originators of the theory (Comrie—Keenan (1979), Comrie (1981), Keenan (1985)). In the present formulation of the hierarchy constraints, I have integrated these. Further contributions have been made by Maxwell (1979), Lehmann (1984), Fox (1987), and Tallerman (1990).

(iii) any relativization strategy must apply to a continuous segment of the Accessibility Hierarchy.
(iv) any relativization strategy may have its cut-off point at any position in the Accessibility Hierarchy, except for the strategy which expresses the relativized position by a pronoun: once this strategy starts, it continues to the last position in the Accessibility Hierarchy which is relativizable at all in the language.
(v) if relativization strategies leave a gap in the Accessibility Hierarchy, then the positions in the gap which cannot be directly relativized may be "promoted" to positions from which they can be relativized.

The combined effect of this theory consists in the claim that for any language all the positions in the Accessibility Hierarchy which precede the final cut-off point for relativization in that language will be relativizable by means of some strategy. From (v) it is apparent that this does not mean that any position can be DIRECTLY relativized by some strategy. The assumption is that, if some position on the Accessibility Hierarchy before the cut-off point is not directly relativizable by some strategy, then it can be promoted to some higher position on the Accessibility Hierarchy which IS relativizable in the language (Keenan—Comrie 1977: 68). For example, if in a given language a Beneficiary term (an Oblique term in Keenan—Comrie's terminology) is not relativizable by itself, but positions lower on the Accessibility Hierarchy are, we may expect there to be a possibility of assigning Subj or Obj function to the Beneficiary, and that the resulting promoted Beneficiary will then be relativizable.

The Accessibility Hierarchy has proved to be a powerful instrument in describing and explaining properties of relativization across languages.[3] It will be argued here, however, that several aspects of this theory are in need of reinterpretation or modification, in part for empirical, in part for theoretical reasons.

---

3. There is also evidence for the psychological reality of the Accessibility Hierarchy. A number of studies on second language acquisition (in particular, Doughty 1991) have shown that the development of the acquisition of relative clause structures in English by second language learners can be described as a progression along the Accessibility Hierarchy. Furthermore, exclusive training in more marked constructions along the Accessibility Hierarchy was found to have a beneficial effect on the acquisition of less marked constructions.

16.4.1.2. Reconsidering the Accessibility Hierarchy. As for the empirical side of the matter, we saw in 4.1. above that there are languages which do not seem to have any kind of relative construction. This means that (32(i)) must be qualified, and that the validity of the Accessibility Hierarchy as a whole must be restricted to those languages which do have such constructions. The constraints are thus not universally valid for all languages, but they may be claimed to be universally valid for all those languages which do have relativization at all.

As for the theoretical side, note that a typological theory phrased in terms of such notions as Subject, Direct Object, etc. presupposes grammars in which these notions have a well-defined status; and such grammars presuppose a general grammatical theory which includes such notions in its vocabulary, and offers criteria for determining when these notions are applicable to given terms.

Keenan and Comrie, however, do not offer such a theory.[4] Rather, they tacitly assume that the grammatical functions used in the Accessibility Hierarchy have universal linguistic validity and can be more or less unequivocally identified in any arbitrary language. In fact, however, this means that the theoretical foundation for the typological generalization is missing. Various difficulties in interpreting and applying the Accessibility Hierarchy originate from this lack of theoretical foundation, as we shall see below. It is useful to first critically consider each of the positions in the Accessibility Hierarchy and compare them with the distinctions which have been made within the framework of FG.

(i) Subject. It is quite clear that the Subject function plays a role in functional constraints on accessibility. Two points should be noted, however, in interpreting the Subject function. Both these points suggest that semantic functions, as well, may play a role in determining accessibility.

In the first place, it is not assumed in FG (as is done by Keenan and Comrie) that the Subject function is universally relevant to natural languages. As argued in *TFG1*: 10.4.1., the Subject function is irrelevant to those languages which have no possibilities of forming passive constructions. In such languages, presumably, the priority claimed for the Subject function in the Accessibility Hierarchy reverts to the Semantic Functions and/or the Pragmatic Functions. Thus, where Subj is not relevant, the first place in the

---

4. Although Keenan (1976) can be seen as an attempt at repairing this situation as far as the notion Subject is concerned.

functional hierarchy will no doubt be taken by the first argument A^1, which has the first position in the Semantic Function Hierarchy.

In the second place, the Subject function in FG can be distinguished according to the underlying semantic function to which it has been applied. Since the assignment of Subject is guided by the Semantic Function Hierarchy, we can set up a derived Subject hierarchy of the following form:

(33) A^1Subj > GoSubj > RecSubj > BenSubj > InstrSubj > LocSubj

Since, according to FG, not all Subjects are alike with respect to their underlying semantic functions, one might in principle expect situations in which a certain operation can be applied only to certain types of Subject, definable in terms of underlying semantic function.

(ii) Direct Object. To Direct Object the same remarks apply, *mutatis mutandis*, as to the Subject function. First, Object according to FG is not necessarily relevant to a language. Where Object is relevant, it will certainly be able to play a role in defining accessibility. Where it is not relevant, the conditioning of accessibility will revert to Goal, as part of the Semantic Function Hierarchy. Second, Objects can be distinguished in terms of underlying semantic function. FG defines the following derivative Object hierarchy:

(34)   GoObj > RecObj > BenObj > InstrObj > LocObj

In the case of this Object hierarchy, there is some evidence that the underlying semantic functions may play a role in co-determining accessibility.

Consider the following example of relativization in Bahasa Indonesia, as presented in Chung (1976). In Bahasa Indonesia, both RecObj and BenObj can be relativized into, as in:

(35)   *wanita   yang   aya   saya   kirim-i   bunga*
         woman   rm   father   I   send-to   flowers
         'the woman that my father sent flowers to'
(36)   *orang   yang   saya   masak-kan   daging   itu*
         man   rm   I   cook-for   meat   that
         'the man that I cooked that meat for'

Chung adds a note, however, to the effect that constructions such as (35) are more common than those of (36), and that native speakers report that although the latter are grammatical, they are avoided in everyday speech. In this sense, then, it is more difficult to relativize into a BenObj position than it is to relativize a RecObj position. This difference can be accounted for in terms of the underlying semantic functions as specified in (34).

(iii) Indirect Object. In FG the notion of Indirect Object has no independent status. The traditional notion Indirect Object is re-interpreted as either indicating the Semantic Function Recipient, or the combination of functions Recipient+Object. In this way, it is possible to account for such oppositions as:

(37) a. *John gave the book* (GoObj) to Peter (Rec).
 b. *John gave* Peter (RecObj) *the book* (Go).

We would thus expect that what is traditionally called an Indirect Object will either behave in the same way as an "Oblique" constituent which has only a Semantic Function, or in the same way as an Object. And this appears to be, in fact, the case:

> The indirect object position is perhaps the most subtle one on the Accessibility Hierarchy. For purposes of relative clause formation, it appears that many languages either assimilate indirect objects to the other oblique cases (...) or to direct objects ... (Keenan—Comrie 1977: 72).

In later work, Comrie (1981: 149) leaves out the Indirect Object function from the relativization hierarchy, and in general expresses doubts concerning the cross-linguistic validity of the Indirect Object function (Comrie 1981: 170), as well as concerning its relevance to the grammar of English (Comrie 1981: 61).

Haberland—Van der Auwera (1990) provide another example of the problematic status of Indirect Objects in the Accessibility Hierarchy. In their discussion of Modern Greek relativization (see the discussion below) they conclude that the Indirect Object is in fact nothing else than a Recipient (or a Beneficiary). It follows that the behaviour of such constituents can only be described in terms of Semantic (and possibly Pragmatic) Functions. Not much seems to be lost, then, in a theory which does not recognize Indirect Object as a grammatical relation of its own. Rather, something is gained, namely the differentiation of the traditional notion Indirect Object into either Rec or RecObj, two types of constituent which have little in common beyond their Semantic Function (Comrie 1981: 61).

(iv) Oblique. Those constituents which are given the function Oblique in terms of the Accessibility Hierarchy can be interpreted within FG as constituents with only a Semantic Function. Again, "Oblique" has no status as a Syntactic Function or grammatical relation of its own, but Obliques are readily identifiable as terms with a Semantic Function which have not received the function Subject or Object.

In those cases in which different "Obliques" display different types of behaviour, such differences can be accounted for in terms of the Semantic Functions of these terms. Consider again the case of Modern Greek. Joseph (1983) had already drawn attention to the recalcitrant behaviour of Modern Greek Indirect Objects in relation to the Accessibility Hierarchy. Joseph, however, rejects the idea of conflating the IO with "Obliques", since Recipient and Beneficiary terms do not behave in the same way as other "Obliques". This, however, can be taken as a sign that "Obliques" must be distinguished as to their Semantic Function. Consider the following phenomena:

— Terms with only a Semantic Function are usually coded by prepositional phrases. Only Recipients and Beneficiaries can also be coded in the socalled "Genitive" case:[5]

(38)	Term	PrepPhrase	Case
	$(Yáni)_{Rec}$	s to Yáni	tu Yáni
	$(Yáni)_{Ben}$	ya to Yáni	tu Yáni
	$(Aθína)_{Dir}$	s tin Aθína	---

— Only those terms which can be expressed by a Genitive may also be represented (or "doubled") by a clitic pronoun in the Genitive ((39b) is grammatical for all speakers, but (39c) only for some):

(39) a. *tu   éδosa   to   vivlío*
         him-gen gave-I   the   book
         'I gave the book to him'
     b. *tu   éδosa   tu   Yáni   to   vivlío*
         him-gen gave-I   him-gen   John   the   book
         'I gave the book to John' (for all speakers)
     c. *tu   éδosa   s   to   Yáni   to   vivlío*
         him-gen gave-I   to   the   John   the   book
         'I gave the book to John' (for some speakers)

---

5. The "Genitive" covers functions which would in other languages be distributed over a genitive and a dative case.

— The same types of terms can be resumed by a Genitive clitic in the relative construction:

(40) Kséro   ton ánθropo pu   tu   éðoses   to   vivlío.
      know.I   the man   rm   him.gen gave.you   the   book
      'I know the man to whom you gave the book.'

— A Recipient and a Beneficiary cannot be "doubled" at the same time (Joseph—Philippaki-Warburton 1987: 213): only one of them can, and it must be the Recipient:

(41) ðóse   tu   to   yá   ména!
      give   him-gen   it   for   me
      'Give it to him for me!'
(42) *ðóse   tu   mu   /   mu   tu   to!
      give   him-gen   me-gen   /   me-gen   him-gen   it
      'Give it to him for me!'
(43) *ðóse   mu   to   s   aftón!
      give   me-gen   it   to   him
      'Give it to him for me!'

From these few facts we may conclude (i) that if we class Indirect Objects with Obliques, we must be able to distinguish Recipient and Beneficiary Obliques from other Obliques, since only they have optional Genitive expression; (ii) that we must also be able to distinguish Recipients from Beneficiaries, on account of the facts of (41)-(43). Both types of distinctions can be made if we take the semantic functions of "Obliques" into account.

(v) Genitive. The grammatical function of Genitive (or Possessor) is not on a par with the other grammatical relations in the Accessibility Hierarchy. So far, the Accessibility Hierarchy has been concerned with terms which can occur as arguments or satellites to the main predicate, and which can then be differentiated qua accessibility in terms of their functional properties.

In the case of Genitive, however, accessibility constraints do not primarily concern the function of the term in question, but rather its hierarchical position within the clause structure. Apart from some rare exceptions the Genitive is not an argument or satellite of the main predicate, but an attribute within a term which itself is an argument or satellite to the main predicate. This means that accessibility of Genitive terms is not only monitored by functional, but also by hierarchical factors. Let us see how the status of Genitive would be interpreted within FG.

First, I should like to replace the term "Genitive" (which is the name of a certain case) by "Possessor", since Possessors may be sensitive to the sorts of constraints involved here, even if they are not expressed in the genitive case. In *TFG1*: 8.6, I suggested that Possessors can be treated as term predicates which act as restrictors within the structure of a term, so that (44a) would be interpreted as (44b), and represented as (44c):

(44) a. *John's dog*
  b. the entity x_i such that x_i has the property 'dog' such that x_i has the property of 'being John's'
  c. $(d1x_i: dog_N: \{(d1x_j: John_N)_{Poss}\})$

It is quite clear, then, that if some operation is to be applied to the Possessor term in (44), this operation must penetrate into the term *John's dog*, and pick out a term position which is contained within that term.

Getting access to the Possessor position is thus, in our terminology, a matter of hierarchical constraints.[6] That the hierarchical status of the Possessor is crucially involved in accessibility is also evident from the fact that in many languages in which Possessors *per se* are not accessible, we find alternative constructions in which the term corresponding to the Possessor occurs as an argument of the main predicate, in which quality it IS accessible to the relevant operations. Keenan—Comrie (1977: 92) note this with respect to such oppositions as those between:

(45) a. The lady's *coat was stolen.*
  b. The lady *had her coat stolen.*
(46) a. *John hit* the man's *head.*
  b. *John hit* the man *on his head.*

In many languages, the constituent in roman typeface in the b-construction is more accessible than that in the a-construction. Note, however, that in an FG analysis of these constructions, the relevant terms in the b-constructions are

---

6. Cf. Tallerman (1990: 303), who mentions this in passing. Haberland—Van der Auwera (1990), in discussing Clitic Doubling and Relativization in Modern Greek, make a distinction between "independent" term positions (= arguments and satellites at clause level) and "dependent" ones (such as Possessors), and then use this distinction to explain the differences in distribution between "doubling" clitics at clause level, and resumptive clitics within relative clauses.

not contained in terms, and do not have the function of Possessor; rather, they are terms by themselves, functioning at the level of the predication on a par with other arguments of the predicate. Thus, the term *the lady* functions as a ØSubj in (45b), and the term *the man* functions as a GoObj in (46b). And in that functional quality, these terms are accessible to the relevant operations:[7]

(47) a. ?*the man whose head was hit by John*
    b. *the man who was hit on the head by John*

We conclude that Possessor constituents do not belong to the same, functionally defined hierarchy as the other terms in the Accessibility Hierarchy.

(vi) Object of comparison. The interpretation of OCOMP, finally, is also a less straightforward matter. The reason in this case is that the notion "Object of Comparison" or "Standard of Comparison" is not a typologically uniform notion: different languages may have quite different types of comparative construction, corresponding to such paraphrases as:

(48) a. *John is taller than Peter.*
    b. *John is tall, exceeds Peter.*
    c. *John exceeds Peter in tallness.*
    d. *John is tall, Peter is not.*

It is clear that, depending on the particular comparative construction that a language has, the Object or Standard of Comparison (*Peter* in (48a-d)) has quite different structural and functional properties. In (48a), *than Peter* is more or less comparable to an Oblique term (but see below). In (48b) and (48c), *Peter* functions as the Object of the clause or Goal of the verb *exceed*. And in (48d), *Peter* functions as the Subject of a clause which is coordinated with the preceding clause.

---

7. Note that this also implies that FG does not recognize a putative rule of "Possessor Ascension", as is commonly assumed in Relational Grammar. According to the FG analysis, the b-constructions are not derived from the a-constructions through some manipulation of the embedded Possessor term, but constitute alternative ways of saying much the same thing as is said in the a-constructions. The rationale for the existence of such alternative constructions may lie precisely in the greater accessibility of arguments of the main predicate than of terms which are in some way contained within arguments to the main predicate.

If, in a language having constructions of the form (48a), one could say something like:

(49) a. *I saw a boy than whom John is taller.*
 b. *I saw a boy who John is taller than.*

then this possibility should be compared to what happens to other Obliques, i.e. other terms with only a semantic function.[8] And if a language having (48b) or (48c) allowed constructions of the form:

(50) *I saw a boy whom John exceeds in tallness.*

this construction should be compared to other cases in which Objects or Goals are relativized. We may furthermore expect that languages having constructions of the form (48d) will not allow relativization into the Standard of Comparison, since what we have there is a coordination (or juxtaposition) of two more or less independent clause structures, in which the actual comparison is left for the interpreter to infer.

In this respect the following statement of Keenan—Comrie's (1977: 74) is significant: "... few languages that distinguish objects of comparison from direct objects or oblique NPs permit them to be relativized." It is thus doubtful whether OCOMP can indeed be regarded as an independent position on the Accessibility Hierarchy.

16.4.1.3. Conclusion. From the preceding discussion we conclude that Keenan and Comrie's Accessibility Hierarchy should in fact be decomposed into two different hierarchies: the Semantic Function Hierarchy and the Syntactic Function Hierarchy given in (29) and repeated in (51):

(51) (i) *the Semantic Function Hierarchy*
  Arg-1 > Go > Rec > Ben > Instr > Loc
 (ii) *the Syntactic Function Hierarchy*
  Subj > Obj > non-Subj, non-Obj

---

8. Cf. Maxwell (1979: 367) who argues for this in general, and Tallerman (1990: 307), who shows that OComp in Welsh is treated in the same way as OBL.

376   *Accessibility*

These two hierarchies and their interaction are to be interpreted as follows: if a term possesses only a Semantic Function, then the Semantic Function Hierarchy may co-determine its accessibility; if a term also has a Syntactic Function, then it will for that reason be more accessible than terms with only a Semantic Function, its accessibility being determined by the Syntactic Function Hierarchy. In that case, its underlying semantic function may co-determine its accessibility, again according to the Semantic Function Hierarchy.

16.4.2. Pragmatic Functions

There is evidence that Pragmatic Functions, too, play a role in determining the accessibility of term positions to various operations. Kuno (1976) and Allwood (1976) were the first to point to the importance of such factors. These factors are also discussed in Grosu (1981) and in Maling—Zaenen (1982).

Kuno (1976) shows that Japanese is rather liberal in allowing Relativization to apply to term positions within restrictors which have already undergone Relativization. Thus, the following construction, which results from such double application of Relativization, is grammatical in Japanese:

(52) *Syuppansita   kaisya   ga   toosansite-simatta hon*
     published   company   Subj   bankrupt-gone   book
        o   yonda
        Go   read
     'I read a book which the company which published (it) went bankrupt'

However, not all products of such double relativization are equally acceptable:

(53) ?*Syuppansita   kaisya   ga   kazi de   yakete-simatta*
      published   company   Subj   fire by   burn-down-gone
         hon   o   yonda
         book   Go   read
     'I read a book which the company that published (it) burnt down by fire'

In order to account for these differences, Kuno hypothezises that in order for some term T, embedded within some predication, to be accessible to Relativization (and likewise to Questioning and Topic assignment), it must be possible to construe this predication as being something which can be predicated in a relevant way about T. In other words, T must be a potential Topic or Theme for the predication.

Maling—Zaenen (1982), elaborating on suggestions contained in Allwood (1976), argue that similar factors play a role with respect to accessibility in the Scandinavian languages. These languages can be characterized as quite liberal with respect to different hierarchical constraints on Relativization and other operations. For instance, they allow Topic assignment into relative constructions, as in the following example from Swedish:

(54) De   blommorna känner jag en man   som säljer.
     These   flowers   know   I   a   man   that sells
     'These flowers I know a man that sells'

Again, however, not all products of this operation are equally acceptable. Compare:

(55) *Lisa   talar   jag med   den poiken   som kysst
     Lisa   spoke   I   with   the boy   that kissed
        (henne).
        (her)
     'Lisa I talked with the boy who kissed'

Again, the difference in acceptability may be dependent on the extent to which the predication can be construed as relevant in relation to the target term. Note, however, that in general we expect the pragmatic factor discussed here to be of a gradual nature, and to be heavily co-dependent on contextualization, that is, on suitable embedding within the pragmatic information of S and A. The stars and question marks on the above examples should for that reason be interpreted in terms of pragmatic coherence rather than of grammaticality.

16.5. Concluding remarks

In the preceding sections we have shown that three types of constraint determine the degree of accessibility of a target term to various grammatical operations. The representations of these three types of constraint are repeated in (56)-(58):

(56)   O (T: <P>)   *Intrinsic constraint*
(57)   O [$_x$ ... (T) ...]   *Hierarchical constraint*
(58)   O (T)$_F$ *Functional constraint*

In describing these three types of constraints we have acted as if they operated independently in order to facilitate their description. It is important to note, as a final point, that the three types of constraint may interact in various ways. Thus, the constraint on AcI-formation in Dutch should in fact be further restricted to embedded Subjects, as in (59):

(59)   AcI [$_{(Sim\ e)}$ ... (T)$_{Subj}$ ...]

(59) combines a hierarchical constraint with a functional constraint. The other two constraints discussed in this chapter should also be reconsidered from this perspective. Similarly, Dative Clitic Doubling in Spanish can be regarded, at a higher level of abstraction, as just one instance of what might be called "Pronominal Doubling", which applies to Subject, Goal and Recipient arguments, with different manifestations and different further restrictions in each case. Pronominal Doubling can then be seen as subject to both intrinsic and functional constraints. Finally, the discussion of the position of terms with Possessor function within Keenan—Comrie's Accessibility Hierarchy in 16.4.1.2. has shown that the somewhat deviant behaviour of terms with this function can be interpreted as the result of a conflict between functional and hierarchical considerations.

17. Extra-clausal constituents

17.0. Introduction

Up to a certain point, any discourse can be ultimately analysed as consisting of a sequence of sentences, where a sentence consists of one independent (main) clause, possibly containing one or more subordinate clauses, or of a coordinated sequence of such main clauses.

Certain linguistic expressions, though not constituting full clauses, can nevertheless be analysed as fragments of clauses, and thus indirectly described with reference to the structure of the clause. Clause fragments are particularly common as answers to questions, as in:

(1) A: *Where are you going?*
     B: *To the library.*

where *to the library* is only a term, not a clause, but can nevertheless be described as a fragment of the clause:

(2) *I am going to the library.*

which might have been produced in the same context. Clause fragments can be produced in circumstances in which the context makes the production of the corresponding full clause superfluous.

Especially in spoken discourse, however, we often produce a variety of expressions which can be analysed neither as clauses nor as fragments of clauses. These expressions may stand on their own, or precede, follow, and even interrupt a clause, being more loosely associated with it than those constituents which belong to the clause proper. These expressions will here be called *extra-clausal constituents* (ECCs).[1]

---

1. Some authors use the term "parenthetical" as more or less equivalent to what I call "ECC" (cf. Ziv 1985). I restrict the term "parenthetical" to those ECCs which interrupt a clause.

380 *Extra-clausal constituents*

For several reasons, ECCs have so far received much less attention in grammatical theory than the internal grammatical structure of the clause proper. Some of these reasons are:

(i) ECCs are especially common in the spoken register, while the attention of grammarians has often been confined to written language.

(ii) ECCs are typical of linguistic expressions used in ongoing discourse, while grammarians have often concentrated on the structure of isolated sentences.

(iii) ECCs are rather loosely associated with the clause, and cannot easily be described in terms of clause-internal rules and principles.

(iv) ECCs can only be understood in terms of pragmatic rules and principles, while grammarians have often pretended that grammar should be described independently of such principles.

It is clear that FG cannot similarly ignore these ECCs, if it wishes to achieve pragmatic adequacy for its linguistic descriptions (cf. Ziv 1985, Hannay—Vester 1987, De Vries 1989, Kroon 1989). Some more specific reasons for paying attention to ECCs are the following:

— these constituents may co-determine the intended interpretation of the clause proper;

— they may interact with the internal structure of the clause in different ways;

— they may diachronically be "absorbed" into the structure of the clause proper, and thus provide an ontogenetic source for certain clause-internal grammatical phenomena.[2]

17.1. On defining ECCs

With respect to the category of ECCs, the following questions present themselves:

(Q1) By what criteria do we determine whether a constituent is, or is not part of the internal structure of the clause?

(Q2) What different subtypes of ECCs must be distinguished?

(Q3) How can the formal and functional properties of each of these subtypes be described?

---

2. This is one aspect of what Givón (1979) has called the shift from the "pragmatic mode" to the "syntactic mode" of linguistic organization.

With respect to question (Q1) we can mention some recurrent properties of ECCs which, though not providing a watertight definition, nevertheless help us in identifying them:

(i) ECCs either occur on their own, or are typically set off from the clause proper by breaks or pause-like inflections in the prosodic contour; they are "bracketed off" from the clause by such prosodic features.[3]

(ii) ECCs are never essential to the internal structure of the clause with which they are associated; when they are left out, the clause still forms an integral whole.

(iii) ECCs are not sensitive to the grammatical rules which operate within the limits of the clause, although they may be related to the clause by rules of coreference, parallelism, and antithesis which may also characterize relations between clauses in ongoing discourse.

In particular languages, more specific language-dependent criteria may be used to determine whether a constituent belongs to the clause or not. For one example, consider constituent order in Dutch main clauses. Main clause constituent order in Dutch can most easily be described in terms of a principle which says that there can be only one clause constituent in the initial position before the finite verb. That constituent is very often the Subject of the clause, but if there is any other clausal constituent in initial position, the Subject will appear after the finite verb. Dutch is, in other words, a rather strongly Verb-second language. Compare:

(3) a. *Jan heeft gisteren een fiets gekocht.*
 John has yesterday a bicycle bought
 b. *Gisteren heeft Jan een fiets gekocht.*
 yesterday has John a bicycle bought
 c. *Een fiets heeft Jan gisteren gekocht.*
 a bicycle has John yesterday bought
 'John bought a bicycle yesterday.'
(4) a. **Gisteren Jan heeft een fiets gekocht.*
 yesterday John has a bicycle bought
 b. **Een fiets Jan heeft gekocht gisteren.*
 a bicycle John has bought yesterday
 c. **Gisteren een fiets Jan heeft gekocht.*
 yesterday a bicycle John has bought
 'John bought a bicycle yesterday.'

---

3. Cf. Cruttenden (1986) and *TFG1*: chapter 18.

382 *Extra-clausal constituents*

Nevertheless, there are quite a few constructions in which two independent constituents seem to appear before the main finite verb:

(5) a. *Die man,   die   heeft   gisteren   een*
       that man,   that.one has   yesterday   a
       fiets   gekocht.
       bicycle   bought
       'That man, he bought a bicycle yesterday.'
    b. *Natuurlijk,   Jan   heeft   gisteren   een*
       Of.course,   John   has   yesterday   a
       fiets   gekocht.
       bicycle   bought
       'Of course, John bought a bicycle yesterday.'
    c. *Nou,   Jan   heeft   gisteren   een fiets   gekocht.*
       Well,   John   has   yesterday   a   bicycle   bought
       'Well, John bought a bicycle yesterday.'

In such cases, as is indicated by the commas, there is typically a prosodic break between the first and the second constituents. This fact, and the rule concerning main clause constituent ordering, allow us to define the initial constituents in (5a-c) as ECCs. On this criterion it follows immediately that what is at first sight the same constituent may sometimes appear as an integrated constituent of the clause, sometimes as an ECC more loosely associated with the clause. Alongside (5a-c), we also have:

(6) a. Die man *heeft gisteren een fiets gekocht.*
       'That man bought a bicycle yesterday.'
    b. Natuurlijk *heeft Jan gisteren een fiets gekocht.*
       'Of course John bought a bicycle yesterday.'
    c. Nou *heeft Jan gisteren een fiets gekocht...*
       'Now John bought a bicycle yesterday...'

In these examples the constituents in roman typeface are integrated parts of the clause. In many cases, however, there are clear communicative differences between the intra-clausal and the extra-clausal occurrences of the same item. For example, the difference between (5b) and (6b) can be described through the following paraphrases:

(5b) 'O.K., I very well know and admit that John bought a bicycle yesterday, but ...'
(6b) 'Of course John bought a bicycle yesterday, how could it be otherwise?'

The differentiation between intra-clausal and extra-clausal occurrences of these constituents can thus be used to account for these communicative differences.

Although there will certainly be situations in which the various criteria which we have mentioned do not provide an unequivocal answer to the question whether a given constituent occurs outside or inside the clause, we shall assume that this question can be satisfactorily answered in most cases.

As for the questions (Q2) and (Q3) above concerning the subcategorization of ECCs and the description of their formal and functional properties, I shall only be able to give a preliminary and no doubt incomplete analysis. Apart from the lack of systematic research in this area, a special problem is the multifunctional nature of many ECCs. This multifunctionality manifests itself in two facts: (i) some of these constituents may have different functions in different contexts of use; (ii) some may simultaneously have several functions in one and the same occurrence.

17.2. Types of ECCs

ECCs can in the first place be distinguished with respect to the place they take in relation to the clause. In terms of this criterion, we can distinguish:
(i) Absolute or free-standing ECCs;
(ii) Preclausal ECCs;
(iii) Clause-internal or parenthetical ECCs;
(iv) Postclausal ECCs.

Some ECCs are by their very function tied to one of these positions; others may occur, with much the same function, in any two, three, or all four of them.

More important than these positional differences are the distinctions which can be made in terms of the functions fulfilled by ECCs. These functions can be associated with some of the distinctions that will be made in the next chapter with respect to the structure and organization of discourse events. I will therefore discuss the different ECC types under the following headings:

(i) *Interaction management*: those ECCs which pertain to the creation and maintenance of the interactional conditions which must be fulfilled for a discourse event to be implemented.

(ii) *Attitude specification*: those ECCs which pertain to the emotional/attitudinal tone in which the discourse is carried out.

(iii) *Discourse organization*: those ECCs which pertain to the organization, the structuring, and the presentation of the discourse content.

(iv) *Discourse execution*: those ECCs which play a role in the expression of the actual content of the discourse.

In the following sections I will discuss these different types one by one.

17.2.1. Interaction management

Several types of ECCs play a role in strategies for getting A's attention and securing his willingness to participate in the discourse event.

— *Greetings and Leave-takings*. Greetings are ECCs through which S acknowledges the presence of A, and signals that he is available as a potential partner for communication.

(7)   *Hello! Hi!*
(8)   *Good day sir, could I ask you a question?*

Leave-takings play an essential role in the closing of most types of discourse event.

— *Summonses*. Summonses are ECCs which serve to draw the attention of some potential A, signalling that S would like to say something to him.

(9)   *Hey there, what's your name?*

Expressions which are basically Greetings are often used in Summons function:

(10)   *Hello there, what's your name?*

— *Addresses*. Addresses are ECCs which may precede, follow, or even interrupt the clause, and which explicitly signal that the utterance is intended for the person named in the Address:[4]

(11) *John, could you give me a hand please?*
(12) *I don't think you should do that, Mary!*
(13) *I don't think, Peter, that it will be easy to get you out of this mess.*

In view of their function, Addresses will often consist of proper names, possibly accompanied by titles, functions, or references to the relation between S and A. Personal pronouns of the second person can also be used in Address function. Languages may furthermore have special devices for marking constituents in Address function. These may consist of special Address particles, as in the English example (14) and the Arabic example (15) (see Moutaouakil 1989):

(14) *O Lord, help me in my misery!*

(15) yā Zaydu, ?ahūka, zārahu 'Amrun.
O Zayd.nom brother.your visited.him Amr.nom
Vocative........ Theme.......... Clause..........................
'O Zayd, (as for) your brother, Amr visited him.'

or the language may have a special case for terms in the pragmatic function of Address: the vocative case.[5]

A, on his part, may use various types of ECC in order to signal that he is ready and willing to participate in the interaction, or that he is still paying attention to what S says, and that S can go on talking. Especially important among the latter are:

— *Minimal Responses*. Minimal Responses typically signal agreement, or at least suggest that what is said is being properly received at the other end of

---

4. Ochs-Keenan—Schieffelin (1976: 355-357) treat Summonses, Addresses, and Expressives together under "attention-getting devices".

5. For the pragmatics of Address, compare Brown—Gilman (1960) and Haverkate (1984: 67-78). For an analysis of Address in Arabic within the context of FG, see Moutaouakil (1989: chapter 5). For the relation between Summons and Address, see also Levinson (1983).

the communication line. Minimal Responses are unique in being verbal utterances which do not count as turns in conversation, nor as attempts on the part of A to obtain a turn. Common Minimal Responses in English are *yes*, *no*, *mm*, *hm*, *mhm*.

At the level of Interaction Management, politeness plays an important role. Both S and A may use several types of ECC (especially excuses) to emphasize the insignificance of S and the importance of A:

(16) A: *Excuse me, Sir, could I have a word with you?*
     B: *By all means, go ahead, take your time!*

17.2.2. Attitude specification

Especially important means of attitude specification are xpressives, which directly symbolize the current emotional state of S, as in:

(17) a. *Ouch, my finger!*
     b. *Damn it.*
     c. *Hurray*!

Although Expressives may occur on their own, they will in fact often be integrated in a wider discourse event, and may then acquire interactive values over and above their role of expressing individual emotions. Most other ECCs are typically used in a discourse context.

17.2.3. Discourse organization

17.2.3.0. Introduction. Once the ground has been prepared for the actual discourse to take place, S may take a number of measures in order to secure a proper organization and a proper receipt of the discourse proper. These measures can be divided over three main (groups of) pragmatic functions: Boundary marking (17.2.3.1), Orientation (17.2.3.2), and Tail (17.2.3.3).

17.2.3.1. Boundary marking. Boundary marking involves all those means which can be used to signal the beginning, the end, and the internal articulation of the discourse as a whole, the different constituent discourse episodes, and the various "moves" which make up these episodes.

— *Initiators*[6]. Initiators precede the clause proper, typically occurring in utterance-initial position. They serve to open up a new discourse, a new episode in an ongoing discourse, or a new turn in an ongoing conversation. The most common initiator in English is *well*:

(18) *Well, ladies and gentlemen, shall we start the game?*
(19) *... until finally I mentioned the financial side of the matter.*
    Well, that turned out to be a touchy point ...

A very common initiator in Dutch is *nou*, used in quite similar ways as English *well*.[7]

— *Topic Shifters*. Topic Shifters (see e.g. Ochs-Keenan—Schieffelin 1976: 348) are ECCs occurring at the beginning of an utterance, by means of which S can indicate that he wishes to broach a new topic of conversation (sometimes the "real" intended topic of the conversation). See Levinson (1983: 313) for some discussion of the use of expressions such as *by the way* and *hey* in this function. Levinson (1983: 314) cites the following example from Owen (1982):

(20) A: *Probably is because of that I should think, yes, mm*
    B: *Mm*
    (1.2)
    B: ((louder)) *By the way, do you want any lettuces*

— *Push and Pop markers*. So-called "push" and "pop" markers (in the terminology of Polanyi—Scha 1983) signal that a subsection, subroutine, or subsequence within an ongoing unit is being entered or left, respectively (see 18.5.1).

— *Finalizers*. Finalizers round off a (topic of) conversation. Leave-takings may have this finalizing effect, but other elements, such as *okay*, *and how about you*, and *anyway* may have a similar function.

17.2.3.2. Orientation. If the content of any utterance is to be interpreted as a contribution to a coherent discourse, it must be possible for A to integrate this content into his antecedent *discourse representation* (cf. Kamp 1984, Vet 1988): the dynamic and cumulative discourse model built up by A as the

---

6. The term "initiator" is from Quirk et al. (1972: 274).
7. For an analysis of Dutch *nou*, see Schep—Vermeulen (1984).

discourse proceeds. Each new contribution to the discourse must be anchored in the discourse representation as built up so far. Consider an utterance such as:

(21)   *He felt awful.*

This utterance has little effect unless A is able to reconstruct the person referred to by *he*, the time referred to by the past tense *felt*, and perhaps also the place where and the circumstances in which (or through which) the person involved felt awful. In other words, coordinates for time, space, discourse topics or participants, and circumstances must have been fixed if an utterance such as (21) is to produce a coherent contribution to the discourse.

ECCs may help A to fix these parameters. They may "orient" A as to the identity of the coordinates essential to a coherent "anchoring" of the content of the proposition. We shall say that such ECCs have the pragmatic function of Orientation[8]. A constituent with Orientation function presents information which orients the addressee to the information to be presented in the clause.

I use the term "Orientation" as a kind of pragmatic superfunction underneath which several more specific types of Orientation can be distinguished. These various more specific types may differ in form as well as in function from each other, and include at least the following:

(22) (i)   Theme
     (ii) Condition
     (iii) Setting, with respect to
           (a) time
           (b) space
           (c) other, circumstantial SoAs

Since Orientation pertains to information that is to follow, constituents with Orientation function typically precede the clause proper. In the following

---

8. I borrow the term "Orientation" as well as its definition (in slightly adapted form) from Hannay—Vester (1987). Other terms with similar import are "Framing" (as used in De Vries 1989) and "Staging" as used by Grimes (1975). See also Brown—Yule (1983: chapter 4). I avoid the term "Frame" as used by De Vries, since I wish to reserve this term for the wider epistemological sense it has acquired in Artificial Intelligence (see 18.6.1), where it is not restricted to ECCs.

discussion of the different types of Orientation, we restrict ourselves to constituents which are outside the (main) clause and precede it.

— *Theme*. A constituent with Theme function specifies an ensemble of entities with respect to which the following clause is going to present some relevant information. The initial constituents in such constructions as the following have Theme function:

(23)   *That guy, is he a friend of yours?*
(24)   *That trunk, put it in the car!*
(25)   *As for the students, they won't be invited.*

In each case, we can understand the structure of the linguistic expression in terms of the following strategy of S:

(26) (i)   here is something (e.g. *the students*) with respect to which I am going to produce some information;
    (ii) and here is what I want to say about it (e.g. *they won't be invited*).

Thus, a Theme constituent orients A with respect to the discourse topics in relation to which the content of the ensuing clause is to be interpreted.

Let us now have a closer look at some of the properties of Themes. The most important property is perhaps that Themes indeed stand outside the structure of the clause proper. Themes are sometimes referred to as "left-dislocated" constituents, with reference to the view of early Transformational Grammar that a construction such as (23) could be derived from the structure underlying (27):

(27)   *Is that guy a friend of yours?*

through a transformational rule placing the subject to the left and "dislocating" it from its source sentence.

Quite apart from the question of why one would want to follow such a course, it is important to realize that in a number of crucial cases the formulation of such a putative transformational rule is impossible. Consider such examples as:

(28) *As for the students, adolescents almost never have any sense.*
(29) *As for Paris, the Eiffel Tower is really spectacular.*
(30) *As for the Center, well, the less said about so-called "think tanks", the better.*[9]

In constructions of this type, there is no natural "source" for the Theme constituent within the clause that follows it, although that clause clearly "bears upon" the Theme in some way or another. Languages differ in the frequency with which they use constructions of this type. Li—Thompson (1976) have introduced the term "Topic-prominent" for languages which make frequent use of this type of organization. Note that what Li and Thompson call "Topic" equals "Theme" in FG, in which a distinction is made between Theme (outside the clause) and Topic (inside the clause). Note also that in evaluating languages with respect to Theme-prominence, one should be careful to compare the spoken registers of these languages with each other. When this is done systematically, I think it will turn out that Theme-prominence is a matter of degree rather than of kind or type. In other words: all languages make use of this type of organization, but some do so more than others.

In languages with a high degree of Theme-prominence, constructions of this type are quite common. Well-known in this respect is the following example from Japanese:[10]

(31) zoo   wa   hana   ga   nagai
     elephant Theme nose   Subj   long
     'As for elephants, noses are long'
     =   'Elephants have long noses'

Since constructions such as (28)-(30) cannot be properly described by rules which extract a Theme from the structure of a given clause, it seems clear that all constructions of the Theme+Clause type must be described in such a way that the Theme is produced independently of the following clause. This not only provides a better account of the grammatical properties of Themes, but above all enables us to understand the pragmatic functionality of this type of constituent.

---

9. (28) and (29) are from Ross (1970). (30) is from Schwartz (1976).
10. From Li—Thompson (1976), who give parallel examples from Mandarin, Lahu, and other languages.

Several properties of Themes point to their independence from the clause which follows them:

(i) Themes usually precede the whole clause, including its illocutionary component. It is not usual for Themes to occur in parenthetical positions. Constrast:[11]

(32)   *As for John, he won't be invited.*
(33) a.   *As for John, I promise you he won't be invited.*
    b.   *?I promise you, as for John, that he won't be invited.*
    c.   *?I promise you that, as for John, he won't be invited.*

(ii) Themes can have their own illocutionary status, different from the following clause:

(34)   *My brother? I haven't seen him for years.*

In terms of the Speaker's strategy presented in (26), one could here assume a variant of the following form:

(35) (i)   You want to know something about Theme X?
    (ii)   Here is what I can say about X: ...

Assuming that it is correct to assign Theme function to *my brother* in (34), the Theme must be outside the following clause, since a clause cannot have two illocutionary values at the same time.

(iii) Themes are often presented in absolute form, that is, either completely unmarked for any kind of semantic or syntactic function, or in that case form which characterizes the most unmarked "citation form" in the given language (typically, the nominative or the absolutive case).[12] Compare the following versions of the same example sentences in English (36), French (37), and Hebrew (38):

(36) a.   *That man, we gave the book to him yesterday.*
    b.   **To that man, we gave the book to him yesterday.*

---

11. For the occurrence of embedded Themes in spoken Dutch, see Dik (1981).
12. This point was made, with these examples, in Schwartz (1971: 159).

(37) a. Cet homme, nous lui avons donné le
       that man   we   him have   given the
       livre hier.
       book   yesterday
       'That man, we gave the book to him yesterday.'
    b. *A cet homme, nous lui avons donné le
       to that man   we   him have   given the
       livre hier.
       book   yesterday
       'To that man, we gave the book to him yesterday.'
(38) a. Ha-iš   ha-ze,   anaxnu natannu lo   et
       the-man   the-that we   gave   to-him Go
       ha-sefer etmol.
       the-book yesterday
       'That man, we gave the book to him yesterday.'
    b. *La-iš   ha-ze,   anaxnu natannu lo   et
       to-the-man the-that we   gave   to-him Go
       ha-sefer etmol.
       the-book yesterday
       'To that man, we gave the book to him yesterday.'

The fact that, in many languages, the Theme must be produced in absolute form is consistent with the view that it is produced in comparative independence from the following clause.

To this it must be added that in certain languages the Theme can ALSO be produced with the case marking which would be appropriate if the Theme did in fact occupy a position within the clause. According to Comrie (1973b) this is the case in Russian, where the following constructions occur side by side:

(39) a. Televizory,   v   ètom   magazine
       televisions-nom   in   this   shop
       ix   mnogo
       3pl-gen   many
    b. Televizorov,   v   ètom   magazine
       televisions-gen   in   this   shop
       ix   mnogo
       3pl-gen   many
       'As for televisions, there are plenty of them in this shop.'

The existence of constructions such as (39b) might be taken as an argument in favour of an analysis which extracts the Theme from its position within the clause. From our point of view we will rather assume that in such cases the Theme may anticipate and formally express the function which it is going to fulfil in the ensuing clause.

(iv) In terms of Speaker's behaviour, finally, it seems correct to say that S will often produce a Theme before he has formed a clear idea of what sort of clause he is going to produce about it. It is quite common to find hesitation phenomena between Theme and clause:

(40) a *As for the students, well, let me see ...*
  b *As for the students, mmm, I don't know really ...*
  c *As for the students, ehm, o.k., let me think ...*

Such hesitation phenomena would be difficult to explain on the assumption that the Theme is extracted from an antecedently completely developed clause.[13]

On the basis of these various arguments it will be assumed here that the Theme originates outside the clause. The Theme is not extracted from the clause; rather, the clause is adjusted to the Theme.

Although Theme and clause are therefore comparatively independent of each other, this does not mean that just any term and just any clause can be combined into a Theme+Clause construction. With respect to possible relations between Theme and clause, two subcases must be distinguished, which can be represented as:

(41) a. $(x_i)_{Theme}$, $(...(x_i)...)_{Clause}$
  b. $(x_i)_{Theme}$, $(............)_{Clause}$

In the first subtype (41a), the Theme is resumed within the clause. This resumption is marked by a personal or demonstrative pronoun coreferential with the Theme, as in:

(42) *As for John, he is crazy about bronze statues.*

---

13. In his discussion of Theme constructions in Hungarian, De Groot (1981c) notes that in certain conditions the case form of the Theme may be explained as a resumption from an earlier clause rather than an anticipation of the following clause.

394 *Extra-clausal constituents*

In the case of this type of relation, the constraints on Theme+Clause combinations can be described in semantic / syntactic terms: the Theme must be such that it could also have occupied the corresponding position within the clause. Thus, the fact that (42) is a well-formed Theme+Clause combination correlates with the well-formedness of:

(43)   *John is crazy about bronze statues.*

Conversely, the relevant selection restrictions have been violated in both (44a) and (44b):

(44) a.   **As for bronze statues, they are crazy about John.*
    b.   **Bronze statues are crazy about John.*

Such selectional relations, however, cannot be established in the case of constructions of subtype (41b), in which the Theme does not recur in the clause. But even in these constructions there are restrictions on possible Theme+Clause combinations. Ross (1970: 231 note 20) contrasted the following examples:

(45) a.   *As for the students, adolescents almost never have any sense.*
    b.   **As for the students, hydrogen is the first element in the periodic table.*
(46) a.   *As for Paris, the Eiffel Tower is really spectacular.*
    b.   **As for Albuquerque, the Eiffel Tower is really spectacular.*

Ross noted that such differences as these cannot be accounted for in purely semantic / syntactic terms, since the evaluation of these Theme+Clause combinations obviously hinges on knowledge of the world rather than on knowledge of the language.

From our point of view this confirms that Theme is a pragmatic function. As such, it is co-dependent on the pragmatic information of S and A, and it stands to reason that the admissible relations between Theme and clause must also be defined in pragmatic terms. Using the pragmatic principle of Relevance in the sense of Grice (1975), we can formulate the following condition:

(47)   For any pair of Theme T and clause C to make sense, it must be relevant to pronounce C with respect to T.

As with most pragmatic conditions, (47) is a matter of more-or-less rather than of all-or-none. Judgements of Relevance will co-vary with the full array of pragmatic information of S and A. For instance, for someone who believes that Albuquerque has its own Eiffel Tower, (46b) is immediately fully acceptable. Such constructions should not be termed ungrammatical, but rather incoherent with respect to a constellation of pragmatic information in which (47) is not fulfilled.

In constructions of subtype (41b), then, the relation between Theme and clause is mediated ONLY via the pragmatic condition (47). In constructions of subtype (41a), this condition is mirrored by the structural relation which links the Theme to the position of (x_i) within the clause. But that structural relation is simply one way in which the pragmatic condition can be fulfilled, because, if the Theme is such that it could in principle also occur within the clause, then that clause must certainly be a potentially relevant thing to say about the Theme.

Note that in languages which allow zero anaphora, the difference between a Theme+Clause construction and a simple clause with preposed Topic may be very slight, reduced to a mere difference in intonation:

(48) a. *That man, I hate Ø.*
b. *That man I hate.*

Conversely, when a language requires a cross-referential element in any main verb corresponding to a certain function in the clause, then again the difference between Theme and Topic may be slight. Compare:

(49) a. *That man, he-hates me.*
b. *That man he-hates me.*

In such cases, then, the prosodic break is the only property distinguishing the Theme+Clause construction from a simple construction with what I will call an "Integrated Theme" below.

— *Condition.* A discourse, discourse episode, or speech act may be introduced by a condition which limits the validity of the ensuing information to a world of which the condition is true. In such cases, the Orientation will typically take the form of a conditional subordinate clause. Consider:

(50) *If you promise to stop crying, then you may have a sweet.*

Note that this usage of the initial conditional has several properties characteristic of the ECCs: there is a break (at least, an inflection) in the prosodic contour and the initial clause is resumed by a pronominal element (*then*) in the second clause. Further, that second clause might, within an appropriate setting, be used all by itself, without the preceding conditional clause.

Conditional clauses may be used by S to "create" a world or "mental model" within which that which is expressed in the apodosis clause is claimed to be relevant or true. If S is uncertain about the truth of the protasis, the result will be a Potentialis construction; if S is certain that the protasis is false, the result is an Irrealis construction:[14]

(51) a. *If John is rich, then he can help us out.* (Potentialis)
    b. *If John were rich, then he could help us out.* (Irrealis)

Note that a conditional protasis may, but need not be realized as a preclausal ECC. The resumptive *then* in (51) points to ECC status; absence of such a resumptive element suggests that the conditional protasis is integrated into the clause structure as a conditional satellite:

(52) a. *If John is rich he can help us out.*
    b. *If John were rich he could help us out.*

In a strongly verb-second language such as Dutch, this difference is confirmed by constituent order.

Several authors have argued for the thesis that conditionals are Topics (e.g. Haiman 1978). I believe the matter is a little bit more complex: first of all, conditionals may occur clause-internally and clause-externally. If they occur clause-externally, they may be formally expressed by the same marker as is also used to characterize Themes. Rather than saying that Conditionals (in this usage) are Themes, we shall assume that the marker in question signals the higher-level Orientation function, which encompasses Themes, Conditions, and Settings. This predicts that in languages in which Themes and Conditions can be marked in the same way, Settings can also be so marked. Below I will present some evidence that this may indeed be the case in certain languages.

— *Setting*. Each subsequent contribution to the discourse must be anchored in the setting as built up in the preceding discourse (Vet 1986a, 1988). At the

---

14. For a fuller discussion of the semantics of conditionals, see Dik (1990b).

beginning of any discourse, if no antecedent expectation pattern has been established, the initial setting is defined by the parameters of the Deictic Centre: Speaker S, Addressee A, Time of speaking t_0 and Place of speaking l_0:

(53)   <S, A, t_0, l_0>

Any discourse contribution may either further specify the setting, or describe some event as occurring against the background of the given setting. Such event descriptions may implicitly modify the setting. I here restrict the notion of "setting" to the time and place coordinates defined explicitly or implicitly in the discourse. ECCs may help to specify these coordinates. Suppose it has been established that we are talking about a John Parker. Then, an utterance such as:

(54)   *John felt awful.*

will make A wonder when and where (and under which circumstances) this was the case. Sometimes, only the time is important:

(55)   *In the beginning of spring, John felt awful.*

Sometimes only the place coordinate is important:

(56)   *In Paris, John felt awful.*

Sometimes both are relevant:

(57)   *In Paris, in the beginning of spring, John felt awful.*

Since every SoA is itself explicitly or implicitly defined by time and space coordinates, a setting may be specified by describing a concurrent SoA:

(58)   *When Mary had left for New York, John felt awful.*

Vet (1988) argues that the difference between the French Imparfait and Passé Simple may be understood in such a way that expressions in the Imparfait contribute to the specification of the setting, whereas expressions in the Passé Simple describe events which occur against the background of the established setting.[15] Since each event may modify the setting, the dynamic progression of the discourse can then be symbolized as a sequence of the form:

(59)   Setting$_0$ - Event$_1$ - Setting$_1$ - Event$_2$ - Setting$_2$ -...

Note that, just as in the case of conditionals, Setting specifications may occur in preclausal Orientation position, but may also be integrated into the clause structure.

— *General Orientation markers*. Certain languages have markers which can be used to characterize Themes, Conditions, and Settings, and which can thus be interpreted as general Orientation markers. Consider the following examples.

Godié (Marchese 1977) has a final marker *n*∧ which can be used both after clauses and after complex terms with the characteristic properties of Orientation. The resulting Orientation constituent also plays a frequent role in Tail-Head linking (see 18.6.5.), thus contributing to the cohesion of Godié discourse. Consider:

(60)   ... *nú*   ∧   *yi*   ɔ   *ní.*   ∧   *ní*   ɔ
         and   I   potential   him   see   I   see-completive   him
         n∧, *nú*   ɔ   *yíí*   *k'o*   *búlú.*
         OR and   he   potential-me   up   take
         '... and I found him. When I had found him, then he took me up ...'

The marker *n*∧, as described by Marchese, has just the range of possible values which we listed as subfunctions of Orientation above. It could be neutrally glossed as 'given ...'. This neutral orienting value will then get either conditional, temporal, circumstantial, or thematic interpretations.[16]

Usan (Reesink 1987) has a postposed marker *eng*, which may be used to mark Themes as well as integrated Themes (or Topics):

---

15. This echoes Quintilian's famous statement on the difference between Perfect and Imperfect in Latin: *Perfecto procedit, imperfecto insistit oratio* 'With the Perfect the discourse proceeds, with the Imperfect it makes a standstill'. Perhaps this makes Quintilian the first to claim that Aspect fulfils discourse functions.

16. Marchese uses "topic" as the general cover term for this type of constituent, but this is a matter of terminology.

(61) a. *Munon eng, wonou bur um-orei.*
man his pig die-3sg.past
'As for the man, his pig died.'
b. *Munon eng wonou bur um-orei.*
man his pig die-3sg.past
'The man his pig died.'

In (61a) the Theme is set off from the clause by a prosodic break; in (61b) the constituent *munon eng* has been integrated into the clause, so that *munon eng wonou bur* 'the man his pig' functions as one unified term.[17]

The marker *eng* has demonstrative properties, and in many cases can be glossed as 'given (that) ...' (cf. Reesink 1983). The structure 'X *eng*, Y' may now also be used with a predication in the position of X (Reesink 1983: 200):[18]

(62) *Wau eâb igor-iner eng, unor mâni*
child cry.ss be-3sg.uf mother yam
utibâ.
she.will.give.him
'Should the child be crying, his mother will give him yam'

This same construction may yield what in English would be paraphrased by means of a relative clause (Reesink 1983: 188):[19]

(63) *Munon qemi bau-or eng,*
man bow take-3sg.past
qemi eng ye me ge-au.
bow I not see-nom
'Given that the man took the bow, I didn't see the bow.'
= 'I didn't see the bow which the man took.'

---

17. Note that integration of a Theme into the clause may be one source of the possessive construction with cross-referential reflection of the Possessor on the Possessed.
18. ss = same subject (see *TFG1*: 13.3.2.); uf = uncertain future.
19. A nominalized form of the main verb appears in negative clauses.

We thus see that predicational Orientations may yield constructions which can be paraphrased as conditionals, as in (62), and that they may also provide a source for the development of a particular kind of relative construction. The latter type of development was discussed in 4.3.3.2.[20] In terms of the present terminology, *eng* could be termed a general Orientation marker.

Zulgo (Haller—Watters 1984) has a particle *ká* which is quite generally used to construe linguistic expressions with the organization Theme *ká*, Clause. The Theme can be any kind of term, corresponding to any kind of function in the clause. With one exception (Instrument), the Theme is not marked for its functional status. Compare:

(64) a. hanáwà á-vəl   síngwè   á   ɔbay   áta.
         Hanawa he-gave money   to   chief   that
         'Hanawa gave money to that chief.'
   b. ɔbay   áta ká,   hanáwà á-vəl-ár   síngwè.
       chief   that Theme   Hanawa he-gave-to.him money
       'As for that chief, Hanawa gave him money.'
   c. *a ɔbay   áta ká,   hanáwà á-vəl-ár   síngwè.
       to chief that Theme   Hanawa he-gave-to.him money
       'As for that chief, Hanawa gave him money.'

Note that the resumptive element *-ár* "to him" in (64b) is suffixed to the verb.

As Haller—Watters show, Zulgo exploits the Theme+Clause construction more than other languages do. There may be more than one term (coordinated) in Theme position, so that we get constructions corresponding to:

(65)   *As for Hanawa and that money, he gave it to the chief.*

The marker *ká* may also follow a full proposition, as in:

(66)   Á-dá   á   dala   kínèhe ká,   aká-lé   áà
       he-went   to   field   now   Theme, he-come.across   at
       mánàhà   gùrùv.
       ripe   figs
       'As he was going across the field, he came across some ripe figs.'

---

20. Similar phenomena from other Papuan languages are discussed in Haiman (1978).

At first sight, *ká* here functions as a temporal or circumstantial subordinator, but Haller and Watters argue that there may be quite different types of semantic relation between two clauses joined in this way, and that the only common factor is, indeed, the common pragmatic function which we have called Orientation.[21]

17.2.3.3. Tails. Just as a clause may be preceded by an Orientation which, in a sense, "sets the scene" for the interpretation of the clause, so it may be followed by loosely adjoined constituents which add bits of information which may be relevant to a correct understanding of the clause. Such constituents may also be added to parts of a clause, for example, to terms.

To such constituents we assign the pragmatic function Tail, defined in general as characterizing constituents which present information meant to clarify or modify (some constituent contained in) the unit to which they are adjoined.

In the following examples the constituents in roman typescript have Tail function:

(67)   *He's a nice chap,* your brother.
(68)   *I didn't like it very much,* that book of yours.
(69)   *I like John very much,* your brother I mean.
(70)   *John gave the book to a girl,* in the library.

In (67)-(69) the Tail constituents add a further specification to a term which is already contained in the clause. It is as if S fears that his initial, rather unspecific term may be insufficient for A to identify the intended referent. In (70) the Tail adds a specification of a location which has not yet been referred to in the clause. However, since any action necessarily takes place somewhere, the added constituent may nevertheless be seen as a further specification of the content of the clause.

Since a Tail constituent most often provides some additional information pertaining to the proper interpretation of the clause as a whole, its typical position is after the clause. However, since a Tail may also pertain to some constituent within the clause, Tails may occur as parenthetical insertions with-

---

21. Haller—Watters use the term "Topic", but explicitly identify this with FG Theme.

in the clause. As such, they will typically be set off from the clause proper by prosodic breaks:

(71)   *I saw John hand it - the money I mean - to the girl.*
(72)   *He pretended that it was there - in the library - that the whole thing took place.*

In fact, we must even allow for the possibility that a Theme will be immediately followed by a Tail, as in:

(73)   *That chap   - your brother I mean -   what's his name?*
       Theme......   Tail..........................   Clause................

Since the Tail is always adjoined to some preceding material, usually the clause, it can always orient itself to the function of that item which it is meant to clarify. This explains why Tails cannot usually be produced in absolute form, but must carry the marking which corresponds to the item in the clause to which they correspond. In this respect they are different from Themes, which take absolute form more often. Consider again the Russian examples in (39), repeated here as (74):

(74) a. *Televizory,*   *v*   *ètom*   *magazine*   *ix*   *mnogo.*
         televisions-nom   in   this   shop   3pl-gen   many
     b. *Televizorov,*   *v*   *ètom*   *magazine*   *ix*   *mnogo.*
         televisions-gen   in   this   shop   3pl-gen   many
         'As for televisions, there are plenty of them in this shop.'

In Russian the Theme can be produced either in absolute form or as marked for its function in the clause. A Tail, however, can only be produced as marked for the function of its equivalent in the clause. Compare the following Russian examples with those in (74):

(75) a. *V*   *ètom*   *magazine*   *ix*   *mnogo,*   *televizorov.*
         in   this   shop   3.pl.gen   many   televisions.gen
         'There are plenty of them in this shop, televisions I mean.'
     b. **V*   *ètom*   *magazine*   *ix*   *mnogo,*   *televizory.*
         in   this   shop   of-them   many   televisions.nom
         'There are plenty of them in this shop, televisions I mean.'

The functional difference between Theme and Tail is thus reflected in this formal distinction.

In a corpus study of Tails in English Geluykens (1987b) established the following points:
— Tails are especially used in unplanned spoken conversation;
— in most occurrences they represent a conversational repair strategy in the sense of Schegloff (1979): S, after having produced a pronominal element in the body of the clause, fearing that the reference may not be clear, adds more explicit identifying information in the Tail;
— the repair is most often 'self-initiated';
— it is usually preceded by a short pause;
— it is often accompanied by a metacommunicative expression such as *I mean*;
— the strategy is typically used when in the eyes of S there may be lack of clarity concerning the reference. This occurs especially when (i) the pronominal element in the clause might be taken as coreferential to more than one entity in the preceding discourse, (ii) when the referent is "inferrable" (SubTopic) rather than explicitly mentioned in the preceding; such SubTopics are typically part new, part given, and S can not always be certain that A has already established the appropriate "bridging assumptions".

17.2.3.4. Integration of Theme and Tail into the clause. In the preceding we have assumed that all languages can make use of a Theme+Clause construction, but that languages may differ in the frequency and the circumstances in which they do so. I believe that a similar assumption is warranted for the Clause+Tail construction. That is, in certain languages this construction will be highly marked or even evaluated as ungrammatical. In other languages it will be a quite normal way to produce linguistic expressions. Compare in this respect the following constructions from English and French:

(76)   *John, he gave it to Peter, your book.*
(77)   *Jean, il l'a donné à Pierre, ton livre.*

(76) is rather highly marked in English, but (77) is a quite normal way of expressing oneself in French. A construction of this type is more highly grammaticalized in French than it is in English. Correspondingly, we may expect that the pragmatic functionality of Theme and Tail in French has lost some of its markedness as compared to the corresponding constructions in English. Such a process of demarking may lead to a situation in which constructions of this type become the normal way of expressing a clause. At that

moment, the status of the pronominal elements within the clause will have changed: they will act as cross-referencing elements rather than as independent pronouns. At the same time, the prosodic breaks will be levelled out, so that we get prosodically unified expressions of the following form:

(78)   *Jean il-l'a-donné à Pierre ton livre.*

This is of course the type of construction which we often find in languages with cross-referencing pronominal elements, or with agreement markers which clearly betray their pronominal origin.

Givón (1976) has advanced the hypothesis that verbal agreement in general originates through developments of this kind. In his terminology, the grammaticalization process can be interpreted in terms of a gradual demarking of an original marked construction with either a topic-shifted constituent (= Theme), or an afterthought-topic (= Tail). For a further elaboration of this subject, see De Groot—Limburg (1986).

Given this demarking process, we may expect intermediate construction types, in which a Theme has already been drawn into the clause, but still has a number of its original Theme properties. In such cases we shall speak of Integrated Themes. There is evidence from different languages that constructions with Integrated Theme may be exploited for special pragmatic purposes. In the same way, overexploitation of the Tail position may lead to absorption of the Tail into the clause, with a possible intermediate stage of a construction with Integrated Tail.

As an example of a language which is characterized by such overexploitation of the Tail function, consider Hixkaryana, as described in Derbyshire (1979, 1981). The Tail position in this language may even consist of sequences of terms, stacked onto each other, each subsequent term providing some further specification of the intended referent: "Such NP sequences constitute the principal means of expressing nominal modification: there are no adjectives or relative clauses of the usual kind." (Derbyshire 1981). An example of this kind is:

(79)   *Wewe   y-ama-xe   ni-nyah-txowi,   noro,*
         tree   3-fell-purp   3Ag3Go-send-past,   he,
         horykomo,   owto   yohi.
         important-man,   village   chief-of
         'In order to fell trees he sent them, he, the important man, the village chief.'

Corresponding to this frequent exploitation of Tails, these Tails may, but need not be set off from the clause by an intonation break (Derbyshire 1981). The resulting construction with Integrated Tail may be presumed to lie at the basis of the uncommon OVS ordering of Hixkaryana.

In a similar way, Hyman (1975) has suggested that the integration of Tails (his "Afterthoughts") into the clause may contribute to a shift from SOV to SVO patterning. Compare:

(80) a. *My sister your brother very much like.* (SOV)
 b. *My sister him very much like, your brother.* (SoV,Tail)
 c. *My sister (him) very much like your brother.* (S(o)VO)
 d. *My sister very much like your brother.* (SVO)

The scenario for such a shift would be as follows. Starting from an SOV pattern as in (80a) we assume that (80b), with postposed Tail and a pronominal object (o) in the main clause, occurs as a pragmatically marked variant. Through overexploitation of this variant, it loses its markedness and correspondingly its typical prosodic structure. The original pronominal element in the clause has now become a redundant cross-referencing element, which may become optional or may disappear. The final result of this would be an SVO pattern as in (80d).

17.2.4. Discourse execution

The last group of ECCs we want to discuss are those which play a role in the expression of the actual content of the discourse.

— *Responses*. Responses are ECCs produced in reaction to what the other participant is saying or has just said. Although languages typically lack specific grammatical sentence types for "answering", they usually have a restricted set of ECCs which have the specific function of providing a reaction to some question, or to any other type of speech act which asks for some kind of response. Such Responses can be distinguished into several types:

(i) Full Responses are responses by means of which S signals agreement / disagreement (full or partial) with what the other has just said. Full Responses count as turns, either by themselves, or in combination with further material from the same speaker. Full Responses which can stand on their own as a complete turn are such English expressions as:

(81) a. *yes, no*
  b. *perhaps, certainly, certainly not, I hope not*
  c. *it is, it isn't, she certainly is*

For the distinction between initiative and reactive speech acts, see Franck (1980). Goffman (1981) distinguishes a subcategory of "Response Cries" such as *gee!, sure!, god!*. One might doubt the ECC status of such expressions as (81c), but note that these expressions are not complete clauses, and can be understood only as signalling agreement or disagreement with that which the other has just said.

(ii) Response Initiators are elements which by themselves do not constitute a Full Response, but serve to introduce (and in certain ways qualify) S's reaction to what the other has just said. Here we meet English *well* again:[22]

(82) A: *What about coming here on the way (.) or doesn't that give you enough time?*
  B: *Well, no, I'm supervising here.*

Such Response Initiators may serve a variety of functions, the common denominator of which would seem to be that they make the answer a little bit less direct. Levinson (1983) at different places mentions the following possible functions of (this usage of) *well*:

(83) *well* signals
  (a) that the response may not be the preferred reaction to the other's question;
  (b) that it may not be the full answer which presumably the other requires (i.e. falls short with respect to Quantity);
  (c) that the answer may not be quite to the point, although potentially relevant to what the other would like to know (i.e. falls short with respect to Relevance).

Example (82B) demonstrates, incidentally, that Response Initiators and Full Responses (such as *no*) can be combined with each other.

— *Tags*. The term "tag" is commonly used for the constituents in roman typeface in such constructions as:

---

22. From Levinson (1983: 335).

(84) *It's rather hot in here,* isn't it?
(85) *It's not very warm in here,* is it?
(86) *Open the door,* will you?

Tags belong to the class of ECCs in that they occur outside the clause proper, typically set off from it by an prosodic break. They were, however, already discussed in 11.5. as a means of converting the basic illocution of the preceding clause into another illocution

17.3. Conclusion

In this chapter we have tried to show that Extra Clausal Constituents fulfil a wide range of functions in the organization of discourse and that their grammatical status cannot be derived from the clause with which they occur. Both these characteristics suggest that Extra Clausal Constituents are best interpreted in the context of a grammatical model that takes levels of linguistic organization higher than the clause into account. The next chapter is meant as a first step towards such a model.

18. Towards a functional grammar of discourse

18.0. Introduction

Functional Grammar wishes to describe and explain natural languages in a way which is pragmatically and psychologically adequate. By pragmatic adequacy we understand the degree to which the linguistic description accounts for the fact that languages are used for communicative purposes in verbal interaction. By psychological adequacy we mean the degree to which the linguistic description is compatible with what is known about the mental processes which are involved in the interpretation and the production of linguistic expressions.

The requirements of pragmatic and psychological adequacy can be summarized by saying that a Functional Grammar should qualify as a component or module in an integrated model of the natural language user (NLU). Together with other modules in such an overall model, it should make us understand how it is that NLUs are able to communicate with each other through verbal interaction.

NLUs do not speak in isolated sentences or clauses, but combine these into longer and more complex stretches for which we may use the general cover term "discourse". A discourse is more (much more) than an arbitrary sequence of clauses. Therefore, even if we had an optimal theory of the clause, this theory would still leave much to be desired when considered as a component in a wider theory of NLU's communicative competence. Moreover, since clauses, in their internal structure, are sensitive to a variety of discourse factors, an "optimal" theory of the (isolated) clause is simply impossible.

It follows that the theory of FG, if it is to live up to its self-imposed standards of adequacy, should in the long run account for the functional grammar of discourse.[1] In other words, it should show how clauses can be combined into coherent stretches of talk, conversation, or written text. At the same time, it is evident that this is a very high aim for a theory of grammar to strive for, and that we have only the bare outlines of what a theory of discourse should look like. Therefore, I will in this chapter restrict myself to

---

1. Cf. Van Dijk (1990) for a recent argument to this effect.

18.1. Intention, content, interpretation, and knowledge

In *TFG1*: 1.3. I sketched a model of verbal interaction of the following form:

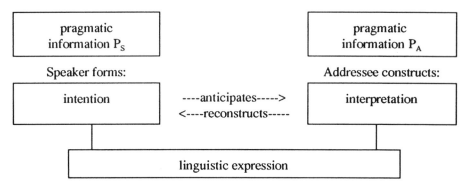

Figure 1. A model of verbal interaction.

Important elements of this model are the following: in any form of verbal interaction, S forms some *communicative intention* which is then partially coded in the content of a linguistic expression. The coding may be more or less explicit. The degree of explicitness is co-determined by S's *pragmatic information*, his full body of knowledge or content of mind at the moment of speaking. This pragmatic information contains, as a proper subpart, a hypothesis on the part of S concerning the pragmatic information of A, and an anticipation of how A is likely to interpret the linguistic expression. A's task, on the other hand, is to try and reconstruct S's intention in his final interpretation of the content. In doing so, A, for his part, is aided by his own pragmatic information which, again, contains a hypothesis about S's pragmatic information as a proper subpart. Pragmatic information is divided into (i) *general information*, (ii) *situational information*, (iii) *contextual information*.

As a general model of verbal communication this model is obviously also relevant for discourse production and interpretation. Most important in this respect is that any discourse is produced from, and projected into, the full pragmatic information of S and A, respectively, and that no discourse is interpretable on the basis of its intrinsic content alone. Even if certain discourse types may be less dependent on discourse-external knowledge than others, any discourse relies, in its development, on contextual information and on the huge body of general knowledge that S and A possess and partially share in their *shared* or *common knowledge*.[2]

In view of the importance of pragmatic information in discourse production and interpretation, it is useful at the outset to be somewhat more specific about the different types of knowledge contained in pragmatic information. Within pragmatic information we can distinguish at least the following types of knowledge:

1 Long-term knowledge
Knowledge which S and A possess before entering a specific communicative event.
   1.1   Linguistic (Knowledge about the language).
          1.1.1   Lexical (Knowledge of the lexical predicates of the language, their semantic and morpho-syntactic properties, and their mutual interrelations).
          1.1.2   Grammatical (Knowledge of the rules and principles which define the underlying grammatical structures of the language, and of the rules and principles through which these underlying structures can be expressed in linguistic expressions).
          1.1.3   Pragmatic (Knowledge of the rules and principles (maxims, conventions), which govern the correct use of linguistic expressions in verbal interaction).
   1.2   Non-linguistic (Knowledge about the world and other possible worlds).
          1.2.1   Referential (Knowledge about entities such as persons, things, places, etc.).
          1.2.2   Episodic (Knowledge about states of affairs (actions, processes, positions, states) that entities have been / are / will be involved in).
          1.2.3   General (Knowledge about general rules and principles (laws, tendencies) governing the world and other possible worlds).

---

2. Compare Van Dijk—Kintsch (1983) for the many cognitive and contextual presuppositions involved in discourse comprehension.

2 Short-term knowledge (Knowledge derived from the communicative event and the situation in which it takes place).
   2.1   Situational (Knowledge derived from what can be perceived in and inferred from the communicative situation, including the basic parameters of the "deictic centre" of the communicative event).
   2.2   Textual (Knowledge derived from the verbal information conveyed in the communicative event).
          2.2.1   Referential (Knowledge concerning entities, as mentioned in the text ("discourse entities / topics")).
          2.2.2   Episodic (Knowledge concerning states of affairs such entities are involved in, as described in the text).
          2.2.3   General (Knowledge about general rules and principles, as mentioned in the text).

In discourse production and interpretation each of these types of knowledge may play a crucial role. Usually, many of these types of information interact in determining the correct interpretation of a discourse, or the correct formulation of what the Speaker[3] is going to say.

18.2. Dynamic Discourse Models

A discourse is a dynamic phenomenon which develops in time. As the discourse unfolds the pragmatic information of S and A is activated and updated continuously in different ways. In the first place, S and A activate and retrieve certain parts of their long-term knowledge to the extent that they are relevant to the production and interpretation of this particular discourse. Secondly, they build up a short-term mental model of what is transmitted in the discourse itself (a *Discourse Model*). Thirdly, the communicative partners may both update their *long-term* knowledge on the basis of the interpreted information which they have gained through the discourse. The latter is the case if they decide (consciously or subconsciously) that the information obtained is important enough to be stored for later usage.[4]

---

3. Wherever Speaker (S) is used this is meant to include the Writer, and wherever Addressee (A) is used this is meant to include the Reader.
4. The decision whether certain information is going to be retained or forgotten is obviously not always a conscious decision on the part of participants.

The Discourse Model which the communicative partners build up is a *partial* and a *dynamic* mental model.[5] It is *partial* in the sense that it never contains (indeed, can never contain) everything there is to know about all possible worlds. It is *dynamic* in the sense that it is continuously updated as the discourse proceeds. This is why later parts of the discourse may rely upon contextual information which has been provided in the preceding context. Following context, however, also plays a crucial role: each step in the discourse typically projects structure onto the discourse that is yet to come; each move creates an expectation pattern about the further steps that are yet to be taken. These forward projections may be explicitly mentioned by S (as in *I should like to tell you a story about what happened to me this morning*, *I have three comments on your proposal*), but even if they are not, the pragmatic long-term knowledge of A includes knowledge of likely continuations of different discourse types. From this it also follows that certain provisional interpretations already made at a given point in the development of the discourse may be clarified or even modified through information which is provided in the further development of the discourse.[6]

A Discourse Model is thus a kind of book-keeping of what the discourse has so far achieved, where we are at this moment, and what is probably yet to come; it serves to help S and A to arrive at an integrated final interpretation of the whole discourse once it is finished. Several attempts have been made to come to grips with such forms of dynamic discourse representation.[7]

---

5. For the notion "mental model" see Johnson-Laird (1983), Van Dijk—Kintsch (1983).

6. While elements referring to or relying on earlier context are termed *anaphorical*, the term *cataphorical* is sometimes used for those devices which point prospectively to elements of the discourse which are yet to come. Seen in this way, all those discourse devices which project structure and expectations on what is yet to come represent cataphorical discourse strategies.

7. See especially the work of Van Dijk and Kintsch (1983). Johnson-Laird's (1983) ideas on the dynamic formation of Mental Models are centrally relevant here. From a more logically oriented point of view Kamp (1984) has developed a "Discourse Representation Theory". See also, within the context of FG, Vet (1986).

18.3. Three perspectives on a functional grammar of discourse

The problems posed by the production, the organization, and the interpretation of Discourse, formidable as they are, can be approached from many different angles. In this chapter I will approach these problems from three distinct but complementary perspectives.

The first perspective takes a constructive approach to the problem, and can be summarized in the following question:

(Q1)   When a discourse event is initiated or being executed, what decisions of S have bearing on whole stretches of clauses rather than on the individual clauses that make up the discourse?

For example, when S decides to "tell the story of his/her life", this decision fundamentally affects a whole stretch of discourse rather than a single clause, both structurally and content-wise. No clause grammar can ever approach an account of the global macrostructure (Van Dijk 1980) which is opened up by this decision.

The second perspective concerns the overall organisation of a discourse, now considered as a finished product. It can be formulated in the following questions:

(Q2)   When a discourse is considered as a finished product, what kinds of structural patterns can be discerned in it? What are the different levels of discourse organisation? What units can be established at these different levels, and how do these different units combine into larger wholes?

The third perspective is concerned with the notion of discourse coherence and can be summarized in the following question:

(Q3)   Which factors contribute to the degree of coherence of a discourse, both locally, as regards the various ways and means which signal higher-level continuity rather than discontinuity between subsequent clauses, and more globally, in the sense in which whole discourse episodes can be said to be coherent or incoherent?

These three questions will be discussed in 18.4., 18.5., and 18.6., respectively.

18.4. Global discourse decisions: scope phenomena in discourse

18.4.0. Introduction

In building up a discourse, S takes many decisions which do not affect just the next single clause, but whole series of clauses of varying length. Such discourse decisions take the whole discourse, or part of the discourse, in their *scope*. In this respect a discourse can in many ways be likened to a piece of music.

At the beginning of a musical score there may, first of all, be a title which reveals something about the type or *genre* of the composition. For example, if the title is "Alegrías", this reveals that the composition represents or is based on one type of Flamenco music. For those who know Spanish the title (*alegrías* 'joys') also reveals something about the *tone* of the composition. Secondly, there is the *key* to the composition; if that key is, for example, A major, this is indicated by a number of sharps which symbolize standard modifications of the relevant tones which they have in their scope. This scope, and this is crucial, extends through the whole composition, and remains valid as long as no contrary information has been provided (when local modifications are required within the composition, these so-called "accidentals" only affect the bar within which they occur: they are short-lived modifications which yield to the global key as soon as their limited scope has expired). Furthermore, there is information on the *timing* and the internal structure of a bar. For example, 3/4 would indicate that there are three crotchets to a bar. What is essential is that, again, this information is held to be relevant for the whole composition, as long as no contrary local information is provided. Further, a composition is usually divided into several subparts, some of which may be defined as partial or full repetitions of each other. Both the composition as a whole and its subparts may carry indications of rhythm, loudness, and performance in such terms as *forte* 'loud' or *allegro* 'lively', 'briskly', which extend across the whole subpart which they have in their scope.

In the same way, the title ("Sonnet") or the introduction (*Do you know this one?*) to a discourse may reveal much about the discourse genre to follow, and many settings are fixed for the discourse as a whole, remaining valid until further notice. Just like a musical composition, a discourse is usally divided into subparts (episodes, sections, paragraphs) which may have their own local settings which extend only across the scope allotted to them, yielding to higher-level settings when that scope has come to an end. Several elements in a discourse may finally reveal the tone with which it is intended to be received.

By *global discourse decisions* we mean such settings as are relevant to the whole discourse or to one of its subparts, rather than accidentally to the wording of a single clause. Let us consider some of these decisions in a top-down way.

18.4.1. Entering a discourse event

At the highest level the primary decision is whether or not to enter into a certain discourse event at all. If one does, one is then committed to a series of consequences which follow from this initial step.

Any discourse is embedded within a discourse event (or speech event, Hymes 1972), within which the discourse content (or discourse in the more restricted sense) is carried out. All through the discourse proper we remain within the discourse event brackets, and a number of activities carried out during the execution of the actual discourse content pertain to the event rather than to the content layer.

A discourse event is a social, interpersonal event defined by conventions and institutions regulating at least the following parameters (cf. Hymes 1972):

(i) the participants (S(s) and A(s)) and their mutual relations.

(ii) the rights and duties of the participants, both with respect to interaction (who may speak when and where?), and with respect to content (who can say what when and where?)

(iii) the time and place and setting of speaking.

Clearly then, the decision to enter a discourse event can normally not be fulfilled by producing only a single clause.

18.4.2. Choosing a discourse genre

When the term "discourse" is used in the general sense in which it was introduced above it will immediately be clear that a number of different types of discourse must be distinguished. Such types or *genres* can be crossclassified along a number of parameters, the most important of which are the following:

(i) Medium: spoken vs. written discourse;
(ii) Participation: monologue, dialogue, polylogue;
(iii) Participant relation: direct (face-to-face), semi-indirect (e.g. through telephone, radio, television), indirect (as in the case of writing and reading a written text);
(iv) Formality: degree of institutionalization of the discourse event, degree of formality of interaction style;
(v) Communicative purpose, for example: passing time, narrative, argumentative, diverting, didactic, aesthetic.

Examples of genre in the sense in which this terms is used here are Conversation, Interview, Lecture, Telephone Call, Sonnet, Meeting, Letter, and Fairy-tale.

The choice of a genre has important implications for the way it can be linguistically construed, both globally (at the level of macrostructure), and locally, at the level of the microstructure of individual clauses or even lower-level constituents.

18.4.3. Choosing a discourse style

The choice of a genre imposes certain limits on the *style* which can be used in implementing the genre. For example, S will not normally start a lecture with *Well, boys and girls, let's have some fun!*. Within the limits imposed by the genre, however, there are usually many choices that can be made concerning the style in which it can be delivered. In this sense "style" may be defined as a sequence of choices through the discourse of means of expression which have consistent values along such polar dimensions as Formality-Informality, Politeness-Familiarity, and Conciseness-Redundancy. Such decisions define settings for the whole discourse, or at least for a substantial part of it (the style may shift during the discourse, but even in that case the style shifts are not determined per clause but rather per discourse phase or episode).

18.4.4. Type of discourse world created

Through the discourse S and A build up a Discourse Model, a mental world against the background of which the successive clauses are to be interpreted. The mental world is never identical to objective reality: even if the discourse pretends to give an objective picture of the outside world, it necessarily does so through the S's conceptualization of that outside world. However, many types of discourse do not even pretend to describe the outside world. They consist in the creation of a world which may have only fictitious, hypothetical, potential, or even counterfactual status. The type of world created in the discourse is partially dependent on the genre chosen. In part, it is determined by the way in which S develops this genre. The choice of the character of the discourse world created is typically made for a whole discourse, or for a phase or episode in the discourse. It essentially affects the ways in which things within this world can be talked about.

For example, if S starts with: *Last night I had a rather intriguing dream ...*, A knows that a dream world is being created within the scope of which a lot of things may be expected, as to both content and verbalization, which would not be expected in a matter-of-fact report on reality.

As a second example, consider S entering a hypothetical argument as in: *Now if X were the case we might expect that Y... However, Y is not the case. Therefore, we may conclude that X is not the case.* The counterfactual conditional at the beginning opens up a bracket within which a hypothetical world is created for as long as the hypothetical argument lasts. Again, the type of world created affects the content and the wording of what goes on inside its scope.

As a third example, consider the introduction of discourse referents (Karttunen 1976). When an entity is introduced into the discourse in a definite or specific mode, that entity receives existential status within the discourse world, and can be referred to again by means of definite anaphorical means:

(1)   *John wants to buy Peter's Volkswagen / a Volkswagen* (specific). *Although second-hand, it is still in good condition. John will get the car next week.*

If, on the other hand, an entity is introduced in a non-specific mode, it does not unconditionally acquire existential status:

(2)   *John wants to buy a Volkswagen* (non-specific). **It is in good condition. *The car will be available next week.*

However, and this is essential here, as long as we stay within the world defined by John's desires, we can refer back to the non-specific entity as if it had existential status within that world:

(3)   *John wants to buy a Volkswagen* (non-specific). *It should be in good condition. The car should be available next week.*

We can thus say: an entity introduced in the non-specific mode does establish a discourse referent as long as we remain within the brackets of the world into which it was introduced. Example (3) shows that the fictitious nature of the world should be re-asserted in each following clause (... *should be* ...), and thus has influence on the wording of the clauses within its scope. Further, the fictitious world creates a bracketing within which anaphorical relations can be established which are not permitted outside the brackets.

18.4.5. Discourse illocution

Each single clause has a certain illocutionary value (see chapter 11 on clause illocution). In fact, however, the illocutionary value of clauses is not arbitrarily fixed per clause. For example, if S decides to tell a fairy-tale, the genre will imply narrative delivery, and thus default declarative illocution throughout the whole discourse. This default declarative illocution may be temporarily suspended when within the narrative the deictic centre shifts to one of the participants in the fairy-tale whose speech acts are reported in Direct Speech. But when this bracketing is closed again, the illocution reverts to default declarative. Whereas the illocutionary value at clause level can be represented as (4a), this *discourse illocution* rather takes a whole (section of) a discourse in its scope, as represented in (4b):

(4) a.   ILL(PROPOSITION)
    b.   ILL(DISCOURSE-EPISODE)

The Discourse Illocution can thus be regarded as a *key* through which the Clause Illocutions of a whole series of clauses are fixed in advance.

The discourse-bracketing nature of illocutionary distinctions also comes out in certain phenomena connected with embedding. Embedding concerns the phenomenon whereby a term containing some clausal, propositional, or predicational structure is inserted into an argument or satellite slot of a higher clause structure; usually we think of embedded constructions in terms of embedded clauses (see chapters 5-7). However, embedding is also relevant at the discourse level. This can be seen from such facts as the following:

(i) *Direct Speech*
In Direct Speech reports, it is a whole discourse rather than a single clause which can be presented as embedded. For example, when we read:

(5)   *After the meeting the minister said: "X"*

we do not usually expect X to consist of only a single clause. X might report a whole speech of the minister in question. Thus, discourses can be embedded in Direct Speech reports.

(ii) *Indirect Speech*
Even in Indirect Speech reports, whole series of clauses rather than single clauses can be embedded. In such a case, later reported clauses are either coordinated to earlier clauses, or take the forms characteristic of Free Indirect Speech. Compare:

(6)   a.   *Peter: "I don't consider this a sound proposal. The budget deficit is not going to diminish through this expenditure. Therefore, I believe we should make do with the old machines."*
      b.   *Peter said that [he didn't consider it a sound proposal, that the budget deficit was not going to diminish through this expenditure and that, consequently, one should make do with the old machines].*
      c.   *Peter said that [he didn't consider it a sound proposal. The budget deficit was not going to diminish through this expenditure. Therefore, one should make do with the old machines].*

When Peter has actually said what is given in (6a), this can be indirectly reported on as in (6b), where several clauses have been coordinated so as to turn them into one (embeddable) compound clause. In (6c), however, only the first clause has been fully subordinated, while nevertheless the following independent clauses have properties (e.g. the Past tense *was not going to*) which reveal that they still belong to the report on what Peter said. Even in that case, therefore, we have to account for the fact that the whole bracketed portion has been embedded. This portion consists of several clauses. Therefore, even in Indirect Speech whole discourses can be embedded.

The same can be illustrated by the rules for Indirect Speech (*Oratio Obliqua*) in Latin. Compare the following:

(7) a. *Ariovistus respondit: "Prius in Galliam veni quam populus Romanus. Quid tibi vis? Cur in meas possessiones venis?"*
'Ariovistus answered: "I arrived in Gaul before the Roman people. What do you want? Why do you trespass on my possessions?"'
b. *Ariovistus respondit [se prius in Galliam venisse quam populus Romanus. Quid sibi vellet? Cur in suas possessiones veniret?]*
'Ariovistus answered that he had arrived in Gaul before the Roman people. What did he want? Why did he trespass on his possessions?'

In (7b), the indirect counterpart of the direct speech report in (7a), the last two clauses of Ariovistus' speech have kept their independent status. But at the same time the verbs in these clauses have shifted from the Present to the Past tense, and from the Indicative to the Subjunctive mood. This mood is required for dependent questions in Latin. Again we see that it is possible for a series of clauses to be embedded under a higher speech act predicate, and thus the embedded unit is a piece of discourse rather than a single clause.

We can relate this embedding of discourse units to the notion of "world creation" discussed in the preceding section: when reporting on what another person has said, we open up a sub-world in which the responsibility for the content is ascribed to that person rather than to the S of the discourse as a whole. Again, we see that the initiation of such a reported world opens up a bracketing which has consequences for both the form and the content of what goes on inside it.

18.4.6. Temporal decisions

When we consider a stretch of discourse we will often find sub-stretches with the same temporal specifications, as in:

(8) Past(X). Past(Y). Past(Z). ...

Clearly, such sequences do not depend on decisions taken per clause. Rather, they follow from a decision on the part of S to relate a certain sequences of past events. At the discourse level, therefore, we could represent (8) as:

(9) Past((X).(Y).(Z)...)

where the Tense operator specifications on successive clauses are inherited from the temporal value which has been fixed for the whole discourse unit. In this way, we could speak of Tense decisions on the discourse level which transcend the Tense specifications on individual clauses.

18.4.7. The introduction and maintenance of Discourse Topics

As we will see in 18.6.3, New Topics are introduced not to live only through single clauses, but to remain available and valid as Given Topics throughout a whole discourse unit or even throughout the whole discourse. When a discourse starts with:

(10)   *Once upon a time there was an ugly duckling.*

we know that not only this or the next clause, but the whole ensuing fairy-tale will be concerned with the duckling in question. Depending on the importance of the entity in question within the discourse, there will be a higher or lower degree of topical continuity (cf. Givon 1983) throughout the discourse unit, i.e., the topical entity will be referred to again and again by anaphorical means through a whole stretch of clauses. In this way, anaphorical chains are created which stretch through whole discourse units and contribute significantly to the coherence of such units. Some aspects of topical continuity were discussed in chapter 10.

18.5. Global structures in discourse[8]

18.5.1. The hierarchical structure of discourse

18.5.1.0. Introduction. In 18.4. we saw that in developing a discourse, S takes a number of decisions which open up a bracketing within which certain things can be done while other things are excluded, both as regards form and as regards content. The highest brackets are those involving the discourse as a whole: entering the discourse event, choosing a genre, and defining a style usually place brackets around the whole discourse. Inside these brackets of the discourse as a whole, discourse sub-units may be created which have a more limited life-cycle, and which yield to higher-level settings as soon as they have

---

   8. For some of the views developed here, compare Komter (1987, 1990) and Polanyi—Scha (1983).

been closed off. Clearly, when we consider the discourse as a finished product, this will have led to such hierarchical structurings as the following:

(11) ENTER 1.
         ENTER 1.1.
            ENTER 1.1.1.
            LEAVE 1.1.1.
            ENTER 1.1.2.
            LEAVE 1.1.2.
         LEAVE 1.1.
         ENTER 1.2.
         LEAVE 1.2.
         ENTER 1.3.
         LEAVE 1.3.
      LEAVE 1.

We may conclude that a discourse has a hierarchical, layered structure. Obviously, this layered structure must be mapped onto the linear order in which the discourse is actually delivered. However, in the actual sequence of clauses it does make an important difference whether the clause belongs to unit 1., unit 1.1., or unit 1.1.1. How do S and A keep track of these levels? Three factors seem to be of major importance in monitoring the hierarchical structure of the discourse through the linear sequence of clauses of which it consists:

(i) Transition phenomena. S may indicate by various means that a transition is being made from one phase of the discourse into another. Such means may signal either an act of Entering into, or an act of Leaving a particular discourse unit.

(ii) Within-brackets features. As we saw in several examples in 18.4., within the brackets of a discourse unit certain things are allowed as regards form and meaning which are not allowed outside these brackets. As long as these features are present in the ongoing discourse, S and A know that they are still within these brackets.

(iii) Metacommunicative explicitation. Discourse Participants may make explicit reference to the kind of hierarchical structure that is being or has been created in the discourse. S may project structure onto the discourse by such metacommunicative contributions as: *I have two questions and one comment on your paper*, or *I can think of three reasons why you should not go to that party*. A, on his part, can call into question certain features of the discourse organization in such metacommunicative contributions as: *Was it still in the summer house that this happened?*, *What was the third reason?*, etc.

The hierarchical structure of the discourse as a whole may in several respects be compared to the structure of the clause. Within the structure of the clause we may distinguish two kinds of complexity. First, we assume that the clause structure as a whole consists of a hierarchically organized design in which higher-level layers include, and thus take into their scope, lower-level layers. Second, there may be various forms of recursion within the clause. We speak of recursion when, within a structure of type X, a new (embedded) structure of type X may be initiated. These two types of complexity can be shown to be also relevant to the discourse level. At this level, as well, we may discern different functionally differentiated layers of organization, such that higher layers take lower layers into their scope. Second, we find certain forms of recursion at the discourse level. We shall consider these two kinds of complexity one by one.

18.5.1.1. Discourse layering. The idea of discourse layering can be conveniently illustrated through the analysis of job interviews presented by Komter (1987, 1990). Komter analysed job interviews in terms of a structure of "boxes within boxes within boxes" of the following general form:[9]

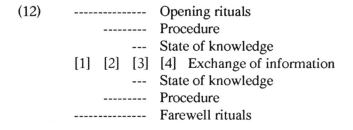

The outer layer [1] concerns the opening and closing moves into and out of the discourse event as a whole, viewed as a social occasion. Within this, at layer [2], there are the procedural steps needed to prepare the ground for and round off the job interview as such. Within this, at layer [3], there is a leveling out of the pragmatic information of the participants as far as it concerns the content of the job interview: at the start, the question is: "do both parties know what they have to know in order to properly conduct the interview?"; at the

---

9. I simplify somewhat by abstracting from some elements more specifically connected with the communicative event "job interview".

end the question is "does any of us have anything more to say or ask before we finish the interview?" The innermost layer [4] deals with the actual subject matter of the interview, that which it is all about. Obviously, [4] may itself consist of different episodes in which different discourse topics or subtopics are treated.

Komter found this type of structure as a recurrent pattern in a great variety of job interviews; she further found that this structure is not simply an observer's artefact, but that it is continuously reflected in the actual behaviour of the participants. Each move of the participants orients to the particular phase they are involved in, and thus contributes to creating and maintaining the structure of the discourse event (Komter 1987: 25). Of particular importance for the structuring of the discourse event were those moves which pertained to transitions from one phase into another.

Just as we have distinguished different functional layers within the structure of the clause, therefore, so we can distinguish different layers in higher-level discourse units. Different types of distinctions can and have been made concerning the layering of discourse. I will here make the following distinctions:[10]

(13) 0. Discourse event
      1. Interpersonal layer
          1.1. Interactional: concerning all those aspects of the discourse which relate to the interaction between S and A.
          1.2. Attitudinal: concerning all those aspects of the discourse which relate to the (emotional or critical) attitude towards or evaluation of the discourse by S and A.

---

10. For different proposals concerning discourse layering, see Halliday (1985), Schiffrin (1987). My account uses terminology of Bühler (1934) and Halliday (1967), more or less in the way in which these were introduced into FG by Hengeveld (1989). Kroon (1989) makes similar distinctions to those in (13). Also relevant to the idea of discourse layering is the work of Komter (1987, 1990) concerning the structure of job interviews.

2. Representational layer
   2.1. Organisational: concerning all those aspects of the discourse which relate to the way the content is organized.
   2.2. Contentive: concerning all those elements of the discourse in which the actual content is transmitted, i.e. the Facts and States of Affairs dealt with in the discourse, including the participants in such Facts and SoAs.

Let us illustrate these different layers and sub-layers with the following example. Suppose I know that my neighbour has caused damage to my car and has not told me about this, and I want to take him to task about this. My first task then is to create the interactional conditions required to achieve my communicative goal. For example, I will have to create a communicative situation in which I get my neighbour's attention as an Addressee. Once the parameters for the interaction have been fixed, a further problem which I have to solve concerns the emotional "tone" to be chosen for this occasion: will I directly and emotionally vent my indignant reproach (risking a flaming row with my neighbour)? Or will I present the facts and my claims in a cool, detached way with a minimum of emotional involvement? Choices among these different attitudinal registers may have important consequences for both the structure and the outcome of the discourse. My next problem is how to organize the actual content of what I want to say. Compare the following alternative introductions:

(14) a. *My car was busted yesterday.*
   b. *I saw you bust my car yesterday.*

In (14a) I present the major fact, leaving room for my neighbour to acknowledge his responsibility. In (14b), on the other hand, I directly accuse my neighbour of the fact in question. Different choices with respect to how to organize what I want to say may again have important consequences for the structure and the effects of the ensuing discourse. Only when the necessary decisions have been taken at these different levels can I start to produce the actual content that I want to talk about.

Corresponding to the different layers distinguished in (13) we may distinguish different strategies that S can deploy in creating a discourse (cf. Van Dijk—Kintsch (1983)):

(15) (1) Interpersonal strategies
- (1.1) Interaction management: strategies which serve to create the interactional conditions which must be fulfilled for a discourse event to be implemented.
- (1.2) Attitude specification: strategies which pertain to the emotional / attitudinal register in which the discourse is to take place.

(2) Representational strategies
- (2.1) Discourse Organisation: strategies which serve to establish the organisation and the presentation of the discourse content.
- (2.2) Discourse Execution: strategies which serve to express the actual content of the discourse.

18.5.1.2. Recursion in discourse structure. Alongside the complexity created through discourse layering (where lower-level units are contained in higher-level units of qualitatively different type), complexity in discourse may also be due to recursion (where higher-level units may contain lower-level units of the same qualitative type).[11] Recursion is involved in any situation in which a unit of type U may contain a sub-unit of the same type U, so that, within U, the organization typical of U may return. For example, a frame story is a story which contains a number of stories as sub-parts. The frame story as a whole must be established as a discourse event, and each sub-story must likewise be so established. Similarly, an argument may contain a number of sub-arguments, each of which runs through the same steps as the argument as a whole. Likewise, a turn sequence may contain a subsequence, and this may in turn contain a subsequence, etc. Thus, recursion creates structures of the general form displayed in (11) above, with the proviso that the sub-units entered and left should be of the same qualitative type.

As noted above, the transitions into and out of such sub-units may be marked by different devices. In the case of recursive discourse organisation, Polanyi—Scha (1983) speak of Push Markers (marking entry into a subroutine) and Pop Markers (marking exit out of a subroutine).

---

11. See especially Polanyi—Scha (1983) and Polanyi (1988). Note also the idea that turn sequences may contain "side-sequences" (Jefferson 1972) or "subsequences" (Weijdema et al. 1982).

In studying recursion a distinction should be made between functional recursion and interruption. In the frame-story example, the recursion is functional: a frame-story by definition contains a number of sub-stories. Interruption rather means that a unit of a given level is broken into by another unit (which may be of the same level), which is a foreign body with respect to the interrupted unit, i.e., has nothing to do with it either in terms of interaction or in terms of content. Polanyi—Scha (1983) give some examples of recursion which should rather be regarded as interruptions. For example, when in a shop one service encounter is interrupted by another (for example, to help a customer who needs only one or two items), then the interrupting discourse event plays no functional role within the interrupted discourse event. Komter (1987) here speaks of intruders. An example would be a job interview interrupted by the arrival of a window-cleaner. In itself it is an interesting fact that participants are able to handle such situations of interruption by suspending their current interaction, dealing with the intruder, and then taking up the main interaction line where they had left off (sometimes after a short *where were we* episode). But this kind of interruption need not play a role in our initial delimitation of the units constitutive of discourse events and discourse content, just as, in studying sentences, we do not need to take care of the fact that two non-related utterances may be simultaneously uttered by two different people.

18.5.2. Discourse units

A discourse event can be subdivided into different types of units of different hierarchical levels, both from the interactional point of view and from the point of view of the content. The most important distinctions would seem to be the following:

(16)
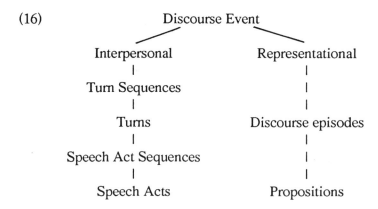

The different units of the interpersonal and the representational level do not necessarily coincide one-to-one. For example, in a conversation a certain discourse episode may be dealt with in a sequence of turns, in which S and A cooperate in treating a certain discourse (sub)topic. On the other hand, a discourse episode may be dealt with in one turn of S, or different such episodes may be combined in one turn. Thus, it is apparent that the structure of the interaction and the structure of the discourse content are partially independent. At the lowest level, again, one speech act may contain a single proposition, or different propositions in some coordinate or subordinate relationship.

18.5.2.1. Interpersonal units. At the interpersonal level the smallest unit is the *speech act*, as represented by a single (simplex or complex) clause. Speech acts may be combined in higher-level *speech act sequences*, sequences of two or more speech acts which in some way or another depend on each other. Consider an example such as:

(17)   *Are you ill? You look so pale.*

The second speech act here provides S's motivation for asking the preceding question, and is thus not interpretable (in the intended sense) outside the context of that question. Kroon (1989) in such cases speaks of "nuclear" vs. "subsidiary" speech acts.

When two or more speech acts form a speech act sequence we can say that there is some kind of functional relationship between them. In (17) the first speech act is a Question and the second speech act is a Motivation for the Question. The relationship between the separate speech acts of a speech act sequence is in many cases close to what could also be expressed by one complex speech act. Compare (17) with:

(18)   *Are you ill, 'cause you look so pale.*

in which the subordinate clause functions as an illocutionary satellite (see *TFG1*: 12.3.3.) to the main clause.

A *turn*, defined as one stretch of talk of the same S, may consist of a single speech act, but also of a series (or sequence) of speech acts. When two turns depend on each other for the proper fulfilment of their function, we speak of an *adjacency pair*.¹² A sequence of Question turn + Answer turn is the paradigm example of an adjacency pair: the question projects the expectation of an answer, and an answer can only be properly understood in the context created by the question. Question + Answer thus constitute an interactional unit above the single turn.

Further work on the structure of conversation has shown that it is often sequences rather than pairs of turns which hang together in this way. Thus, some *adjacency sequences* consist of three, some of five turns. For example, Houtkoop (1987) analyses sequences in which some kind of agreement is established as five-part sequences, as exemplified in:

(19) A: *Would you like to have dinner with us?*
    B: *That's a good idea.*
    A: *Yes?*
    B: *Yes!*
    A: *O.K.*

Note that such discourse sequences typically serve to establish one discourse episode, in this case 'establishing agreement on a dinner invitation'.

18.5.2.2. Representational units. Within the discourse event as a pattern of social interaction the actual discourse (content) is executed. From the content perspective, again, the discourse has an organized hierarchical structure in which different "layers" can be distinguished.

The smallest units of discourse content organisation are the propositions and predications contained in simple or complex clauses. Propositions capture the potential facts that S and A talk about, predications the States of Affairs which form the content of these facts. Together, predications and propositions are used to build up the mental model which reconstructs the discourse world.

The discourse content as a whole may be divided into different episodes and sub-episodes, much as a book is divided into chapters, chapters into sections, sections into paragraphs, and paragraphs into clauses. One way of distinguishing discourse episodes is in terms of the roles they fulfil in constituting the full discourse content. For example, once S has entered a discourse event of "telling a story", he will have to run through different episodes which together constitute the actual story. Several authors have tried to develop a general

---

12. A central notion introduced in Conversation Analysis.

models for how stories can be constructed.[13] Disregarding differences between these various models, the following general picture of the form of a story can be given:

(20)
1. Opening
2. Abstract
3. Orientation
   — Setting: Time, Place, and Circumstances
   — Characters
   — Problem
4. Events and Evaluation
5. Resolution
6. Epilogue: Conclusion
7. Closing

18.5.3. Discourse relations

In the preceding section we looked at the structure of discourse from a structural point of view: what types of constituent units can be discerned in a discourse, and how do these units follow one another in time? We can also look at discourse structure from a relational or functional point of view, in terms of the question: what functional relations hold between units in a discourse, and how do these functional relations serve to define the local and global integrity of the discourse?

This functional point of view has been developed in "Rhetorical Structure Theory" (Mann—Thompson 1987, Matthiessen—Thompson 1988). This theory can be briefly summarized as follows. Each basic discourse unit (roughly: each clause) entertains a certain functional relation with the unit which precedes or follows it. There are two basic relations: parataxis and hypotaxis. In parataxis, two or more units are equal partners in a list which as a whole stands in a functional relation to the surrounding units. In hypotaxis, one unit can be termed the nucleus, the other the satellite. There is a limited number of functional relations that satellites can entertain with the preceding

---

13. See, e.g., Labov—Waletzky (1967), Labov (1972), Rumelhart (1975), Clark—Clark (1977: 168-170), Lalleman (1986). See also Marchese (1988) on narrative structures in Godie. For critical discussion of "story grammars", see Johnson-Laird (1983).

or the following unit. These relations may hold between basic units, but also between units of higher level which themselves can be ultimately decomposed into basic units. The relational structure of discourse is thus hierarchical. Functional relations may pertain to the level of the rhetorical act (the interpersonal level) or to the level of the subject matter (the representational level).

To give an impression of these various functional relations, consider the following examples:

(21) The interpersonal level
    a. U_1 *motivates* U_2
    b. U_1 *provides background for* U_2
    c. U_1 *gives an antithesis to* U_2
    d. U_1 *gives a solution for* U_2

(22) The representational level
    a. U_1 *elaborates on* U_2
    b. U_1 *enables* U_2
    c. U_1 *specifies a condition for* U_2
    d. U_1 *specifies the purpose of* U_2
    e. U_1 *specifies a circumstance of* U_2
    f. U_1 *is a concession in relation to* U_2

It is clear from these examples that the functional relations at discourse level overlap with the semantic relations of satellites at clause level. This is no coincidence, since the theory includes the idea that units which are usually regarded as subordinate clauses do indeed function at the discourse level.

I do not go along with the idea that clausal, propositional and predicational satellites should not be treated as subordinate or embedded at the clause level. But I do believe it is a good idea to assume that intraclausal functional relations of this kind can be projected onto the discourse level. Just as we speak of the clause nucleus which can be modified and specified by a variety of clausal satellites, so we can speak of a discourse nucleus which is modified and specified by a variety of discourse satellites. In order to distinguish the latter from the former, we can speak of "D-nucleus" and "D-satellite". The general picture seems to be that all intraclausal nucleus-satellite relations can also be found at the interclausal level, where they can be extended with a number of functional relations which are specific to the discourse level. In this sense, again, the clause structure model can be taken as a partial model of the discourse as a whole.

18.6. Discourse coherence

18.6.0. Introduction

The third perspective from which we approach the structure of discourse is through the notion of *coherence* (see Halliday—Hasan 1976, Halliday 1985, Longacre 1983). In the preceding we have seen ample evidence that a discourse event is structured at different layers or levels of organization. When a discourse is properly construed it will be coherent in the sense that the different constitutive parts will follow each other in a natural, interpretable way. This holds both for the local sequencing of clauses (*local coherence*) and for the sequencing of more global discourse units (*global coherence*). If either at the local or at the global level the principles of natural sequencing are not observed, the discourse will be, in that respect, incoherent and difficult or impossible to interpret.

In considering the notion of coherence we must remember that the Addressee is an active interpreter of verbal information which necessarily underspecifies the final interpretation arrived at. The Addressee is out to arrive at a coherent interpretation of the text. To the extent that the text offers its own coherence signals, so much the better. But if it does not, A will try to link the bits and pieces by so-called "bridging assumptions" so as to arrive at a coherent interpretation after all. Only when even such bridging assumptions fail to create coherence should we say that the text as such is incoherent.

In this section we consider the question of what factors contribute to discourse coherence. In the discussion I do not make a sharp distinction between devices used to establish local and those establishing global coherence, since it seems in general to be the case that the same devices are used at both levels. For example, a connector which can locally connect a clause to a preceding clause can usually also be used to connect a following clause to a preceding higher-level discourse unit. Where this is not the case it will be explicitly mentioned.

18.6.1. Frames as a source of coherence

Suppose I am in a spacious room with bookshelves all along the walls. I take a book from the shelves, go to a desk near the door, and engage in the following exchange with person X:

(23) I: *Can I borrow this book until next week?*
X: *Sir, this is a bookstore, not a library!*

Now I find myself in a quite similar situation. Again, I walk up to the desk, and this is what follows:

(24) I: *I'd like to buy this book.*
X: *Sir, this is a library, not a bookstore!*

In both cases, my move does not fit into the setting in which I find myself. This setting may in the two cases be physically quite similar or even identical; institutionally, it is quite different: I find myself in the institution bookstore in the first case, and in the institution library in the second.

Institutions of this kind are such that certain things can or must be done or said, and other things cannot or should not be done or said. Most people are well aware of the institutional setting in which they find themselves, and therefore miscommunications such as those of (23) and (24) will seldom occur. The things that can or cannot be done within the particular institutional setting are a matter of common knowledge: unless I find myself in a foreign country or in unusual surroundings, I will not ask what sorts of things are allowed / forbidden in a library or a bookstore. I know these things. On the basis of this knowledge I can generate the behaviour which is acceptable in the setting, and I have an expectation pattern about what other people can do or say in that setting.

The organized knowledge concerning what can be done and said within a given institutional setting can be called a "frame" in the sense of Minsky (1977). A frame can then be described as a structured mental representation of acceptable actions and speech events in relation to a given institutional setting. A frame is organized in such a way that if some part of the frame is activated, the rest of the frame is at least potentially activated as well.

We can distinguish different types of frames. If the frame concerns an institutional structure which consists of a standard *sequence* of events it is often called a "script". For example, in baking a cake I have to go through a sequence of actions, the order of which cannot be randomized. Only when certain steps are taken in a certain order will the final product be a cake. If I am able to bake a cake, I know the script for baking a cake. If I am unable to bake a cake, I can learn the script from a cookery book. In other words, a recipe is a representation of a script.

Frames can be further distinguished into structure frames and content frames.[14] The difference can be seen as follows: I can ask someone to write a sonnet about unrequited love. For the sonnet the person needs a structure frame which specifies what number of lines, divided into how many stanzas, and with what kinds of rhyme schemes between the verses, count as a well-formed sonnet. The structure frame allows for a certain degree of variation within the limits of what counts as a sonnet. But it excludes many sequences of verses as being decidedly non-sonnet. Content-wise, as well, the theme "unrequited love" generates certain expectations concerning the subject matter to be described or alluded to in the poem: the theme elicits a content frame within which certain things can be done and said, but other things are excluded.

It may be assumed that discourse participants have a repertoire of structural and content frames stored in their long-term general knowledge. Such frames may be used for two purposes:

(i) to evaluate the coherence of a given discourse in terms of compatibility with the conditions imposed by the relevant frames;

(ii) to create coherence in a discourse by filling in bridging assumptions from the frame concerning things which have not been made explicit in the text.

18.6.2. Iconic sequencing

One source of discourse coherence is provided by certain default principles of iconic sequencing. Such principles say that, without overt indications to the contrary, the order of mention of certain items may be assumed to reflect the order of these items in reality or in our conceptualization of reality.

Temporal iconicity implies that, without indications to the contrary, when event E_1 is mentioned before event E_2, it may be assumed that E_1 took place before E_2 in time. Compare the following examples:

(25) a. *Mary ate clams and fell ill.*
    b. *Mary fell ill and ate clams.*
(26) a. *Mary fell ill. She had eaten clams.*
    b. *Before falling ill, Mary had eaten clams.*

---

14. Cf. the distinctions between (formal) "superstructures" and (content-oriented) "macrostructures" in Van Dijk—Kintsch (1983).

(25a) can only be interpreted in the sense that Mary first ate clams and then fell ill (due to a general principle of *post hoc ergo propter hoc*, the former will easily be interpreted as providing the cause of the latter). (25b) cannot be interpreted as describing the same course of events, since there are no overt indications that the order of mention does not reflect the temporal order.

(26a-b) can be so interpreted, but in both cases there are overt contra-indications: in (26a), the tense marking *had eaten* places the second event before the first in time, and in (26b) this is overtly signalled by *before*. Both construction types may be evaluated as being marked in comparison with (25a), in which the default ordering is applied.

Iconic ordering may also rest on some natural cognitive or conceptual principle. For example, the following define cognitively-based default orderings:

(27) cause → effect
      event → result
      condition → consequent
      action → purpose

Thus, as long as the ordering within the discourse is in accordance with these natural defaults, this adds to the overall coherence. Where such orders are shifted around, overt markers must warn the interpreter of this marked situation.

18.6.3. Topical continuity

An important factor defining the degree of coherence of a text is its degree of topical continuity (see Givón ed. 1983). In *TFG1*: 13.3. I discussed the notions "Topic" and "topicality" from a discourse perspective. The following basic strategies were distinguished:

 (i) Introducing a New Topic (NewTop) into the discourse;
 (ii) Maintaining a Topic, once introduced, as a Given Topic (GivTop);
 (iii) Inferring a Sub-Topic (SubTop) from a Topic;
 (iv) Reviving a Topic as a Resumed Topic (ResTop).

Especially the last three strategies greatly contribute to the topical continuity of a discourse, and thus to its degree of coherence.

Topic maintenance is achieved by a variety of means:[15]
— Different forms of anaphorical reference;
— Syntactic parallelism;
— Switch reference mechanisms;
— Obviation.

These different means (in the languages that use them) can be interpreted as signalling that the speaker is still talking about the same things.

Given Topic - Sub-Topic relations likewise contribute to topical continuity, but in a less direct way, mediated through frames which allow for bridging assumptions in which missing links are reconstructed. A Given Topic — Sub-Topic sequence is interpreted as coherent if the interpreter, aided by his frame knowledge, can reconstruct the step(s) which allow S to assume that, once the Given Topic has been established, the Sub-Topic may be assumed to be available as well.

Given Topic - Sub-Topic relations may also play a discourse-organizing role at a higher level of analysis. Suppose we ask a person to describe his apartment (cf. Linde—Labov 1975, Linde 1974). This question calls for a Frame in which such entities as a living room, a bedroom, a kitchen, etc. occur as expectable Sub-Topics. We may thus expect a description in which a sub-episode is devoted to each of these Sub-Topics, which themselves will be introduced as if they were given right from the start. Another important point found by Linde and Labov was that Ss, when asked to perform this kind of task, do not simply give a random enumeration of the different SubTops, but present these in terms of some organizing principle. One recurrent organizing principle for apartment descriptions was to order the description as if S was giving A a guided tour through the apartment. The organizing principle then provides a structural frame within which the content frame can be executed.

A quite similar example of this kind of discourse organisation is quoted in Pinkster (1988: 377) from the Latin author of *De Architectura* ('On architecture'), Vitruvius, where he described the construction of a Roman bathhouse. In both cases, the Discourse Topic, together with its structure and content frames, projects a natural organisation onto the discourse.

---

15. See *TFG1*: 13.3. for more detailed description.

18.6.4. Focality

Focality plays a role in co-determining the coherence of a discourse, in that a discourse should be focality-coherent. For a simple example, consider the following Question-Answer (Q-A) sequences:

(28) Q: *Who is Kohl going to meet in Gdańsk?*
    A1: *Kohl is going to meet WAŁĘSA in Gdańsk.*
    A2: **Kohl is going to meet Wałęsa in GDAŃSK.*

Note that in the context of (28Q), answer (A1) is coherent, while (A2) is incoherent. The focality which is predefined in the question by the question word *who* must be reflected in the answer by a parallel Focus assignment, which will be prosodically expressed as in (A1). Q-A pairs such as (28Q)-(28A1) are well-formed adjacency pairs, while pairs such as (28Q)-(28A2) are ill-formed. Thus, the correct assignment and expression of Focus function contributes to the well-formedness of the discourse.

In general, the topical or focal status of discourse elements may influence the constitution of individual clauses in the following ways:

(i) it may co-determine the selection of the predicate frame around which the clause is construed;

(ii) it may co-determine the choice of construction type of the clause;

(iii) it may co-determine the expression of the underlying clause structure.

18.6.5. Tail-Head Linking

One device for creating coherence in a discourse both at the local and the global level consists in what has been called Tail-Head Linking (cf. De Vries 1989, with reference to Thurman 1975). In Tail-Head linking a clause starts with a constituent which briefly summarizes a crucial part of the preceding clause or context. This may be done through an anaphorical term, as in:

(29)   *After a long journey they came to a small village. In that village /*
       There they found a place where they could spend the night.

It may also be done through a brief summary of the SoA described in the preceding clause:

(30)   With much effort they crossed the river. Having crossed the river / Having done so they finally found the main road.

De Vries (1989) shows that this type of verbal linking is especially common in Papuan narrative. For example, the following is the translation of part of a Kombai story discussed in De Vries (1989: 206):

(31)   ... they held a meeting in the house of the headman. They held a meeting and the wife of the headman started speaking angrily against her husband. She spoke angrily and the headman started to hit his wife. He started to hit and she became unconscious, spreading her arms and legs ...

Kombai has a special "generic" or anaphorical verb meaning 'to do thus', which is often used in this function, as in the following example (De Vries 1989: 208):[16]

(32)   Khumolei-na   ifamano.
         die.3sg.nf-conn.ds   bury.3pl.nf
         'He died and they buried him.'
         Ma-na   khwaimigi   mene   luwano.
         do.3sg.nf-conn.ds   foreigner   this   say.3pl.NF
         'When they had done so, the foreigners spoke thus: ...'

This example also displays an additional function of such initial constituents, as pointed out by De Vries: note that non-final verbs are marked for switch reference in Kombai (ds = the next verb is going to have a topic different from the present verb), but final verbs such as *ifamano* do not carry such information. By summarizing the content of the final verb in a medial verb at the beginning of the new clause, the expression of topical (dis)continuity becomes possible. We now know that *khwaimigi* 'the foreigners' are not the same as those who buried the person who died in the first clause.

Similar strategies are common in other languages. Latin, for example, makes frequent use of the ablative absolute in such clause-initial expressions as *hoc facto* 'this having been done', or *his verbis dictis* 'these words having been said'. Note, however, that these expressions more often link the clause to a preceding discourse episode than to a preceding clause (Pinkster 1988:

---

16. nf = non-future, ds = different subject, conn = connective.

373). Thus, *his verbis dictis* will typically be used after some protagonist has delivered a speech, in order to signal, first, that the (report of the) speech is over, and second, that the next discourse episode has started.[17]

18.6.6. Connectors

A further means of creating coherense are *connectors*, which occur in patterns of the form:

(33)   Preceding Clause(s). Connector, New Clause.

where the Connector has the primary roles of linking the New Clause to the Preceding Clause(s) while at the same time specifying a semantic / pragmatic relation between the two. An example would be:[18]

(34)   *It was a very difficult examination. Nevertheless, he passed it with distinction.*

The semantic / pragmatic relation could here be described as follows:

(35)   *Nevertheless* announces that the New Clause is contrary to what A might have rightfully inferred from the Preceding Clause.

These elements are known under a wide variety of names in the literature.[19] I follow Pinkster (1988) in calling them "connectors". Pinkster divides connectors into the following semantic types:[20]

---

17. For examples of Tail-Head Linking in Godie (Eastern Kru, Ivory Coast), see Marchese (1988).

18. From Quirk et al. (1972: 523).

19. For example, as "conjuncts" in Quirk et al. (1972); "discourse markers" in Schiffrin (1987). The application of these terms is not co-extensive with these various authors.

20. For another, partially overlapping taxonomy, see Quirk et al. (1972: 520-523).

(i) additive (*and, also*);
(ii) adversative (*but, however*);
(iii) disjunctive (*or*);
(iv) causal (*for, because*);
(v) consecutive (*so, therefore*)
(vi) continuative (*and then*).

It is to be understood that connectors are not to be equated with coordinators, which function intra-clausally, even if they are segmentally identical to connectors.[21]

18.7. Conclusion

In this chapter we have tried to systematically describe the various features of discourse that have to be taken into account in the creation of a grammatical model that takes entire discourses rather than clauses as its input. In view of its own standards of adequacy, FG should ultimately develop into such a model. It is evident that this is a very high aim for a theory of grammar to strive for, and that what we have offered here is only a starting point. Recent work in FG has shown, however, that the challenge posed to a grammatical theory by the structure of discourse is being taken seriously. For some first results in this area, the reader is referred to Connolly et al. eds. (1996).

---

21. Compare Schiffrin (1987: chapter 6) for an analysis of the relations between *and*, *but*, and *or* as coordinators in sentence grammar and their usages as discourse markers.

References[1]

Adelaar, Willem F.H.
   1990   "The role of quotations in Andean discourse", in: Pinkster—Genee (eds.), 1-12.

Afman, Liesbeth
   1985   "Les constructions pronominales en français", *WPFG* 6.

Akmajian, Adrian
   1970   "On deriving cleft sentences form pseudo-cleft sentences," *Linguistic Inquiry* 1: 149-168.

Ali, Saeed—Yero Sylla
   1977   "Perceptual transparency in relativization; a case study in Fula", *Studies in African Linguistics* Supplement 7: 1-10.

Allwood, Jens
   1976   "The Complex Noun Phrase Constraint as a non-universal rule", *Occasional Papers in Linguistics* 2. [University of Massachussetts, Amherst.]

Anderson, Stephen R.
   1985   "Typological distinctions in word formation", in: Shopen (ed.), vol. 3, 3-56.

Asher, R.E.
   1982   *Tamil* (Lingua Descriptive Studies 7). Amsterdam: North-Holland.

Austin, John L.
   1962   *How to do things with words*. Cambridge, Mass.: MIT Press.

Auwera, Johan van der
   1984   "More on the history of subject contact clauses in English", *Folia Linguistica Historica* 5: 171-184.
   1985   "More predicative relatives in French; the 'l'homme que je dis qui ressemble a un chat' construction", in: Jan Nuyts (ed.), *Antwerp Studies in Functional Grammar.* (Antwerp Papers in Linguistics 39). 13-48. Antwerp: Antwerp University.
   1992   "Free relatives", in: Fortescue—Harder—Kristoffersen (eds.), 329-354.

Auwera, Johan van der—Louis Goossens (eds.)
   1987   *Ins and outs of the predication*. Dordrecht: Foris.

---

1. *WPFG* = Working Papers in Functional Grammar, available from IFOTT, University of Amsterdam, Spuistraat 210, NL-1012 VT Amsterdam.

Bach, Emmon
    1971   "Questions", *Linguistic Inquiry* 2: 153-166.
Baker, C. Leroy
    1970   "Notes on the description of English questions: the role of an abstract question morpheme", *Foundations of Language* 6: 197-219.
Barker, J.W.
    1957   *Teach yourself Portuguese*. London: The English Universities Press.
Berg, Marinus van den
    1989   *Modern standaard Chinees; een functionele grammatica*. Muiderberg: Coutinho.
Besnier, Niko
    1988   "Semantic and pragmatic constraints on Tuvaluan raising", *Linguistics* 26: 747-778.
Bever, T.G.
    1970   "The cognitive basis for linguistic structures", in: J.R. Hayes (ed.), *Congnition and the Development of Language*, 279-352. New York: Wiley.
Bierwisch, Manfred—Karl Erich Heidolph (eds.)
    1970   *Progress in linguistics*. The Hague: Mouton.
Bokamba, G.D.
    1971   "Specificity and definiteness in Dzamba", *Studies in African Linguistics* 2: 217-237.
Bolkestein, A. Machtelt
    1976   "The relation between form and meaning of Latin subordinate clauses governed by *verba dicendi*", *Mnemosyne* 29: 155-175 and 268-300.
    1979   "Subject-to-Object raising in Latin?" *Lingua* 49: 15-34.
    1981a   "Embedded predications, displacement and pseudo-argument formation in Latin", in: Bolkestein—Combé—Dik—De Groot—Gvozdanović—Rijksbaron—Vet, 63-112.
    1981b   "Factivity as a condition for an optional expression rule in Latin: the *ab urbe condita* construction and its underlying representation", in: Bolkestein—Combé—Dik—De Groot—Gvozdanović—Rijksbaron—Vet, 205-233.
    1985   "Discourse and case marking: three-place predicates in Latin", in: C. Touratier (ed.), *Syntaxe et latin*, 191-225. Aix en Provence: Université de Provence.
    1987   "Discourse functions of predications: the background / foreground distinction and Tense and Voice in Latin main and subordinate clauses", in: Nuyts—De Schutter (eds.), 163-178.
    1990a   "Sentential complements in Functional Grammar; embedded predications, propositions, utterances in Latin, in: Nuyts—Bolkestein—Vet (eds.), 71-100.

1990b "Unreportable linguistic entities in Functional Grammar", in: Pinkster—Genee (eds.), 13-26.
1992 "Limits to layering: locatability and other problems", in: Fortescue—Harder—Kristoffersen (eds.), 387-407.
Bolkestein, A. Machtelt—Henk A. Combé—Simon C. Dik—Casper de Groot—Jadranka Gvozdanović—Co Vet
1981 *Predication and expression in Functional Grammar*. London: Academic Press.
Bolkestein, A. Machtelt—Michel van de Grift
1994 "Participant tracking in Latin discourse", in: Joseph Herman (ed.), *Linguistic studies on Latin*, 283-302. Amsterdam: Benjamins.
Bolkestein, A. Machtelt—Rodie Risselada
1985 "De tekstuele funktie van valentie: Latijnse drieplaatsige predikaten in kontekst", in: Dik (ed.), 161-176.
Bolkestein, A. Machtelt—Casper de Groot—J. Lachlan Mackenzie (eds.)
1985a *Syntax and pragmatics in Functional Grammar*. Dordrecht: Foris.
Bolkestein, A. Machtelt—Casper de Groot—J. Lachlan Mackenzie (eds.)
1985b *Predicates and terms in Functional Grammar*. Dordrecht: Foris.
Borkin, A.
1974 "Raising to object position", *Papers in Linguistics* 7.2.
Bossuyt, Alain
1982 *Aspekten van de geschiedenis van de negatieve zin in het Nederlands*. [Ph.D. dissertation, Free University Brussels.]
1983 "Historical Functional Grammar: an outline of an integrated theory of language change", in: Dik (ed.), 301-325.
Bresnan, Joan .W.
1970 "On complementizers: toward a syntactic theory of complement types", *Foundations of Language* 6: 297-321.
Brömser, Bernd
1985 "On the derivation of English compounds", in: W. Kürschner—R. Vogt (eds.) *Grammatik, Semantik, Textlinguistik*. (Akten des 19. Linguistischen Kolloquiums. Vechta, 1984.) 99-113. Tübingen: Niemeyer.
Brown, D. Richard
1985 "Term operators", in: Bolkestein—De Groot—Mackenzie (eds.) (1985b), 127-145.
Brown, R.—G. Gilman
1960 "The pronouns of power and solidarity", in: Sebeok (ed.), 253-276.
Brown, Gillian—George Yule
1983 *Discourse analysis*. Cambridge: Cambridge University Press.
Bühler, Karl
1934 *Sprachtheorie*. Jena: Fischer.

Carnap, Rudolf
  1937   *The logical syntax of language*. London: Routledge & Kegan Paul.
Chastain, C.
  1975   "Reference and context", in: K. Gunderson (ed.), *Language, mind and knowledge*, 194-269. Minneapolis: University of Minnesota Press.
Chomsky, Noam
  1964   *Current issues in linguistic theory*. The Hague: Mouton.
  1965   *Aspects of the theory of syntax*. Cambridge, Mass.: MIT Press.
  1970   "Remarks on nominalization", in: Roderick A. Jacobs—P.S Rosenbaum (eds.) *Readings in English Transformational Grammar*, 184-221. Waltham, Mass.: Ginn and Co.
  1973   "Conditions on transformations", in: Stephen R. Anderson—Paul Kiparsky (eds.), *A Festschrift for Morris Halle*, 232-286. New York: Holt, Rinehart and Winston.
Chung, Sandra—William A. Seiter
  1980   "The history of raising and relativization in Polynesian", *Language* 56: 622-638.
Clark, Eve V.
  1971   "On the acquisition of the meaning of *before* and *after*", *Journal of Verbal Learning and Verbal Behaviour* 10: 266-275.
Clark, Herbert H.—Eve V. Clark
  1977   *Psychology and language; an introduction to psycholinguistics*. New York: Harcourt Brace Jovanovich.
Cole, Peter
  1982   *Imbabura Quechua*. Amsterdam: North-Holland.
  1987   "The structure of internally headed relative clauses", *Natural Language and Linguistic Theory* 5: 277-302.
Cole, Peter (ed.)
  1978   *Pragmatics*. (Syntax and Semantics 9.) New York: Academic Press.
Cole, Peter—Wayne Harbert—S. Sridhar—S. Hashimoto—C. Nelson—D. Smietana
  1977   "Noun phrase accessibility and island constraints", in: Peter Cole—Jerrold M. Sadock (eds.), *Grammatical relations*. (Syntax and Semantics 8.) New York: Academic Press.
Cole, Peter—Jerry L. Morgan (eds.)
  1975   *Speech acts*. (Syntax and Semantics 3.) New York: Academic Press.
Comrie, Bernard
  1973   "Clause structure and movement constraints in Russian", in: Claudia Corum—T. Cedrik Stark—Ann Weiser (eds.), *You take the high node and I'll take the low node; papers from the Comparative Syntax Festival 'The differences between main and subordinate clauses'*, 291-304. Chicago: Chicago Linguistic Society.

1976a "The syntax of action nominals: a cross-language study", *Lingua* 40: 177-201.
1976b *Aspect*. Cambridge: Cambridge University Press.
1985 *Tense*. Cambridge: Cambridge University Press.
1981 *Language univerals and linguistic typology*. Oxford: Blackwell.
1989 "Haruai attributes and processing explanations for word order", in: F.J. Heyvaert—F. Steurs (eds.), *Worlds behind words*, 209-215. Leuven: Leuven University Press.

Comrie, Bernard—Edward L. Keenan
1979 "Noun phrase accessibility revisited", *Language* 55: 649-664.

Connolly, John H.—Roel M. Vismans—Christopher S. Butler—Richard A. Gatward
1996 *Discourse and Pragmatics in Functional Grammar*. Berlin: Mouton de Gruyter.

Cornish, Francis
1986 *Anaphoric relations in English and French; a discourse perspective*. London: Croom Helm.

Coulmas, Florian
1986a "Reported speech; some general issues", in: Coulmas (ed.), 1-28.
1986b "Direct and indirect speech in Japanese", in: Coulmas (ed.), 161-178.

Coulmas, Florian (ed.)
1986 *Direct and indirect Speech*. Berlin: Mouton de Gruyter.

Cruttenden, Alan
1986 *Intonation*. Cambridge: Cambridge University Press.

Dahl, Östen
1971 *Nouns as set constants*. (Gothenburg Papers in Theoretical Linguistics 3). Gothenburg.
1979 "Typology of sentence negation". *Linguistics* 17: 79-106.

Davies, John
1981 *Kobon*. Amsterdam: North-Holland.

Davison, Alice
1978 "Negative scope and rules for conversation; evidence from an OV language", in: Cole (ed.), 23-45.

Derbyshire, Desmond C.
1979 *Hixkaryana*. Amsterdam: North-Holland.
1981 "A diachronic explanation of the origin of OVS in some Carib languages", *Journal of Linguistics* 17: 35-45.

Dijk, Teun van
1990 "Issues in Functional Discourse Analysis", in: Pinkster—Genee (eds.), 27-46.
1980 *Macrostructures; an interdisciplinary study of global structures in discourse, interaction, and cognition*. Hillsdale, N.J.: Lawrence Erlbaum.

Dijk, Teun van—Walter Kintsch
1983 *Strategies in discourse comprehension*. New York: Academic Press.
Dik, Simon C.
1968 *Coordination; its implications for a theory of general linguistics.* Amsterdam: North-Holland.
1979 "Raising in a Functional Grammar", *Lingua* 47: 119-140.
1980 *Studies in Functional Grammar*. London—New York: Academic Press.
1981 "Embedded Themes in spoken Dutch: two ways out", in: Bolkestein—Combé—Dik—De Groot—Gvozdanović—Rijksbaron—Vet, 113-124.
1985a "Formal and semantic adjustment of derived constructions", in: Bolkestein—De Groot—Mackenzie (eds.) (1985b), 1-28.
1985b "Valentie en valentie operaties in Funktionele Grammatika", in: Dik (ed.), 95-114.
1985c "Progress in linguistics", in: T. Hägerstrand (ed.), *The identification of progress in learning*, 115-139. Cambridge: Cambridge University Press.
1990a "Some developments in Functional Grammar: predicate formation", in: F. Aarts—T. van Els (eds.), *Contemporary Dutch linguistics*, 58-79. Washington: Georgetown University Press.
1990b "On the semantics of conditionals", in: Nuyts—Bolkestein—Vet (eds.), 233-261.
1992 *Functional Grammar in Prolog; an integrated implementation for English, French, and Dutch*. Berlin: Mouton de Gruyter.
Dik, Simon C. (ed.)
1985 *Valentie in Functionele Grammatika*. (Tijdschrift voor Taal- en Tekstwetenschap 5.2). Dordrecht: Foris.
Dik, Simon C.—Jadranka Gvozdanović,
1981 "Subject and Object in Serbo-Croatian", in: Hoekstra—Van der Hulst— Moortgat (eds.), 21-39.
Dik, Simon C.—Kees Hengeveld
1991 "The hierarchical structure of the clause and the typology of perception verbs", *Linguistics* 29: 231-259. (= *WPFG* 37).
Dik, Simon C.—Kees Hengeveld—Elseline Vester—Co Vet
1990 "The hierarchical structure of the clause and the typology of satellites", in: Nuyts—Bolkestein—Vet (eds.), 25-70.
Dixon, Robert M.W. (ed.)
1972 *The Dyirbal language of North Queensland*. Cambridge: Cambridge University Press.
1976 *Grammatical categories in Australian languages*. Canberra: Australian Institute of Aboriginal Studies.

Doughty, Catherine
1991 "Second language instruction does make a difference: evidence from an empirical study of SL relativization", *Studies in Second Language Acquisition* 13: 431-469.
Downing, Bruce T.
1978 "Some universals of relative clause structure", in: Greenberg (ed.), vol. 4, 375-418.
Eemeren, Frans van—Rob Grootendorst
1982 "The speech acts of arguing and convincing in externalized discussions". *Journal of Pragmatics* 6. 1-24.
Falster Jakobsen, Lisbeth
1978 "Der dänische Satzknoten - mit Anleitungen zu seiner Übersetzung ins Deutsche", *Kopenhagener Beiträge zur germanistischen Linguistik* 14: 83-134.
Fodor, J.A.—T.G. Bever—M.F. Garret
1974 *The psychology of language; an introduction to psycholinguistics and generative grammar*. New York: McGraw-Hill.
Fortescue, Michael—Peter Harder—Lars Kristoffersen (eds.)
1992 *Layered structure and reference in a functional perspective*. Amsterdam: Benjamins.
Fox, Barbara
1987 "The noun phrase accessibility hierarchy reinterpreted: subject primacy or the absolutive hypothesis?", *Language* 63: 856-870.
Franck, Dorothea
1980 *Grammatik und Konversation*. Königstein/Ts.: Scriptor.
Frantz, Donald G.
1973 "On question word movement", *Linguistic Inquiry* 4: 531-534.
Gary, Judith O.—Saad Gamal-Eldin
1982 *Cairene Egyptian colloquial Arabic*. Amsterdam: North-Holland.
Geest, W.P.F. de
1970 "Infinitiefconstructies bij *verba sentiendi*", *Studia Neerlandica* 3: 33-59.
Complementaire constructies bij *verba sentiendi* in het Nederlands. [Ph.D. dissertation, University of Nijmegen.]
Geluykens, Ronald
1987a "Intonation and speech act type: an experimental approach to rising intonation in queclaratives", *Journal of Pragmatics* 11: 483-494.
1987b "Tails (right-dislocation) as a repair mechanism in English conversation", in: Nuyts—De Schutter (eds.), 119-129.
Givón, Talmy
1973 "Opacity and reference in language; an inquiry into the role of modalities", in: J.P. Kimball (ed.), *Syntax and Semantics* 2. New York: Academic Press.

1976 "Topic, pronoun, and grammatical agreement", in: Li (ed.), 151-188.
1979 *On understanding grammar*. New York: Academic Press.
1983 "Topic continuity in spoken English", in: Givón (ed.), 347-363.
Givón, Talmy (ed.)
1983 *Topic Continuity in discourse: a quantitative cross-language study*. Amsterdam: Benjamins.
Goffman, Erving
1981 *Forms of talk*. Oxford: Basil Blackwell.
Gorbet, Larry
1976 *A Grammar of Diegueño nominals*. New York: Garland.
1977 "Headless relative clauses in the Southwest: are they related?", *Berkeley Linguistic Society* 3. 175-181.
Gordon, David—George Lakoff
1975 "Conversational postulates", in: Cole—Morgan (eds.), 83-106.
Goossens, Louis
1991 "FG reflections on 'Tobacco is said to be harmful'", *Cahiers de l'Institut de Linguistique de Louvain* 17: 65-74.
Greenberg, Joseph H.
1966 *Language universals*. The Hague: Mouton.
Greenberg, Joseph H. (ed.)
1978 *Universals of human language*. 4 volumes. Stanford: University Press.
Grice, H.P.
1975 "Logic and conversation", in: Cole—Morgan (eds.), 41-58.
Grift, Michel van de
1987 *Zero, is, hic, ille; pragmatic constraints on the use of Latin subject expressions*. [M.A. thesis in Latin, University of Amsterdam.]
Grimes, Joseph H.
1975 *The thread of discourse*. The Hague: Mouton.
Groot, Casper de
1981a "Sentence intertwining in Hungarian", in: Bolkestein—Combé—Dik—De Groot—Gvozdanović—Rijksbaron—Vet, 41-62.
1981b "The structure of predicates and verb agreement in Hungarian", in: S. Daalder—M. Gerritsen (eds.), *Linguistics in the Netherlands 1981*, 149-158. Amsterdam: North-Holland.
1981c "On Theme in Functional Grammar; an application to some constructions in spoken Hungarian", in: Hoekstra—Van der Hulst—Moortgat (eds.), 75-88.
1984 "Totally affected; aspect and three-place predicates in Hungarian", in: De Groot—Tommola (eds.), 133-151.
1986 "Hongaren en Nederlanders smeren niet hetzelfde", in: E. Mollay (ed.), *Németalföldi-Magyar kontrasztiv filológiai tanulmányok*, 4-18. Budapest: Elte.

1987 "Predicate formation in Functional Grammar", *WPFG* 20.
1989 *Predicate structure in a Functional Grammar of Hungarian.* Dordrecht: Foris.
Groot, Casper de—Machiel Limburg
1986 "Pronominal elements: diachrony, typology, and formalization in Functional Grammar", *WPFG* 12.
Groot, Casper de—Hannu Tommola (eds.)
1984 *Aspect bound; a voyage into the realm of Germanic, Slavonic, and Finno-Ugrian aspectology.* Dordrecht: Foris.
Groot, Wijnie de
1982 De SJA-werkwoorden in het Russisch. [M.A. thesis in General Linguistics, University of Amsterdam.]
Grosu, A.
1981 *Approaches to island phenomena.* Amsterdam: North-Holland.
Guéron, J.
1980 "On the syntax and semantics of PP extraposition". *Linguistic Inquiry* 11: 636-678.
Gundel, J.K.
1977 "Where do cleft sentences come from?", *Language* 53: 543-559.
Gvozdanović, Jadranka
1981 "Word order and displacement in Serbo-Croatian", in: Bolkestein—Combé—Dik—De Groot—Gvozdanović—Rijksbaron—Vet, 125-141.
1990 "Predicate formation in Bantawa", in: Hannay—Vester (eds.), 41-49.
Haberland, Hartmut
1986 "Reported speech in Danish", in: Coulmas (ed.), 219-253.
Haberland, Hartmut—Johan van der Auwera
1990 "Topics and clitics in Greek relatives", *Acta Linguistica Hafniensia* 22: 127-157.
Haiman, John
1978 "Conditionals are topics", *Language* 54: 564-589.
Haiman, John—Sandra A. Thompson
1988 *Clause combining in grammar and discourse.* Amsterdam: Benjamins.
Hale, Kenneth
1976 "The adjoined relative clause in Australia", in: Dixon (ed.), 78-105.
Haller, Beat—John Watters
1984 "Topic in Zulgo", *Studies in African Linguistics* 15: 27-46.
Halliday, M.A.K.
1967 "Notes on transitivity and theme in English", *Journal of Linguistics* 3: 37-81 and 199-244; *Journal of Linguistics* 4: 179-215.
1985 *An introduction to Functional Grammar.* London: Arnold.

Halliday, M.A.K.—R. Hassan
   1976   *Cohesion in English*. London: Longman.
Hankamer, Jorge
   1974   "On the non-cyclic nature of wh-clefting", *Chicago Linguistic Society* 10: 221-233.
Hannay, Mike
   1985   *English existentials in a Functional Grammar*. Dordrecht: Foris.
Hannay, Mike—Elseline Vester
   1987   "Non-restrictive relatives and the representation of complex sentences", in: Auwera—Goossens (eds.), 39-52.
Hannay, Mike—Elseline Vester (eds.)
   1990   *Working with Functional Grammar; descriptive and computational applications*. Dordrecht: Foris.
Harries-Delisle, Helga
   1978   "Contrastive emphasis in cleft sentences", in: Greenberg (ed.), vol. 4, 419-486.
Hattori, S.-K. Inoue (eds.)
   1983   *Proceedings of the XIIIth International Congress of Linguists*. Tokyo.
Haverkate, Henk
   1979   *Impositive sentences in Spanish; theory and description in linguistic pragmatics*. Amsterdam: North-Holland.
   1984   *Speech acts, speakers and hearers; reference and referential strategies in Spanish*. Amsterdam: Benjamins.
Hengeveld, Kees
   1989   "Layers and operators in Functional Grammar". *Journal of Linguistics* 25: 127-157 (= *WPFG* 27).
   1990   "The hierarchical structure of utterances", in: Nuyts—Bolkestein—Vet (eds.), 1-24.
   1992a   "Parts of speech", in: Fortescue—Harder—Kristoffersen (eds.), 29-55.
   1992b   *Non-verbal predication; theory, typology, diachrony*. Berlin: Mouton de Gruyter.
Hewitt, B.G.
   1979   *Abkhaz*. Amsterdam: North-Holland.
Hoekstra, Teun—Harry van der Hulst—Michael Moortgat (eds.)
   1981   *Perspectives on Functional Grammar*. Dordrecht: Foris.
Hoffmann, Maria E.
   1984   "Latin negation and illocutionary force", in: J. Veremans—F. Decreus (eds.), *Acta Colloquii Didactici Classici Decimi* (Didactica Classica Gandensia 24-25), 268-278. Gent.
   1987   *Negatio contrarii; a study of Latin litotes*. Assen: Van Gorcum.

Houtkoop-Steenstra, Hanneke
    1987   *Establishing agreement; an analysis of proposal-acceptance sequences*. Dordrecht: Foris.
Houtlosser, Peter
    1989   "Negatieve proposities aan negatieve standpunten", *Tijdschrift voor Taalbeheersing* 11: 293-298.
Hyman, Larry M.
    1975   "On the change from SOV to SVO: evidence from Niger-Congo", in: Li (ed.), 113-147.
Hymes, Dell
    1972   "On communicative competence", in J.B. Pride—J. Holmes (eds.), *Sociolinguistics*, 269-293. Harmondsworth: Penguin.
Jacobsen, B.
    1977   *Transformational-generative Grammar; an introductory survey of its genesis and development*. Amsterdam: North-Holland.
Jakobson, Roman
    1960   "Linguistics and poetics", in: Sebeok (ed.), 350-377.
Jefferson, Gail
    1972   "Side sequences", in: David Sudnow (ed.) *Studies in social interaction*, 294-338. New York: The Free Press.
Johnson-Laird, Philip N.
    1983   *Mental Models*. Cambridge: Cambridge University Press.
Johnson-Laird, Philip N.—P.C. Wason (eds.)
    1977   *Thinking: Readings in Cognitive Science*. Cambridge: Cambridge University Press.
Jong, Jan de
    1981   "On the treatment of Focus phenomena in Functional Grammar", in: Hoekstra—Van der Hulst—Moortgat (eds.), 89-115.
Joseph, Brian D.
    1983   "Relativization in Modern Greek; another look at the Accessibility Hierarchy Constraints", *Lingua* 60: 1-24.
Joseph, Brian D.—Irene Philippaki-Warburton
    1987   *Modern Greek*. London: Croom Helm.
Junger, Judith
    1985a   "Morphological causatives in Modern Hebrew", in: Bolkestein—De Groot—Mackenzie (eds.) (1985b), 235-257.
    1985b   "Valentiereduktie in het Modern Hebreeuws", in: Dik (ed.), 141-160.
    1987a   "Agentless passives in Modern Hebrew", *Acta Linguistica Hafniensia* 20: 55-79.
    1987b   *Predicate formation in the verbal system of Modern Hebrew*. Dordrecht: Foris.
Kahrel, Peter
    1985a   "Some aspects of derived intransitivity", *WPFG* 4.

1985b "Afgeleide intransitieven in het Nederlands en het Engels", in: Dik (ed.), 115-126.
1987 "Derived statives in Saramaccan", in: M. Alleyne (ed.). *Studies in Saramaccan language structure* (Carribean Cultural Studies 2), 53-70.

Kamp, Hans
1984 "A theory of truth and semantic representation", in: J. Groenendijk—T.M.V. Janssen—M. Stokhof (eds.), *Truth, interpretation, and information*, 1-41. Dordrecht: Foris.

Karttunen, Lauri
1971 "Implicative verbs", *Language* 47: 340-358.
1976 "Discourse referents", in: James D. McCawley (ed.), *Notes from the linguistic underground.* (Syntax and Semantics 7.) New York: Academic Press.

Keenan, Edward L.
1972 "On semantically based grammar", *Linguistic Inquiry* 3: 413-461.
1975 "Logical expressive power and syntactic variation in natural languages", in: Edward L. Keenan (ed.), *Formal semantics of natural language*, 406-421. Cambridge: Cambridge University Press.
1976 "Towards a universal definition of 'subject'", in: Li (ed.), 303-333.
1985 "Relative clauses", in: Shopen (ed.), vol. 3, 141-170.

Keenan, Edward L.—K. Bimson
1975 "Perceptual complexity and cross-language distribution of relative clauses and NP-question types", in: Robin D. Grossman—L. James San—Timothy J. Vance (eds.), *Papers from the parasession on functionalism.* 253-259. Chicago: Chicago Linguistic Society.

Keenan, Edward L.—Bernard Comrie
1977 "Noun phrase accessibility and universal grammar". *Linguistic Inquiry* 8: 63-99.
1979 "Data on noun phrase accessibility hierarchy", *Language* 55: 333-351.

Keizer, Evelien
1991 "Referring in Functional Grammar: how to define reference and referring expressions", *WPFG* 43.
1992a "Predicates as referring expressions", in: Fortescue—Harder—Kristoffersen (eds.), 1-27. Amsterdam: Benjamins.
1992b Reference, predication and (in)definiteness in Functional Grammar. [Ph.D. thesis, Free University of Amsterdam]

Kendall, Martha B.
1974 "Relative clause formation and topicalization in Yavapai", *International Journal of American Linguistics* 40: 89-102.
1976 *Selected problems in Yavapai syntax; the Verde Vallay dialect.* New York: Garland.

Kiparsky, Paul—Carol Kiparsky
    1970   "Fact", in: Bierwisch—Heidolph, 143-173.
Kirsner, Robert S.—Sandra A. Thompson
    1976   "The role of pragmatic inference in sentences: a study of sensory verb complements in English". *Glossa* 10: 200-240.
Komter, Martha
    1987   Conflict and cooperation in job interviews; a study of talk, tasks and ideas. [Ph.D. dissertation, University of Amsterdam.]
    1990   "The discourse structure of job interviews", in: Pinkster—Genee (eds.), 165-181.
Koopman, Hilda
    1984   *The syntax of verbs; form verb movement rules in the Kru languages to universal grammar.* Dordrecht: Foris.
Kraak, A.
    1966   *Negatieve zinnen; een methodologische en grammatische analyse.* Hilversum: De Haan
Kroon, Caroline
    1989   "Causal connectors in Latin; the discourse function of *nam, enim, igitur* and *ergo*", in: M. Lavency—D. Longree (eds.), *Actes du V*^{e} *Colloque de Linguistique Latine*, 231-243. Louvain-la-Neuve: Peeters.
Kučanda, Dubravko
    1984   "On Subject assignment in Serbo-Croatian within the framework of FG". *Lingua* 64: 99-114.
    1987   "On Serbo-Croatian 'true' reflexives and pseudo-reflexives", in: Auwera—Goossens (eds.), 77-92.
Kuno, Susumu
    1973a   *The structure of the Japanese language.* Cambridge, Mass.: MIT Press.
    1973b   "Constraints on internal clauses and sentential subjects", *Linguistic Inquiry* 4: 363-385.
    1976   "Subject, theme, and the speaker's empathy - a reexamination of relativization phenomena", in: Li (ed.), 417-444.
    1978   "Japanese: a characteristic OV language", in: Winfred P. Lehmann (ed.), *Syntactic typology*, 57-138. Austin: University of Texas Press.
Kuno, Susumu—Jane J. Robinson
    1972   "Multiple wh-questions", *Linguistic Inquiry* 3: 463-487.
Kwee Tjoe Liong
    1981   "In search of an appropriate relative clause", in: Hoekstra—Van der Hulst—Moortgat (eds.), 175-189.
Labov, William
    1972   "Where do grammars stop", *Georgetown Monograph on Languages and Linguistics* 25: 43-88.

Labov, William—Joshua Waletzky
   1967   "Narrative analysis", in: June Helm (ed.), *Essays in verbal and visual arts*, 12-44. Seattle: University of Washington Press.
Lalleman, Josine A.
   1986   *Dutch language proficiency of Turkish children born in the Netherlands*. Dordrecht: Foris.
Langacker, Roland W.
   1966   "Les verbes *faire, laisser, voir*, etc.", *Langages* 3: 72-89.
Langdon, Margaret
   1977   "Syntactic change and SOV structure: the Yuman case", in: Li (ed.), 255-290.
Lees, Robert B.
   1966   *The grammar of English nominalizations*. (Fourth printing.) The Hague: Mouton.
Lehmann, Christian
   1984   *Der Relativsatz. Typologie seiner Strukturen, Theorie seiner Funktionen, Kompendium seiner Grammatik*. Tübingen: Narr.
   1986   "On the typology of relative clauses", *Linguistics* 24: 663-680.
Levinson, Stephen C.
   1983   *Pragmatics*. Cambridge: Cambridge University Press.
Li, Charles N. (ed.)
   1976   *Subject and topic*. New York: Academic Press.
   1977   *Mechanisms of syntactic change*. Austin: University of Texas Press.
Li, Charles N.—Sandra A. Thompson
   1976   "Subject and topic: a new typology of language", in: Li (ed.), 457-489.
   1978   "Relativization strategies in Wappo", *Berkeley Linguistic Society* 4: 106-113.
Linde, Charlotte
   1974   The linguistic encoding of spatial information. [Ph.D. thesis, Columbia University.]
Linde, Charlotte—William Labov
   1975   "Spatial networks as a site for the study of language", *Language* 51: 924-939.
Longacre, Robert E.
   1076   *The grammar of discourse*. New York: Plenum.
Lyons, John
   1977   *Semantics*. 2 vols. Cambridge: Cambridge University Press.
McCawley, James D.
   1976   "Relativization", in: Masayoshi Shibatani (ed.), *Japanese Generative Grammar*. (Syntax and Semantics 5). 295-306.
   1978   "Restrictive relatives in surface constituent structure", *NELS* 8: 154-166.

Mackenzie, J. Lachlan
1984 "Communicative functions of subordination", in: J. Lachlan Mackenzie—H. Wekker (eds.), *English language research; the Dutch contribution*, vol. 1, 67-84. Amsterdam: Free University Press.
1985a "Nominalization and valency reduction", in: Bolkestein—De Groot—Mackenzie (eds.) (1985b), 29-47.
1985b "Genominaliseer", in: Dik (ed.), 177-198.
1987 "Nominalization and basic constituent ordering", in: Van der Auwera—Goossens (eds.), 93-105. Dordrecht: Foris.

Mackenzie, J. Lachlan—Mike Hannay
1982 "Functional predicates and focus constructions in a Functional Grammar of English", *Lingua* 56: 43-57.

Maes, Alfons
1987 "The pragmatic value of cataphoric relations", in: Nuyts—De Schutter (eds.), 131-146.

Maling, Joan—Annie Zaenen
1982 "A phrase structure account of Skandinavian extraction phenomena", in: P. Jacobson—G.K. Pullum (eds.), *The nature of syntactic representations*, 229-282. Dordrecht: Reidel.

Mallinson, Graham
1986 *Rumanian*. London: Croom Helm.

Mallinson, Graham—Barry J. Blake
1981 *Language typology; cross-linguistic studies in syntax*. Amsterdam: North-Holland.

Mann, W.C.—Sandra A. Thompson
1987 "Rhetorical Structure Theory: a framework for the analysis of texts", *Papers in Pragmatics* 1: 79-105.

Marchese, Lynell
1977 "Subordinate clauses as topics in Godié", *Studies in African Linguistics*. Supplement 7,: 157-164.
1988 "Sequential chaining and discourse structure in Godié", in: Haiman—Thompson (eds.), 247-273.

Mardirussian, Galust
1975 "Noun-incorporation in Universal Grammar", *Chicago Linguistic Society* 11: 383-389.

Matsumara, Kazuto
1983 "Mari (Cheremis) 'pseudo-relatives'", in Hattori & Inoue (eds.).

Matthiessen, Chr.—Sandra A. Thompson
1988 "The structure of discourse and 'subordination'", in: Haiman—Thompson (eds.), 275-329.

Maxwell, Daniel N.
1979 "Strategies of relativization and NP accessibility", *Language* 55: 352-371.

Merlan, Francesca
    1982   *Mangarayi*. Amsterdam: North-Holland.
Minsky, M.
    1977   "Frame-system theory", in: Johnson-Laird—Wason (eds.).
Mithun, Marianne
    1988   "The grammaticalization of coordination", in: Haiman—Thompson (eds.), 331-358.
Moreno, Juan Carlos
    1990   "Impersonal constructions in Spanish", in: Hannay—Vester (eds.), 31-40.
Moutaouakil, Ahmed
    1984a   "Pour une représentation adequate de la force illocutionnaire en grammaire fonctionnelle" [Paper, University Mohamed V, Rabat.]
    1984b   "Le Focus en Arabe: vers une analyse fonctionnelle", *Lingua* 64: 115-176.
    1986   "Les constructions causatives en arabe: approche fonctionnelle". [Paper, University Mohamed V, Rabat.]
    1987   "Valency changing rules in Arabic". [Paper, University Mohamed V, Rabat.]
    1989   *Pragmatic functions in a Functional Grammar of Arabic*. Dordrecht: Foris.
    1990   *Essais en Grammaire Fonctionelle*. Rabat: SMER.
Munro, Pamela
    1973   "Reanalysis and elaboration in Yuman negatives", *Linguistic notes from La Jolla* 5: 36-62.
    1976   *Mojave syntax*. New York: Garland.
    1977   "From existential to copula: the history of Yuman *be*", in: Charles N. Li (ed.), 445-490.
Muysken, Pieter
    1978   "Three types of fronting constructions in Papiamentu", in: Frank Jansen (ed.), *Studies in fronting*, 65-79. Lisse: De Ridder.
Noonan, Michael P.
    1981   Lango Syntax. [Ph.D. dissertation, University of California at Los Angeles.]
    1985   "Complementation", in: Shopen (ed.), vol. 2, 42-140.
Nuyts, Jan—A. Machtelt Bolkestein—Co Vet (eds.)
    1990   *Layers and levels of representation in language theory*. Amsterdam: Benjamins.
Nuyts, Jan—Georges de Schutter (eds.)
    1987   *Getting one's words into line*. Dordrecht: Foris.
Ochs-Keenan, Elinor—Bambi B. Schieffelin
    1976   "Topic as a discourse notion; a study of Topic in the conversation of children and adults", in: Li (ed.), 335-384.

Orlandini, Anna
   1980   "On rhetorical questions", in: G. Calboli (ed.), *Papers in Grammar*, vol. 1, 103-140. Bologna: CLUEB.
Ortiz de Urbina, Jon
   1989   *Parameters in the grammar of Basque*. Dordrecht: Foris.
Owen, M.L.
   1982   "Conversational topics and activities: final report to the SSRC of the project on Topic Organization in Conversation". *Mimeo*, University of Cambridge.
Payne, John R.
   1985   "Coordination", in: Shopen (ed.), vol. 2, 3-41.
Penchoen, Thomas G.
   1973   *Tamazight of the Ayt Ndhir*. Los Angeles: Undena Publications.
Peranteau, Paul M.—Judith N. Levi—Gloria C. Phares (eds.)
   1972   *The Chicago which hunt; papers from the relative clause festival*. Chicago: Chicago Linguistic Society.
Pepicello, W.J.
   1977   "Raising in Latin." *Lingua* 42: 209-218.
Peres, Joao Andrade
   1984   *Elementos para uma gramática nova*. Coimbra: Livraria Almedina.
Pinkham, Jessie—Jorge Hankamer
   1975   "Deep and shallow clefts", *Chicago Linguistic Society* 11: 429-451.
Pinkster, Harm
   1972   *On Latin adverbs*. Amsterdam: North-Holland.
   1988   *Lateinische Syntax und Semantik*. Tübingen: Francke Verlag.
Pinkster, Harm—Inge Genee (eds.)
   1990   *Unity in diversity; papers presented to Simon C. Dik on his 50th birthday*. Dordrecht: Foris.
Platero, Paul R.
   1974   "The Navajo relative clause", *International Journal of American Linguistics* 40: 202-246.
Polanyi, Livia
   1988   "A formal model of the structure of discourse", *Journal of Pragmatics* 12: 601-638.
Polanyi, Livia—Remco Scha
   1983   "On the recursive structure of discourse", in: K. Ehlich-Henk van Riemsdijk (eds.), *Connectedness in sentence, discourse and text*, 141-178. Tilburg: Tilburg University.
Quirk, Randolph—Sidney Greenbaum—Geoffrey Leech—Jan Svartvik
   1972   *A grammar of contemporary English*. London: Longmans.
Reesink, Ger P.
   1983   "Switch reference and topicality hierarchies", *Studies in Language* 7: 215-246.

1987 *Structures and their functions in Usan, a Papuan language of Papua New Guinea.* Amsterdam: Benjamins.

Reinhart, Tanya
1976 The syntactic domain of anaphora. [Ph.D. dissertation, MIT.]
1983 *Anaphora and semantic interpretation.* Chicago: University of Chicago Press.

Rijk, R.P.G. de
1972 "Relative clauses in Basque; a guided tour", in: Peranteau—Levi—Phares (eds.), 115-135.

Rijkhoff, Jan
1986 "Word order universals revisited: the principle of Head Proximity". *Belgian Journal of Linguistics* 1: 95-125. (= *WPFG* 14).
1992 The noun phrase; a typological study of its form and structure. [Ph.D. dissertation, University of Amsterdam.]

Rijksbaron, Albert
1981 "Relative clause formation in Ancient Greek", in: Bolkestein—Combé—Dik—De Groot—Gvozdanović—Vet, 235-259.

Risselada, Rodie
1987 "Voice in Ancient Greek: reflexives and passives", in: Auwera—Goossens (eds.), 123-136.
1988 Subjectpronomina in direktieve zinnen. [Paper, Department of Classics, University of Amsterdam.]
1990 "Illocutionary function and functional illocution", *WPFG* 34.

Ross, John R.
1967 Constraints on variables in syntax. [Ph.D. dissertation, MIT, Cambridge, Mass.]
1970 "Gapping and the order of constituents", in: Bierwisch—Heidolph (eds.), 249-259.

Rumelhart, D.E.
1975 "Notes on a schema for stories", in: D.G. Bobrow—A. Collins (eds.), *Representation and understanding; studies in cognitive science*, 211-236. New York: Academic Press.

Sadock, Jerrold M.—Arnold M. Zwicky
1985 "Speech act distinctions in syntax", in: Shopen (ed.), vol. 1, 155-196.

Saltarelli, Mario
1988 *Basque.* London: Croom Helm.

Sasse, Hans-Jürgen
1977 "A note on wh-movement", *Lingua* 41: 343-354.

Schaaik, Gerjan van
1983 A functional analysis of aspects of Turkish grammar. [M.A. thesis in General Linguistics, University of Amsterdam.]
1985 "Valentiereduktie in het Turks", in: Dik (ed.), 127-129.

Schachter, Paul
  1973 "Focus on relativization", *Language* 49: 19-46.
  1977 "Constraints on coördination", *Language* 53: 86-103.
Schaub, W.
  1985 *Babungo*. London: Croom Helm.
Schegloff, E.A.
  1979 "The relevance of repair to syntax-for-conversation", in: Talmy Givón (ed.), *Discourse and syntax*. (Syntax and Semantics 12.) New York: Academic Press.
Schep, Antonet—Wiepke Vermeulen
  1984 'Nou en?': een onderzoek naar het functioneren van het woordje *nou* in gesprekken. [M.A. thesis in General Linguistics, University of Amsterdam.]
Schiffrin, Deborah
  1987 *Discourse markers*. Cambridge: Cambridge University Press.
Schwartz, Arthur
  1971 "General aspects of relative clause formation", *Working Papers on Language Universals* 6: 139-171.
  1976 "On the universality of subjects: the Ilocano case", in: Li (ed.), 519-545.
Scott, Eugene—Donald G. Frantz
  1974 "Sharanahua questions and proposed constraints on question movement", *Linguistics* 132.: 75-86.
Searle, John
  1969 *Speech acts; an essay in the philosophy of language*. Cambridge: Cambridge University Press.
  1976 "A classification of illocutionary acts", *Language in Society* 5: 1-23.
Searle, John—Daniel Vanderveken
  1985 *Foundations of illocutionary logic*. Cambridge: Cambridge University Press.
Sebeok, T.A. (ed.)
  1960 *Style in language*. Cambridge, Mass: MIT Press
Seuren, Pieter
  1976 "Echo: een studie in negatie", in: Geerd Koefoed—Arnold Evers (eds.), *Lijnen van taaltheoretisch onderzoek*, 160-184. Groningen: Tjeenk Willink.
Shopen, Timothy (ed.)
  1985 *Language typology and syntactic description*. Vol. 1: Clause structure, vol. 2: Complex constructions, vol. 3: Grammatical categories and the lexicon. Cambridge: University Press.
Sie Ing Djiang
  1989 The syntactic passive in Bahasa Indonesia; a study in Government-Binding theory. [Ph.D. dissertation, University of Amsterdam.]

Siewierska, Anna
    1988   *Word order rules.* London: Croom Helm.
    1990   "The source of the dative perspective in Polish pseudo-reflexives", in: Hannay—Vester (eds.), 1-15.
Solé, Y.—C. Solé
    1977   *Modern Spanish syntax.* Lexington: Heath and Co.
Stanchev, Swillen
    1990   "Bulgarian *se*-constructions", in: Hannay—Vester (eds.) 17-30.
Steever, Sanford B.
    1977   "Raising, meaning, and conversational implicatures", *Chicago Linguistic Society* 13: 590-602.
Stockwell, Robert P.—Paul Schachter—Barbara Hall Partee
    1973   *The Major Syntactic Structures of English.* New York: Holt, Rinehart and Winston.
Tagashira, Y.
    1972   "Relative clauses in Korean", in: Peranteau—Levi—Phares (eds.), 215-229.
Tallerman, Maggie
    1990   "Relativization strategies: NP accessibility in Welsh", *Journal of Linguistics* 26, 291-314.
Thompson, Sandra A.
    1971   "The deep structure of relative clauses", in: Charles J. Fillmore—D. Terrence Langendoen (eds.), *Studies in Linguistic Semantics*, 79-94. New York: Holt, Rinehart and Winston.
Thurman, R.C.
    1975   "Chuave medial verbs", *Anthropological Linguistics* 17: 342-352.
Touratier, Christian
    1980   *Le relative; essai de théorie syntaxique.* Paris: Klincksiek.
Tweehuysen, Rolandt
    1988a   Verbale suffigering (*s*-vorm) in het Zweeds. [M.A. thesis in General Linguistics, University of Amsterdam.]
    1988b   Rijzing en causatief in het Nederlands en het Zweeds. [M.A. thesis in Scandinavian Languages, University of Amsterdam.]
Ultan, Russell
    1969   "Some general characteristics of interrogative systems". *Working Papers on Language Universals* 1, 41-63.
Vester, Elseline
    1983   *Instrument and manner expressions in Latin.* Assen: Van Gorcum.
    1987   "A representation of Latin relative clauses", in: Auwera—Goossens (eds.), 153-162.

Vet, Co
1981 "Subject assignment in the impersonal constructions of French", in: Bolkestein—Combé—Dik—De Groot—Gvozdanović—Rijksbaron—Vet, 143-163.
1985 "Passive, reflexive, and causative predicate formation in French," in: Bolkestein—De Groot—Mackenzie (eds.) (1985b), 49-69.
1986a "A pragmatic approach to Tense in Functional Grammar", *WPFG* 16.
1986b "Les constructions causatives et réfléchies en français", *Actes du XVIIIe Congrès International de Linguistique et Philologie Romane*.
1986c "Causatieve constructies in het Nederlands", in: Cor Hoppenbrouwers—Ineke Schuurman—Ron van Zonneveld—Frans Zwarts (eds.), *Syntaxis en lexicon*, 62-75. Dordrecht: Foris.
1988 "Temps verbeaux et compléments adverbiaux de temps: leur contribution à la cohésion du texte", in: Henning Nølke (ed.), *Opérateurs syntaxiques et cohésion discursive*, 87-97. Copenhagen: Nyt Nordisk Forlag.

Vries, Lourens de
1989 Studies in Wambon and Kombai; aspects of two Papuan languages of Irian Jaya. [Ph.D. dissertation, University of Amsterdam.]
1990 "Some remarks on direct quotation in Kombai", in: Pinkster—Genee (eds.), 291-309.

Wachowicz, Krystyna
1974 "Against the universality of a single wh-question movement", *Foundations of Language* 11: 155-166.

Walusimbi, Livingstone—Talmy Givón
1970 "Conjoined and stacked restrictive relative clauses; deep and not-so-deep constraints in the light of Luganda data", *Studies in African Linguistics* 1: 157-183.

Watters, John R.
1979 "Focus in Aghem: a study of its formal correlates and typology", in: L. Hyman (ed.), *Aghem grammatical structure*, 137-197. Los Angeles: University of Southern California.

Weijdema, Willy—Simon C. Dik—Margo Oehlen—Clara Dubber—Akke de Blauw
1982 *Structuren in verbale interaktie; strategieën van sprekers en hoorders in het taalgebruik*. Muiderberg: Coutinho.

Wolfart, H.C.—J.F. Carroll
1981 *Meet Cree; a guide to the Cree language*. Edmonton: University of Alberta Press.

Yallop, Colin
1982 *Australian aboriginal languages*. London: André Deutsch.

Zimmermann, Luke
1985 "Subordinate clauses in Australian aboriginal languages", *WPFG 5*.

Ziv, Yael
    1985   "Parentheticals and Functional Grammar", in: Bolkestein—De Groot—Mackenzie (eds.) (1985a). 181-199.

Index of languages

Abkhaz 238
Aghem 278, 279, 286
Algonquian 17
Aoban 49
Arabic 2, 193, 198, 199, 238, 250, 289, 337, 338, 345, 385
Australian 73, 83, 275
Babungo 137, 324
Bahasa Indonesia 40, 276, 369
Bantawa 2
Bantu 323
Basque 64, 76, 280
Berber 328
Breton 327
Bulgarian 3
Chinese 33, 176
Cree 17, 18
Czech 288
Danish 211, 212, 331, 343, 349
Diegueño 65, 68
Dutch 3, 7, 9, 15, 16, 55, 56, 74, 77, 78, 80, 81, 104, 109, 138, 146, 149, 151, 153, 154, 156, 166-168, 175, 179, 187, 211-214, 225, 233, 244, 246, 247, 248, 273, 286, 287, 305, 306, 310, 363, 364, 378, 381, 387, 391, 396
Dyirbal 275
Dzamba 323
English 1, 3, 9, 12, 13, 15, 16, 30, 33-37, 39, 47-50, 52, 56, 61-63, 68, 76, 79, 82, 99, 117, 127-132, 135-140, 144, 146, 147, 156, 160, 161, 163, 165, 167, 168, 170, 179, 182, 187, 190, 191, 198, 199, 203, 210-212, 225, 227, 233, 237, 242, 247, 248, 270, 272, 275, 276, 281, 282, 283, 284, 287, 293, 295, 298, 300, 302, 304, 305, 307, 309, 314, 315, 316, 318, 326-328, 344, 346, 350, 353-355, 358, 367, 370, 385, 386, 387, 391, 399, 403, 405, 406
French 1, 3, 9, 19, 20, 35, 36, 152, 310, 326, 391, 397, 403
Fula 53
German 55, 56, 138, 247, 310
Godié 398, 431, 440
Greek 3, 335, 337, 370, 371, 373
Hebrew 3, 50, 391
Hindi 69, 185
Hixkaryana 72, 238, 404, 405
Hungarian 3, 17, 19, 128, 129, 280, 288, 340, 342, 349, 393
Imbabura Quechua 64, 67, 87, 135
Japanese 59-61, 105, 117-119, 130, 136, 157, 170, 376, 390
Kobon 238
Kombai 97, 439
Lango 321-323
Latin 3, 16, 17, 19, 41, 69, 101, 146, 147, 156, 180, 208, 215, 221, 250, 251, 332-334, 336, 340, 342, 350, 354, 355, 398, 420, 421, 437, 439
Luganda 27, 33, 34, 36, 37
Mangarayi 83, 85, 86, 238
Melanesian 49
Mojave 65, 308
Murinypata 67
Navajo 86, 87, 362
Ngaanyatjara 275
Niuean 346, 347
Papiamentu 317
Papuan 97, 400, 439
Persian 39, 336
Polish 3, 288
Polynesian 346, 347

Portuguese 146, 147, 306, 307
Quechua 64, 67, 87, 97, 135, 136, 139, 238
Romance 12
Romanian 49
Russian 3, 12, 288, 392, 402
Scandinavian 377
Serbo-Croatian 3, 340, 349
Spanish 3, 110, 141, 227, 360, 361, 378, 415
Swahili 323
Swedish 3, 377
Tagalog 309
Tamazight 328
Tamil 59, 130, 139, 238, 280, 281
Turkish 1, 3, 57, 58, 62, 279, 280
Tuvaluan 347, 348
Urdu 185
Usan 67, 85, 185, 398
Vata 316, 317
Wappo 66, 68, 89
Welsh 328, 375
Yavapai 65
Yuma 65, 66
Zulgo 400

Index of names

Adelaar 97
Afman 3
Akmajian 302, 304
Ali 27, 53
Allwood 376, 377
Anderson 10, 327
Asher 59, 130, 238, 280
Austin 230, 233, 234, 252
Auwera 35, 38, 48, 370, 373
Bach 277, 323
Baker 277
Barker 146
Berg 176
Besnier 347, 348
Bever 139
Bimson 53, 281
Blake 25, 38, 40, 67, 76, 189, 207, 208, 212
Bokamba 323
Bolkestein 3, 16, 100, 101, 103, 123, 197-199, 221, 229, 250, 332, 334, 340, 342, 343, 350
Borkin 350
Bossuyt 171
Bresnan 277
Brömser 3
Brown, D. 181
Brown, G. 388
Brown, R. 385,
Bühler 239, 425
Carnap 266, 267, 284
Carroll 18
Chastain 218, 226
Chomsky 129, 156, 165, 340, 361, 363
Chung 327, 346, 369
Clark, E. 133, 139, 431
Clark, H. 133, 139, 431

Cole 64, 67, 87-89, 135, 238, 362
Comrie 25, 39, 49, 51, 52, 55, 69, 72, 75, 76, 83, 99, 163, 336, 355, 357, 365, 366-368, 370, 373, 375, 378, 392
Connolly 441
Cornish 215
Coulmas 96-99, 103, 105
Cruttenden 381
Dahl 32, 184
Davies 238
Davison 185
Derbyshire 72, 238, 404, 405
Dijk 409, 411, 413, 414, 426, 435
Dik 3, 6, 10, 11, 20, 101, 104, 108, 110, 116, 158, 167, 189, 191, 193, 194, 210, 327, 345, 351, 352, 355, 364, 391, 396
Dixon 218, 275
Doughty 367
Downing 25, 45, 49, 56, 68
Eemeren 173
Falster Jakobsen 331, 343, 349
Fodor 139
Fox 366
Franck 259, 406
Frantz 277
Gamal-Eldin 238
Garret 139
Gary 238
Geest 353
Geluykens 246, 403
Gilman 385
Givón 27, 34, 36, 50, 221, 222, 380, 404, 422, 436
Goffman 406
Goossens 345
Gorbet 65, 68

Gordon 249
Greenberg 45, 46, 132-134, 285
Grice 394
Grift 221
Grimes 123, 218, 388
Groot, C. 3, 17, 44, 47, 128, 280, 288, 330, 340, 342, 349, 351, 393, 404
Groot, W. 3
Grootendorst 173
Grosu 376
Guéron 342
Gundel 310
Gvozdanović 2, 3, 340, 349
Haberland 98, 100, 370, 373
Haiman 396, 400
Hale 73, 82, 83
Haller 400, 401
Halliday 425, 433
Hankamer 287, 310
Hannay 38, 81, 296, 353, 380, 388
Harder 204
Harries-Delisle 294, 310
Haverkate 250, 252, 385
Hengeveld 102, 108, 110, 116, 180, 203, 224, 229, 236, 352, 355, 364, 425
Hewitt 238
Hoffmann 173, 178-180
Houtlosser 175
Hyman 405
Hymes 416
Jacobsen 35, 43, 311
Jakobson 239
Jefferson 427
Johnson-Laird 413, 431
Jong 229, 239
Joseph 371, 372
Junger 3
Kahrel 3, 13
Kamp 387, 413
Karttunen 114, 115, 418
Keenan 25, 41, 46, 48, 49, 51-53, 55, 69, 79, 184, 185, 281, 319, 320, 357, 362, 365-368, 370, 373, 375, 378, 385, 387
Keizer 203, 212, 224, 307
Kendall 65
Kintsch 411, 413, 426, 435
Kiparsky, C. 108
Kiparsky, P. 108
Kirsner 353, 355
Komter 422, 424, 425, 428
Koopman 316, 317
Kraak 187
Kroon 380, 425, 429
Kučanda 3
Kuno 75, 117-119, 130, 286, 287, 376
Kwee 30, 31
Labov 431, 437
Lakoff 249
Lalleman 431
Langacker 361
Langdon 65, 89
Lees 80, 81, 164
Lehmann 25, 38, 45, 65, 69, 257, 336, 337, 366
Levinson 235, 237, 249, 385, 387, 406
Li 66, 390
Limburg 44, 330, 404
Linde 437
Longacre 433
Lyons 42, 169, 172, 173, 176, 217, 233, 248
Mackenzie 3, 123, 162-164, 166, 167, 296
Maes 213
Maling 376, 377
Mallinson 25, 38, 40, 49, 67, 76, 189, 207, 208, 212
Mann 55, 431
Marchese 398, 431, 440
Mardirussian 10
Matthiessen 431

Maxwell 50, 52, 366, 375
McCawley 41, 59
Merlan 83, 84, 238
Minsky 434
Mithun 190, 192
Moreno 3
Moutaouakil 2, 189, 193, 198, 199, 229, 239, 250, 289, 337, 345, 385
Munro 65, 308
Muysken 317
Noonan 57, 95, 106, 110, 115, 140, 141, 321, 322, 324, 353, 364
Ochs-Keenan 385, 387
Orlandini 250
Ortiz de Urbina 280
Owen 387
Payne 189, 191
Penchoen 328
Pepicello 334
Peres 229, 306, 307
Philippaki-Warburton 372
Pinkham 310
Pinkster 41, 77, 193, 336, 437, 439, 440
Platero 86, 362
Polanyi 387, 422, 427, 428
Quirk 39, 155, 156, 211, 244, 248, 314, 387, 440
Reesink 67, 85, 123, 185, 398, 399
Reinhart 361
Rijk 64, 175
Rijkhoff 64, 76, 339
Rijksbaron 38, 44, 335, 336
Risselada 3, 16, 229, 237, 250
Robinson 286, 287
Ross 42, 43, 54, 211-214, 234-236, 240, 361, 390, 394
Rumelhart 431
Sadock 237, 238
Saltarelli 64
Sasse 277
Scha 387, 422, 427, 428
Schaaik 3, 57, 63, 279, 280

Schachter 193, 310
Schaub 137, 324
Schegloff 403
Schep 387
Schieffelin 385, 387
Schiffrin 425, 440, 441
Schwartz 25, 390, 391
Scott 277
Searle 173, 230, 234, 236
Seiter 346
Seuren 171
Sie Ing Djiang 40
Siewierska 3, 342
Solé, C. 360
Solé, Y. 360
Stanchev 3
Steever 350
Stockwell 33
Sylla 53
Tagashira 59
Tallerman 366, 373, 375
Thompson 41, 43, 66, 353, 355, 390, 431
Thurman 438
Touratier 38
Tweehuysen 3
Ultan 285
Vanderveken 173, 236
Vermeulen 387
Vester 38, 81, 106, 193, 380, 388
Vet 3, 152, 153, 387, 396, 397, 413
Vries 97, 380, 388, 438, 439
Wachowicz 286, 288
Waletzky 431
Walusimbi 27, 34, 36
Watters 278, 400, 401
Weijdema 231, 233, 427
Wolfart 18
Yallop 275
Zaenen 376, 377
Zimmermann 82, 83
Ziv 379, 380
Zwicky 237, 239

Index of subjects

absolute construction 82
accessibility 51-53, 218, 219, 270-276, 348, 357-378
   hierarchical constraint 51, 270, 357, 361-364
   intrinsic constraint 357, 359-361
   functional constraint 357, 365-377
Accessibility Hierarchy 51-53, 366-376
accusative *see* case, accusative
accusativus cum infinitivo 147, 333, 334, 355, 363, 364, 378
address 385
adjacency pair 259, 430
adjective 23, 26, 27, 33-35, 39, 75, 159, 163, 207, 225, 312, 354
adjoined clause *see* clause, adjoined
adnominal modifier 24, 33
adpositional predicate 309-312
adverbial clause *see* clause, adverbial
advice 249
affixation 21
Agent 20, 157
agent noun 1, 3-5
agreement 140, 146, 302-307
anaphora 30, 41, 54, 78, 86, 87, 89, 136, 149, 150, 156, 204, 210-228, 301, 302, 358, 418
anaphorical chain 218, 221, 222, 422, 436, 437
animacy 18, 359-361
answer 259, 261, 323
apposition 63, 64, 72, 73, 338, 404
argument 11
   first 12, 13, 95, 122, 150, 333-335, 334, 335
   second 17, 19, 95, 122, 150, 162, 334, 335
   third 95, 122
aspect 17, 29, 57, 58, 140, 211, 212, 397, 398
attitudinal satellite *see* satellite, level 3
attitude specification 386, 427
auxiliary 22
boundary marking 386, 387
case 163, 391, 392
   accusative 16, 17, 343
   genitive 5, 157-163, 371-373
   vocative 104, 105, 385
cataphora *see* anaphora
causative predicate formation 1, 9
Causee 15, 20
circumstantial satellite *see* satellite, circumstantial
clausal term *see* term, clausal
clause 228
   adjoined 73, 83-85
   adverbial 95
   embedded *see* embedded construction
   independent 42, 43, 65
   matrix 95
   subordinate *see* embedded construction
clause fragment 379
cleft construction 265, 291-330
clitic doubling 360, 361, 378
coherence *see* discourse coherence
cohesion 17
comparison 374, 375
complementary formation 178
completive predicate formation 15-17

complex term *see* clause, embedded
complexity 126-131, 300, 312
Condition 395-396
conditional clause 132-135
conjunction *see* subordinator
connector 440, 441
contra-factivity *see* factivity
contrary formation 179, 180
control 102
conversion *see* zero modification
coordination 105, 189-214
    clause 196-199, 210
    function 207, 208
    metalinguistic 207, 208
    multiple 209-214
    operator 207, 208
    predicate 203-205, 209
    predication 200, 210
    proposition 200, 210
    restrictor 205-207
    sentence 196-199
    simple 196-208
    simultaneous 212-214
    term 201-203, 209
coordinator 190-192
copula 295, 305-308, 317, 326, 327
coreferentiality 147, 148, 216-219, 393
cross-reference 403, 404
de-actualization 14, 15
declarative 237, 239-248, 253, 254
definiteness 159, 160, 185-187, 208, 218, 294, 321, 350, 359-361
deictic centre 96, 99, 100, 102, 236, 397
deixis 219
demonstrative 71, 77, 78, 80, 128, 208, 221-223, 271, 272
denial *see* negation, propositional
dependent question 69, 70, 79-82, 101, 251, 263, 270, 320
derivation *see* predicate formation

derived illocution *see* illocutionary conversion
diachrony 76-92, 129, 192, 380, 403-405
diminutive formation 7
direct speech 96-105, 420, 421
discourse coherence 433-441
discourse decisions 414-422
discourse event 416, 425, 426, 428
discourse execution 405, 406, 427
discourse genre 416, 417
discourse model 412, 413
discourse organization 386-405, 427
discourse referents 418
discourse relations 431, 432
discourse structure 409-441
discourse style 417
discourse unit 428-431
discourse world 417-419
discrepancy 331-356
    formal 332-338, 342, 343
    positional 333, 338-343
    structural 333, 351-356
disjunctive question 257, 263
displacement 339-344
dummy element 63, 127, 128, 132, 292, 296-298, 305, 314, 318, 326, 337
dynamic discourse model *see* discourse model
embedded construction 43, 44, 58-63, 65-67, 79-82, 83, 90, 91, 93-168, 197-200, 250, 251, 339-356, 419-421, 431
    finite 144, 145, 310, 340
    infinitival 145-154, 251, 363, 364
    nominalization 71, 89-92, 130, 131, 136, 157-168
    non-finite 334
    participial 154-157, 354
entity type 93, 94, 153, 220, 223-228, 351-356

episode 428-430
ergativity 162, 346, 347
exlamation 103, 238-240, 243, 244
Experiencer 14
expression rule 3, 6, 21, 22, 167, 170, 317, 336
expressive 386
extra-clausal constituent 103-105, 197, 198, 379-407
   attitude specification 386
   discourse execution 405, 406
   discourse organization 386-405
   interaction management 384-386
extraction 54, 74, 341, 342, 362
factivity 108-110, 124
finalizer 387
finiteness 138-140, 144-168
first argument reduction 12, 13
Focus 171, 172, 175, 199, 223, 264, 265, 278, 279, 282, 283, 288, 291-330, 341, 351, 438, 438
focus construction 257, 291-330
   interrogative 318-324
frame 433-437
free indirect speech 100
fund 2, 165
gender 163, 359
genericity 14, 15, 149, 150
genitive *see* case, genitive
genre *see* discourse genre
Given Topic 294-302, 307, 308, 314
Goal 5, 13, 15, 20, 336, 345
goal incorporation 11
grammaticalization *see* diachrony
greeting 384
habituality 14, 15
iconicity 133-137, 435, 436
identifying construction 293-297, 310-312
illocution 42, 43, 100-102, 172-174, 198, 199, 229-260, 391, 419-421
illocutionary conversion 240-252, 254, 255, 258
   grammatical 240-252
   pragmatic 241, 242, 249, 250
illocutionary operator *see* operator, level 4
illocutionary satellite *see* satellite, level 4
imperative 102, 103, 111, 229, 237, 239, 240, 243, 246, 248
implicative predicate *see* matrix predicate, implicative
incorporation 10-12
indirect object 369, 370
indirect speech 96-105
indirect speech act 230, 251, 252, 420, 421
infinitival construction *see* embedded construction, infinitival
information 410-412
   contextual 410
   general 410
   situational 410
initiator 387
Instrument 400
intention 410
interaction management 384-386, 427
interrogative clause 104, 237, 239-251, 257-289
interrogative focus construction *see* focus construction, interrogative
interrogative predicate *see* predicate, questioned
interrogative pronoun *see* pronoun, interrogative
interruption 428
job interview 424, 425, 428
knowledge 411, 412
layering
   clause 93-95, 169, 170, 224
   discourse 422-431
leave-taking 384
lexical priority 4
lexicalization 4, 5, 19, 20

lexicon *see* fund
LIPOC *see* complexity
litotes 179, 180
markedness shift 325-330
matrix predicate 95
   achievement 113-115
   commentative 113
   communication 97, 102, 104, 199, 233, 250-254
   direct perception 112, 113, 118, 119, 200, 351-355, 363, 364
   directive 110, 111
   implicative 114-116
   knowledge 107, 109
   mental perception 108, 119, 200
   objective modal 114
   phasal 113
   practical manipulation 111, 112, 116, 200, 201
   pretence 109
   propositional attitude 97, 106-110, 200, 201
   propositional manipulation 107, 116
   volitional 112, 132
medial verb 439
minimal response 386
mitigation 124
modal particle 244-246
modality 124, 169, 177, 245, 246
mood 140, 141, 251
mutation 21
narrative construction 146
negation 124, 125, 169-187
   illocutionary 172-174
   predicate 178-180
   predicational 175-177, 183-187
   propositional 174-177
   term 41, 180-187
nominalized restrictor *see* verbal restrictor, nominalized

nominalization *see* embedded construction, nominalization
nominativus cum infinitivo 350
non-verbal predication 307
noun 23
number 160, 163, 208
Object 35, 128, 129, 219, 331, 333-335, 347, 358, 366, 369
open predication *see* predication, open
operator 170, 171, 207, 208
   level 1 180
   level 2 176, 177
   level 3 28, 109, 176
   level 4 229, 239, 240, 265-267
Orientation 69, 81, 85-92, 132, 387-401
parataxis 72, 77, 78, 431
parenthetical 44
part of speech *see* predicate, type
participant identification 24, 25, 73
participial construction *see* embedded construction, participial
participial restrictor *see* verbal restrictor, participial
performative analysis 234-236
performative statement 173, 174, 230, 232-236, 252-255
person 359
personal pronoun *see* pronoun, personal
polarity 169-187, 248
   negative *see* negation
   positive *see* positive polarity
politeness 105, 386
pop marker 387, 427, 428
positive polarity 175-177
possessive pronoun *see* pronoun, possessive
Possessor 271, 273, 334, 335, 373, 374

posterior 111, 239
potentiality 14, 15
pragmatic function 123-125, 131, 132, 171, 172, 175, 193, 365, 376, 377
pragmatic information *see* information
predicate 286
   adpositional *see* adpositional predicate
   complex 211
   form 6, 21, 22
   matrix *see* matrix predicate
   questioned 274-276
   type 7
   valency *see* valency
predicate focus 313-318
predicate formation 1-22, 153, 154, 165-168, 178-180, 205-207
predicate frame 2, 6, 17, 165, 203, 204
predicate operator *see* operator, level 1
predicate satellite *see* satellite, level 1
predicate schema 204
predicate variable 203, 204, 217, 224
predication 28, 226, 229
   closed 58-63, 82, 147-150, 155
   half-open 92
   open 29-31, 82, 147-150, 155
predication operator *see* operator, level 2
predication satellite *see* satellite, level 2
predicational term *see* term, predicational
Principle of Domain Integrity 339, 341
Principle of Formal Adjustment 20, 158-164, 335

Principle of Increasing Complexity 341, 342
Principle of Logical Variants 320
Principle of Pragmatic Highlighting 341
Principle of Semantic Adjustment 20
Processed 15
processing 53, 75, 133, 139, 282, 283
productivity 4, 165, 166
pronoun
   interrogative 69, 71, 80-82, 260, 263-289, 339, 341, 358, 376
   personal 30, 46, 48-55, 69, 71, 86, 216-221, 403
   possessive 221
   reflexive 219-221
   relative 30, 46, 48-51, 54, 55, 69, 71, 80-82, 221, 227, 310, 335-338
pronoun retention 283, 284
property assignment 311
proposition 227, 229
proposition operator *see* operator, level 3
proposition satellite *see* satellite, level 3
propositional term *see* term, propositional
prosodic contour 39, 245, 246, 264, 381, 396, 402, 405
prosodic modification 21
pseudo-cleft construction 291, 292
pseudo-passive 10
pseudo-relative 60
psychological adequacy 19
purpose clause 132, 150, 151
push marker 387, 427, 428
quantification 160, 169, 180-187, 271-273

question, independent *see* interrogative clause
question, dependent *see* dependent question
question word *see* pronoun, interrogative
question word question 257, 260, 263-289
  multiple 281, 286-289
raising 144, 145, 152, 344-351, 358
Recipient 20
reduplication 21
reference 40, 93, 217, 225, 226
reflexive pronoun *see* pronoun, reflexive
reflexivization 10
relative attraction 335-338
relative clause *see* verbal restrictor
relative pronoun *see* pronoun, relative
Relator Principle 46, 136, 137
repair strategy 403
reported speech 96-105
request 243, 246-250
restrictor 23, 24, 27, 29, 60, 62, 83, 92, 205-207, 270-273
  stacking 31-38, 205
response 405, 406
response initiator 406
rhetorical question 243, 244, 251
satellite 170, 171
  circumstantial 73, 82-92, 155, 353
  embedded construction 122
  level 1 11
  level 3 28, 41, 42
  level 4 41, 42, 229
script 434
second argument reduction 13, 14
selection restriction 17, 18, 31, 32, 68, 101, 164, 300-302, 394
semantic function 15-17, 121, 122, 132-135, 192, 193, 202, 208, 365-376
Semantic Function Hierarchy 68
sentence type 236-239, 254
sequence of tenses 98, 99
Setting 396-398
simultaneous 112, 364
specificity 183-185, 360, 361, 418, 419
speech act 229-260, 428, 429
speech act variable 229
stacking of restrictors *see* restrictor, stacking
story 431
style *see* discourse style
Subject 34, 56, 57, 65, 67, 123, 128-130, 132, 219, 222, 270, 303, 304, 308, 321-324, 331, 333-335, 345-348, 358, 366-369
subordinator 48, 97, 98, 100, 117-119, 135-137, 144, 310, 328, 364, 401
Sub-Topic 216, 217
summons 384
syntactic function 37, 123, 128-130, 192, 365-376
tag question 178, 241, 247, 248, 406, 407
Tail 129, 248, 329, 401-405
tail-head linking 438-440
tense 29, 47, 57, 58, 107, 108, 112, 113, 140, 421, 422, 435, 436
term 357-378
  clausal 96-105
  complex *see* clause, embedded
  predicational 110-119, 315
  propositional 106-110, 116-119, 331, 350, 355
term formation 32, 36-38
term operator 41, 101, 158, 180-187, 266, 267
term predicate 8, 23, 39, 150, 151, 203, 314, 319
term structure 23, 24, 158

Index of subjects 477

Theme 329, 388-395, 402, 403-405
Theme-prominence 390
Topic 222, 223, 288, 322, 341, 351, 376, 377, 395, 422, 436, 437
topic chain *see* anaphorical chain
topic continuity *see* anaphorical chain
topic shifter 387
transitivity 10, 18, 314
turn 429, 430
universality 71-73
valency
    extension 8, 9
    quantitative 8-15
    qualitative 15-18
    reduction 9-15, 154
verbal noun 159, 168
verbal restrictor 23-92, 258, 358, 362, 366-378
    appositive 63, 64, 73
    circumnominal 45, 64-68, 71, 85-92, 355, 356
    correlative 68-70, 82
    finite 25-28, 45-47, 55, 59, 64, 281, 284
    headed 298-300
    headless 80, 294, 297-300, 336
    nominalized 28, 45, 46, 57-59
    non-restrictive 38-44, 338
    participial 26, 28, 45, 46, 55-57
    postnominal 45-55, 71
    prenominal 45, 46, 55-64, 71
vocative *see* case, vocative
voice 57
volition 14, 15
warning 242
word class *see* predicate, type
word order 45-49, 53-57, 61-69, 71-76, 78, 126-139, 164, 213, 214, 265, 276-289, 295, 298-300, 322-330, 339-343, 381-383
X-bar syntax 165
yes-no question 257, 260, 262, 263

Zero 15
zero modification 21
zero quantification *see* negation, term